THE AMERICAN IMPACT
ON
GREAT BRITAIN

THE
AMERICAN IMPACT
ON
GREAT BRITAIN
1898-1914

A Study of the United States in World History

By

RICHARD HEATHCOTE HEINDEL

1968
OCTAGON BOOKS, INC.
New York

Reprinted 1968
by special arrangement with the University of Pennsylvania Press

OCTAGON BOOKS, INC.
175 FIFTH AVENUE
NEW YORK, N. Y. 10010

LIBRARY OF CONGRESS CATALOG CARD NUMBER: 68-16775

Printed in U.S.A. by
NOBLE OFFSET PRINTERS, INC.
NEW YORK 3, N. Y.

To

WILLIAM E. LINGELBACH

PREFACE

I CLING to the illusion that it is vitally important that the United States understand itself as a factor in world civilization. Historians have not given sufficient attention to the part we have had in European life and opinion. Quite rightly, they have studied European contributions to the United States, but have neglected, either as a problem of cultural history or as a matter of daily increasing national importance, the impact of American civilization abroad. This volume, one of a projected series *The United States in World History*, was designed to be a brief part of the story of American influence on the Old World, a contribution through national history to the study of international history, and a supplement to the familiar diplomatic chronicle. The pages should contribute to many aspects of British and American personalities, and to domestic history, and add to the history of such subjects as technics, science, education, medicine, and the law. It is probably one of the first efforts on a broad scale to see how one nation gets its ideas about another, and what use one nation makes of another's experience. This should prove stimulating to the propagandists.

I do not share the common belief that Anglo-American studies are complete or that the relationships are such that nothing more need be said about them. Nearly everyone will commit himself with startling authority to an opinion on Anglo-American affairs; such is probably the disadvantage of a common language. One is almost tempted to conclude that our historical scholarship has done more well-rounded work on our relations with other foreign countries. It is easier to be safe about the psychology governing cousin and cousin or a poor relation than that affecting a mother and an illegitimate daughter. Consequently, I hope the volume will add more reality to Anglo-American discussions.

Not all the implications of the study can be described and argued at every instance. But something of value can be said of America's impact without pretending to follow such influence in all the innumerable phases of human effort and thought to a definite resting place in British civilization. The archaeologist may not be satisfied in chronicling the diffusion of culture unless he is able to handle a concrete object or trace a distinctive motif. But, where material is so abundant and rapidly merging unidentified into the national culture, must we restrict ourselves to these palpable evidences? I think not, even though archaeologists rambling over the remains of the two countries some millennium hence may think otherwise.

Further, had this volume been labeled "America in British Public Opinion" many criticisms could have been forestalled and fertile points of attack sacrificed. But I intended that the volume should be put forward as more than a study in public opinion. While I can see some reasons for informing another country what we have meant to it, I see no reason to belittle the multitude of ideas and attitudes which was its heritage or the result of stimulation from a complex world. I believe the true significance of a volume such as this for international history will become clearer when we have similar works covering almost countless relationships.

By the very nature of the study a chapter would be needed to record the advice, encouragement, and time given to the author, who has been left with a feeling of disproportion between the results of the study and the delightful obligations incurred in carrying it on. My thanks go to some thousands of Britons who were disturbed in one way or another, to scores of those gentlemen of state who unburdened themselves under the inevitable pledge of anonymity, to American diplomatic representatives and members of the American colony in the British Isles, and to teachers and scholars on the interchange scheme. In Great Britain I recall with pleasure the help given me by the Chambers of Commerce, Rotary, the American University Union, the English-speaking Union, and the Foreign, Home, Colonial, and General Post Offices. Scores of organizations coöperated in the friendliest fashion, and I have drawn upon the Immigration and Naturalization Service, U.S. Department of Labor, and the U.S. Department of Commerce, the State Department, and numerous publishing houses. Among the many personal obligations, I wish to record the kindnesses of Viscountess Bryce and the Marquess of Lansdowne for permission to quote from collections in their possession, and to recall the aid given by the Marquis of Salisbury, H. G. Wells, Professor H. Hale Bellott, Sir Michael Sadler, Sir Philip Hartog, Thomas Stephenson, "Augur," Willard Connely, Ferdinand Kuhn Jr., Donald Gill, F. A. Southard Jr., Harwood L. Childs, C. Mace Thomas, and especially Miss Elsie Fisher. A fellowship from the Social Science Research Council and the Penfield Fellowship in International Law, Diplomacy, and Belles Lettres of the University of Pennsylvania gave me time to complete the study. I want to note the coöperation of the staff at the British Museum, the Royal Society, Royal College of Surgeons, Royal Astronomical Society, the London School of Economics, the Institute of Historical Research, the Library of Congress, the Mercantile Library, and the Library of the University of Pennsylvania. My colleagues at the University have been patient and helpful, and throughout the years the assistance of Professors A. C. Howland, Conyers Read, Roy F. Nichols, Richard Shryock, A. P. Whitaker, Leonidas Dodson, Thomas Woody, and the Hon. Roland S. Morris has meant much. To Professor William E. Lingelbach, unsparing in time and unselfish in the promotion of scholarship, any merits of this volume are due. The coöperation of Elizabeth Calvert Heindel, a joyous companion in all my studies, made even footnotes a pleasure.

This manuscript was finished June 1938. The outbreak of the Second World War strengthens my suspicion that we have reached an epoch in which Americans and foreigners must consider seriously the United States in World History.

RICHARD HEATHCOTE HEINDEL

University of Pennsylvania
May 1940

CONTENTS

I

INTRODUCTION [1]

IT is too early in the history of the United States to expect that much has been done to estimate the American impact upon other countries. The possibilities of the subject have been only touched. Journalists have for the greater part made the most of the sensational aspects; novelists have become swamped in the psychological complexities brought about by the interrelations. Some of the most brilliant and unsatisfactory history has been written in the study of the impact of one race upon another, nation upon nation, and all the other groupings that come quickly to mind. A study of the American impact can escape none of the difficulties.

Henry James, who toyed with this subject, and some of whose complicated prose may be due to the subtleties such a topic is likely to inspire, expressed the problem in his volume on W. W. Story (1903):

> The old relation, social, personal, aesthetic, of the American World to the European . . . is as charming a subject as the student of manners, morals, personal adventures, the history of taste, the development of a society, need wish to take up, with the one drawback, in truth, of being treatable—but in too many lights. The poet, the dramatist, the critic, would alike, on considerations, find it to bristle with appeals and admonitions. It has, in short, never been "done" to call done, from any point of view.

Despite the suggestion thrown out by the famous imperial historian J. R. Seeley in his *Expansion of England* (1883), "There is no topic so pregnant as this of the mutual influence of the branches of the English race. The whole future of the planet depends upon it," very little has been attempted in studying the American influence upon Great Britain. Seeley himself, perhaps not completely non-insular, dismissed the problem by making a lesson of the American Revolution for contemporary imperial discussions, intimating the conclusion of a broader vision by saying that the United States "exerts a strong influence upon us by the strange career it runs and the novel experiments it tries." Actually he complained of the irrational historical treatment of the American Revolution which made that event less pregnant for the British than it really was.

James Bryce has warned:

Now and then we may directly claim transatlantic experience as accrediting or discrediting some specific constitutional device or the policy of some enactment. But even in these cases he who desires to rely on the results shown in America must first satisfy himself that there is such a parity of conditions and surroundings in respect to the particular matter as justifies him in reasoning directly from ascertained results there to probable results in his own country.

Yet Bryce does say: "America has in some respects anticipated European nations. She is walking before them along paths which they may probably follow." One must record, as Bryce did, a useful caveat: While there may be a parallelism between the two countries, the correspondence may rather be due to the "simultaneous action of the same causes than to any direct influence," one country upon another.

"American" has been broadly interpreted to include all the emanations of influence or stimuli coming from the United States, and it has been used to describe the activity, outlook, and experience of, and contributions by, the people of the United States. These developments may not be original with us. Placed as we have been within the tradition of Western Europe, as part of Atlantic civilization, America's career did not, except in details here and there, thrust itself upon Britain as a mighty force completely alien to her own tradition. There are many instances where an American would deny vehemently the homogeneity of American life, and yet the foreigner may, in his simplification of observation, designate as "American" that which we would prefer to describe as an importation, as local, or as atypical.

It is convenient, and only what can be expected, that at a mental and spatial distance, the term and the country it covers are treated as a unit, and the term may be loosely applied, becoming less meaningful as one turns, for example, from diplomacy to the complexities of social life. What is important is to see what and how traits, values, objects, or activities described as "American" have been received abroad. The changes or applications of a descriptive adjective may not be momentous, but one can observe that they have an accumulative effect of some value in estimating the reception by one nation of another's methods, styles, or ways of life; and an adjective, as when loosely applied to such things as "American business morality," helps to build up a British mental image of our civilization which may give us more credit for originality and distinctiveness than is our due.

Under the word "impact" this study deals with three things: the knowledge of or interest in the United States, the opinions and attitudes about it, and the imitation, modification or use of the American example. Impact includes slow, subtle permeation as well as the more startling spasms of influence which the British press has loved to call "the American invasion." An impact (as broadly defined) may exist without influence, hence the word is usually to be preferred to "influence." "Collision," an overtone inherent in the word, has not been unduly stressed. It would be folly to presume that the American impact meant many startling changes in the history of the United Kingdom, but it has been more significant than the author anticipated. British readers need not assume that I am trying to prove that the impact was and is entirely dependent upon American initiative or conquest; it may well be related to a state of mental breadth which exists in Great Britain. Further, such impact, although frequently not free from evil, may imply a desire to profit from another's experience. Indeed, it is important for America to know whether the impact has been for good or evil. Whether the phrase "American impact" may possess more significance and originality in the future rests with the Fates.

The United States has been a frontier to Great Britain, and just as the significance of the frontier in American history has been a fertile clue, *mutatis mutandis*, one may reflect that meditations on the hypothesis may well wander eastward, beyond the seaboard states, on across the Atlantic Ocean, and, in point of time, on beyond the first century and a half of plantations in America, perhaps the more obvious period of European repercussions. Even though the American frontier in its special sense of available free land (which likewise possessed Old World importance) had disappeared by 1890, the conception of the American nation as a frontier influence affecting Great

Britain, at least up to the World War, contains just enough meaning to make it tolerable history. One is not surprised to see G. K. Chesterton, William Archer, and G. B. Shaw in cowboy dress cavorting on an Essex field. However, I am impelled to add here the extreme observation made by P. A. Sorokin: "Racial, national, geographic, and other differences of the groups that are the bearers of the culture rarely change the essential nature and destiny of the culture. They call forth and lead to many variations in the *secondary* characteristics of the culture."

It would have been misleading in this specialized topic to confine attention to England, and just as confusing not to recognize that differences exist in Wales, Northern Ireland, and Scotland. The emphasis that is given to England is excusable, partly because the material so warrants and partly because Parliament and London are the natural focus of international movements. The shades of difference within England itself, Lancashire and Cornwall for example, in response to something as foreign as the United States cannot be constantly differentiated; but the reader will keep in mind the possibility of such niceties which are not often of paramount importance unless there is a crisis, such as occurred during the Civil War when Lancashire mills suffered from the cotton blockade. In the pre-war period, what is now the Irish Free State can hardly be completely omitted, for there is no doubt that it was Ireland which directed much British attention to America, and Americans who made Ireland a world problem. However, the American impact on Ireland and by way of Ireland must await another volume. More important than the geographical distinctions are the stratifications in social life.

One may legitimately doubt whether "public opinion" should be used to describe the general or specific expressions made by the British upon the United States over a long period of time. The reaction of Britain to America, usually centering upon episodes, has a body of symbols, prejudices, and traditions which it is hard to call public opinion inasmuch as it may not be generally expressed at each episode. For that reason I have frequently preferred to speak about the knowledge of or interest in the United States rather than speak only of public opinion. Until we know British attitudes (a term much battered about), we cannot learn how American influences might have come in. Perforce, it is impossible to say as much as one should about the slumbering impressions which have got into the inarticulate masses.

Some early American travelers once advanced the amusing theory that the interval of space which separated the two countries might function as an interval of a century, and that American judgment was therefore in some respects a prophecy of the judgment of posterity. This statement, if reversed to English judgment on American civilization, would contain the same amount of untruth. Yet foreign opinion of our country is vital to us for many reasons, because it modifies the influence or prestige we may have in the world, is a clue to the study of national characteristics, and furnishes a stimulating guide to our own domestic problems. The cynic might decide that at the most the intervening space of the Atlantic Ocean encouraged harsh British expressions which in time became more general in our own country.

A word may be said about the period selected for study. Historical analyses that have been made which would directly, but usually indirectly, impinge upon the subject of the American impact center mostly on the American Revolution or the Civil War. These usually emphasize diplomatic relations or the state of public opinion in Great Britain. The years from 1865 to 1898 (which the author plans to treat elsewhere) are not unimportant; indeed, that period conditions the mental outlook as it is to be found at the outset of the present discussion. The years 1898 to 1914 form a logical block of time. The Spanish-American War stimulated attention to the United States in many fields besides diplomacy. The World War years, with their special stress and strain, are better treated as the foundation for a contemplated study of the American impact since 1918. The time division does not have the same validity in all the fields of activity that are discussed here, but this is true of any topic like the present which is somewhat tangent to the life and being of a nation.

To make the complexity of history comprehensible, events have been given causes, and the influence of one civilization upon another has often been cited with marvelous courage. If we ask the question, what impact the Occident has had upon the Orient, it is assumed because of their dissimilarity that it is easier to identify reciprocal influences. But with utter disregard for the greater difficulties of working within a more common heritage, historical pages have been filled with the impact of ideas, geographical environment, and so forth. Such pages devoted to the interweaving of influences usually inflame the imagination and never quite satisfy the critical intellect, either because the sweep for material has not been very broad or because there has been a tendency—frequently made vicious by a motive of boosting or depreciating a hero or nation—of confining attention to smaller and smaller units until we get an analysis of the response of a third-rate English writer to a fourth-rate Frenchman.

The dangerous leanings of these studies may be summarized: excessive nationalism or racialism, over-generalization, a confusion between opinion and imitation, the excusable inability to isolate one stimulus from another, the use of over-specialized historical sources, an assumption of static or mature or dead civilization or civilizations, an emphasis on material objects (e. g., the spread of gout in England because of a change in Anglo-Portuguese trade relations), a disregard of the fact that the origins of methods or ideas may soon be forgotten, and too much stress on the crises or major events of history. Perhaps in order to avoid the pettifogging pitfalls that a social scientist thinks he sees in many advanced studies of literature, he turns in despair to analyses of public opinion. Such analyses, while part of the story of reaction to stimuli, are still only part of the larger problem of the reception and adaptation of another's aims, thoughts, and achievements.

What are the guideposts for writing about impacts? There is a subtlety in such research which comes as a relief from a strict narrative of action. Placing one object in relation to another allows for closer approximation to the real nature of each separate object, no matter whether the object be a nation or a philosopher. Such epics developed in bygone ages in order to glorify the home folks. So it is that in this very day when internationally minded workers gather material for the relationships and interacting (no matter how feebly) unity of mankind, the chauvinist can turn the same material to his own desires, to whip or crown his fatherland. The fact that one or both civilizations appear to have passed an apogee usually inspires efforts to evaluate influence or contributions. But perhaps the very entrance of America into the British horizon, even apart from the chance that it has been too busy to develop a rounded culture, exerted an influence which was so strong that nothing we may do in centuries to come could equal it.

Partly in the belief that most stimuli are personal, the individual thinker or traveler has been given almost unwarranted attention. This has given rise to bibliographies and analyses of travelers to the States, and to a lesser degree, to the study of an American abroad, whether Cooper, Emerson, or a missionary in China. The constant speeding up of international communications may diminish the need for such studies; but it is not likely, with the vastness of physical and mental oceans, and the barriers of hatred and ignorance, that we shall ever lack variety, and the airplane and the radio will merely produce a different methodology, not an abolition of the problems themselves. But to return to the matter at hand, to estimate American contributions abstractly is not enough. Charles W. Eliot's *American Contributions to Civilization* (1898) may be logical and entirely correct for domestic consumption, but are these contributions convincing without estimating their permeation to other countries?

The contacts and channels of information existing between the two countries are basic to the nature of our influence, consequently I have devoted much time to an evaluation of their present effectiveness. A field program was designed as supplementary to the more orthodox historical research, setting the problem of how one may obtain a broad perspective of the public opinion or attitude of one country regarding another. Inquiry as to the strength of the channels which aid in forming British opinion about the United States naturally combined an analysis of contemporary British attitudes toward the States. Such contemporary examination, besides fortifying historical caution, furnished comparisons to illuminate many problems of the earlier period, and helped to explain the content of the concepts. The very changes in the channels of information, once the differences are estimated, account for much.

It is difficult to decide when opinion becomes public opinion, but not so difficult to include everything which might form it. As Stuart Rice has defined it, opinion need not be the result of a rational process, need not include an awareness of choice, and must be sufficiently definite to create a disposition to act upon it under favorable circumstances. British opinion may be definite, but opinion on such a subject as the United States is usually acted upon through diplomatic channels unless we descend to the disposition which prompts the reading of an American book, a walk to Bond Street to see an American cartoon, or the purchase of an American typewriter. The term "attitude," of which opinion may be the verbal expression, is a useful postulate for classification of human behavior.

Particularly in this study it has been desirable to proceed quantitatively, but such quantitative measurements were not always possible; however, the effort to proceed quantitatively brought about useful conceptual reformulation of the subject matter. L. R. Thurstone's elaborate quantitative measurements were not easily used for gaining knowledge from England, especially since it is difficult with them to distinguish between factual-judgment opinions and attitude-representation opinions. The latter no doubt predominate in international relations. The American heritage in Britain—the element in the composite picture which was pre-existent and stored up for our own period—may be called the stereotype and shall be duly considered. All this governs the infiltration of things American, which, it is true, may be used or resisted by the British without an expression of opinion.

As a practicable approach, this study began as an attempt to analyze British reaction to American imperialism, but it was felt increasingly that what could be said thereon must be related to a more general picture, a synthesis which would be full of fertile explorations. Without the aid of many monographic studies, there can be no pretensions of exhausting the many topics discussed. Among the vital subjects that have not been given proper attention here are the rôles played by members of the Empire, the useful contrast between the American impact upon the Empire and upon the United Kingdom, and the essential meaning of a German or a Colonial impact upon Great Britain as compared with the picture drawn in these pages.

Wandering about in Britain with a special purpose is always a pleasure, but especially so since the repeated inquiries were thought to be of doubtful usefulness and strangely American. By innumerable conversations, questionnaires, and surveys, an effort was made in some seventeen thousand miles of British travel to draw upon ten thousand British, a "sampling" (including over eight hundred selected and pre-arranged interviews) in such a way as to exploit the variations in the social and economic structure, pressure groups, and territorial divisions. Both the knowledgeable and the innocent were approached, questions respecting the channels of information and America being modified to fit the immediate circumstances.

The abundance of commonplace nonsense concerning the alleged characteristics of the Briton and the American, and the peculiar idiosyncrasies of Anglo-American relations make it difficult for a personal study to avoid the traditional claptrap. The gentle art of being insular is no prerogative of the British, and if such does govern the attitude to America, it also affects the British Empire, or Yorkshire's views on Cornwall. No matter what may be the envious accusations of Continental diplomatic opinion respecting British machinations, the more subtle art of being gentle with a sting is not pertinent to this study except in so far that an American, at the end of interviews or speeches, constantly finds himself forced to defend American civilization. This may be turned to value for the study of stereotypes. The regional differences of Britain are startling, and it is difficult for the American to believe that the British cannot understand the sectional variations of the United States. Many difficulties exist because of the heritage that has been left by interminable discussions of racial and lingual unity; even if taken seriously up to a point, the verbiage is most confusing. The date of the field work, August 1936 to August 1937, was as satisfactory as any one year could be, and as typical. The abdication of Edward VIII, exaggerated by Americans as an Anglo-American event, did not fundamentally distort the results of the field program.[2] More to the point was the increasing political tension in Europe, and the alignment of fronts of Fascism and Communism. Such developments stimulated an interest in the function of the United States.

The British belief has been growing that the English and American democracies have a united duty in preserving a common civilization. This approach, which is presented with many variations, now supersedes the appeals of race or language. One suspects that the English desire to improve their understanding of American history and literature depends more upon the belief that the political understanding of democracies must be fortified on the cultural side than upon any advance since 1914 in the culture or refinements of American life. The contemporary interest (which naturally affected the field work), one may fear, relies too heavily upon a surge of political feeling. Substantial improvement to knowledge will come only when the British feel that American civilization must be appreciated as a subject of knowledge and world history, without any dependence upon a feeling which national interests might conceivably destroy. So many British efforts to reach a better non-political understanding have impressed Americans more than the British. There is an expectation of substantial American contributions. And it seemed that talking and thinking about America have become, even amid the distracting realities of the Continent, a katharsis for the British. The interest reminds one of the attraction exerted by some mystifying writing on the wall. Herr Hitler decided in *Mein Kampf* that England differed from any other state in Europe if only because of her linguistic and cultural communion with us.

[1] Henry James, *William Wetmore Story and his Friends* (Edin. & Lond., 1903), I, 5–6; J. R. Seeley, *Expansion of England* (Boston, 1901), p. 150. Bryce, *American Commonwealth* (1927 ed.), I, 9; II, 656, 847, 851; cf. his *Social Institutions of the U.S.* (New York, 1891), 270. Note J. B. Botsford, *English Society in the Eighteenth Century, as Influenced from Oversea* (New York, 1924); it is not always easy to see the connection between the society and overseas in this interesting volume. A detailed study of the allusions to Colonial experience in 19th and 20th century England would be useful. Stuart A. Rice, ed., *Statistics in Social Studies* (Philadelphia, 1930), 177, 179–80, 194; also Rice's *Methods in Social Science* (Chicago, 1931) and *Quantitative Methods in Politics* (New York, 1928). L. R. Thurstone, "Attitudes can be measured," *Amer. Journ. of Sociology*, 1927, 33:529–45. For other methods see G. B. Neumann, *A Study of International Attitudes of High School Students* (Teachers College, *Contribution to Education*, No. 239, Columbia Univ.); J. L. Woodward, *Foreign News in American Morning Newspapers* (New York, 1930). Woodward prefers the term "Public Attitude" to "Public Opinion"; of 40 individual papers, each weighted by its own circulation, the proportion of space devoted to foreign news was 5.15%—the A.P. furnishing 58.5%. The attention-compelling value of that space must also be considered. J. D. Whelpley, *British-American Relations* (Boston, 1924), impressionistic. P. A. Sorokin, "Socio-Cultural Trends in Euro-American Culture during the last hundred years," address at Duke University, 1938.

[2] The gentleman's agreement of the British press was remarkably effective; direct circulation of American newspapers and news magazines can be discounted as a mass force in this instance. Provinces were in more darkness than London; surprise increased as one descended the social scale. When American clippings were

produced, they brought forth such remarks: "Oh, that's from an American paper—just gossip!" Letters from relatives in America helped information to filter through. The Dominions were more susceptible to stories carried in the American press, and served as an indirect source of American information. See author's comments, *Journalism Quarterly*, June 1937, pp. 210–11.

II

AMERICA AND THE PRESS

THE historian is primarily concerned with newspapers—the completed process of journalism; but by so confining himself, he easily overlooks what influence journalism may have upon the historical narrative.[1] If the British press is too sensational or too degenerated, it is said to be "Americanized." It is significant that this permeating channel of Anglo-American information is so accused. One-half of the British journalists interviewed were inclined to agree with this accusation; a larger percentage thought this opinion was prevalent in other social groups. American journalists, familiar with the British press, preferred to maintain that the American influence had been merely toward brighter make-up and easier reading.

In 1920 it was said:

Time was when the average British newspaper represented a high standard of accuracy, fairness and literary ability, but since the importation of many doubtful American methods, the character of the press has to a large measure degenerated.

The full outcry began much earlier. Sir James Henderson lamented the American sensationalism of the British press in his inaugural address to the Institute of Journalists in 1900. Before the Society of Women Journalists, Mr. Zangwill deplored the Americanization, from which only *Punch* escaped, by which the press was losing its prestige. To the same Society Lady Auckland described in 1909 her nightmare experiences with New York reporters. An American police reporter for a London paper broke so many rules of English libel law that he had to skip out of England. In the course of ex-American William Waldorf Astor's libel action brought against the *Daily Mail* for its story of a dinner party, the Lord Chief Justice said:

One cannot fail to see that there is growing in the English press, copied from a Press with which Mr. Astor is better acquainted than we are—(laughter)—a practice of inserting personal paragraphs which is very annoying.

The *Manchester Guardian,* which agreed with the statement that the American press "is a reflex of the nation rather than a leader of it," said in a leading article:

The Americanization of the British newspapers is a favorite theme whenever any detail of simplification or elucidation is attempted here, and it may be admitted at least that some civilised Americans do not think very well of their newspapers.

On October 31, 1900, the same paper began an editorial:

Those who have learned to discount, as a rule, bad news from America will be disappointed in the latest accounts of the New York explosion.

That such explanation had to be made would point to faulty press coverage, or a reliance upon newspapers which were not held in high esteem by the British press.

At the Newspaper Press Fund dinner the American Ambassador, Whitelaw Reid, deprecated English imitation of the constant, almost incredible, corruption of the English language in American colleges and on American streets. When the *Daily News* complained in 1907 of vulgarity, sensationalism, and a moral menace, it added: "The Press in this country has developed every attribute that we used to consider peculiarly American." The "sheer Billingsgate" of the American press, cried the *Scotsman,* would not be tolerated in Scotland. "That it is tolerated in America seems to show that in point of manners and in regard to the decencies of controversy our kinsmen have yet much to learn."

American press machinery and administration served as models. American companies pushed the linotype in England (about 1889) and the monotype. With American experience Robert P. Porter returned to the *Times* and inaugurated its famous supplements. The City of London School's experiment with classes in journalism arose out of a casual conversation between a prominent London journalist and a friend who told him what America was doing. The President of the Conference of Institute of Journalists in 1903 declared that England must be willing to learn, otherwise American journalists would come over to delight the British public. Thus, from about 1895 onwards, the British press was drawing heavily upon American experience. It is therefore surprising that when British journalism is so well acquainted with the attributes of the American press, it is so frequently opened to the criticism, by British and Americans alike, that never has England's press been adequate in its treatment of the United States.

Attention will be directed to what the British considered to be American public opinion.[2] British views in this respect would affect vitally any impact. James Bryce throughout the various revisions of his *American Commonwealth* spoke with diffidence about the American press, apparently tending toward leniency in his views. He considered the American newspapers powerful as "narrators, as advocates, and as weathercocks," and concluded,

Taking the American press all in all, it seems to serve the expression, and subserve the formation, of public opinion more fully than does the press of any part of the European continent, and not less fully than that of England.

As a supplement to his volumes, as well as some slight indication of British diplomatic opinion and practice concerning the American press, it is instructive to note the papers and periodicals which were cited most in Bryce's dispatches during his Ambassadorship in Washington, 1907–13. They were the *Literary Digest*, the *New York Evening Post*, *Herald*, *Journal of Commerce*, *Times*, and *Tribune*, the *San Francisco Chronicle*, the *Outlook*, the *New York World*, and the *Washington Post*. The predominance of New York is very marked, and is like the emphasis of quotations in the British press during these same years (and to an extent, up to the present) on opinion of the eastern seaboard. But Bryce himself was aware of the dangers and limitations of this preoccupation.

The press of the United States and the "organization of a powerful news agency called the Associated Press" formed the subject of a long report prepared by His Majesty's Embassy at Washington in 1908. Mr. H. G. Watson, then a secretary, later minister to Helsingfors, wrote this acute analysis, of which Bryce said:

Mr. Watson has couched his comments in a language whose moderation I appreciate all the more because I should have felt inclined to paint in darker colours the reckless irresponsibility of a large section of the American press.

Watson had concluded, "The press is very powerful in the United States, more so perhaps than in England. . . . Of all the many features of American life, the press is the most discouraging."

The complaint of the inadequate treatment of the United States by the British press has become almost traditional.[3] Lodge complained to A. J. Balfour, whose first important speech on foreign affairs as a Minister was largely devoted to Anglo-American relations, that England had kept herself ignorant; "Until very lately your newspapers gave us less space than to Belgium and Holland." Hay informed Roosevelt as late as September 29, 1897, "There is never a civil word about England printed in America, and rarely a civil word about us printed in England. Whether this ill-wind is all historical or partly prophetical, I cannot say." W. H. Page, one of those who highly valued Shakespeare as a link, was amazed at the mutual ignorance and dumbfounded by the profound effect of the yellow press, including American correspondents of London papers, upon the British mind. Obviously James Bryce was not alone in the opinion he offered to Roosevelt, August 19, 1904:

I am anxious to get to understand the present position of politics on your side. It is impossible to gather them from the scanty and far from impartial accounts which the English newspapers give us.

Of 520 representative and educated Britons questioned by the author, 410 relied upon the British press to keep them informed about America. Four hundred of those replying felt that the presentation of American life in the British press was inadequate. Justifying reasons for this state of affairs were advanced by over two hundred and fifty persons. British journalists were less severe on their product, only eighteen of fifty admitting that the treatment was inadequate. Those who depended on other sources of information—travel, professional contacts, etc.—still relied to a large extent upon the press. There were no marked differences in the replies from the provinces. Seventy-nine per cent declared that the cinema was for the rest of the community, preëminent as a permeating channel of information. But for steady formation of opinion among the more educated, the press would appear to be as significant as it was in the decades before the World War.

The late Ambassador Bingham, himself a newspaper man, in pointing an extreme case alleged that American papers in cities of 150,000 carried more news about Great Britain than the best English papers do about the United States. Traveling and resident Americans in England were almost unanimous in their complaint: of 190 American residents of three years standing, 170 thought the press defective. American journalists in England were not so critical.

America is recognized as a "Reporter's Paradise," but British journalists, it is said, even though sent out to cover the country, soon exploit only the richer routines—New York, Washington, and, more recently, Hollywood—and become affected by their sensational contemporaries in the States. Many special correspondents have been sent to cover Hollywood, a fact which lends plausibility to the newspaper men's complaint that American films stimulate their readers' news appetite. Discretion is left with the foreign correspondent, but some whose experiences span the years 1898 to 1938 have felt that England has not been interested in American news, although they sense an increased interest since 1914. Where our foreign affairs may affect England, or where our domestic affairs and policies have foreign repercussions, the journalists assert that the treatment is adequate, but usually no news follow-ups are wanted. The manager of the *Times*, Moberly Bell, whose first American visit in 1901 made him profoundly distressed with British conditions, concluded that the task of the foreign correspondent in America was difficult:

> The province of a correspondent is to describe facts as they are, and not as he wishes they were, and in no country of the world have I met so much frankness in describing things as they are as in America, combined with a unanimous desire that they should be described as they are not.

America is more strongly represented in news-gathering agencies.[4] There are ten or more American papers and seven news services

with offices in London. The Associated Press recently entered the
European field and is now supplying news to many leading British
papers. Seven British papers have membership in the Association
of Foreign Press Correspondents in the United States, several
Americans making up the representation. Reuter's, the British
United Press Limited, and Central are the principal agencies. The
first resident British correspondent came to the States shortly after
1900; not until after the World War did several leading British
papers send correspondents. Apparently only the *Times* and *Daily
Telegraph* have full-time correspondents in more than one place
in the United States. Quantitative measurements here as in the
measurement of news space may be misleading; however, some
are offered. In 1937, if the author's interviews were weighted, most
reliance in Great Britain was placed upon the American news in the
Times, Daily Telegraph, Morning Post (now defunct), the *Manchester Guardian,* the *Observer,* and possibly the *News-Chronicle.*
The reporting is done differently to satisfy the type of reader, as
illustrated by the cables to the *Times* and the *Daily Mail.* The
importance of this subject was shown in 1936 by the American
Government which undertook a survey of news space devoted to
America, a survey of more value to the diplomat than to the historian.[5]

In reading the British press from 1898 to 1938 for the purpose
of historical work, this writer feels that there has not been much
change quantitatively or qualitatively since 1918. The more sober
morning papers might be analyzed approximately as follows:
America receives 8 to 16 per cent of the total foreign news space.
Domestic news tends to occupy a higher total percentage, although
it is important to note that American news in the financial page is
bulky, and that feature articles (frequently approaching fiction)
about us are increasing. These features may be about giantism,
crime, or Hollywood. The more conservative provincial papers
probably print less American news. As a working classification
American news space may be listed as follows:

Government and policies	25 per cent
Finance and commercial	15 " "
Sensation and crime	30 to 40 per cent
General	20 to 30 " "

More elaborate analyses are possible.[6] The proportion of domestic news space is higher in the evening papers, but America receives about one-ninth to one-fifth of the total foreign news space. The Sunday press cannot be said to complete any gaps, and background material is offered only to a slight degree.

One may conclude that American crime receives more space than all the crime of the rest of the world, and so does American sex life. But such a paper as the *Manchester Guardian* may treat crime as a social phenomenon because of the semi-political aspects it seems to have. American kidnappings were considered better "stories" than simultaneous English kidnappings. Reports of the Thaw trial were more detailed and disgusting than those published in American papers. But as an editor of a London daily told the author: "You make your crime more spectacular—and we lay the stress as do your own papers." Europe does not yet feel any responsibility for America.

Without holding, however, to the harshest criticisms or indulging in national comparisons, one may conclude that the reporting of America for Britain, before and after the War, left much to be desired. Because of the centralization of the press in London, papers are unable to distribute the cost of an American service. After an acute analysis of their press (1938), a British non-partisan group of economists, scientists, and others (known as Political and Economic Planning) declared that American news was worth more space and staff than were allowed for it, that a national paper could well afford £15,000 a year for a first-class service.

A strong force in British journalism, Sir Arthur Pearson, who was always interested in America, started in 1898 the American Pearson Publishing Company with the idea of issuing his periodicals in the United States.[7] But this venture failed like other similar schemes of British publishers. Curiously for such a shrewd publisher, he once contemplated a daily paper in London for Americans to make up for what he thought inadequate treatment of American news. His *Daily Express* appeared April 24, 1900; on its staff was Sir Percival Phillips, a former American. Ralph Blumenfeld, another American, joined in 1902 and became editor in 1906. The *Express* and *Standard* preached the gospel of tariff reform and protection to which Pearson had become more strongly attached by his American visits. Pearson went so far as to suggest to Joseph Chamberlain that he should record his speeches for smaller audiences on gramophone, a campaign device he learned from us. The *Express* picked out America's oddities for its readers, except when tariff issues were involved. An editorial of August 29, 1907, was therefore not surprising:

Are we the victims of an exaggerated incredulity, or can we claim justification for our attitude of suspicion towards the news which comes from America? Day after day, the cables bring us well-rounded reports of remarkable doings from Over There, and the unkind thought constantly flashes across our minds as we read them in their artistic completeness— Is it possible that so many quaint things happen Over There of which we never see the like Right Here?

The halfpenny, morning *Daily Mail*, established in 1896 as an independent paper, either because of our sensational offerings or because of Northcliffe's interest in the United States, ranked almost with the *Times* and *Manchester Guardian* during the pre-1914 years in stimulating awareness to America. The *Mail* about 1897 was the first British paper to be brought into direct telegraphic contact with New York. It went into mourning for McKinley. The paper gave good position to American news and feature articles which decreased somewhat between 1906 and 1914. It illustrated how American news could be made to interest English readers—and to satisfy Northcliffe's desires. Considering the paper's policies, it gave little attention to the career of Roosevelt. Northcliffe himself was on the alert for American journalists. In his effort to "Americanize" the *Mail* and *Evening News* and other Harmsworth publications, he brought over Pomeroy Burton from Hearst's *Evening Journal*. Burton was described as a typical American who would probably not succeed in London because he would find no hustling reporters. Northcliffe once said, "Every young man ought to go to the United States. . . . But it is ridiculous to rush it." Before establishing the *Mail*, Northcliffe made his first visit to the United States, where he talked with editors and owners, went through offices, and studied printing plants; he became convinced of the value of having his staff know the mechanics of press production. "He also found," according to Fyfe, "much to admire in the American presentation of news, but he did not think British readers would care for it." His *Weekly Despatch* was often spoken of as a copy of an American Sunday paper. Tom Clarke records that Northcliffe spent money so that his staff could visit the United States to study methods of business and our outlook.

Spring-Rice in 1892 wrote, "It is quite absurd to see the enormous importance attached to the slightest word of the *Times* or of an English statesman. Americans are still very colonial." This comment, at least for the *Times*, remained true for several decades. The *Times*, with its influential status lending prestige to its American news, had correspondents who frequently offered criticism within their news dispatches, and it was unusual for editorials to diverge from their observations. This was dangerous if the correspondents were misleading, as Henry Cabot Lodge was pained to see in August 1895 when G. W. Smalley was telling England that Americans did not care about the Monroe Doctrine or Venezuela. On October 17, 1907, appeared the first Marconi dispatch, and thereafter during 1908 longer accounts were coming through this way. The *Times's* presentation was incomplete for the West and Middle West and any cultural activities.

The thoroughly liberal and eminent provincial journal, the *Manchester Guardian*, with an editor determined to keep out Americanisms, gave throughout the period a comprehensive picture of America and revealed Manchester's interest in the South. Because of its hostile attitude to imperialism, it devoted excellent reporting to America's overseas expansion. Its interest in the functioning of democracy prompted a fairly complete coverage of American governmental policies. It frequently quoted the New York *Journal of Commerce*, the *Commercial and Financial Chronicle*, and the *Nation*. It was apparently the only non-Labor paper which gave a full account of the Idaho labor trials in 1907. The morning *Standard*, suffering a checkered career under the same management as the Conservative *Evening Standard*, did not commit itself in editorials, but used them instead to give analyses of American activities. There was ample news space without stress on the piquant. And though there was not the same space as given by the *Times* and the *Westminster Gazette* in 1900–03 to American trade and competition, for polemical reasons it led in news about Canadian-American rela-

THE PRESS21

tions in 1910–11. Serious American news after 1911 was supplemented with exotic features and humor. J. A. Spender, one-time editor of the *Westminster Gazette*, a Liberal evening paper, told the author that "It was difficult to get readers interested in the better things of the States." This paper, carrying on the political life of the *Pall Mall Gazette*, gave most of its slight American space to politics, without ignoring crimes, disasters, and lynchings. Its editorial policy was usually tolerant, and though its "notes" helped to propagate comments on fads and notions, it was usually with a smile rather than a sneer. Mr. Dooley's observations were a feature. It frequently relied upon the American news of the *Times*.

The *Scotsman* (Liberal Unionist), without granting so much space as the *Times*, had well-selected news, particularly from 1898 to 1901, on imperialism and finance; the independent *Glasgow Herald* ranked with it in this respect. The *Birmingham Post* and the *Yorkshire Post* gave to their communities a fairly representative selection of American news. Much less space is to be expected in other provincial papers such as the *Sheffield Daily Telegraph*. Two evening papers, the *St. James's Gazette* (Independent Conservative) and the *Globe* (Conservative), stressed oddities, although the former claimed to give special attention to American news. W. T. Stead, who may share the honor with R. Blathwayt of introducing the interview to England in the late eighties and all the evils it implied to the English, was at one time editor of the *Pall Mall Gazette*. The *Daily Telegraph* (Unionist) and the *Morning Post* (Unionist) which claimed wealthy readers, were much alike in their American news; the former offered comprehensive reporting on the Spanish-American War. The *Labour Leader* (Socialist) had little space to devote to American news, and despite a certain provincialism in what it did print, the paper kept up with American labor by the pens of Keir Hardie, Upton Sinclair, and others.

The Anglo-American papers, which served the traveling American or the semi-permanent hordes of American residents, conformed to a mental need and assuaged nostalgia, and have been discussed elsewhere.[8] Such numerous publishing ventures and failures indicated the migratory habits of Americans. Those with the more nauseous social "puffs" have happily disappeared. The American Colony in Britain never had enough cohesion or distinctiveness to support a paper for any length of time, or else it felt it was well served by the British press. Paris, not London, is the strategical publishing center for such enterprises.

The *Chicago Tribune* and the *New York Herald-Tribune* have been the more conspicuous successes in the field of European editions. James Gordon Bennett II established the European edition of the *New York Herald* in 1887 at Paris; in a fit of pique he moved it to London where he published it for several months in 1888–89, daily and Sunday. There was resentment in journalistic circles against the publication of an American newspaper, and a deeper opposition to a seven-days-a-week paper. Fortunately for the paper, Bennett settled his dispute with the French authorities and closed down in London. Frequently these papers were designed to capitalize on a surge of friendly political feeling. The *Bond* (1899) was devoted "to the moral federation of the English-speaking Peoples," and extolled the civilizing effect of Anglo-Saxon commerce. A paper founded in 1905 under the editorship of Charles Damiens said in May 1913:

> The *Anglo-American Times* is now the sole organ voicing the aspirations of the two great English-speaking peoples in whose power lie the destinies of the world, old or new, if united, to uphold the traditions and share the sorrows and glories of the Anglo-Saxon race, wherever met between Peary and Scott's tents.

The War brought to a close most of these fitful efforts at Anglo-American chitchat. The Anglo-American community of interests evidently does not call for a significant specialized journal.

As an informative and effective channel, British and American magazines must not be exaggerated.[9] However, American journals circulating in England should be viewed as a source of undiluted, intensified stimulation to things American, the British journals more as spasmodic reflections and reactions to the American scene. The American magazines not only conveyed impressions but also influenced their competitors.

William Archer stated in 1900, "I am much mistaken if there is a single club in London where American periodicals are so well represented on the reading-room table as are English periodicals in every club in New York." If they were supplied, he thought, they would be read. But Gertrude Atherton observed:

All the magazine writers are almost as well known in Great Britain as in the United States, for the British prefer our magazines to theirs; the literary quality is not as high, but the world is yet a child and loves good pictures . . .

Harper's Young People met with such favor that it was published simultaneously in England; in 1880 the English *Harper's* was started. In 1881 E. A. Abbey declared that everyone was enthusiastic over American magazines, particularly *Scribner's*. England and Europe were impressed by the illustrations, the wood engraving, and the rapid fine-art printing of the periodicals. "Ian Maclaren" judged the *North American Review* in 1903 the best edited magazine of public criticism. Sir Walter Besant even asserted:

We have many things to learn from America. The maintenance of the honour and the reputation and the authority of the critical columns of our journals is one of these things.

Harper's, Scribner's, the *Atlantic, Century,* and a few other quality magazines had a fairly large circulation in England at the turn of the century. The success of these led Sir George Newnes to start the *Strand Magazine.* Chalmers Roberts brought Heinemann the idea of publishing an English edition of *The World's Work* about 1901, and under the editorship of Sir Henry Norman the American practice of a general get-together meeting of the staff was imitated. The founding of *Country Life* was due to Lord Riddell, who directed Mr. Hudson's attention to American developments in fine printing. From his trips to the States, Allen Thorndike Rice helped to make the "symposium" a feature among magazine editors. William Archer urged "McClure methods" for the dramatic presentation of social politics in the sixpenny class.

American magazines with London addresses have almost tripled since 1914.[10] Trade journals of American origin sometimes created and sometimes followed the attention given to our technical development. Probably the best-selling journals have been in the engineering and electric industries. The *American Machinist* (1877), which dropped the adjective in its European edition, gained steadily from 1900 in connection with the great interest taken in American machinery. British editorial matter and advertisements had to be inserted, as in other similar journals, to meet the accusation that it was too American. One machinist who was hunting subscriptions in England out of zeal for American methods wrote in 1905:

> If they happen to see it is an American paper from which you got your information, they will tell you at once that American tales are not to be trusted . . .

The *American Referee* (1897) became the *Cycle Referee* in 1898 to ride along on the American cycle invasion. The former made a graceful bow, May 13, 1897:

> There have been established within the past two years hundreds of agencies for the sale of the product of American makers. . . . *The Referee* will not argue that because you fail to appreciate some American ideas you are necessarily wrong.

Americans in these journals were less reticent; consequently, the British benefited by their disclosure of industrial practices. But it is noticeable also from 1900 onwards that British trade journals were becoming more crisp and breezy in the face of our trade journal competition.

At the present American magazines in England are more than a flash of home to the American traveler. They form for certain classes of English people a fountain of Americanism and ideas or misconceptions about the United States. They assume importance as objects by which to compare the language, the current taste, and the mentality of two groups of English-speaking peoples. Apart from a few of the more famous periodicals which have their own distributing centers, four rather unpretentious agencies circulate the bulk of our magazines. Some of these firms have a history reaching back before the War, but distributing then was not highly organized. The earlier period saw fewer American magazines, but the proportion of quality magazines was higher. London and a few provincial cities get most of the American magazines.

Our fashion magazines possess a steady appeal, especially since

English women can profit by the dress-pattern service offered by these periodicals. One experienced distributor placed our geographical magazines next in appeal, and to be ranked with the *Saturday Evening Post,* which may be found among enterprising advertisers. Our curt news magazines now have several English imitations. Digests of magazine articles have appeared. In style and format the pocket magazine has been followed. A few others have tried to capture the atmosphere of the *New Yorker.* The home, cooking, and housekeeping magazines must be Anglicized, since the ways of the English household are different. The English housewife until recently did not go readily to a mechanical ice-box or trouble herself with the intricate problems of central heating. Except for Christian Science publications, there is little interest in our religious journals. One of the most eminent of American Anglican journals has but three subscribers in Britain.

Movie and radio magazines have had good sales. True romances and true love were Anglicized and sometimes translated from the American; sweetheart stories run a fickle course from month to month. Illustrations were frequently changed to avoid unintentional humor—lovers cannot kiss good night on porches, for there are no porches in England. It does not matter that the stories were read five months before in the States; hence there arose deputations to the Board of Trade protesting against the dumping of old American magazines. Our war-story magazines did not become popular until the publication of *All Quiet on the Western Front;* an armament program created a demand for heroic, paper-backed tales of the air. Sport magazines will not be popular until the sports of the two nations converge; baseball is not cricket. The file of our "saucy," "spicy" magazines is complete. The international understanding of a ribald joke or lewd cartoon passes belief even though we don't agree on general humor magazines. Experiences of distributors would seem to prove that where the American periodical is equal to the English in price, the American magazine is often preferred. One agent explained this by suggesting that many of our magazines are specific—all-west, all-horror, all-action—which appeals to the English reader who wants variety within a very narrow range.

The circulation of American magazines and papers in Great

Britain might be disregarded, but the influx into Canada from 1900 onwards raised widespread agitation and fears.[11] Chambers of commerce, the Victoria League, the British Empire League, the Royal Colonial Institute, and members of Parliament heralded the dangers to trade, imperial loyalty, and ideals if American literature bearing advertisements were to flood Canada because imperial postal rates were exorbitant. Printed matter which cost one cent a pound between Canada and the United States cost eight cents a pound from England to Canada. The *Times* warned in February 1906:

> It means really an immense preference to American periodical literature. . . . Canada thus gets her comments and her ideas from American sources; and, though the tone of American opinion towards this country is happily very different from what it used to be, no patriotic citizen of the Empire can regard such a state of things with indifference.

Moved by this threat, members of Parliament urged the Postmaster-General in 1905 to lower the postage to Canada. Parliament discussed the danger in 1906; said Sir Gilbert Parker:

> Canada was swamped with American literature which represented the commercial and social life of the United States and dealt with the attitude of Canada as a Colony towards this country. This constant influx of American literature and its influence in Canada tended to devitalize the loyalty of the Colony.

One M.P. who had the temerity to suggest that Americans were succeeding because their magazines were better raised cries of "Oh, Oh!" It was a pity that the old *Life* circulated rather than *Punch!*

The proportion of British to American periodicals in Canada had been about 5 per cent to 95 per cent; after reduced rates had been in force for several years an estimate showed the proportion to be 40 per cent to 60 per cent in 1914. In 1908 the British publications sent yearly to the Dominion jumped from three million to nine million copies. But as late as 1914, during the Post Office Vote in Parliament, Mr. L. C. M. S. Amery insisted that the cheap magazine rate to Canada was essential unless American ideals were to dominate. The threat of Americanization could come in roundabout ways. This episode illustrates how Great Britain may be reminded of the United States by the British Empire.

A devoted reader of several British weeklies, monthlies, and quarterlies might still find himself unaware of many American developments.[12] But among the weeklies (which exercised in pre-war days an influence not appreciated in this country) the *Spectator* prided itself upon its presentation of America and its conviction of the peace-compelling virtues of the English-speaking peoples. Leo Maxse, editor of the *National Review*, believed John St. Loe Strachey, editor of the *Spectator*, was taken in by the Americans. When Hay was Secretary of State he wrote to Strachey,

I read the *Spectator* every week, and am glad to think that in this way I sometimes hear your voice and exchange ideas with you. You are always just to us. Sometimes you do us a little more than justice.

The *Saturday Review*, coming under Lord Hardwicke when Frank Harris sold it in 1898, watched hawk-like for America's defects and became a counterblast to the *Spectator*. The *Economist* frequently carried acute interpretations of American affairs, and was one of the calm journals in face of the American invasion of 1900–02. Massingham chose *The Nation* as the new name for his magazine in 1907.

The "wild man" of English journalism who talked like an American, W. T. Stead, had an influential whim which was America. He felt it was the proper interest of his *Review of Reviews* to bring the English-speaking people together, and though in 1903 he might confess to the loss of one great illusion—his overreliance upon the English-speaking people—he continued to be one person in the magazine world who described many American activities. The *Fortnightly Review*, the *Nineteenth Century*, and the *Contemporary Review* led their rivals in articles relating to America. Among lighter magazines with frequent comments on American life were T. P. O'Connor's *M.A.P.* and *T.P.'s Weekly*. O'Connor made an unsuccessful American marriage, was quite early susceptible to our journalistic influences, longed for separate seats and desks in the House of Commons as in Congress, and enjoyed Americans because they were unlike the English. Many technical and professional journals of different degrees of influence kept their readers informed of special developments. The *Dental Record* was at first more conscious of America's existence than the prominent medical journal, the *Lancet;* the *Engineer* and *Engineering* preserved intellectual contacts which bore fruit. The *B.M.G.,* specializing in banjo, mandolin, and guitar, was published with the most pertinent use of the motto "Hands Across the Sea." The *Era* had full reports on American amusement as a guide primarily for British entertainers. The British ladies' magazines and illustrated society journals, as if in a conservative protest, never stressed the United States. Religious journals followed the activities of their brethren quite spasmodically, the Baptists and Quakers perhaps more than others. As *Punch* warned, Americans should not take British humor too seriously, but in its instinctive English feeling it found enough American curiosities to stimulate its funny bone. Generally, the emphasis upon the ridiculous in the States seemed to decline after 1905. The effectiveness of a mass of jokes, squibs, or cartoons cannot be ignored, for many ideas about persons and countries are lightly gained. Traditional ideas, surrounded by a halo of ignorance, feed upon humor.

Both cables and postal communication may well be discussed here.[13] Cables are important enough as links of international communication to arouse diplomatic anxiety about the control thereof, an uneasiness which implies that the news about a country or its business may be discolored by an unfavorable or snooping control. American complaints have been heard from time to time. Melville Stone thought that before 1898 all foreign news had a British slant; William W. Hawkins, president of the United Press Association, described how American news to South America was boiled down via London. At the very extreme it has been said that it would be possible to get over the cables of the Western Union and Commercial only such intelligence as any principal British minister of state would deem harmless or promotive of British interests. It is therefore revealing to turn to British complaints in pre-war years.

The British were not concerned with what came from the United States over the cables; they were interested in seeing what and how much went to the States, Canada, and the rest of the Empire.[14] Henniker Heaton said in 1907 that five million dollars were spent telegraphing to the United States; when the Institute of Journalists in 1910 wanted cheaper cable rates and a non-American news service to Canada, Heaton observed that the carrying capacity to

America and Canada was three hundred million words per annum, but only twenty-one million words were sent. Charles Bright had urged in 1898 an All-British or Anglo-American Pacific Cable to bind English-speaking countries together. The *Times* accepted the working agreement of the Anglo-American Telegraph Company with the Western Union Company, December 20, 1910, as marking the transfer of control of the only remaining British Atlantic cable to American hands. Sir Gilbert Parker expressed his concern in Parliament. The *Saturday Review* complained in 1912: "All the thirteen Atlantic cables—every one made and laid by this country—are now under American control." Cables were discussed at the Imperial Conference, but it did not end anxiety, and in 1912 Parliament was urged to plan a state cable over the Atlantic.

Once again the relationship between Canada and America had stimulated discussion. It was argued in England that the news service as it existed in 1910 between Canada and the United States was inadequate, since no Canadian newspaper maintained a special correspondent in the States and therefore Canada had to depend upon our news services which spread American influence and gave a fillip to our merchandise. An M.P. was of the opinion that all the cabled news in the Dominion's journals passed through American sources and "gets considerably muddier in the process"; the *Saturday Review* added:

If the effect produced on the mind of the Englishmen settled in Canada is one of resentment or irritation, that on the future generation of native-born Canadians is likely to be more serious and even disastrous.

Thus it was, as the *Spectator* observed in 1910, that cables carried the evidences of British self-depreciation to American papers who took it all seriously and passed it on to Canada and the British West Indies. Sir Evelyn Wrench admitted in 1914 that the Imperial Press Conference of 1909 had done some good, but the fact remained that too much Canadian news came through American sources.

Cable traffic figures are not of a nature to warrant detailed comparisons. The total traffic now carried by United States carriers (radiotelegraph and cables) would probably be thirty-five to forty million words a year from the United States to Great Britain;

about five to ten million words would constitute the press messages [15] or enough to fill thirty to sixty weekday issues of the *New York Times*. Press messages from Great Britain to the United States are greater than the eastward flow. This traffic no doubt exceeds any pre-1914 figures.

The pleasure of receiving letters from the United States does not correlate with any informative content.[16] The influence of postal communications between the United States and Great Brittain is vague, but the channel does not upon observation appear to bulk large in molding opinion. One finds in districts of heavy emigration to America some detailed experience and knowledge about small regions which were secured from American letters. Of some two thousand persons questioned in South Wales, only two hundred were influenced in any significant way by such correspondence; the proportions were similar in Edinburgh. Particular correspondence may be of real importance in the interchange of ideas and methods, but in general the importance of this channel, as compared with the force of other forms of communication, appears to be decreasing. The higher one goes in the social scale, the more frequent becomes the emphasis upon the value of personal correspondence, and where such communication does exist, there is almost a snobbish belief that only such a channel is reliable. But if one may judge from American and British biographies, this source of information could not have been persistent or widely effective.

The arguments for cheaper postage to the United States indicated the belief that it was one definite way to improve mutual understanding. Henniker Heaton made his first voyage to the States in 1890 and began a friendship with John Wanamaker. America from the first was anxious to have the penny postage which was established on the first of October 1908 on the same lines as the imperial penny post. But Heaton complained in 1910 that after seventeen years of effort his Government had consented with ill grace.

About 4,058 short tons of letters and postcards were sent from the United States to Great Britain between 1898 and 1914. The tables show that in 1901 the volume of letters and postcards and other articles dispatched from the United States for the first time surpassed the westward traffic; in letters and postcards the eastward traffic remains greater, with few exceptions, than the westward traffic. There is a steady increase from 1894 (accelerated in 1909 by the cheaper postage) until the War; the increase is renewed in post-war years until the severe drop in eastward letters and postcards in 1933, and in other articles in 1931. The eastward traffic in letters mounts slowly thereafter; the westward traffic does not. The greatest eastward traffic in letters is in 1929 (25,400,000 items), that of other articles, in 1931 (10,720,000 items). By 1920 the letters sent to Great Britain had more than doubled the volume of 1894. But there was about as much letter traffic between 1910 and 1914 as in any peak years after the War. Prosperity affects communication, and some of the mail must be accounted for by the increase of American business in Great Britain and the hordes of tourists. However, it would be most unimaginative for one looking at the years 1920 to 1936 to deny that a stack of letters and postcards from the United States 276 miles high would not have some effect upon Great Britain! It undoubtedly helped to supplement the press.

¹ L. M. Salmon, *The Newspaper and the Historian* (New York, 1923), 38; *The Newspaper and Authority* (New York, 1923), 409. Zangwill, *Times*, June 21, 1911; Elizabeth Banks, "American 'Yellow Journalism,'" *19th Cent.*, 1898, 44: 329; Lord Chief Justice, *D. Mail*, Feb. 8, 1899, p. 6. See G. W. Smalley, *Anglo-American Memoirs* (London, 1912, Second Series), II, 271–73. Astor, sometimes nicknamed "Walled-off Astor," spent £30,000 to keep H. M. Hyndman out of Burnley, according to Frances, Countess of Warwick, *Discretions* (N.Y., 1931), pp. 120–22. Reid, *Times*, May 21, 1906, p. 6; Conference of Journalists, *Times*, Sept. 2, 1903; schools of journalism were frowned upon by the majority of British journalists questioned. Charles Whibley in *Blackwood's Edin. Mag.*, 1907, 181:538. The *Newsagents Bookseller's Review* (Jan. 6, 1906, p. 12) declared that American methods, disliked by newsagents, of direct subscription for and supply of daily newspapers were beginning to tempt British publishers; *Times* and *Glasgow Herald* were the chief offenders. American workmen frequently got laurels in Britain for fitting of press machinery. R. H. Heindel, *Journ. Q.* XIV: 82.

² For details see author's article, "A Pre-War British Analysis of the American Press," *Journ. Q.*, Dec. 1937, 361–63, based partly upon answers to questions addressed to the British Foreign Office; cf. author's "Press References in Pre-War Diplomatic Documents," *Journ. Q.*, Sept. 1937, 297. Bryce, *Amer. Commonwealth* (2nd ed., Revised, London and N.Y., 1891), II, 263, 267, 645; there are slight changes in later revisions. *U.S. Dept. of State, G.B.*, Vols. 191–213. By comparison, judging merely from the incoming diplomatic dispatches of our Embassy in London (between 1898 and 1906), one is likewise not much impressed by American analysis of British public opinion or observations on the press and general affairs. The *Times* was giving amazing leadership as a reflection of public opinion by Hay, White, Choate, and Reid; the *Daily News, Chronicle, Standard, Telegraph*, and the *Morning Post* trailed at a great distance, approximately in the order named.

³ Blanche E. C. Dugdale, *Arthur James Balfour* (London, 1936), I, 226; W. R. Thayer, *John Hay* (2 vols., Boston, 1915), II, 335; Hendricks, *Page*, I, 248–49, 162; III, 44, 46; Price Collier, *England and the English from an American Point of View* (London, 1911), 185; Bryce Mss. Collection; E. H. C. M. Bell, *The Life and Letters of C. F. Moberly Bell* (London, 1927), 222; confidential report of a discussion held Jan. 14, 1937, English-speaking Union, London, on "The Press as an Agency of British-American Understanding."

⁴ A.P. has 14 men in London, U.P., 12, Hearst, 12. Fifteen American newspapers were represented in London in 1901. Reuter's handled A.P.'s American material for England, with 25 staff men and 75 string men. *Daily Mail* may send about 800 words a day. P.E.P. (Political and Economic Planning), *Report on the British Press* (London, April, 1938), 55–56, 160–61, 267, 292–93.

⁵ Government survey was Request No. 2673, June 25, 1936, "News Survey." I have used approximately 30 London and provincial papers, and others for special purposes. A writer in the *Newspaper World* (July 17, 1937) makes an analysis of the *Daily Telegraph* for 1936, revealing total American news was 300,000 words, only 6.3 per cent dealing with crime. John S. Steele, "Why Not More American News?" *Anglo-American News*, Sept. 1936, 363–64; author's "U.S. and the British Press," *Public Opinion Q.*, April 1939.

⁶ Reuter's files of American news, London, were examined, covering dates April 1935 to October 1936. The principal interests, in the order named, were: disasters, finance, legislative bodies and elections, matrimony and divorce (frequently of Hollywood), disorders and strikes, government, commerce and trade, personals (frequently cinematic), crime, aviation, theatre and cinema, and foreign relations. This file combines cables and news sent by post. At the bottom in interest are: charities, fine arts, religion, societies and conferences. See also, J. L. Woodward, *Foreign News in American Morning Newspapers* (New York, 1930), 67, and G. A. Schreiner, *Cables and Wireless and Their Role in the Foreign Relations of the United States* (Boston, 1924), 169, 180, 189.

Difference in time between New York and London may affect news-treatment; thus, American news developing up to noon suffers in the British evening papers. June to September are the dull months. One of the arguments against the Daylight Saving Bill in 1909 was that it would inconvenience those handling American quotations and securities.

⁷ Sidney Dark, *The Life of Sir Arthur Pearson* (London, n.d.), 72, 87, 89, 106–07, 111; Tom Clarke, *My Northcliffe Diary* (New York, 1931), 10, 167; Hamilton Fyfe, *Northcliffe, an Intimate Biography* (London, 1930), 66; on Moberly Bell see Allan Nevins, *Henry White, Thirty Years of American Diplomacy* (New York and London, 1930), 22; when Spring-Rice introduced Mr. Chirol to Roosevelt he stressed Chirol's support and the *Times's* coöperation during the Spanish-American War, Stephen Gwynn, *The Letters and Friendship of Sir Cecil Spring-Rice, A Record* (2 vols., Boston and N.Y., 1929), I, 119, 432–33; F. A. McKenzie, *The Mystery of the Daily Mail, 1896–1921* (London, 1921), 18–19.

The *Times* correspondents in the United States have been: G. W. Smalley, Feb. 1895–May 1906; W. L. Crippen, R. H. Porter, C. R. Hargrove, Arthur Willert during 1906–1910; Arthur Willert, 1911–20; Willmott Lewis, 1920–.

⁸ Author's "Bibliography of the Anglo-American Press," *Anglo-American News* (American Chamber of Commerce in London), December, 1937. Louis Jennings, M.P., was editor of the *Tribune's* London edition; Jennings had been a *Times*

correspondent in U.S. and returned to London in 1876 to found *The Week*. Bennett was one of the first Americans to be a feature of the Midlands. One of the more significant efforts to serve the community of interests was Ford Madox Ford's *Transatlantic Review* (1924) which did not survive. Its purpose was purely literary and to make England, France, and the United States acquainted with the intellectual achievements in the countries united by the North Atlantic Ocean. See also *Revue anglo-américaine*, Paris, 1923, etc., edited by L. F. Cazamian and Charles Cestre. R. D. Blumenfeld, *Press in My Own Time* (London, 1933), 157–58.

⁹ W. Archer, *America To-day* (London, 1900), p. 76 and "The American Cheap Magazine," *Fort. R.*, 1910, 87:321; Atherton, "The American Novel in England," *Bookman*, Feb. 1910, pp. 637, 638; E. V. Lucas, *Abbey*, I, 110–11; J. H. Harper, *The House of Harper* (N.Y. and London, 1912), 461, 475; John Lillie was the first English editor of *Harper's*. Hulda Friederichs, *Life of Sir George Newnes* (London, 1911), 111; Lord Riddell, *More Pages from My Diary, 1908–1914* (London, 1934), 15–16; Escott, *National Links*, 212; Besant, *Autobiography*, 195; Frederic Whyte, *William Heinemann: A Memoir* (London, 1928), 217–19. The author's "Circulating America," *Landmark*, Mar. 1937, 145–47.

¹⁰ Bancroft's *Directory, 1903* cites 23 American magazines with London offices; cf. lists in *Willing's Press Guide* for 1898, 1914, and 1937. The *American Machinist* was in such demand during the height of German submarine warfare that it was permitted to be exported by the special permission of the British Government; see interesting booklet "Appreciations" (McGraw-Hill, London). Pages for European consumption were added to the *Am. Mach.* in Apr. 7, 1900, XXIII, No. 12. *American Gentleman* on fashions first published in England, Aug. 1908, *Delineator* about Jan. 1893; *Vogue*, about May, 1916; *American Furrier*, Jan. 1907. See also the *American Humorist*, Feb. 18–Nov. 1888, discontinued. In the list of American magazines circulating before the War one should not overlook *St. Nicholas, Smart Set, Success, Youth's Companion, Chautauqua Magazine, Cosmopolitan*, and the *Nation*.

¹¹ *Times*, Feb. 24, 1906, an ed. inspired by Alfred Mosely; *P. Debs.*, 1906, 159: 407, 395, 419, 431; 162:1363; 164:1458; 1908, 186:1086–87; 1914, Commons, 64:773; Sir Frank Newnes, *Times*, Apr. 4, 1914; Buxton, *Times*, July 14, 1906, p. 12.

¹² Strachey in 1897 followed two supporters of the Northern cause, Richard Holt Hutton and Meredith Townsend; he was followed by Sir Evelyn Wrench in 1925 and the present editor, Willson Harris—all with practically the same views on the United States. Circulation of *Spectator* in 1903 was 22,000; see W. B. Thomas, *The Story of the Spectator* (London, 1928) and Amy Strachey, *St. Loe Strachey: His Life and His Paper* (London, 1930), 135. A. M. Low, Sydney Brooks, and H. W. Horwill were frequent contributors to British magazines on American affairs. Frederic Whyte, *The Life of W. T. Stead* (2 vols. London, 1925), II, 55, 226, 232. Hamilton Fyfe, *T. P. O'Connor* (London, 1934), 141, 191, 220, 223, Chap. XV; he wanted interviews when they were frowned upon as "very American." J. M. Richards, American business man and father of Mrs. Craigie, was proprietor of the *Academy* from 1888 to 1905. The ephemeral *Photo-Bits* and *Snap-Shots* used American females to point pointless jokes. Jokes clipped from New York journals may be found in almost every English "comic" paper.

¹³ Cables are an expensive form of communication, consequently the mass of people would be affected mainly by the coloring that cable control would give to

the press. Melville Stone, *Fifty Years a Journalist* (London, 1922), 244; he quotes Lowell, "What's good's all English; all that isn't, ain't." Will Irwin says Wolff, Havas, and Reuter's suppressed or cut to the bone the good news from the U.S., *Propaganda and the News* (New York and London, 1936), 123, 201. President of Western Union reported that 95 per cent of his cable employees are British; see Schreiner, *Cables and Wireless*, 176, 115, 122–23, 126, 184.

[14] *P. Debs.*, 1907, 174:390–91; 1911, Commons, 25:437–38; 32:2142; 1912, Commons, 36:1194; 38:1619, 1628, 1634. Heaton was optimistic enough to suppose the Anglo-American Telegraph Union would lead to a Telegraph Union of the World. Stone assured the English in 1906 that American news service to Canada did not contain advertisements.

[15] Based upon 2 seven-day periods in 1936 and 1937, "Statistics of International Telegraph Traffic Reported by United States Carriers," Federal Communications Commission, Washington. Averages are hardly possible. In the 1937 study (7 days in September), words in press messages, U.S. to G.B., were 128,490 as compared with 1936 (7 days in March), 104,017. In 1936 words in press messages, G.B. to U.S., were almost double those of eastward traffic. Great Britain in 1937 period received 53,000 more press words than France, next among the European nations.

[16] Based on statistics kindly supplied by the Public Relations Department, General Post Office, London, E.C.1. Under Heaton's efforts, the undecipherable smudge on English stamps gave way to an imitation of clean canceling used in America. In July 1909, the Bishop of Hereford, in a deputation to the Home Office, pointed out that in U.S. and Australia, Post Office facilities were refused to professional betting firms. Wanamaker was the first American elected to the Carlton Club. See Mrs. A. Porter, *Life and Letters of Sir J. Henniker Heaton* (London, 1916), 83, 85, 135, 192; *P. Debs.*, 1908, 190:53–54.

III

FACE TO FACE

AMERICANS resident in Great Britain may be viewed as sources of information and influence, but perhaps the personal element of cultural contacts does not seem so influential as, for example, in the westernization of Asia.[1] The group does not indulge in much self-expression; it has never had a historian. A prominent English statesman has said, "Certain individuals by spasmodic circulation among various important groups play a significant rôle, but we never think of an 'American Colony.' " One senses, however, a certain cohesiveness in the mental outlook of this Anglo-American group. By contrast with illusions of Anglo-American coteries still resident in America, it is more realistic, allows more for divergent viewpoints, and is less oleaginous.

The number of American citizens resident in the United Kingdom has probably not changed much since 1900. A large number have been British subjects by birth, but this would not necessarily imply a lessening of American influence. Excluding the Irish Free State, there was from 1922 to 1933 an average of 19,768 registrants (residence of three months or more); since 1933 British-born women, even though American citizens by marriage, have not been registered, and the average fell to 12,924 persons. The London area holds almost 50 per cent of the group in England and Wales; Scotland has 10 per cent of the total, Northern Ireland, 11 per cent. These figures may be contrasted with the estimate in 1931 of twenty-five thousand Americans residing permanently in France, and an estimate in 1928 which showed a total of seventy-seven thousand Americans resident in Great Britain, France, and Italy.

The mental approach of this group is conditioned slightly by being "outside" in spite of frequent interpenetration, and by the belief that it is necessary to return to the homeland in order to preserve anything resembling an American outlook. International cosmopolitans are rare. The individual may warp himself by conforming or by trying to keep himself American. But one should add that Britons who believe in the value of personal contacts for international understanding grant to the resident American much credit, as contrasted with their almost constant disapproval of the American tourist. Fully 80 per cent of those affected even slightly by personal contacts thought our migratory compatriots gave false and unhappy impressions (which might or might not decrease their possibilities of influence). Forty per cent of the total questioned had contacts with resident Americans and nearly all of these thought their general influence was corrective and reliable. Weighed against other channels, it is probable that the American Colony was more effective in pre-war years.

About 1870 "American smartness" began to be noticed and to be something of a social force in fashionable England. For decades after the Civil War the English favored the Southerner. It was the time when Americans apologized for being American by calling themselves Southerners. One of the earliest Yankee "tame cats" in great English houses was the friend of Lord Rosebery, the lobbyist Sam Ward. Edmund Hodgson Yates (1831–1894), who founded the *World* (1874) with money made on an American tour, entertained Americans to get that personal touch, the first person singular, which he had come to appreciate while working on a New York paper. Diplomat Henry White's entrance into the "Souls," a group surrounding Arthur Balfour, Margot Tennant (later Mrs. Asquith), Curzon, St. John Brodrick, and Lord Elcho, enabled him to hear and be heard. Hay spoke of Whitelaw Reid, Ambassador from 1905 to 1913, as "the delight of the nobility and the gentry." It was recorded that Princess Louise, fourth daughter of Queen Victoria and wife of the Duke of Argyll (who hunted in the West), had been especially kind to Americans.

By 1936 there were nineteen American clubs and organizations, mostly in London. It was Ambassador Choate who suggested that American women should do away with their disorganized condescension. In 1898 preliminary steps were taken to form the Society of American Women in London; it functioned more vigorously by 1916. There is now some contact with similar British groups, but there has always been a tendency for American wives of foreign husbands to shy away from such organizations. The Society has been interested in Anglo-American scholarship schemes and women's newspapers. By 1900 many plans for organizations were in the air: a Washington Society and an Anglo-American Millionaire's Club. An Anglo-American Club announced its opening in Mayfair in 1908; in 1910 an American Universities Club opened in Pall Mall. In 1922 the American Luncheon Club (formed during the War) and the United States Navy League, London section (formed in 1903, with an annual banquet on Washington's Birthday), merged with the American Society of London which had been organized in 1895, under the chairmanship of Benjamin F. Stevens. At present there are such groups as the American Circle of the London Lyceum Club Ltd. (for good fellowship); the English "Mayflower" Club (founded in 1913 to honor the Pilgrim fathers); the American Golfing Society; the American Legion (1919); the London branch of the American Overseas Memorial Day Association (1926); the American Relief Society (1925), and the Masons (whose keynote in 1899 was Anglo-Saxon unity). The Ends of the Earth Club, an outgrowth of the friendliness of 1898 and American initiative, entertains distinguished American and Colonial guests. By trying to foster reciprocal trade the American Chamber of Commerce (1916) has been very active and influential.

By celebrating our national festivals these organizations have reminded the British of the Fourth of July and Thanksgiving Day which have been occasions for fuzzy Anglo-American speeches and candied sweet potatoes. In 1898 July the Fourth was celebrated for the first time throughout Great Britain. W. T. Stead and Walter Besant wanted Independence Day to be an international day of celebration, particularly of Anglo-American solidarity. The *Times* was surprised at the hearty reception given this fête, and explained that Englishmen must have thought it saved their liberty, but more probably it was because of "the singular deficiency of our people in the sense and pride of history." Support for an Empire Day was drawn from these celebrations. The American Embassy and Consulate are also social spearheads (less so, in British opinion, than embassies of other nations), and our ambassadors, who have differed greatly in this respect, may do much to direct attention to America outside the realm of diplomacy.

By their very composition Anglo-American associations have been designed to facilitate social contacts. Nearly all of them have functioned upon the basis of personal contact, preferably between the leading citizens of both countries who are fed upon dinners, guided tours, speeches, and frequently synthetic hospitality. There has been cultural inbreeding in such groups which usually have preached to the converted. Their enthusiasm has relied heavily upon racial mottoes and linguistic unity. The "society" appeal was perhaps forced upon them because originally only the more wealthy Americans traveled. Branch activities have been more easily set up in tourist haunts which are not necessarily of social or economic significance. Nevertheless, these organizations must be discussed because they reflect historical circumstances.

One of the earliest of these bodies was the Anglo-American Association which published its aims on January 25, 1871.[2] Mr. Thomas Hughes, chairman, predicted that similar societies would be started in the United States and Canada; he added: "The lamentable ignorance of contemporary American history, which exists in England even amongst otherwise well-instructed politicians, is too notorious . . ." The group was to concentrate upon carefully prepared statements on Anglo-American issues and correspondence with American citizens. Such persons as Herbert Spencer, Sir Charles Wolseley, John Westlake, and John Morley were members. The excitement of the Spanish-American War and the persistence of American expansion and travel stimulated the growth of similar bodies. Anglo-Saxonism, with clonic spasms, had a field day.

Shocked by the war threat over Venezuela, Britons began to realize that traveling Americans should know the best of England. The Atlantic Union was originally designed for those who molded opinion in both countries and to put Americans into touch with the right aspects of British life.[3] One of the prime movers was Sir Walter Besant, who was convinced of the value of learning from America. After a visit in 1893 he had concluded that a federation of the English-speaking nations was a task worthy of a man's whole life, and to be forwarded by private contacts and constant advocacy in the press. One enthusiasm he expressed: "Except with those who, like me, have been fed with the poetry and literature of America, this romance is impossible." The first annual dinner in 1901 received little publicity; the third year's work consisted mostly of entertaining 260 Americans. During 1908, five hundred members and visitors had joined together in the Union's purpose; Lord Crewe, its president in 1910, observed, "There was something in our national character that made such societies all the more necessary." Prominent among its supporters were Lords Kinnaird, Monkswell, Crewe, Coleridge, Aberdare, and Brassey. The British Empire League also started a fund for entertaining Americans and Colonials.

The birth of the Anglo-American League at Stafford House, July 13, 1898, revealed that British friendship cut across party lines.[4] The organizing committee had earlier contemplated a protest against European interference in our war, and the whole movement had rather outrun any reciprocating response in America. Under the presiding care of the Duke of Sutherland, Lord Brassey, seconded by Mr. Ismay, moved for every effort to cement the two nations; the motion affirmed that both nations were closely allied by blood, literature, law, and world interests. Among those interested were James Bryce, Horace Plunkett, George Wyndham, T. Lee Roberts, Dr. R. C. Maxwell, Randal Cremer, and Sir Frederick Pollock. Although the League became inactive after 1900, one must record a proposed scheme in 1899 for "diffusing accurate information collected and set forth in an impartial spirit," and another in 1902 for a series of lectures upon American life. An Anglo-American Alliance Society of 1898 soon disappeared.

The Pilgrims (now designated as the Pilgrims of Great Britain) was formed at the Coronation of Edward VII. The first president, Lord Roberts, who frequently referred to blood kinship, described how General Joseph Wheeler and Harry E. Brittain (probably influenced by the Clover Club of Philadelphia) had discussed the formation of a club where Americans and Englishmen could discuss their affairs.[5] The membership which was based on public service was to extend throughout the English-speaking world. The eminence of its speakers secured a good press. These mutual interests enabled people to dine together, but the *Westminster Gazette* once remarked it didn't matter what was said there. The Sulgrave Manor Board, which supervises Washington's ancestral home, was the outgrowth of the centenary of the Treaty of Ghent. The English-Speaking Union, a post-war product, continues many of the traditions of the Atlantic Union.[6] The World War convinced Sir Evelyn Wrench, its founder, of the important closeness of these people. American members outnumber English and Colonials. The Union in America has rather tended to restrict English travelers' impressions. Recently the London group has instituted a series of important discussion panels on Anglo-American affairs.

The fitful contacts between the Protestant churches of the two countries have been systematized since the War by the establishment of the Council on Interchange of Preachers and Speakers. The personal contact in religious influence may be important; the achievements of such American visitors have been mildly beneficial if not lasting. The returning British interchanges may be even more effective factors in cultural exchange. The Congregationalists and Presbyterians appear especially eager to have Americans fill their pulpits. The Methodist circuit system has made it difficult to place colleagues in prominent pulpits. The exchanges take place in summer months when many parishioners are away; politics are permitted only outside the pulpit. A Council publication declared: "English religious books are more widely read in America, and vice versa, than any other literature. The language of religion is almost the only language of both countries which does not require re-interpretation." This is doubtful, and implies an exaggerated awareness to America's religious life and problems.

In May 1937 a movement was started under the mystic name of the Three-Fold Cord with the aim of setting up contacts between England, America, and a dominion. Carrying out a suggestion by John Buchan (Lord Tweedsmuir), the North American Committee in the House of Commons, with Sir Austen Chamberlain as chairman, held its first meeting on December 18, 1936; about ninety interested members can study and discuss Anglo-American problems and talk privately with any distinguished Americans "wishing to get into touch with political thought in this country." The Associates for Anglo-American Understanding reported "quiet" work since 1931 "to interpret American and British problems through a programme of talks and discussions"; an American lecturer devoted himself to this work. A few less specialized organizations occasionally offer platforms for American expressions—the Royal Institute of International Affairs (Chatham House), the St. George's and St. David's Societies of New York, and the British Empire Chamber of Commerce, established at New York in 1920 partly as a copy of the American Chamber of Commerce in London. Rotary in Great Britain and Ireland does not function vitally in this respect, but sometimes affords an interchange of views. Anglo-American associations were probably less effective before 1914.

American shrines in Great Britain, usually symbols of blood heritage, influence American visitors more than natives; they evoke no definite images and suggest very little American history to British passers-by.[7] Many of them have been consecrated by American initiative, and have the indirect effect of attracting tourists. Marie Corelli, forgetting her dislike of American habits, persuaded a Chicagoan to buy Harvard House, Stratford, to be "a link with John Harvard's University and a sign of friendship between the two nations." Exchange greetings have been organized by the Namesakes Towns Association which was launched in May 1932 under the auspices of the English-Speaking Union; at the beginning of 1935, fifty British cities and towns had enrolled with 579 namesakes in the United States.

Francis Bacon once wrote, "We have twelve that sail into foreign countries . . . Merchants of Light." He was optimistic. As if to grasp something concrete, cultural historians and internationalists have been led into strange paths in booming the value of mass tourist traffic, granted always so many conditions: that the correct people travel to the right places with the proper frame of mind. Britons have constantly declared that Englishmen should visit America as much as Americans visited England. But this much is already obvious, that Americans abroad make impressions and contacts which can affect the reception of American civilization. Furthermore, the British urge to travel or emigrate is evidence that an impression about America has been created, as an opportunity, adventure, relief, or fashionable haunt. Many Atlantic cross-ings, such as the hundred indulged in by Moreton Frewen, develop intimate contacts hard to estimate. The Italian historian Ferrero once asked:

What means the strange and incessant coming and going over the Atlantic; the restless stream from continent to continent, neither of which can apparently exist by itself any longer, nor yet merge itself completely in the other?

One might suggest that American journeys warm the English ego.

For our purposes the figures indicating all possible types of migratory movements between the two countries would be the most illustrative, but thousands would have to be ruled out as non-effective in contributing anything to the American impact on Great Britain. In addition there is a type of sublimated gaseous consciousness (sometimes called the "traveler's mentality") which is not indicated by statistics. Ninety per cent of the Britons questioned who had not toured America viewed our tourist as more effective in molding opinion than the British traveler returned from the States, and 80 per cent somehow concluded that the results were injurious. Forty per cent added that they were better prepared to believe British travelers, who actually were a primary source of information for only 2 per cent. Nearly all suspected that travel to America, even short of three months, would be the most effective means of improving understanding and gaining from American experience. Eighty per cent revealed an acute desire to travel to the States and to turn their itinerary from Europe to America. Inquiries addressed to Britons who had visited us suggested mental revolutions more remarkable than those usually found in travel books. Perhaps British travel since 1918 is a stronger, more healthful channel of information than that between 1898 and 1914.

Between 1898 and 1914, over a million British nationals entered the United Kingdom after embarking from the United States, a large number of possible narrators.[8] The boom years of this traffic were 1904, 1907, 1911–14. But more significant are the emigrant aliens who did not care to stay here, and departed for permanent residence in the British Isles.[9] Between 1908 and 1937, 262,486 returned to the British Isles, including all of Ireland: England,

155,509; Scotland, 48,803; Wales, 3,371; and Ireland, 54,803. Based on the length of their residence here, they took about 1,500,-000 years of American experience with them, plus some dollars. As the peaks of such movements were often related to depressed economic conditions here, one may guess that many disturbing stories were told. These emigrant aliens, representing such occupational classes as professional engineers, farmers, agents, actors, and teachers, were most familiar with life in the eastern seaboard States.

In addition, between 1918 and 1936, a total of 17,279 American citizens (native-born and naturalized) took up permanent residence in the British Isles. Their lengthy American sojourn would make them fertile channels even though they might choose their new residence because of disillusionment or dissipation. Proportionately, Scotland received slightly more than the Irish Free State and three times more than England. Possibly those who left before the depression of 1929 carried suggestions for raising Britain to American standards of efficiency. Although similar figures do not exist before 1918, such citizens no doubt accounted for many signs of American influence.

Approximately 18 per cent of the American citizens who indulged in foreign travel went to ports in the British Isles. A minimum of 317,240 Americans visited there between 1910 and 1914; those entering England via Europe would raise the total considerably. Their pre-war tourist expenditure in the United Kingdom possibly varied from fifteen to twenty million dollars a year. Such sums dropped from $40,788,000 in 1927 to $18,000,000 in 1933—a fact of great importance in cultural history. Another money tie which stimulated interest in this country was the remittances to foreign countries by aliens and other residents; the drop from $7,825,000 in 1927 to the United Kingdom to a much smaller figure in post-1929 years caused heartaches.

The exodus to London began in the sixties; by the end of the century the American hordes aroused extensive comment.[10] They toured well-beaten paths where efforts were made to cater to their needs; when tourists' routes changed, regional attitudes respecting America also changed. Gertrude Atherton described her search for atmosphere in the village of Haworth:

I never got inside the parsonage. The incumbent had been so exasperated by tourists that he had conceived an unpriestly hatred of all Americans, and vowed that not another should cross his threshold.

In 1906 the *Daily Mail* decided that the latest tourist was a cultural improvement on the old, but actually criticism was harsh because hotel managers and cabmen complained that Americans were not spending enough. Britons wagered that they could follow our routes in the provinces merely by detecting poor service and familiar incivility among the natives. Wealthy Americans who made England a playground inspired personal interest and as many jokes as our own "traveling salesman" or the penny-pinching Scotsman. These travelers ("the most senseless type of human nature," according to W. S. Blunt) were stereotypes, and the British reaction was commonplace. Americans, however, did not rush into print about their English travel in pre-1914 years; consequently, England suffered less than we did from travel literature. They propagandized newer plumbing, central-heating, breakfast foods, fruit juices, and cocktails. Frequently our condescension struck a chord of excited wonder which led to more serious investigations of American life. One may conclude that the importance of American tourists did not change much in post-war years.

It is difficult to prove conclusively that British emigration contributed to a better British understanding of American affairs or an Americanizing influence.[11] In a sense, the successful lure of America was by itself a tremendous, incalculable influence which sometimes caused bitterness. The vast numbers who departed before 1898, and after, took burdens and experience from the British Isles. From knowledge or guesses, thousands ventured the ocean voyage. The flood of persuasion books and pamphlets, "gold rush" literature, blurbs of land and steamship agents, and non-polemical British weeklies, lectures in rural districts and squibs in agricultural journals to get farmers for the South—all these may have been successful without contributing a whit to knowledge. In fact, one of the arduous tasks undertaken by G. J. Holyoake was the education of the British emigrant. No worthy guidebooks on Canada or the United States existed in 1882 when he tried to fill the gap. Our London legation wrote home in 1879:

It is remarkable how ignorant even the educated classes in this country are of the geography, history, and vital statistics of the United States, and how few books can be found here, within the reach of persons intending to emigrate, which will satisfy their reasonable curiosity in respect to the routes they should take after landing on the other side . . .

However, this state of affairs, which did not change remarkably up to 1914, affected our impact, and the available information was just as potent in over-stimulating British imagination as if it had been correct and complete. Jack London and Bret Harte made San Francisco a "dream city" to many others besides Kipling and Conan Doyle. The fact that many regretted their migration influenced those who remained behind when confronted with admonitions to "See what the United States is doing." But this "mother-land complex" (not strictly dependent, at least in the latter half of the nineteenth century, upon the political separation of the United States) could not resist infiltrations. The emigrants' preference for the United States instead of the British Colonies awakened the British Emigrants' Information Office. Between 1891 and 1900, 72 per cent of the emigrants had come here. In 1907 the question was raised in Parliament whether public money should "issue a handbook extolling the advantages of the United States as a field of emigration . . ." The Under Secretary of State for Colonies replied that accurate information could not be denied. Lord Curzon disliked this wholesale migration because British citizens "would be swallowed up in the whirlpool of American cosmopolitanism or would be converted into foreigners and aliens"—an observation that weakened the concept of blood being thicker than water. But not all ties with the homeland were severed, and family letters, perhaps even the begging notes of the "remittance men," accounted for regional differences, as in South Wales where many persons knew the physical and economic details of Pennsylvania. In general the Welsh and Scotch relied more than the English on such contacts which probably meant more before 1914.

Until recently, Britain's upper classes did most of the traveling to America; the vastness of the continent and expense severely limited the areas generally covered. About 80 per cent of such travel is for pleasure, and this proportion is probably increasing.[12] Our expansion and competition stimulated westward travel. No doubt these visitors aroused that attention to America so remarkable between 1900 and 1903. In those four years respectively came 25,822, 29,148, 30,744, and 23,013 non-immigrant aliens, an average of about four thousand coming each year from all of Ireland. The total for 1902 has not yet been surpassed. In two sixteen-year periods, 1899–1914, 1921–1936, about 279,000 and 250,000 Britishers traveled here; as yet there would seem to be no marked quantitative improvement in these contacts. The Scotch traveled slightly more than the English, as much as the Irish in the pre-war period and twice as much since; the English more than four times as much as the Welsh. Northern Ireland traveled slightly less than the Irish Free State whose share has been slowly decreasing. Thousands of British skilled mechanics also came as migratory labor to New England, returning home, no doubt, with more than dollars. But more important than all this was the fact that between 1820 and 1919 almost twelve million British citizens came here to settle. It was as late as the eighties that the first real impulse to migrate struck Scotland, a movement of great consequence to that country.

When two people come face to face one usually makes a speech.[13] Our compatriots have not been so effective in England as England's "subsidized bores" here. Yet the windy, sententious American became a stereotype. Only a few Americans like Moody the evangelist had large audiences. Roosevelt's Guildhall speech in 1910, with pithy comments about Egypt, was one of the few to make a national impression. One of the unsung heroes of cultural communication was Major J. B. Pond (1838–1903) who guided the lecturing destiny of many Britons. Matthew Arnold (seldom heard beyond the first row) was pitied for having fallen into his company, but Arnold "always found him a very kind man and strictly honourable." A wit suggested that Ian Maclaren should write his biography. This market for speeches (and books) exerted a tremendous influence upon authors and men of affairs, and still gives the British mind a sense of security, like a pension. The lecturers gained as many impressions and conceits as their audience. Our atmosphere unloosed hundreds of taciturn Britons, a carousal which may be classed as an American influence.

[1] Figures on Americans supplied by the Home Office, Whitehall. There was a marked drop from 21,061 in 1927 to 18,846 in 1928. In 1936, 1800 Americans were listed in the *Anglo-American Year Book, 1936, Directory and Guide to London, Americans with British Titles and the Anglo-American Who's Who* (London, 1913–). See also Basil and G. C. Bancroft, eds., *The American Blue Book* (London, 1905–06); W. B. Bancroft's *Directory of Americans in London* (London, 1901–1906?); *The Anglo-American Annual* (Paris, 1896–1905, etc.); and, for some activities, L. F. Lightfoot, *Some well-known Englishmen and Americans on the Continent* (Nice, 1894); J. J. Conway, *Footprints of Famous Americans in Paris* (New York, 1912); and P. Neagoe, *Americans Abroad: An Anthology* (The Hague, 1932) for post-war writers. American residents in England probably increased 30 per cent in 1899 and 1900.

[2] T. H. S. Escott, *Society in the Country House* (London, 1907), 421; A. Warren, *London Days: a book of reminiscences* (Boston, 1920); Mrs. Hugh Reid Griffin was one of the Americans responsible for the Society; see *Times*, Mar. 5, 1902, p. 4; Mar. 3, 1908, p. 10. The present American Club was opened by the Am. Ambassador in 1919; the Harvard Club was formed, July 1913; British-American Phi Beta Kappa Assoc., 1925, meets once a year. Crossed flags and clasped hands usually decorate the menus. The American Circle of the Lyceum Club once had the novel idea of giving a dinner to descendants of statesmen who championed America in 1775.

[2] From a pamphlet, *The North American Fisheries* (London and Cambridge, 1870) once belonging to Sir Philip Egerton, M.P. Passing notice may be given to the Anglo-American Y.M.C.A. established in 1868 and the British and American Mission Homes and Christian Associations in Paris, 1876. The latter was founded by Miss Ada Leigh (Mrs. Travers Lewis). Some London clubs have a corresponding membership with American clubs; Whitelaw Reid thought it important enough to mention in 1905 that the Lotus Club had such affiliations with the Savage Club, London. Reid had also been interested in a dining club called "The Kinsmen," an Anglo-American club of painters, actors, and writers with a symbol designed by E. A. Abbey showing John Bull and a Red Indian fraternizing with glass in hand. Note also the amusing account of an "Anglo-American School of Polite Unlearning" (London) to be found in S. McChord Crothers, *Among Friends* (Boston, 1910), 37; Lucas, *Abbey*, I, 120.

[3] Besant, *As We Are and As We May Be* (London, 1903), 222, 244; Besant, *Autobiography*, chap. xv; *Forum*, Oct. 1900, pp. 245–56. The British American Union (San Francisco) and the Transatlantic Society (Philadelphia) were among the imitators.

[4] Members of the executive committee of the League may be found in *Times*, July 14, 1898; attendants at the Anglo-American Banquet, *Times*, June 14, 1898; Justin McCarthy of the Irish party was in favor of the League: *U.S. Dept. of State, G.B.*, Vol. 192, No. 381.

[5] The speeches throughout the years reveal little variety. J. D. Squires, *British Propaganda at Home and in the United States from 1914 to 1917* (Cambridge, Mass., 1935), 55; New York responded in 1903.

[6] Membership in British Isles in 1918 was 757, in 1927, 8,630; *An.-Am. Year Book, 1936*, 107–110; John Evelyn Wrench, *Struggle, 1914–1920* (London, 1935). Wrench lists among those vitally interested in British-American coöperation:

A. Balfour, the two Lords Grey, Moreton Frewen, Bryce, Stead, Waldstein, and Northcliffe. Alex. Smith Cochran, the American millionaire, he called the fairy godfather of the E.S.U. and the Overseas League; Ireland was regarded by Wrench as "an essential link in Anglo-American friendship."

In New York the Committee on Interchange of Preachers was organized by representatives of the World Alliance for International Friendship, the Church Peace Union, and the Federal Council of the Churches of Christ in America. See *Council on Interchange, etc.* (n.p., 1931) and *Retrospect and Prospect, 1935–36* (n.p., 1936). British ministers may return with ideas; e. g., an Anglican who wished to see the English youth movement carried out on a larger scale on a diocesan basis, and election in parishes by choice of vestrymen. Note Rotary convention in Edinburgh in 1921. Fifteen British representatives were present at the International Council, Chicago, 1925.

[7] Funds may be sought because of this feeling of kinship; e. g., Rev. Heathcote Smith appealed to us to rebuild St. Michael's Church, Princetown, Dartmoor, originally built by American sailors who were prisoners there! British movement for memorial to Washington began in 1898. Marcus B. Huish, *American Pilgrim's Way in England* (1907); Ward and Locke, *London* (47th ed., London, 1929), 1–2; L. Russell Muirhead in *An.-Am. Year Book, 1936*.

[8] Based on *Statistical Abstracts for the U.K.* Moreton Frewen, *Melton Mowbray and Other Memories* (London, 1924).

[9] *Annual Reports of the Commissioner General of Immigration* (Washington, D.C.); also communications from the U.S. Immigration and Naturalization Service, Dept. of Labor. *The Balance of International Payments of the U.S. in 1933* (U.S. Dept. of Commerce, Washington, 1934). Returned emigrant became important figure in literature; note Shan F. Bullock's *Dan the Dollar* (Dublin, 1905); K. G. Soanes and E. C. Kenyon, *Uncle Jack from America: Story of a Poor Relation* (1899), stereotype—having made a "pile," hero returns to Old World.

[10] Atherton, *Adventures of a Novelist* (London, 1932), 239; R. B. Mowat, *Americans in England* (London, 1935), vi; Spiller, *American in England . . .* (New York, 1926), viii; *Punch,* Apr. 9, 1898, p. 159; Oct. 16, 1901, p. 283; Feb. 22, Sept. 20, 1905.

[11] G. J. Holyoake, "Emigrant Education," *19th Cent.,* Sept. 1898, 427–36; R. E. Macnaghtan in *Econ. Rev.,* Jan. 1898; H. A. Vachell, *Sport and Life on Pacific Coast* (London, 1900), 6–7; *P. Debs.,* 1907, 170:470; Curzon, *Spec.,* Dec. 14, 1907, 973–4. P.P., 1897, LXXXVIII, No. 404, Mis. Series (also No. 423), *Report on Distress Caused to British Emigrants to California by Fraudulent Land Syndicates and Emigration Agencies.* Cf. P. C. Weber, *America in Imaginative German Literature in the first half of the nineteenth century* (New York, 1926), stresses improvement in understanding due to emigration.

[12] Based on figures supplied by U.S. Immigration Service.

[13] J. B. Pond, *Eccentricities of Genius* (London, 1901), *passim;* Sir Henry Lucy, *The Diary of a Journalist* (London, 1920–23), I, 264; III, 82; Nicoll, *Ian Maclaren,* 210; Dean S. R. Hole, full of Irving and Cooper, came seeking funds to restore Rochester Cathedral; see his *Little Tour in America* (London, 1895), four months; also his *More Memories: Being Thoughts about England spoken in America* (London, 1894). George Dawson (1821–1876) was one of those who helped to spread Emerson's teachings in England. F. W. Farrar visited U.S. in 1885; eulogized Grant in Westminster Abbey, Aug. 1885; astonished by growth of U.S.

It is not clear how much the visit affected his ideas on social and temperance reform; see *Men I Have Known* (New York, 1897) and Reginald Farrar, *Life of Dean Farrar* (London, 1905). Sir Edwin Arnold was surprised that he was known here; the trip helped him in England. David Christie Murray, novelist, was careful not to criticize before he came to lecture in 1894–95; in spite of this bias, see his *Cockney Columbus* (London, 1898) in which he says a broad view is more accessible in the U.S.

IV

ANNUS MIRABILIS

1898

Yes, this is the Voice on the bluff March gale,
We severed have been too long:
But now we have done with a worn-out tale,
The tale of an ancient wrong,
And our friendship shall last as long as
Love doth last,
And be stronger than death is strong.
"A Voice from the West," ALFRED AUSTIN, 1898.

THE comments on our foreign relations throughout this period equaled in bulk the attention given to all other aspects of American history. It is therefore essential that the diplomatic background be related to the rest of international history. This is not a chronicle of detailed diplomatic negotiations, but the next three chapters on American diplomacy should prove valuable. It is not necessary, nor particularly fruitful at this late date, to reanalyze British opinion merely to see how friendly it was to imperialistic ventures such as the Spanish-American War. The objects of an analysis must go deeper than that. What did the new imperializing nation mean to the British? How intelligent and far-seeing was the British reaction to 1898? How did imperialism affect the American impact in other phases of experience? What was the meaning of Anglo-American relations? And finally, what was the content and nature of British attitudes to American antics in foreign affairs?

Although wars, economic imperialism, and trade expansion may be shadows one of the other, no harm is done by treating these subjects in different places. That minor conflict, the Spanish-American War, perhaps of less fundamental economic, political, or spiritual significance to Britain than our Civil War, aroused a popular interest which in these days of violence seems disproportionate. For Britain that interest was conditioned by its temporary dissatisfaction with its Continental neighbors, a renewed analysis of its own imperialism, an alteration in the world outlook, a rediscovery of America, and the minor joys of an assumed, vicarious motherhood to an imperial youngster. There was an element of originality, for England did not feel that American efforts would be a distinctive contribution to old-fashioned imperialism. The growth of the idea of imperialism in the United States was welcomed, if not its concrete manifestations. The war acted as a cathartic for race sentiment. The weary Titan contemplated a new ally, and both nations emerged from isolation at the same time. The reaction was not so blindly enthusiastic as legend has embalmed. While the war might not be of great cultural significance, it was a dramatic shock which prepared the way for Britain's increased interest in America. As Henry Adams had perceived, England had been brought into an "American system." While trying to remove obstacles in Anglo-American diplomacy, Great Britain came to appreciate a common front with America. Her desire to use us affected vitally many steps in British diplomacy, and in spite of the American Senate and isolationism, she tried to make American expansion a counterweight to European competition and a reinsurance of the *status quo* satisfactory to Great Britain.

Our tariff policies, the threat to the gold standard, the Bering Sea controversy, and especially Cleveland's warlike message of 1895 about the Venezuela boundary, had not been forgotten. British public opinion had not been prepared for this hostile threat from Washington. Bryce, who was astonished at our ill-will, told Roosevelt that not one in ten in the House of Commons knew that Anglo-American trouble was brewing over Venezuela.[1] Coupled as it was with British difficulties in South Africa, where some linked the failure of the Jameson Raid to the coolness of its American participants, this event revealed Britain's isolation. British opinion was more awake to the approaching Spanish-American War. Halévy, the French historian, has described the meaning of that war for England: "Both parties alike were suffering from anaemia. . . . Just then an event took place . . . which with dramatic suddenness awoke British imperialism to new life."

In order not to lose sight of the personal factors in the reception of America's growth, let us pause to examine a few British men of affairs.[2] J. L. Garvin, who neglects to say much about important American influences upon Joseph Chamberlain, concluded that "He did not merely welcome the rise of American power: he gloried in it." Halévy declared, "Chamberlain there [at Washington] learnt to interest himself in colonial questions and, without abandoning all his democratic opinions, became a missionary of British imperialism," and also found an accredited interpreter in A. T. Mahan. Chamberlain played a prominent part in the Venezuelan squabble when he urged upon Secretary Olney the value of frank intercourse between the two powers. In contrast with his later desires for fiscal reform, Chamberlain had written to Queen Victoria, September 10, 1896: "Mr. McKinley is a bigoted Protectionist, and is said to be surrounded by advisers who are unfriendly to England." To Her Majesty he described a political situation "not at all creditable to a nation which boasts of its intelligence and public spirit." But it is possible that Chamberlain, who was known early in his career for "Birmingham caucus work," a type of activity then smiled at, learned some political tricks from America.

Sir Cecil Spring-Rice, Ambassador to the United States during the World War, had ideas about America similar to Chamberlain's. His friendships in this country were with an important group, the Roosevelts, Camerons, Lodges, Henry Adams, and a host of others. Always feeling at home here, he constantly spoke of "our race"; but he also added, "America is not in the least like France, to be won over by social attentions." He wrote to Roosevelt, May 1898, about the so-called Anglo-American hypocrisy in foreign dealings, namely, the appeal to rights and ideals: "I daresay the British part of the common heritage is going down hill; all the more reason to look after the other." During 1898 he wrote frequently to Hay, encouraging our imperialism; from Berlin, April 30, 1898, he advised that Hawaii be annexed immediately, otherwise at the end of the war Germany would demand compensation, perhaps Samoa. He explained further to Senator Lodge, July 8:

I can't tell you with what pleasure I see that Hawaii is at length to be annexed. . . . I think that there can be no doubt that there is an in-tention (and a natural one) to depose English civilization (I mean yours as much and more than mine) from the Pacific. . . . I don't believe that England, the island, is strong enough, or will remain comparatively strong enough to defend English civilization alone . . .

The English historian, John Richard Green, had declared earlier that the future history of the English-speaking race would be unrolled on the shores of the Hudson and the Mississippi rather than on the Tweed and the Thames. W. T. Stead wrote to Morley, "I feel as if the centre of the English-speaking world were shifting westward, and I feel this so strongly. . . ."

James Bryce, who preceded Spring-Rice as Ambassador to Washington, could not believe that our internal administration would be improved by imperialism. H. A. L. Fisher writes:

> He held that it was not to the interest of the United States to acquire or to maintain an empire overseas. The tasks which confronted the American government at home were sufficiently complex and formidable without the additional burden of foreign possessions. . . . It was, in his view, a wild paradox to maintain that the American union required additional territory.

Because of Bryce's knowledge of American affairs, his views on our expansion were important. He wrote to Roosevelt, September 12, 1898, about the great alteration in world affairs:

> In the interests of the United States I am uneasy at the change, because these new enterprises you will enter on are enterprises for which your Constitution and Government have not been framed, and mistakes may be made, many and serious, before you develop the institutions needed.[3]

He preferred Americans, who had no machinery to control provincial governors, to apply themselves to domestic problems, but if there were colonies, he wanted them ruled by a "steady government" without Congressional interference. He added: "You will have noticed that nearly everyone here applauds your new imperialistic departure. Smarting under the weakness of Salisbury's government, we are here more imperialistic than ever." He doubted whether the Philippines could be left to themselves. To look forward for a moment, he wrote to Woodrow Wilson, December 19, 1913:

I can hardly think of any greater misfortune for the United States than to be obliged to set up a government which it would have to maintain, or to become directly responsible for the administration of any South American country.

Here, as on other subjects, the revisions of his influential *American Commonwealth* are pertinent. Bryce noted the decline of imperialistic impulses, but the suddenness of our move in 1898 had made him extremely wary. Diplomatic caution no doubt led him to drop a sentence of the 1909 edition concerning administrative posts in dependent countries:

> Nearly all the work which the Federal authorities had to do of this kind has been badly done, and has given rise to scandals.

And we read in 1909, but not in the 1913 or 1923 revisions:

> Eight millions of recently enfranchised negroes (not to speak of recent immigrants from Europe) are a heavy enough load for the Anglo-Americans to carry on their shoulders without the ignorance and semi-barbarism of the mixed races of the tropics.

Another lawyer, A. V. Dicey, whose interest had developed out of his sympathy with the North in the sixties, was Bryce's companion in the American visit of 1870, and kept a close watch on American life which was always an important element in his study of law and constitutions. While he was not so pessimistic about our imperialism as his American host, C. E. Norton, he did not believe the United States would benefit by imperialism in general, or by the Philippines in particular. Events in Cuba had strengthened T. P. O'Connor's conviction of the stupidity of using force in international quarrels. He wrote of the Spanish-American War: "War is a crime against civilization, even when waged for the best of causes. . . ." Leslie Stephen, a close and cautious follower of American life who never thought we were unpopular in England, expressed himself to C. F. Adams, February 2, 1899, on imperialism: "The people who still call themselves liberal here disavow all the doctrines which used to be called liberal in my youth." Undoubtedly, America helped along this change. Like Balfour, the fifth Earl of Rosebery's initial intervention in foreign affairs was prompted by Anglo-American affairs, June 4, 1872; his numerous visits or holidays (he couldn't avoid seeing Mormons) in 1873, 1874, 1876, and 1882, encouraged him to interpret America. William Vernon Harcourt, who when writing to Chamberlain would say "we semi-Americans" since he too had married an American, was intensely interested in Anglo-American relations. We may close with Sir Henry Campbell-Bannerman, the future Prime Minister, who wrote to Carnegie, January 20, 1899, a letter which Carnegie whimsically passed on to President McKinley with directions to destroy:

Now that your great Republic has gone in for a big Army, a powerful Navy, numerous colonies, and all the other appurtenances of Empire, you will encounter some of the difficulties for which our cast-iron system has been created. We all wish you luck in your new career; but if you had all our experiences there would be more support given to yourself and those who are with you in trying to preserve your happy immunity.[4]

In January 1898 the *Times,* diverted momentarily from the Dreyfus trial, declared that because of the Republican disorganization and the inability of the "sound money" men to retain authority among the Democrats, an "immense advantage has certainly been given to the anarchical and predatory tendencies that have recently become so formidable in American society. . . ." McKinley's administration, weakened by the silver wedge, might be precipitated into rash decisions concerning Cuba; the intrigue of politicians, not the deliberate judgment of the people, would tolerate annexation. The Unionist press was sceptical about our viewpoint. There was dislike on all sides for our diplomacy prior to the outbreak of the war.[5] The destruction of the *Maine* caused little excitement. What strikes one at the outset was the lack of enthusiasm for any potential, empire-building qualities of the kin across the sea, a British attitude which had to change slightly to appear friendly.

On March 19 the *Economist* predicted that England would side with America, but there was an undercurrent of suspicion that we possessed no rights of intervention and that our expansion might lead to unexpected consequences. Even the *Spectator,* which recognized such rights, disliked our vacillation. The *Daily Mail* hoped for peace as late as April 11, but lamented that not more preparation had been made for a possible war from which we would gain little. Other papers suggested that McKinley wanted peace because he felt the weakness of his case. The *Times* began on March 29 to stress sympathy and common interests under the spell of Alfred Austin's verses; Hay sent back a *Times* leader of April 1 as marking the favorable change which had come over important London financial circles. The *Westminster Gazette* (April 14) observed:

There is in fact something more than ridiculous in the solemn lectures which are now being administered to American Jingoes by patriotic British newspapers which a few weeks ago were clamouring for war on minor points in the remote East.

Nor could that paper see why the *Standard* referred to the belligerent Senate as a shining example of the merits of a second chamber. The liberal *Manchester Guardian* quite early predicted the war and the annexation of Cuba, partly because many odious figures in American public life wanted to stop domestic reform; the *Guardian* outlined its future tone:

The American Jingo, who is very like our own, pleads that he is only robbing the Hawaiians of Hawaii because their ignorance renders them utterly unfit to govern it or say how it ought to be governed.

By the end of April British opinion seemed to desire a Cuba independent of Spain and expressed the view that Anglo-American amity really dated from the beginning of trouble in the Far East. At this date the jaundiced *Saturday Review* concluded that only the ravings of the *Chronicle* and the faddism of the *Star* indicated that America had England on her side. Many papers were disappointed by the evidence "of a growing militarism in the great industrial Republic," and yet many friends were surprised at America's military weakness. The general opinion was that the war would last a long time, and that the fruits of a Cuban or Philippine campaign would be bitter. Such observations were determined frequently by distrust of America's political and social life and the belief that we had no administrators to compare with Lord Cromer and his subordinates. Surprisingly little was said about the Monroe Doctrine. What America wanted or would do seemed remarkably unpredictable, but opinion was sufficiently innocuous or favorable to convince Americans that they had nothing to fear from England, and it seemed very possible to the English that a Spanish-American war would not harm them. Our war victories and Britain's diplomatic difficulties fostered sympathy.

Salisbury told the Queen, May 25, 1896, "The United States will do all the mischief they can without going to war," and that England would give any assistance to the Queen Regent of Spain consistent with neutrality. On April 1, 1898, he added that any remonstrance might arouse American anger to no advantage. Salisbury doubted the expediency of any concerted action from Europe, but England could not refuse to join in any course taken by all the other powers.[6]

Much ink has been spilled over Sir Julian Pauncefote's conduct as British Ambassador at the outbreak of the war. Just what was his attitude to the intervention of the Powers? A. J. Balfour evidently thought that Pauncefote rather approved of the Joint Note to the United States, and tried to tone down this attitude. He replied to Sanderson, then Permanent Secretary to the Foreign Office, April 15:

I confess to be in great perplexity. The Representatives of the Powers at Washington and the Austrian Ambassador in London appear to wish us to give the United States a lecture on international morality. If Pauncefote had not associated himself with this policy I confess I should have rejected it at once; but he knows our views, he is on the spot, and he is a man of solid judgment.

Chamberlain, who suspected we would feel that England had interfered, wrote April 17 to Balfour: "Your instinct was much better than Pauncefote's 'experience and judgment.'" So if there was this uncertainty among British officials, there was sufficient excuse for the misconceptions which prevailed in foreign countries about this episode. Holleben, April 14, informed Bülow, German Secretary of State for Foreign Affairs, ". . . very surprisingly the English ambassador took the initiative for a new joint action of the representatives of the Great Powers" in Washington. Hay concluded, June 15, that only Austria was trying to exert pressure.

Whether the German Government really resented a hostile German press is doubtful; what is certain is that England made the most of that hostile press. Somehow the British publicly convinced themselves, aided by Americans, by continual harping from 1898 to the present, that Germany had taken the lead in intervention and that there was real danger of a German-American conflict over the Manila episode. The German documents in *Die Grosse Politik* showed at least that Germany was not prepared to make Manila a *casus belli* and that Britain's attitude left nothing to be desired. Queen Victoria wrote sharply in her journal, April 21: "It is monstrous of America." But nothing was done about it.

It is not correct to say that the British news from America was accurate because late.[7] Nothing is more noticeable than that the British press during the Spanish War admitted it was not free from wild stories and rumors, and indeed, the year 1898 marked an intensification of America's love for sensation which the British press was not able to overcome. Although diplomatic comments were hardly more numerous than those on the Mexican situation in 1913–14, the war captured attention through the press, innumerable speeches, and organizational activities. The *Daily Mail* commented March 18: "The average Englishman may be pardoned if he fails to understand all he hears from America." Other papers remarked on the scantiness of American opinion which crossed the Atlantic; three conservative New York papers (fair or friendly to England) were usually quoted in London. The Secretary of the Anti-Imperialist League wrote correctly:

The important movement in opposition to the annexation policy of the Administration seems not to have received in England the attention which it deserves.

The *Saturday Review* declared the English press had suppressed all accounts of American military cowardice. Finally in despair, *Punch* commented on war news: "Sampson has slain his thousands, thanks to the jaw-bone of an ass."

There was almost an overabundance of Continental opinions and reactions to the war printed in British papers which devoted numerous editorials to this subject.[8] They frequently emphasized German, French, Austrian, and Russian hostility. Such garnered opinion seemed to isolate the Anglo-Saxon race in order to force the two nations together. The English press in July was using Germany as a bugbear. The European press soon became aware of England's sympathy and pointed sceptically to the value of racialism and the "bitter-sweetness" of much of the British comment. Judging from the English press, one would conclude that Europe took very seriously the possibilities of an Anglo-American alliance. Some of the foreign correspondents—and editorial comments did not depart much from their views—were far from impartial. The *Times* Paris correspondent, accused of bias, admitted that he regretted we had entered the imperialistic fold; the Spanish correspondent was unfriendly. The *Revue des deux Mondes* and *Journal des Débats* complained that England was denouncing France to the United States. Delcassé and Jules Cambon were so perturbed by this British nuance which ultimately affected American papers that they willingly paved the way for the establishment of an Associated Press bureau in Paris in 1902.

The war stimulated discussions on the question of capture of private property at sea.[9] Lord Charles Beresford proposed an international conference to define the rights of neutral states. Sir George Baden-Powell wanted to treat privateers as pirates, and urged England to stand by the Declaration of Paris, to which the United States had not adhered; but the Government rather sided with T. E. Holland and others who were more mild. Nor did the Government apparently fall in with the German Ambassador's suggestion to ask Washington and Madrid to abandon the right of searching neutrals. What exercised the Foreign Office most were questions of contraband and neutrality. The bulk of this legal work came from the pen of Sir William Edward Davidson, the overworked Legal Adviser to the Foreign Office. It was to be expected that because of British interests in Sicily, the Government wanted certain war materials withdrawn from Spain's prohibited list. Generally the Government gave no opinion on contraband to the numerous firms which made inquiries. British interests in Spain expressed fear that they might suffer because Spain considered the Government sympathetic to America. So great was the alarm in England over American proposals to make large increases in the Tonnage Tax on shipping arriving in American ports that the *Daily Mail* (April 29) had to explain that it did not mean hostility. Claims against Americans for cutting cables in Manila Bay which belonged to the Eastern Extension Australasia and China Telegraph Company were put forward slowly by the British Government, partly because there were no precedents and partly, no doubt, because of the growing Entente Cordiale. When the claims were made, the British case was to be based on equity. The glorious legend of the intervention of Captain Chichester of the *Immortalité*, which prevented a conflict between Dewey and the German Diederichs, was not originally emphasized by the British, and his actions were based merely on the law of blockade which allowed visits to men-of-war to establish nationality, but not the right of search. Apropos of this incident, Mr. Mackinder enunciated the curious theory in Parliament in 1912 that Manila was one of the victories of the British Navy where her silent coöperation "practically secured our markets in South America." The *Times* thought the war a pleasant one, as far as neutrals' rights were involved.

Hay summed up the feeling in London: "I wish you would take Cuba at once. We wouldn't have stood it this long"; Hay also believed Britain wanted us to keep the Philippines.[10] But this failed to note the "bitter-sweet" comments. Several papers felt that too much nonsense had been written concerning a "benevolent" British neutrality. The *Globe* advised America not to let Spain surpass her in courtesies of war; "the Americans ought to put a curb upon that nervous excitability of theirs which occasionally leads them to behave in a rather unseemly manner." Nor did the *Manchester Guardian* claim we excelled in humanity. *Blackwood's Edinburgh Magazine* acknowledged the war as perfectly natural, but the influential *Morning Post* considered that we had precipitated a conflict which might lead to a collision with England; hence, British sympathy with aggression was unintelligible. The *Birmingham Daily Gazette* wanted America to learn the sorrows of glory-hunting; the *Scotsman*, although it found British opinion favorable partly because of racial ties, declared us "wantonly offensive and aggressive." Further, said the same paper, "It is noteworthy that the British people, who have most to fear from the example of a success for the Monroe Doctrine, are, perhaps, most in sympathy with the American view." The *Daily Mail*, which in April had been disappointed with the harsh lectures of the London press, watched the new imperialism with favor, and commended in June the *St. James's Gazette* for changing its attitude by welcoming the acquisition of Hawaii. The *Daily Graphic, Morning Leader, Daily*

Chronicle, and *The Speaker* saw no reasons to decry America's motives; in addition the *Chronicle* was pleased to see Australia's enthusiasm for our undertaking. The attitude of the *Labour Leader* reminded one of the *Revue Socialiste,* which in denouncing capitalistic wars in general seemed less harsh on America; this British Socialist paper, which regretted that it stood alone in the Socialist ranks which had echoed the Yankee cackle, knew that American capitalists wanted compensation in Cuba, that American workers would have to double time for the same wages, and that Americans probably blew up the *Maine.* While advising an early peace, *Punch* objected to swashbuckling jingoism, and decried Spain, as a fifth-rate adversary, and the value of Cuba and the Philippines; but it praised the war for revealing to America her true friends, and published "Blood is Thicker than Water" cartoons.

Actually there seemed to be little difference between Conservative and Radical papers, except that the latter, when enthusiastic, were more ecstatic. The public and many of its leaders sometimes appeared to outrun the press in sympathy; but former friends might be sincerely chagrined by action which carried out the imperial idea. It will be remembered that Bryce told Roosevelt, February 28, 1897, that Americophils had been annoyed by the Senate's reaction to the Arbitration Treaty, which did not violate the Monroe Doctrine and seemed "as virtually admitting that doctrine further, especially as coupled with the Venezuelan treaty, than anyone could have expected Britain to do ten years ago." While many Liberal Imperialists derived encouragement, other Radicals were displeased. An active Liberal on April 28 objected to Herbert Gladstone's speech at Cambridge: "To read some comments which have been made in this country, it might be supposed that in the high interests of humanity America had proclaimed a holy war to save the Cubans from every imaginable horror. But is not this the veriest claptrap?" [11] Among other groups the formula was different; the bankers concluded: American victories—higher prices; Spanish victories—lower prices. Our victories impressed England more quickly than the Continent. By the end of June there was irritation that the war continued. Throughout the struggle there does not seem to have been any discrepancy between public opinion and the Government.

Sir William Harcourt found the sympathy of the Liberals and the nation with the foe favoring freedom, i. e., the United States, and reported that everyone felt that Anglo-Saxons all over the world were behind us.[12] Lord Salisbury on June 29 told the United Club about America's "elevated philanthropy" in waging the war. While W. E. H. Lecky did not feel that we should benefit by territorial acquisitions, he almost believed that our increased intervention would benefit civilization.

Resolutions of sympathy and support poured upon the Embassy from the Congregational Union of England and Wales, the Liberal Churchmen's Union, the head branch of the Irish Independent League, the Men's Union of London, pastors and delegates of the Baptist Union, and the Synod of Primitive Methodists. Protestant denominations had a field day; religious journals were especially bellicose. At the Congregational Union in the City Temple in May, Dr. Charles Leach of Manchester and Rev. Bernard Snell put a typical motion before the assembly:

In view of the close relations between this Union and the Congregational Churches of the United States, this assembly . . . recommends our churches to offer special prayer on their behalf, that even the events that seem to be adverse may be over-ruled for the furtherance of the Gospel and the establishment of truth and righteousness in the world.

The Baptist Union passed a similar resolution, but the mover asserted that he was not motivated by race or religion. The Baptist Missionary Society at Nottingham learned that now the two flags might be planted beneath the Cross. The *Freeman*, a Baptist organ, found Spain "a striking object lesson of the evils of Romanism." At the Church Congress the Bishop of Hereford asserted: "We hold the United States did the work of a Christian nation." The *Saturday Review* smiled at the Presbyterian General Assembly for asking the President not to fight on Sunday. The Dean of Ripon concluded that Washington Gladden's pro-Anglo-Saxon speeches in England had vindicated the "pureness" of America's aims. It was alleged that English Catholics and their organ, the *Catholic Times*, were supporting Spain; no prominent Catholic leader had been on the Anglo-American Committee until Father Vaughan joined belatedly. But his pastoral letter to his congregation, January 1, 1899, cited the value of closer Anglo-American relations, and intimated that American experience would be valuable for the Church's mission in the Far East and Africa.

The oratorical distinctions between friendship, unity, and alliance were fragile.[13] Few denied the value of closer Anglo-American relations. America's new sentiment was the only bright spot in a depressing year, according to Grey. The Unionists claimed credit, if for nothing else, as Lord Selborne put it, for this improvement. The Government, when it got started, tried to outrun the Liberal Opposition in its advocacy of a vigorous friendship. In the matter of alliances, Chamberlain outran his colleagues, the Government outran the people, both passed the press, and everybody was ahead of the United States. This friendship, based upon national interests which were overlaid with racial enthusiasm, by springing out of an imperialistic year could not but be by a very short, logical step an imperialistic friendship. English conditions had changed since 1863, as Bryce pointed out, and there was now a natural affinity, since the two countries were not jealous of each other; but one senses, when Bryce speaks of "America at the parting of the ways" and England and America as belonging to the "living nations," that men of every political color were indulging in a luxurious weakness which momentarily wanted romping America to inspire the English heart. It is difficult to escape a feeling of unreality in all this talk.

Buds of friendship had of course been in sight before the first months of 1898. By March some of the Radical press were talking of an Anglo-Saxon alliance. By the time of our victory at Manila Bay the talk became more concrete. In April the *Times* had not thought highly of an alliance; the *Daily Mail* sensibly observed: "The disproportion indeed between our mission and America's makes one impossible." Although the force of events foreshadowed an increase in our mission, the press was never clear about the meaning or the possibility of an alliance.

The Anglo-American arbitration treaty of 1897 had perished without leaving a deep impression on the Anglo-Saxon press. Despite the growing friendliness, Sir Randal Cremer of the International Arbitration League doubted in May 1898 whether a Member of Parliament should ask about a similar treaty, because such questions furthered the League's opponents. To date the Liberals had considerably outnumbered the Conservatives in advocating such measures. But the new feeling seemed promising. Justin McCarthy wrote on July 4:

My own conviction is that a thoroughly good understanding between England and the United States would inevitably tend to promote the cause of Home Rule for Ireland. The American Republic is founded on the principle of Home Rule, and the influence of American precept and example cannot fail to impress upon England the justice and practicability of that claim for domestic legislation which is accorded to every State of the American Union.

The idea of coöperation with the United States, made feasible by our entry into a larger world, was closely related to the idea of a Federated British Empire, and as an expert in colonial affairs put it, such a federation would probably lead to an alliance with the United States for a "Pax Britannica." Returning from Australia, Lord Brassey reported, May 6, 1898, "The community of Australia would cordially welcome any understanding which would mean common action in the larger affairs of the world." He told the Colonial Club, June 13: "The notion of an Anglo-American friendship was not incompatible with that deep purpose which had brought them there—to do all that in them lay to promote the unity of the British Empire." At the Anglo-American meeting in the same building, the Bishop of Ripon had proposed a toast, "Our Kin Beyond the Seas," for the fight for freedom had drawn the two nations together; Professor Dicey proposed "Our Common Language and Letters."

Chamberlain had put the word "alliance" into common circulation. Contemporary cartoons showed him dancing with the Stars and Stripes and the Union Jack, and talking too much. In a startling speech at Birmingham, May 13, which was a bid for support of the Government's foreign policy, he aroused European chancelleries as much as England. Thoroughly imbued with the validity of the Anglo-Saxon racial theory and the ties of laws and ethics, he put forth a dramatic bid for American friendship—"They speak our language, they are bred of our race"—which caught off guard many staunch friends of America. The Continent suspected that Chamberlain had revealed the weakness of his country, disputed the identical

interests, and called him a "civilian Boulanger." Such speeches convinced German officials that

> For England an alliance with the United States . . . would create
> an absolutely ideal situation. . . . It is thus almost hopeless to bring
> the English statesmen to any voluntary renunciation of this grand pur-
> pose. England will only become available for other political combinations
> when her present hope of an Anglo-American alliance is shattered.

In general, the greater the European tension, the more England
and Germany sought to attach America. (Lord Lansdowne in 1901
even visualized dropping Germany on account of America.) Henry
White detected some efforts in January 1899 to stir up ill will in
England. But Chamberlain had enough English critics.

The *Globe* disbelieved in such an alliance because it would bring
Britain nothing; we would not support a big navy and our army
could not help! The *Manchester Guardian* thoroughly disapproved
of his attitude, and significantly pointed out that now one could see
that English Tories had become sympathetic with America's conservative institutions. In Parliament Labouchere smiled at Chamberlain for crediting himself with Anglo-American amity since the
people had always been for it. Sir Charles Dilke declared that no
one wanted a war alliance; Mr. Schwann reminded the Government that America had forced Salisbury to settle the Venezuelan
controversy, and that it was non-official Britons such as Pease and
Cremer who had advocated arbitration. Irish members suggested
that Chamberlain might do more for an alliance by healing the Irish
question. Another member added on June 10: "I can readily imagine circumstances in which our power or interests would clash
with those of the United States more almost than with any other
power." Herbert Paul told the Women's National Liberal Association that Chamberlain's proposal was not sufficiently disinterested
to capture us. What Morley and Harcourt feared—two persons who
had worked for a "virtuous" alliance—was a jingoistic entente. The
alliance idea had indeed become popular. The Prince of Wales
bought some "alliance" cravats which combined both flags, and
Smith's Advertising Agency in London issued a clever booklet,
The New Anglo-American Alliance and the American Market.
Printers produced advertising seals which showed clasped hands.

In early June the Executive Committee of the "Liberals Forward," who had G. W. E. Russell and Lord Coleridge as leaders, passed the following premature resolution:

That it is the imperative duty of Her Majesty's Government to render all possible support to the United States in the event of German interference with American action in the Philippine Islands . . .

At the World's Sunday School Convention in July a prayer besought Americans to "rise to their responsibility for the Christianizing of the islands," for an Anglo-American alliance would be one "saturated with the spirit of universal evangelization." This was possible because men like Rev. Joseph Parker declared that they had never read anything "so affecting, so pathetic, as the patience, the forbearance, the magnanimity, and the noble generosity of the United States of America in the present war." The *Christian World* had early suggested an alliance. Thus minority groups helped to build the "alliance" atmosphere. Although some papers believed in a tacit alliance and reported American opinion as favorable, more papers were sceptical and counseled less speed.

Chamberlain kept talking about alliances. At Manchester, in what Labouchere described as "swaggering speeches," he predicted that Germany, America, and England would draw closer together; but he also added, "A combination between the two great English-speaking peoples is a combination which would fear no other alliance." At Wakefield he talked of seventy million Americans as "chiefly Anglo-Saxons." Although admitting all the forces making for union, Campbell-Bannerman told his constituents in December "to avoid shaking in the face of other nations the American fist which we did not yet quite hold in our hands." In answering Chamberlain Mr. William M'Ewan told his constituents in Edinburgh that since Germany and America "will be our chief opponents in the industrial war which is expected, the proposal seems to be ill-conceived and quixotic." However, the year closed on a peaceful note, for some Britons now felt that the Empire and the Republic could coöperate on the Tsar's disarmament proposals.

The meaning of all this is as much mental as political. A great amount of talk arose from spontaneous combustion, for it is difficult to see what Britain had sacrificed for this lush growth of kinship.

America had made an impression, and the current of these tributes to her power developed a readiness to expect great things. England had projected the United States upon an Old World background. There was little careful analysis of American public opinion. Germany was elevated temporarily into the position of bugbear. There was a feeling of inevitability in any discussion of Anglo-American relations, discussions as repetitious as English travel books about America. The course of practical politics and all this sentiment offered humorous disparities. This new horizon created by America was opened to public contemplation and momentarily accentuated England's addled subjectivity.

This elevated plane of thought encountered difficulties the moment it struck upon some concrete manifestation of our imperialism in colonial administration and overseas expansion.[14] Britons looked upon Hawaii as a liability to any but a strong naval power. Even after the battle of Manila, British interests in Honolulu desired neutrality; but England had no *locus standi* in Hawaii to protest against excessive enthusiasm for American troops on the way to the Philippines. Except perhaps for allowing the *Bennington* to remain in neutral waters, England could discover no breach of neutrality. The acquisition of Hawaii was accepted as inevitable, but some papers like the *Economist* were reserved, because it seemed to fortify the principle that to win markets one must annex them.

By May 9 the *Standard*, the *National Review*, and particularly the *Times* had considered the annexation of the Philippines as the best solution. The *Spectator*, anticipating and insisting, decided we must keep the Philippines, and suggested a model based upon Ceylon or an Indian province; the *Daily Mail* asserted that the "Philippines once conquered can never be surrendered." Although up to August journals believed we had not grasped unanimously the concept of imperial expansion, it was felt that we recognized that the *status quo ante bellum* was impossible. The *Scotsman* asserted that America must carry through the work of colonial government, otherwise it would be guilty of a blunder "that the lapse of centuries will not wipe out." Some papers and publicists which were not certain about annexation suggested an exchange might be made with England. The *Times* took the lead in connecting the Philippines with British interests in China.

But when the *Times* asserted November 14, "We would rather see the Philippines in the hands of our American friends than in those of any European power," it had already argued constantly that the Open Door must apply to the islands. When German critics insinuated that English hopes were doomed, the *Times* rather feebly replied that with the American tariff all would be on an equal footing. Other papers were disturbed lest the islands should be closed. The *Economist* had constantly expected that the war might force American finances to a sounder basis, and even viewed as possible a modification of our tariff system. By the end of the year the press had become displeased with events in the Philippines. The *Manchester Guardian* declared their annexation would be a crime like the rape of Alsace-Lorraine. But it was expected we would demand the whole archipelago.

Evidently Hay had thought by the end of July that the British Government wished the United States to retain the Philippines or, failing that, to secure an option on them. Otherwise, as Balfour intimated, Germany would get a footing. Salisbury had looked with disfavor on retaining only Luzon, for we should "undoubtedly have had another Kiau-chau very soon on our hands." By early November the Government had decided that, failing annexation, it was safe to assume that the United States would establish some form of protection over the Philippines. But Britons had not been sleeping. As early as April petitions were circulating in Liverpool, Manchester, and Birmingham which demanded that the Government protect British interests in the Spanish colonies. St. John Brodrick had told Henry White of England's intense anxiety in maintaining the Open Door, even in the Philippines; in November he described the flood of appeals and protests over the probability that America would establish differential duties and extend her navigation laws to her new possessions. Both Brodrick and Balfour naturally felt that such steps would convert England to a lukewarm or even hostile attitude.

The year 1898 had given England little opportunity to talk about colonial administration. Although England reminded itself of remarkable qualities inherent in the Anglo-Saxon race, the press kept warning us of the need for sound management in imperialism, of the great administrative tasks which only professionals could accomplish. The inefficiency of the War Department was a dangerous omen. The *Daily News* added:

The Washington Government will have quickly to create a new Colonial Department. It will be interesting to see whether in doing so they find they can improve on the British model.

Many of the opponents of annexation agreed with Henry M. Stanley, the explorer:

It seems to me this Imperialism is going to prove costly and disturbing to America, and her well-wishers are in doubt whether it be wise in her to take upon herself the task of regenerating the Philippines.

But the predominant opinion was that America had by the end of the year accepted in full the task of imperialism.

The pattern for discussions and actions upon a basis of the similarity of national interests had been formed early in 1898, and in this respect the British diplomats and the public were again ahead of the United States, and drew encouragement from a very little amount of American opinion.[15] In addition to the Far East, which conditioned part of the response to our war, there were added more general phrases which we, in our infancy as an imperializing nation, could better understand. A common background might explain this similarity; Edward Dicey wrote in September:

Feeling as they do that democratic institutions are no longer a panacea for the cure of social discontents, the Americans resort most naturally to the remedies which under like circumstances have commended themselves to their English forefathers—that is, to foreign trade, to emigration, and to the establishment of a colonial empire.

Thus there were common destinies in the underlying imperial motives of the two nations. The press soon identified Continental hate towards England and the United States as spiritually and practically the same thing. Almost before we had become a colonizing nation, the press hit upon the very sensible suggestion that as a colonizer we should be better able to understand the difficult, historic rôle of Great Britain.

Lord Kimberley felt that the extension of American operations would benefit England; Asquith uttered strange views in the face of world history:

I am one of those who believed, paradoxical as it would seem, that the more points of contact we had with America, the fewer would be the points of collision.

Before a large gathering of the Primrose League, Lord George Hamilton in July pointed out that so long as the United States confined itself to the North American continent, Britain was the only power whatsoever which could cross her path; outside of that, their interests were alike. Stead even went so far as to hope that our flag would float over a protected Liberia. So strong was the feeling that Sir Edward Grey said in April:

The struggle in which the United States is engaged must be one to stir up our blood, and makes us conscious of the ties of language, origin, and race.

He added in June: "It was remarkable how a war of this kind unearthed and brought to the top feelings which had been overlaid." Only a deep conviction that America's earth hunger was easily satisfied, or a sincere belief in the youthful timidity of a new world power, or finally and traditionally, only the great mutual respect of the two nations could account for Asquith's paradoxes, which at the time did not seem to apply to any other phase of diplomatic relations.

Early in the year the British view was that only the United States would be with them in supporting the Open Door for China. White wrote to Hay, March 6, 1898:

I don't know whether I wrote you that Joseph Chamberlain in addition to Arthur Balfour had spoken to me of the importance of our taking some sort of action in support of England's policy in China.

The Government received a cool reply, but the press continued in this vein. Almost unanimously the press anticipated the benefits to be derived from America's interest and coöperation in China. In March Sir William Des Voeux, former governor of Hong Kong, advised England to secure American friendship to help solve the Chinese question. Consequently any American diversion from the principle of an Open Door aroused anxiety, whether by laws which confined our coasting trade with Puerto Rico, Cuba, and Hawaii to vessels of American registry, or colonial tariff systems which possibly the Democrats might modify more to British pleasure. Although the *Times* did not object to an affirmative maritime policy, it declared in December:

It must not be supposed that we are prepared to approve the adoption of an exclusive policy in regions with regard to the destinies of which we might have claimed a voice.

Nevertheless it was of international importance that here were two nations whose purposes were allegedly alike as peas in a pod.

The elusive racial melody was also wedded to national interests with the highest contrapuntal skill. Surprisingly little was said about what might appear more clear-cut—political affinity.[16] The year 1898 was viewed as a definite break with our political traditions. It seemed hardly possible to the British that we could escape politically from the effects of an imperialistic war. While anti-imperialists considered the war a failure of republicanism, others, as during our Civil War, declared that it put democracy to a test which it must weather.

Chamberlain and the imperial publicist, A. R. Colquhoun, viewed one aspect alike; Colquhoun asserted:

One result of American expansion is to make the republic both more interesting and more intelligible to British people. . . . America, on her part, is able to appreciate and understand far better the circumstances of our national life.

Perhaps the first sentence was most valid. Mr. Courtney suggested that Britons now thought it might be unwise to let popular assemblies vote on war and peace. Many papers argued that the final steps in Congress did not inspire general respect for the American Constitution. The *Scotsman* had observed, April 18:

The eyes of the world are turned towards the Congress of the U.S.A., but not in admiration. . . . The American Constitution is now on trial, as it were, before the public opinion of Christendom.

Further, the huge war expenditures were "a piece of brag." Although the war would play havoc with American traditions, the *Manchester Guardian* (April 15) explained:

That is a very different thing from charging democratic institutions of America with the responsibility for Jingoism and for disorder in debate,

as some Conservative writers in England are doing now. . . . Every
enemy can have a stick to beat democracy with, because it does its work
in public.

Chamberlain, whose American visit was an exciting event at this
time, was certain that a colonial policy would, as in Britain, elevate
the entire national character; Bryce did not agree.

The *Spectator*, which viewed our system as weakest in foreign
affairs, continued to emphasize the healthful results of imperialism.
Pre-war events had not, however, blinded it "to the fact that America's representatives have been . . . on a question of vital interest,
'on the stampede.' " While urging us to take colonies to learn how
to govern, it added:

> The future of the world will depend greatly upon the political char-
> acter of Americans. . . . It is because Americans will need great poli-
> ticians, great diplomatists, great administrators, that we desire to see
> them come out of themselves and take up their share of the world's gov-
> erning work.

With some amusement Sir Edmund Monson discussed the term
"new diplomacy" which owed its originality and its "openness" to
the restless American mind and which "will perhaps end by improving diplomatists of the old school off the face of the earth."
(This we failed to do even by participation in World War diplomacy.) The *Times* concluded that the war had renovated our
national unity and removed the "perilous unrest" caused by a lack
of political issues. With ill-concealed surprise, Lecky the historian
summed up events:

> Here I think we were most struck by the skill and resolution with
> which on the American side the war was conducted, and by the humanity
> and self-restraint shown by American public opinion.

However, the discussion of political affinity had not been pleasant
or fruitful, and the two peas in the pod were far from being alike.

It is hardly possible to say that in 1898 the British had erected
a philosophical justification for American imperialism. But first
among the theoretical factors were "inevitable destiny" and the
will of Providence. To a lesser degree, our imperialism was rational-
ized as an exercise of international police power. The conception

of the "white man's burden" was not yet predominant. And practically nothing was said of the justifying ideas of geographical predestination, the mission of regeneration, or natural growth. Benjamin Kidd, who was undoubtedly influenced by America's expansion, preached the English-speaking peoples' special duties of developing the tropics as a trust for civilization; his argument of the "destined use of the soil" had by 1899 become one of the foremost moral pleas in England.

The lessons and importance of 1898 were therefore tremendous. America had acted as a much-needed tonic. America's example, coupled no doubt with Britain's anomalous position in Egypt, gave renewed life to her belief in manifest destiny, that glorious "fit of absent-mindedness" which built the Empire. Had our foe been stronger, England would have been more impressed, but the war and its aftermath excited British attention and made life more complicated with the emergence of a new world power. Acquiescence in our new imperialism struck the British as being the best bid for Anglo-American friendship. Naturally many who had been early advocates of closer relations disliked this approach.[16]

An increase in America's army and navy was expected.[17] In fact England warned America to develop stronger fighting arms. The *Standard* asked:

What may not be looked for when the vast population has developed a taste for fighting, and finds itself one of the great naval Powers of the earth?

The *Times* viewed the war as of greater importance than the campaign on the Nile, and the imperialism which had sprung into life with "the vigor of Jonah's gourd" was the harbinger of new things. By sea power the transmarine empire of the United States had been inaugurated, and the lessons were not lost upon the British Navy. The *Times* declared, August 16:

Never were the eternal principles of sea warfare more instructively illustrated than by the nation which has produced their most philosophical exponent [Mahan].

Nor did the British think the full import of such a lesson would be lost upon all Powers which cherished transmarine ambitions or expansive impulses. The war had also aroused interest in an inter-oceanic canal, which necessitated a reëxamination of old treaties. Part of the press began to think of changes; the *Times* hinted on December 6:

> If the freedom of the water-way were secured to ships of all nations, as in the case of the Suez Canal, we do not see what object we should have in standing strictly upon claims which originated when the circumstances were altogether different.

Such problems of Anglo-American diplomacy were placed in a new setting after the war.

On Lord Mayor's Day, November 9, six horses, led by "Carters in uniforms," pulled a float which demonstrated that "Blood is thicker than water," and Salisbury was about to stir the chancelleries of Europe. After speaking of the Tsar's disarmament proposals, he continued:

> In some respects the era of this great proposition has been marked by unhappy omens. It is the first year in which the mighty force of the American Republic has been introduced among the nations whose dominion is expanding and whose instruments, to a certain extent, are war. . . . No one can deny that their appearance among the factors of Asiatic, at all events, and possibly of European diplomacy, is a grave and serious event, which may not conduce to the interests of peace, though I think that in any event it is likely to conduce to the interest of Great Britain.

The Russian circular and proposed conference prompted Lord Ripon to express himself to Lord Kimberley, September 7, 1898, in a significant letter which explains the rediscovery of America.

> I do not . . . see that such a limited arrangement as this can be come to unless the United States are admitted to the Conference. . . . I cannot doubt that they will make such an increase in their permanent fleet as will place them amongst the principal powers of the World. If they become so, their navy must be taken into account before we and the French could agree to fix a maximum for our fleets. I should be glad to see the United States admitted to a place among the "great powers" and so should hail their presence at the Conference apart from any other considerations. Not that I delude myself with any idea that they would always side with us, but they would help to deliver us from the groove

(shall I say, rut) into which the European Powers have got their affairs. But be this as it may, their Military and Navy strength can no longer be disregarded in fixing the armaments of the world.[18]

Although British attitudes toward other aspects of American civilization may not have been fundamentally altered, the events of 1898 demonstrated that the United States had become an important factor in British life, and had prepared the way for an increased American influence.

[1] *Bryce Mss. Coll.*, Jan. 1896; Élie Halévy, *A History of the English People*, Epilogue, Vol. I, 1898–1905 (London, 1929), 24, 63, 432. R. C. K. Ensor, who is very critical of Cleveland, in *England, 1870–1914* (Oxford, 1936), suggests (pp. 230–31) the speech may have helped to precipitate Cecil Rhodes and divide the Rand plotters; but see *The Autobiography of John Hays Hammond* (New York, 1935), I, 361, II, 409–10; also J. H. Latané, *A History of American Foreign Policy* (New York, 1927), 479–88; Nevins, *White*, 108 n.9, 115–18, 124–25, 129–33. Whyte (*Stead*, II, 78, 84, 87) says W. T. Stead was the first to mark rising of the trouble over Venezuela. Stead considered that the Anglo-American Arbitration campaign, launched March 3, 1896, was not brilliant except for the work of Herbert Spencer, William Watson, Dr. W. E. Darby of the Peace Society, and W. Randal Cremer of the Inter-Parliamentary Conference. The diplomatic story may best be followed in a Canadian account, *The Rise of Anglo-American Friendship, a study in world politics 1898–1906* (London, 1938) by Lionel M. Gelber who shows the American influence on British diplomacy.

[2] J. L. Garvin, *Life of Joseph Chamberlain* (London, 1933–34), III, 301, 167, 296; Chamberlain had an article in *19th Cent.*, Dec. 1890, "Shall We Americanise our Municipal Institutions?" and another in *Forum*, Nov. 1892. Henry White wrote (Nevins, *White*, p. 111), "I also discovered that Joseph Chamberlain put himself forward in the Venezuelan business unknown to Lord Salisbury, with a view to getting the credit of patching it up, and that he was set upon by Lord Salisbury." Halévy, *op. cit.*, 24, 67; unfortunately, Sir Willoughby Maycock's *With Chamberlain in the United States and Canada: 1887–88* (London, 1914) is mostly small talk. G. E. Buckle, ed., *Letters of Queen Victoria* (3d. series; London, 1930–32), III, 75. Stephen Gwynn, *Letters and Friendships of Sir Cecil Spring-Rice* (Boston, 1929), I, 3, 61, 246–50; Roosevelt and Lodge usually agreed because of optimism with Spring-Rice's conception of the future of the English-speaking peoples. Whyte, *Stead*, 25; H. A. L. Fisher, *James Bryce* (New York, 1927), II, 12–13, 44, 211; he did, however, write to Mr. Storey in 1919 urging us to take responsibility for Christian races in Western Asia. Cf. Lubbock, *Henry James*, I, 316.

[3] *Bryce Mss. Coll.* See *Am. Comm.* (1909), II, 531, 533; (1928), II, 573. Bryce once suggested common citizenship for the two countries. George Peel (*Friends of England*, London, 1905, pp. 188, 190) did not agree with Bryce's view that Am. possessed no earth hunger. See also, Fyfe, *O'Connor*, 210; Maitland, *Stephen*, 451, 467; Robert S. Rait, ed., *Memorials of Albert Venn Dicey* (London, 1925), 53, 74, 154, 155, 166–68; A. G. Gardiner, *Life of Sir William Harcourt* (London, 1903), I, 429, 522–23; II, 60–61, 396.

⁴ In *McKinley Papers*, Vol. 24; Library of Congress.

⁵ For details and different conclusions, see B. A. Reuter, *Anglo-American Relations during the Spanish-American War* (New York, 1924), esp. chap. vi; oversimplification is sometimes misleading. For example, speaking of *hostility*, which in itself is an over-simplification, she cites the appraisal of the *New York Times* (May 1, 1898) which found only the *Morning* and *St. James's Gazette* (Reuter adds the *Sat. Rev.*) as hostile to the U.S.; pp. 128–29. Miss Reuter's volume is significant, however, as reflecting Am. opinion of British opinion, a secondary approach which may after all be of great importance. The eleven English papers used by her are a curious mixture. The *Scotsman* expected war as early as April 1. *Globe* (Apr. 2) talks about "Munroe" (*sic*). There was apparently an Eng. edition of *Cuba* (London, Jan. 12–Apr. 13, 1898), a political weekly edited by Cubans in the interests of a self-governed Cuba.

Dicey, *19th Cent.*, 1898, 44: 501; B. Willson, *New America*, 29. The *Stand.* (Apr. 2) sagely announced: "America, we are sure, does not want either to annex Cuba or to have an Independent Republic established at its doors." Sir Algernon Barthwick wanted to open his *Morning Post* for relief subscriptions for victims of *Maine* disaster. The Irish view on the growing friendliness in Parliament is expressed by Michael Davitt in answer to the Crown Speech, Feb. 9, on question whether U.S. would join Eng. in a war with Russia: "I know something about the U.S. . . . The American people are not in the habit of prowling around the world stealing countries and carving out continents. . . . I am certain they will never lend their arms, or the prestige of their name, to a policy of brigandage such as England is carrying out in Africa and in India." *P. Debs.*, 53: 153. F. Sheehy Skeffington, *Michael Davitt* (London, 1908), 74ff., 110ff., 128, 199–200.

⁶ Buckle, *Letters of Queen Victoria*, III, 45, 239, 244; but see *Brit. Doc.*, II, No. 302, p. 254. Dugdale, *Balfour*, I, 262, 263; R. B. Mowat's *Life of Lord Pauncefote* (Boston, 1929), says practically nothing about Pauncefote's views on the U.S.; but see chap. xx. Curiously, even Hay's telegram of April 6, 1898 to Sherman was at first garbled in deciphering, which left a question: "What would be agreeable to the President?" It should have read that Pauncefote's instructions were "to do nothing except what would be agreeable to the President." See *U.S. State Dept., G.B.*, Vol. 191. L. B. Shippee's article written in 1925, "Germany and the Spanish-American War," *Am. Hist. Rev.*, xxx, 754–77, cautious in accepting the British version, remains essentially correct in spite of recent diplomatic publications. J. F. Rippy comes to same conclusions in "The European Powers and the Spanish-American War" in *James Sprunt Historical Studies, U. of N. Car.*, xix, No. 2, 1927, 22–52. Vol. 5 of E. P. Oberholtzer's *History of the United States* (New York, 1937), repeats the British position in the most favorable light. In 1902, Mr. Norman's question in the Commons, considered academic by some, was replied to by Lord Cranborne (now Marquess of Salisbury): "Whatever opinions were expressed by Lord Pauncefote during the discussion, which was of an informal character, were personal to himself and not in pursuance of any instructions from Her Majesty's Government," and the British declined to assent to any proposal of intervention. See *P. Debs.*, 1902, 102: 992; 103: 38; 104: 10; 107: 1082; 108: 1533. Lord Salisbury in a letter to the author, June 10, 1937: "I know that I have always held the view that the best relations between this Country and the United States are of vital importance." Henry White seemed to think that the British Ambassador to Spain, Sir

Henry Drummond-Wolff, was friendly to the U.S.; Chamberlain apparently did not. Cf. Nevins, *White*, 131, and Garvin, *Chamberlain*, III, 297. G. L. Beers in *The English-Speaking Peoples* (New York, 1917), a war-time book which argued that America was morally negligent in not making the Anglo-Saxon block more than a cultural block, quotes Earl Grey (p. 102) as saying to Hay on the eve of the Sp.-Am. War, "Why do not the U.S. borrow our navy to make a quick job of Cuba? They could return us the favour another time."

[7] Reuter, *op. cit.*, p. 109; author's article, "Pre-War British Analysis of the American Press," *Journ. Q.*, Dec. 1937, 361–63. *Times*, Dec. 27, 1898. Among the few historical novels making use of Sp.-Am. War material are Capt. F. S. Brereton, *Under the Spangled Banner* (1903) and "Harry Collingwood" (W. J. C. Lancaster), *Cruise of the Thetis* (1910).

[8] The French press seemed about equally divided in viewing the struggle as one of Latins against Anglo-Saxons. See also Charles W. Porter, *The Career of Théophile Delcassé* (Philadelphia, 1936), 158–59; A. L. P. Dennis, *Adventures in American Diplomacy* (New York, 1928), 77–78, 85–86, 91, 98.

[9] Interviews. *P. Debs.*, 1898, 56: 663, 1398ff.; 1912, 41: 920. *Times*, July 7, 9; Apr. 16, 1898; Mar. 6, 1914. T. A. Bailey, "Dewey and the Germans at Manila Bay," *Am. Hist. Rev.*, Oct. 1939, 59–81.

[10] Hay's Mansion House speech in April was made on the advice of leading Englishmen. Thayer, *Hay*, II, 166, 168; Nevins, *White*, 131, 133–37; Hay to Day, June 25, 1898, No. 437, *U.S. State Dept.*, G.B.; *Bryce Mss. Coll.* In Aug. the *Daily Mail* criticized Leonard Courtney's "New Policy of the U.S." in *London Review* in which he stigmatized imperialism as based on greed and productive of misery. *Labour Leader*, May 7, 21, June 21. Note Keir Hardie in *Lab. Lead.* who believed Henry Norman (who had attended college in Am.) had gone to the U.S. to negotiate an alliance. *Lab. Lead.* often quoted from the New York *People*.

[11] In uncatalogued *Herbert Gladstone Mss. Coll.* at Brit. Museum.

[12] Ideas similar to Harcourt's were held by the Bishop of Ripon and the Marquis of Ripon; Harcourt, *Times*, May 9, referred to debate and division at the Cambridge Union which condemned Am. conduct. Note Rev. Mackennal's sermon, *Manch. G.*, Aug. 15; Am. experience of Dr. Charles Berry, *Freeman*, May 13, also May 6; Washington Gladden, *England and America* (Columbus, Ohio, 1898), p. iii; G. C. Musgrave, *Contemporary R.*, July 1898; *Westminster R.*, 160: 246–58, 357–74; Lecky, *Independent*, July 1898, 15–17; Vaughan, *Manch. G.*, Dec. 31, 1898; Baptists, *Manch. G.*, Sept. 28.

[13] Throughout it will be noticed that Chamberlain made great use of Am. examples; already in this year he asserted the U.S. did not hesitate to give countervailing duties similar to those which could benefit the W. Indies. *P. Debs.*, 54: 1526; 55: 562; 58: 1335, 1376–77, 1386, 1407, 1421, 1436–38; 60: 458; 63: 891. Lansdowne, *Brit. Documents*, Nov. 11, 1901, II, No. 92, p. 78; *Die Grosse Politik*, XV, p. 49, July 6, 1898, Richthofen to Hatzfeldt; Nevins, *White*, 204; McCarthy, *Times*, July 5. The reader should turn to D. Jordan and E. J. Pratt, *Europe and the American Civil War* (New York, 1931), 121; "America was the field of many a light skirmish between the party of progress and the party of resistance."

On arbitration: The address to Cleveland in 1887 from the Commons was signed by 175 Liberals, 44 Liberal Unionists, 13 Conservatives; a Parliamentary memorial to the President in November, 1894, was signed by 232 Liberals, 71 Nationalists,

38 Unionists, and 21 Conservatives. A. C. F. Beales, *The History of Peace* (London, 1931), 219; Howard Evans, *Sir Randal Cremer* (London, 1909), 26–29, 150ff., chap. xxi.

Sir Francis and Lady Cook gave a garden party to the idea of an Anglo-American Alliance. *The World's Third Sunday School Convention: London, July 11th to 16th, 1898* (London, n.d.), viii, 160, 28, 45, 30, 32, 76, 55ff., 217, 227, 242, 246, 289, 290ff.; Frederick Greenwood in *19th Cent.*, 1898, xliv: 1–11; Bryce, "Essential Unity of Britain and America," *Atlantic Monthly*, July, 1898, 22–29; Lord Kimberley disparaged the alliance; H. M. Stanley didn't think either country needed it. Chamberlain, in *Scribner's*, Dec. 1898; *Times*, Nov. 7; Dec. 9, 14. Selborne, *Times*, Dec. 20; "Liberal Forwards," *Times*, June 17; Paul, *West. G.*, May 17; *Quart. Rev.*, 188:264; *Christ. World*, Mar. 31; Apr. 21, 28; Dec. 15; *Punch*, June 4, p. 254; June 11, p. 271; Nov. 26, p. 246. Note peace meeting held on Dec. 18, *Times*, Dec. 19; Bowen, *Times*, June 3; Campbell-Bannerman, *Scots.*, Dec. 7; M'Ewan, *Scots.*, Nov. 23.

14 Based partly upon questions addressed to the Foreign Office. Nevins, *White*, 137, 140, 165–66; Dennis, *op. cit.*, 81, 85; Stanley, in J. B. Pond, *Eccentricities*, 285; Willson, *New America*, 51ff.; *Econ.*, July 9, 23; Nov. 5, 26; note G. J. Younghusband, *Philippines and Round About* (London, 1899); *P. Debs.*, 63: Aug. 1. The *Times* complained that no career diplomat such as Henry White was ever appointed ambassador.

15 Dennis, *op. cit.*, chap. viii; Nevins, *White*, 162, 164–65, 172, 181, 202; Dicey, *19th Cent.*, Sept. 1898, p. 495; Asquith, *Times*, Sept. 10, Dec. 16, 17, 19, 20; Grey, *Times*, Apr. 23, June 6; Max Pemberton in late April showed surprise at statement that commercial classes sided with Spain. Hamilton, *Times*, July 8.

16 A. R. Colquhoun, *Greater America* (New York and London, 1904), 416; this view is repeated by an American, W. A. Dunning, *British Empire and the United States* (New York, 1914), 347; cf. D. S. Jordan, *Imperial Democracy* (New York, 1899), 51. Chamberlain, while open to suggestion, considered any application of tariff to our colonies a blunder. The *West. G.* may be added to those who disliked our diplomacy. Courtney, *Times*, Apr. 14; Low, *Natl. R.*, 31:261; Chamberlain, *Scribner's*, Dec. 1898, 674–82; *Times*, Aug. 5. Eliz. Lecky, *A Memoir of W. E. H. Lecky* (London, 1909), p. 323. For a philosophical analysis of American imperialism (in American thought), see A. K. Weinberg, *Manifest Destiny: a Study of Nationalist Expansionism in American History* (Baltimore, 1935).

17 *Stand.*, Apr. 29; *Times*, Aug. 16, 17, 25, 27; Nov. 28; Fowler, *Times*, Nov. 19; Balfour, *Times*, Dec. 21; note that on July 16, even the *Sat. Rev.* had said, "This fact that the two nations which stood against each other at the beginning of the nineteenth century now stand together as friends, if not as allies, will probably turn out to be the most important fact of the twentieth century." But cf. the review of E. L. Godkin's *Unforeseen Tendencies of Democracy* in the same issue, p. 85. The *D. Mail* in December wanted joint construction of canal; cf. *Manch. G.*, Dec. 6.

18 *Ripon Collection*, Brit. Museum Add. Mss. 43540, Gen. Correspondence, 2nd Series.

V

SAID THE LION OF THE EAGLE

1899–1903

FORTUNATELY for imperialism and the effect of it upon England and Anglo-American relations, it did not seem to matter that England could work up no praise or enthusiasm for our management of the spoils of war.[1] Our conduct in the Philippines and Cuba brought again to the surface the suspicion of our political incapacity. Party politics, blundering altruism, windy sentimentality, and inefficient hustling were observed in our colonizing, and decreased the significance of our imperialism for the British. But our colonial ventures could not be ignored, and played a minor part in a renewed analysis of imperialism. Once again British opinion was not sharply divided along party lines. Those Americans who had conceived of a natural kinship with English Liberals suffered some rude jolts during our overseas ventures.

It was soon realized that American experience was too limited to have given us much insight into the problems facing the scattered British Empire. This was expressed by Sir Edward Grey and A. E. Duchesne; the latter's reasoning was curious:

We shall not gain much light from the history of American *colonial* administration when we reflect that all such is in federal hands, and that the President is more truly autocratic than the king of England, while the democratic element of the constitution rests with the individual states and is concerned purely with state domestic matters.

The press relied for a time on Anglo-Saxon instincts to carry us over difficulties; hence the pattern of colonial work might well follow England's. The *Economist* (February 23, 1901) put the argument in another way: "The real question is whether American political morality will surmount supposed American political interests."

79

For several years following the war it was often repeated that the new colonial efforts would influence American attitudes. The *Quarterly Review* decided that it would improve the home government and even raise the standard of American journalism in relation to foreign affairs; others hoped it would improve our sense of international courtesy and propriety. The *Times* (November 1899) concluded:

> In proportion as America assumes proprietorship beyond the original limits of her territory, it will become more and more necessary that there should be complete unity in the attitude of the nation towards its new acquisitions, and this necessity will manifestly tend towards the increase of the national or Republican spirit in other directions also. . . . America cannot escape her destiny. . . . The idea of preserving her isolation is a dream.

Chamberlain, who kept heralding the adoption of the Open Door in the new possessions, wrote to Hay, July 5, 1902: "I am primarily convinced that this extension of American rights and dimensions will make for the happiness of the native populations," and enable Americans to understand Britons. Chamberlain bolstered his arguments for a native hut tax by citing the approval of the "admirable . . . very practical" American missionaries in Sierra Leone. What the *Westminster Gazette* expected, however, was that "We shall see the British Jingo raised to the power of New York."

The British freely offered advice. Professional men were needed, but as the ex-Governor of Borneo explained, "America is so rich, so under-populated, so full of boundless opportunities, that I cannot see how a young American can be expected to accept lifelong banishment in an uncongenial climate." The *Spectator* wanted a native army, a governor-general with a free hand to teach the Filipinos to expect permanent occupation, and Roosevelt as pro-consul. Sir George Clarke advised America to follow the experience of Britain in the Malay Peninsula. The *Times*, fearful that the new imperial policy would be discredited by mismanagement, suggested in 1899 a civil service for the Philippines, a reasonable tariff system, and military victories before concessions; "The Americans will, doubtless, proceed . . . as we have done in similar lands, and as we are now proceeding in the Sudan and Nigeria," that is, extend good government by arms. Indeed, when "America is on her trial in the eyes of the world as an Imperial Power" it could do no better than follow the British system. The *Times* also warned that we might find it difficult to realize that citizens in a field army are on a "different footing from citizens going to the ballot-box at home."

When the *Times* praised Mr. Gould's achievements in Cuba they were described as the "result of the qualities which have made English Imperial policy, in Admiral Dewey's words, so great a factor in the civilization of mankind." While *Punch* often satirized our imperialistic methods and gains, others predicted that our treatment of the Negro augured ill for America's future relations with Cubans and Filipinos, partly also because Americans were indifferent to personal prestige in dealing with natives. But in "General Leonard Wood," commented Sidney Brooks, "the Americans have discovered a second Cromer. . . ." The *Scotsman* early in 1899 was happy to see that Americans followed England in common-sense adaptations of political principles. Curiously enough, the Supreme Court decisions on the "Insular Cases," which legalized American imperialism in the sense that Congress now had a right to make laws for all dependencies, aroused little interest and were slightly unintelligible. Several papers concluded that the decisions would make the annexation of Mexico and Nicaragua much easier. Mr. Alleyne Ireland's realistic colonial investigation sponsored by the University of Chicago received some press notice; Sir Frank Swettenham, former Governor of the Straits Settlements, approvingly declared, "That course was characteristic of the American people."

Opinion hesitated to take seriously the self-denying ordinance which guaranteed Cuba's independence. When attention could be diverted from the South African conflict, fears were expressed over America's commercial penetration. The *Scotsman* had observed:

It is eminently creditable to American methods that the transference of Cuba from Spain to the States should have been accomplished with so little friction.

Cuba suggested the formula for American expansion into Latin America. In 1901 Lionel Carden reported that Cuba was prospering under American control; the *Times* concluded that everything was improved except the judiciary and municipal system. If one were inclined to describe the treatment of Cuba as selfish and shameless (over sugar and tobacco), said Neville Lubbock, British treatment of her own West Indies was even less liberal. By June 1902 England through Carden made advances to Cuba for a reciprocity treaty. The following year deputations from chambers of commerce waited upon Lord Lansdowne because of anxiety over the Cuban-American reciprocity treaty. The press decided in 1906 that the annexation of Cuba would inevitably follow any disturbance, and even the *Manchester Guardian* acquitted the American Government of any undue acquisitiveness. The *Standard* preached: "Either the 'white man's burden' must be shouldered manfully, or it should not be taken in hand." Reports from *Guardian* and *Times* correspondents that our business men had financed the rebellion made the press less favorable. However, departing from its original opinions, the *Daily Express* (August 30, 1907) even added: "The only hope for Haiti and San Domingo is American administration. . . ." Viscount Elibank, who for many years had been trying to direct more attention to the West Indies, declared, almost as a threat to British indifference, "The policy of the U.S.A. towards their Dependencies in the Caribbean waters and in the Pacific has been both broad-minded and generous."

England did not believe self-government possible in the Philippines, which captured most attention.[2] Nor did it seem possible that the rush to Americanize without a capable civil service would bring success. Although originally the *Manchester Guardian* did not want an independent republic, as soon as America had difficulties it suggested that the Philippines be granted complete autonomy with an American veto on foreign treaties: "We hope to have heard the last of the argument that America, of all nations, must stifle liberty because if she does not somebody else may." In 1899 the *Times* and *Daily Mail* took the lead in predicting a serious struggle, but the *Times* explained it was not motivated as were German criticisms by a spirit of malicious joy. The *Mail* added: "We are seeing day by day the fatal results of sending an army into the field imperfectly organized and improperly armed." The press was surprised by the middle of 1899 that all had not been settled. The general opinion was that America was trying to govern the Philippines "as though it were a larger Wisconsin."

Acting-Consul Sinclair had written quite accurately from the Philippines in 1901: "The gigantic nature of the task before the United States authorities in these islands is probably not understood in the United Kingdom." Although he did not suggest withdrawal, F. H. Sawyer's *Inhabitants of the Philippines* (1900) had been accepted as showing how, with a little sense and tact, an American protectorate over the islands could have been established without friction. The *Guardian* could not discover a more shabby war; the army's conduct led the *Scotsman* to complain of the pro-Boer feeling in the States: "Why should not these American humanitarians look nearer home?" Under the title *Filipino Martyrs* (1900), Richard Brinsley Sheridan indicted the United States in theory and practice. Major Younghusband found America completely unprepared. A. Savage Landor's *Gems of the East* (1904) viewed us as poor colonizers. Although his over-emphasis on America's future in the Pacific was hard to accept because of the gloomy outlook, Colquhoun's *Mastery of the Pacific* (1902) and *Greater America* (1904) demonstrated that it was difficult to approve of the Philippine adventure, that America was masquerading as an apostle of liberty rather than as an order-loving Anglo-Saxon people, that too much was made of native education, and finally, that "The desire to rule is not implanted in the American heart." Much of the press agreed that Americans had never shown any capacity for governing an inferior race. The *Westminster Gazette* (February 10, 1902) observed: "The way of safety must in South Africa as in the Philippines be the way of self-government." The extreme gloom of 1902, according to the press, had shocked profoundly the American people, but had not killed the taste for imperialism. By 1904 more hopeful articles described American achievements in agriculture and education. A few voices even suggested that the British system might well move as swiftly in developing social and industrial capacities of communities within the Empire. But the *Annual Register* of 1904 pointed to mismanagement in education, investment, and marriage laws in the island of Guam "as a striking illustration of the impractical side of the American as a colonizer."

Various journals had always insisted that the Philippines must benefit by the American connection, otherwise imperialism would mean nothing. British commercial interests might suffer. Concern had already been expressed in 1902 about the trade in hemp; the Chamber of Shipping in 1904 urged the Government to protest the proposed exclusion of British vessels from commerce between the islands and ourselves. The Earl of Selborne, mindful of the current fiscal discussions, reminded the Lords of the loss of markets in our new possessions; Lord Muskerry wanted to retaliate, but Lord Lansdowne could find no way of doing so. Thus our colonial fiscal arrangements, linked with American and German competition, fanned the discussion of fiscal reform in England.

After 1904 the observations on our colonial administration could hardly be called "public opinion." The *Westminster Gazette* in October 1907 argued at length that "the first attempt ever made to 'hustle' and Americanize the East looks like breaking down." Mrs. Campbell Dauncey in her *Englishwoman in the Philippines* (1906) was sorry a country had been laid waste "for the sake of a windy theory" of sentiment and false promises. Articles carried in the *Times* in 1910 showed great disappointment with America's inability to inculcate respect in the islands. So the annexation of the Philippines—"hardly a deliberate act of policy, but a logical result of American expansion," as the *Morning Post* described it in 1907 —had inspired no British admiration, and made Englishmen peculiarly sensitive to our criticism of their own colonial achievements, whether it was Bryan on India or Roosevelt on Egypt.

However, a few looked for some positive lessons. In 1904 the *Spectator* viewed Mr. Root's report to the President as worthy of England's attention,

. . . for, apart from the work of Army reform, the American experiment in reconstruction is closely analogous to our work in South Africa during the last three years. . . . The most friendly observer might have assumed that they would err in trying to transplant American ideas of government to soil not yet fully prepared for them. But the United States Government made no such mistakes.

The *Birmingham Post* (March 10, 1906) even gave credit for insight: "Presumably, the commercial gains are expected to compensate for the expenditure." During the Colonial Office Supply debate in 1911, Sir Max Aitken said that the American possessions had developed well as compared with British territories; further, "The United States Government has developed its Colonial systems along lines which are at least worthy of investigation by the Commission which the Imperial Conference proposes to set up." While advocating measures to combat opium-smoking, Mr. Theodore Taylor described what we had accomplished in the Philippines. Mr. Harcourt added: "When American care and genius have turned Panama into a health resort, there need be no limit to our hopes in the future."

Our ventures again raised the question whether Democracy and Empire were compatible. The *Guardian* asked, "What is to become of the root ideas of the American Republic?" Even the *Saturday Review* had hoped that imperialism would impart to our administrative machine "a stability which it at present lacks." Although it was expansion by explosion, J. A. Hobson viewed the economic basis of imperialism as "strikingly illustrated" by American events; Cuba and Hawaii were "but the *hors d'œuvre* to whet an appetite." Actually, very little was said about the domestic effects of imperialism after 1902. Those who opposed our new imperialism from unselfish motives had not been deceived. Continental and British reactions were fundamentally alike, but British journals and writers interpreted for us this Continental suspicion.

In an analysis of the imperial song predominant between 1899 and 1903 one can find that our expansion by explosion was still explained as inevitable destiny.[3] England, in urging America forward, whipped up her own enthusiasm. She became aware of a new imperial power without falling into a general panic; no political danger was discoverable in American imperialism. But the "American peril," a term more used on the Continent, did not fail to penetrate the British Isles; if it did nothing else, the foreign opinion quoted in the British press covered all our threats to Old World polity.

Our national pride no doubt tingled at the space given to us in British speeches. When the Duke of Devonshire spoke before the Birmingham Chamber of Commerce in 1899, he declared that only England had viewed the imperial venture with "real and active sympathy," and that American interests "will mainly, if not in every particular, coincide with our own and that of all our colonies." At a Conservative and Unionist demonstration organized by the Primrose League, January 1899, Sir Matthew White Ridley found the past year a remarkable one in history because "it had witnessed a great growth of Anglo-Saxon influences." For Chamberlain, whom Gladstone once described as the most American of English statesmen, the year 1898 marked the close of the period associated with the Manchester school of economics, brought American influence to bear on English imperial policy, and prepared the way for tariff reform. Like Walter Long, he had no doubt of the civilizing rôle of Anglo-Saxons or the need of enlisting Americans in controlling the tropics; in January 1899, he said, "It will not be any longer the Imperial policy of England alone."

The *National Review* belabored Carnegie, who disagreed, for misleading his countrymen because he connected America's annexation of the Philippines with a European quarrel; the *Review* insisted that British opinion held that the struggle would come if there was not annexation. Chamberlain still dropped easily into such topics as "alliances" and America's pro-British sympathy in the Boer War, much to the sceptical amusement of American opinion, foreign journals, and English radical papers. Another Lord Mayor's banquet found him and Salisbury praising the Anglo-Saxon peace which benefited civilization. Labouchere concluded that Chamberlain envisaged a heavenly mission to conquer all tropical countries, but doubted whether we would pull chestnuts out of the fire for England.

Enthusiastic reports which favored American imperialism had been coming from British possessions. The reciprocity treaties between the West Indies and the United States did not excite much attention; the "Looker On" in *Blackwood's* favored their annexation to the United States. A book like J. W. Root's *The British West Indies and the Sugar Industry* (1899) prompted some journals to consider the desires of those islands for annexation. Reports that America planned to improve Pago Pago harbor did not alarm the British, according to the German Ambassador in London, because the Australians, who influenced British policy in such matters, objected to Germans, not Americans, as neighbors. But a few journals argued that the United States was a more dangerous rival than Germany. The *Westminster Gazette* suggested in 1900 that "America had much better let Denmark keep her islands." Further American expansion was expected. To Cecil Rhodes the Philippines were a mere bagatelle because America would conquer most of South America. The *Times* (February 20, 1899), which disclaimed any desire to incite Americans to additional ventures, was correct in part when it said:

With regard to the tasks that America is now taking up, there is greater sympathy and comprehension in this country than Americans perhaps fully recognize.

England's general election in 1900, which paralleled in nature the American elections, produced few comments. The *Westminster Gazette* (June 16, 1900) reflected:

In our own controversies about Imperialism and expansion it is not amiss to spare a moment . . . to observe the corresponding debate which is in progress in the United States. . . . Even those who are Imperialists in this country may sympathize with a protest against Imperialism in a country of the nature and extent of the United States.

In spite of all that Little Englanders could find, and no matter what was the real meaning of McKinley's success in 1900, the results of the American election were hailed in England as a "Victory of Imperialism." It was natural, therefore, that interested groups stressed America's anti-imperialistic feeling and lamented our indulgence in armaments and aggressiveness which had not added to America's beneficent world rôle. According to Goldwin Smith, an Englishman fascinated by America's power since 1861, we had been inspired by plutocracy and militarism; he proclaimed America's threat to Canada to his friend Lord Rosebery in England, and warned us in his *Commonwealth or Empire* (1902) against imperial responsibilities. It was important for Anglo-American diplomacy that England was soon wondering whether Roosevelt was a dangerous Monroeist and whether he might be compared with Palmerston.

British opinion which seeped into the thinking of professional diplomats seemed unwilling to believe that America did not want an alliance or feel the need for one.[4] To be sure, there were voices which predicted a gigantic struggle for the sovereignty of the seas, but during the years 1899 and 1900 the idea that the peace of the world rested in Anglo-American hands was perhaps as strong as it ever has been. The moral superiority of such a combination was unquestioned; the physical superiority appeared less and less probable. Balfour professed to view relations with the United States from no selfish basis; Captain Bagot, mover of the Address in the Commons in 1899, included among the guarantees of peace an understanding between the two countries. Arnold White, Cecil Rhodes, Lord Beresford, and a host of others were for an alliance and deemed it possible; Beresford, proud of the coöperation England had already shown, discovered in the new sentiment at least a chance for a vital commercial understanding. G. S. Clarke argued that united action was possible without a formal alliance. A. V. Dicey, who had advocated a common citizenship in 1897, and Sir Charles Dilke, who had reported in 1898 that English opinion hoped America would be satisfied with a protectorate over the Philippines, did not believe an alliance possible, but a good understanding was a necessity. The feeling which encouraged an alliance, however, was better expressed in the vaguer terms of Kipling, the great expounder of Empire:

After a nation has pursued certain paths alone in the face of some slight misrepresentation, it is consoling to find another nation (which one can address without a dictionary) preparing to walk along the same lines to, I doubt not, the same ends.

But alliances were not so constructed. The Liberal press professed joy that early in 1899 the American Ambassador "gave no encouragement to Anglo-Saxon rowdyism." In all this outburst of feeling the movement for a general arbitration treaty lagged.

Mutual difficulties made American imperialism and sentiment bulk large during the very British problem of the Boer War.[5] Americans had participated in some of the earlier maneuvers in South Africa; more recent American events accounted for fundamental discussions which amounted almost to a comparative, practical study in expansion. England had become more sensitive to America's criticism, expected much from it, and had an opportunity to estimate the real nature of America's imperialistic impulses and her feeling towards Anglo-American diplomacy. American opinion competed for first place with European comments in news columns and leading articles. In the face of European press hostility, England may have linked her troubled circumstances too closely to recent American history, but this was understandable since many of the accusations were bombs hurled at both countries. Perhaps the *Times* in 1901 was not talking useful nonsense but outlining the pattern for subsequent world history when it declared:

The jealousy of the prosperity and expansion of the Anglo-Saxon race which is at the root of the virulence of the criticism directed against this country abroad is a main element also in the bitterness against "Americanism" on the Continent.

European journals felt that England was misleading a youngster and prejudicing us against Europe.

By October 1899 affairs in the Philippines and South Africa had, as the *Times* suggested, "a curious resemblance." The press intimated, however, that Americans favorable to Aguinaldo were more influential than the pro-Boer British! England expected American opinion to be sympathetic, and generally it was so reported by sources as diverse as the *Scotsman*, Chamberlain, and the Poet Laureate. The difficulties just faced by America, "the common battles for freedom and civilization," and common interests—not to mention England's aid in saving us from European blood-lust —suggested what should be the tone of American opinion. Oddly enough, the two Americans whose support received most attention were A. T. Mahan, the naval historian, and John Hays Hammond, an American engineer who had been active in South Africa! To repay the religious approval of the English churches in 1898, American Methodists who attended the Œcumenical Conference in 1901 thanked God for British victories. That not all Britons were pleased was reflected in rhymes by "O.S." in *Punch:*

How served the Anglo-Saxon bond for bar
'Gainst Europe's intervention, proving blood
Thicker than water? Babble o' sentiment.
Mere unction good at after-dinner hours

To ease exchange of yachtsmen's courtesies;
Not to be understood the serious way
By public men with Celtic votes to catch.

It was these American friends, not the Kaiser, who transmitted the Boers' mediation proposals to London.

H. H. Asquith expressed to Campbell-Bannerman, October 14, 1899, what was a common, significant interlocking of ideas:

Our title of intervention [in South Africa] was far stronger, both legally and morally, than that of the United States in the case of Cuba. And yet the action of the latter was almost universally approved in Great Britain.[6]

One might speculate a long time over this observation. Had statesmen mistaken a desire to express and secure American friendship for a renewed approval of imperialism? Had England been misled by the depth of American imperialism? Both seem possible.

The Boer War stimulated interest in American history.[7] Salisbury and Wyndham preferred to discuss our Civil War (rather than the War of 1776) as analogous to the Boer War even though John Redmond, who quoted Burke and Chatham, had spoken of 1776 to show that peace would not follow such a bloody struggle. Lloyd George concluded that England had followed in South Africa the Spanish policy in Cuba which had aroused Americans. Salisbury reminded his listeners that several years elapsed before the Civil War had been brought to a conclusion; Spenser Wilkinson compared the two wars as both of gradual growth. Military strategy of the Civil War had been brought to British attention by Colonel George Henderson, eminent military historian, whose *Stonewall Jackson and the American Civil War* (1898) helped to shape Lord Roberts' campaigns. The Boers' tactics were said to have been consciously modeled on Jackson by way of General Joubert.

Amid many interruptions, Balfour read to Parliament United States Army regulations to show that if persons rebelled in occupied territory the population lost the army's protection and disorganized bands were treated as pirates. T. M. Healy, who thought our conduct less justified than England's, found it an "unhappy omen" that the Government, in order to support its policy, had to turn to "America in the miserable squabble with the Philippines." In the next year, 1901, while justifying a policy of banishment should the Boers not surrender, Chamberlain, who had chided Irish politicians for not complaining more about America's war, asked:

To whom of all the great nations of the world would one go if he wanted an example of honourable treatment to an honourable foe? I imagine he would go in the first instance to the United States.

In the Civil War Americans exceeded such things as farm-burning, he explained, and in the Philippines there were General Arthur's proclamations which were applicable to the Transvaal—guerrillas became mere bandits. Some disliked comparing the Boers with the Filipinos, and Bryce found the reference inaccurate, partly because American public opinion did not tolerate Arthur's proclamations. The view was widely held in England that the North had made wholesale confiscation of rebel property in 1865, and extremists had referred persistently to the Civil War to condone farm-burning. Bryce reminded Parliament of the amnesty given by the North; John Hays Hammond, who advised a moderate peace, put forward Grant's generous terms to Lee. Others followed the suggestion, and during the peace negotiations the Duke of Devonshire devoted much attention to the example of General Lee, who preferred surrender rather than guerrilla warfare. Part of the press complained that England had failed to learn the lessons of the campaigns in Cuba and the Philippines. The Civil Lord of the Admiralty, Mr. Pretyman, thought England might take comfort from the fact that we had failed to subdue the less formidable Filipinos who had no De Wet or Botha and no Mausers or artillery. Brodrick decided the British were more efficient. Thus our imperialism soon had practical implications.

We have already seen that the situation in the Far East influenced the British response to American imperialism.[8] If America could not be stimulated to action before April 1898, it seemed much more likely that with obligations in the Philippines thrust upon us, we would look to the Pacific. British opinion hoped for this, and anticipated Hay's note of September 6, 1899, which requested a declaration from foreign powers concerning their interests in China. America's new influence in the Pacific was acknowledged, but one can hardly conclude that British opinion was completely satisfied with our diplomacy in the Far East. Beresford, who was advised by Hay to call on America, had a great reception in his trip across the continent; when he spoke before the American-Asiatic Association in early 1899 he advised the Open Door. At the New York Chamber of Commerce he pointed out the increase of our trade. Within four years the imports of American cotton had increased 121 per cent in quantity while the import of British cotton decreased 13 per cent; this might alarm the British manufacturer, he said, but not the British merchant in China. Beresford talked about the United States almost as much as Chamberlain; his arguments convinced many in England because he demonstrated our stakes in the Chinese question. American people agreed that the doors should be kept open, he argued, but they naturally felt that the country with 64 per cent of the foreign trade should take the lead, and he tried to use American opinion as a lever to get action in England.

The press the year before, particularly the *Times* and the *Statist*, had decided that there was no connection between high tariff and the Open Door; one was not incompatible with the other. British traders watched with some fear the application of this logic in our new possessions. But the Pacific was to be a bond between the two nations, and the will of the English-speaking people, if united, would be paramount there. Spring-Rice and Gerald Balfour recognized this unity of interests and reported that America wanted parallel action. The *Daily Mail* (March 28, 1900) viewed America's desire for the Open Door with enthusiasm: "Nothing that it has hitherto done in international affairs can in the least compare with the result of its present action." As a Member read the American statement on the Open Door he told Parliament that the British Government would probably not have our coöperation in its policy of "spheres of interests," as in the Yangtze valley. Mr. Brodrick replied that "There is a great difference between what was agreed upon between the British Government and the United States Government as to the open door and dealing with the Chinese Government." Dilke suggested that Brodrick "altogether minimized the new departure in the policy of the United

States," which also wanted Chinese reforms. American opinion had been brought to England in 1898 by John Barrett, American Minister to Siam, who talked with several Members of Parliament in Committee; he explained that coöperation was to be based upon dollars and cents rather than on "Anglo-Saxondom." American activities, as well as German and Japanese efforts, encouraged the formation in England of the China League and the China Association.

British opinion was extremely doubtful in 1900 and 1901 whether we had a Chinese policy. The *Labour Leader* (December 8, 1900) concluded that we had sided against Britain throughout the Chinese crisis. John Hay was sorry that some of the British press had taken this view. The *Economist* believed that too much had been said in England about our Chinese policy, which at best was vague. Hesitancy in China created the impression in Europe that America was difficult to negotiate with because she didn't know her own mind and because of the peculiarities of the American Constitution, e. g., the Senate's power over treaties. The *Saturday Review* added, "Of course the trouble in this matter as with every other foreign interest . . . is the ignorance and apathy of all the best Americans," and also a badly informed populace. Several papers urged England not to drift from the United States because of a more forward policy. Ultimately, the lack of American coöperation led to the Anglo-Japanese alliance of 1902.

English opinion is excellently summed up in a letter which the Prime Minister, A. J. Balfour, dictated from his sick bed, February 11, 1904, to Lord Lansdowne, Foreign Secretary.[9] He was preoccupied with the questions raised by us concerning Chinese neutrality in the course of the Russo-Japanese conflict. He continued:

The success of Russia in the war with Japan means, to an absolute certainty, war with China—the immediate annexation of Manchuria, and other consequences not less serious, to follow. *Are the Americans prepared to help us by force of arms to prevent this?* [Underlined in pencil, probably by Lansdowne.] I do not know that it is worth bringing them up to this fence too quickly; but you and I ought not, at all events, to be under the illusion that anything *short* [underlined in ink] of this will be of the slightest value or that mere diplomacy will snatch from Russia the fruits of her victories, if victories she is destined to obtain.

If the Americans would so far violate their traditions as to make any suggestions of an alliance for the purpose of *preserving by arms* [underlined in pencil], if necessary, the integrity of China, it would open a new era in the history of the World. It seems all important to induce them, however, to make the [proposal—crossed out] first move; if *we* start it the Senate are sure to upset the scheme.

. . . all American negotiations drag so that [we had better know our own minds, at all events, as soon as possible—crossed out] the sooner we begin to feel our way, the better.

The Russian defeat and the Japanese alliance, renewed in 1905, answered the letter.

Inasmuch as subsequent American activities in the Far East did not bulk large in British opinion, we may violate chronological divisions for a moment.[10] The Anglo-Japanese alliance was signed January 30, 1902. There was some British anxiety at the possible reception of this treaty in America. The attitude of the imperial conferences served to a degree to remind Britain that the Colonies, at the outset appreciative of their new relations to Japan, demanded that the United States must also be considered. Mr. Norman was told by Lord Cranborne that we had been informed of the treaty prior to publication, but had made no comment on it. It was Norman's opinion that "The interest of America and our own have been identical with those of Japan, and the obvious course would be to endeavour to take step by step in this matter with America." The British press reported correctly that American opinion was favorable.

Roosevelt's rôle as peacemaker in the Russo-Japanese conflict attracted attention. In 1905 the United States seemed more eager for peace than England. Several journals were happy to see that their new ally regarded Americans as potential friends. Spring-Rice wrote to Mrs. Roosevelt, August 10, 1905, that an old wish of his was "to see the President acting the part of a practical and disinterested preacher and example, in the world at large as well as in America—a living influence and force for all good things." Balfour had written to Lansdowne, January 17, 1905, that since

Roosevelt was feeling the ground for peace in an unofficial way, Britain ought to follow his example.[11] Lansdowne wrote to Balfour, September 3, 1905:

Like you, I am a little puzzled by the suddenness of the Japanese climb-down. They may have been to some extent convinced by Roosevelt's powerful argument, but I suspect that there is something more behind it, and that Ito and his friends, who certainly were at one time very Russian in their proclivities, have prevailed.

The *Saturday Review* might call Roosevelt the "Pope of Oyster Bay," but in general the British press was kind to his ambition to extend America's good influence. Despite many variations of policy, American war loans to the Japanese brought Anglo-American views closer together to form the basis of the Far Eastern settlement. In revising the Anglo-Japanese alliance, which was made public in September 1905, the mutual naval obligations, the British held, were not to take into account any threat from the American fleet. The racial problem of the Japanese in California was not minimized, and the trouble rather suggested that a stronger Federal government was needed. Such news was difficult to discuss, and there were numerous warnings that British journalists should control themselves, for portions of the Empire, particularly Australia, might act the same way.

Although little that was definite had been achieved in all these prospects of similar interests, Sir Edward Grey, still in the Opposition in 1905, approved of British foreign policy based upon three points: the Japanese alliance, the entente with France, and an Anglo-American understanding. Just as England had in 1900 and 1901 viewed America's policy in China as dangerously hesitant, again in 1910 it viewed that policy as unreal, particularly Knox's proposals to take the Manchurian railroad out of politics. This uncertainty concerning our policy in the Far East vitally affected many subsequent British moves in that region.

Now with obligations in both oceans the United States contemplated an interoceanic route between the Atlantic and the Pacific.[12] British opinion accepted this revived enthusiasm as a direct result of the new imperialism. The Clayton-Bulwer treaty, signed April 19, 1850, had joined the United States and Great Britain in any canal enterprise, and the protection and neutralization thereof. Maturity altered American desires. The original draft of the Hay-Pauncefote treaty was signed February 5, 1900; it did not provide for the abrogation of the Clayton-Bulwer treaty and it failed to secure for us the sole right of neutralization and control. The Senate's handiwork on the amended treaty was rejected by Great Britain. The new draft, which was a compromise ratified by the Senate, December 16, 1901, removed diplomatic obstacles from the construction of the canal. During 1900 and 1901 British opinion was not excited over this problem of Panama or Nicaragua; in turn it was about as ill informed as it was in the Venezuela crisis of 1896 regarding American aims. The British had hoped in vain to link the concessions on Panama with an adjustment of the Alaskan boundary which satisfied the Canadians. These concessions brought about a vital alteration of British naval strategy which left reinsurance in the western hemisphere to an expanding and friendly American navy.

Throughout 1899 and 1900, articles had appeared calling British attention to the importance of the canal scheme. Although the canal would probably lead to the control of Central America as the Suez Canal led to English control in Egypt, the *Times* (February 14, 1899) recognized the claims for revisions of the Bulwer treaty; but England's calm was not to be misconstrued as indifference. The *Saturday Review*, directly opposed to the *Spectator*, which had early advocated the abrogation of the treaty, declared: "The Senate . . . in its present condition is certainly not a body with which any self-respecting government would attempt to reason." Other papers declared that the mysteries of party strife in America were "unfathomable" to an English observer. The press had expected trouble in the Senate and also Britain's rejection of the Senate amendments. It rather felt that the interests of all concerned could have been just as well secured without the abandonment of the principles of the Bulwer treaty; in general, the Liberal press objected less strenuously to the proposed alteration of power.

The seizure of the Canal Zone and the Panama Revolution in November 1903 did not elicit severe criticism in the British press. Several of the leading papers could not see America's hands in the rebellion. However, the *Scotsman* looked upon the episode as

a high-handed, strong-armed policy which set a dangerous precedent; the *Guardian* doubted whether with "booty so profitable" we
would submit Colombia's grievance to The Hague. The Government was more aware of the facts.[13] The British Acting Consul at
Panama, Mr. Rohrweger, telegraphed November 7, 1903:

> The attitude of the United States Government throughout the revo-
> lution was one of more than benevolent neutrality towards the seced-
> ing province . . .

He also suggested to Lansdowne that the "key to the situation
should be sought for in Washington. . . ." Consul Mallet added,
November 23, 1903:

> However much the conduct of the United States Government in
> this affair is open to criticism, for it is quite certain their actions have
> not been governed by international usage, the fact remains that they
> are now placed in a position to dictate their own terms of ownership,
> construction, and maintenance of the Panama Canal.

America had played the rôle of international policeman, a form
of responsibility that England urged upon us in Latin America.

The British public was advised from time to time to look to the
opportunities in South America, but perhaps European fear of
American aggression there was given more prominence than any
similar British apprehension.[14] British papers had held, with less
vehemence than the Continental press, that American imperialism
weakened the validity of the Monroe Doctrine. A few influential
voices admitted the value of our influence on the minor states. The
Times (August 23, 1901) explained:

> Central and South American states may learn also that they have
> nothing to fear from the moral hegemony which the United States can-
> not but exercise over their destiny . . .

But the value of Pan-American congresses and the conception of
Pan-Americanism were not taken very seriously.

The Monroe Doctrine came in for a greater share of attention in
1901 and 1902. Generally, England meant it to imply America's
responsibility for the actions of weaker states. Balfour and Lord
Avebury wanted us to adjust difficulties between Europe and South
America; the former wrote to Carnegie, December 18, 1902:

"These South American Republics are a great trouble, and I wish the U.S.A. would take them in hand." The *Spectator* argued that the Monroe Doctrine guaranteed British possessions in the American continent. It also praised Sir Frederick Pollock, who interpreted the Doctrine as an English-speaking determination to preserve political and spiritual freedom, and a defensive measure which might even be adapted to certain portions of the British Empire. The *Times* regretted that Mahan, writing in the *National Review*, denied the corollary that we were obligated to see that weaker states carried out their duties. In addition, Continental hostility to us had been quoted so much that portions of British opinion were beginning to believe that Germany feared America more than England as a rival; several shrewd observers wondered whether it would be prudent for America to keep Germany out of South America.

But it is difficult in the face of all this and many diplomatic documents to see what evaluation either of British or American public opinion induced the British Government to join with Germany in forcing Venezuela to meet her obligations, coöperation which by December 20, 1902, had resulted in a state of belligerency with Venezuela. Lord Lansdowne and Villiers, the British Under-Secretary of State, were certain that the United States would not interfere; the British Ambassador at Washington reported, December 29, 1902, a complete "absence of apprehension as to the course pursued by Great Britain." To be sure, Hay and Roosevelt, as Professor Perkins demonstrates, had given both countries assurances that they might discipline Castro with impunity. "It is possible, moreover," writes Perkins, "that Villiers, and the chief whom he represented, Lord Lansdowne, were not unaware of the advantages that coöperative action against Venezuela might bring as regards the United States." It is difficult to discover the advantages.

On August 7, 1902, the British Ambassador in Berlin was informed that his government was willing to coöperate. In the spring of 1902 British investors had first suggested control of the customs; this proposal was soon dropped. While the press hoped that America would not make the Monroe Doctrine a shield for chronic dishonesty, it also believed that England would do better by acting alone. Others suggested a triple protest as conjectured by

Lansdowne early in August. Pertinent discussion began in Parliament on December 15, 1902. Although the Government was reminded that when America previously asked for arbitration "Britain ate dirt," many members were quite disturbed. Mr. Schwann (Manchester) explained:

The Monroe Doctrine has many times been used for Presidential election purposes, and, consequently there may at any time be a change in American sentiment.

In advising arbitration Mr. Norman added:

With regard to the position of the United States, the most important point is the great weight public opinion has there. . . . The American Government is peculiarly susceptible to public opinion, and public opinion may from one week to another take a much keener interest in this matter, which makes the position more serious for this country.

Arbitration was probably not accepted under American pressure. The United States began to intervene through its minister, Herbert W. Bowen. Lansdowne, January 23, 1903, expressed anxiety to Balfour about telegrams from Washington: "I am disturbed by Herbert's reports of Bowen, who is, I am afraid, not behaving well. . . . The tone of Bowen's language strikes me as most objectionable." [15] Herbert wrote to Lansdowne, February 7, 1903:

The time has almost come in American opinion for us to make the choice between the friendship of the United States and that of Germany.

Difficulties were overcome, and during the summer of 1903 mixed commissions sat to determine the amount of claims against Venezuela.

The *Scotsman* in commenting upon arbitration said:

One does not even see where the Monroe Doctrine comes up at all, except in the way of making it more clear where and when, even in American apprehension, it is excluded.

Lord Rosebery had been fearful of British treatment on "the very tenderest point of American susceptibilities"; Sir Edward Grey proclaimed that "it was public opinion which got the Government out of the mess." It is significant that an acute Foreign Office career man, Sir Eyre Crowe, in an elaborate departmental analysis of February 1907, could recall only two cases where the foreign policy of his Government had been directly influenced by public opinion as expressed in newspapers and magazines—the Bagdad railway and this Venezuelan imbroglio. But assurances to America were forthcoming. The Duke of Devonshire said England accepted the Monroe Doctrine "fully and unreservedly." In a speech at Liverpool Balfour declared, February 3, 1903:

We know that American public opinion is naturally sensitive upon what is known as the Monroe Doctrine. But the Monroe Doctrine has no enemies in this country that I know of. (Cheers) We welcome any increase of the influence of the United States of America upon the great Western Hemisphere. (Hear, hear.)

The inability to settle the Alaskan boundary dispute between 1898 and 1903 did not discourage British opinion.[16] The American view of the dispute was adequately presented to the public long before January 24, 1903, when a convention was signed to refer the dispute to a mixed commission composed of three Americans, two Canadians, and an English jurist (Lord Alverstone). Coming at a time when British opinion was urging the Government to retreat from the Venezuelan affair to preserve American happiness, the position of Lord Alverstone was very delicate. The Colonial Office had expected that trouble would arise from the composition of the tribunal, especially in the event that Alverstone agreed with the American arguments, as turned out to be the case. A Secretary in the Colonial Office wrote to Lansdowne, January 6, 1903:

I cannot help thinking that Sir Michael Herbert is a little influenced by the idea of a great Anglo-American Supreme Court, though he does speak of it as Utopian.

Some "philo-American furor" had to be whipped up by the press to make the award pleasant to Britons; England dared not be enthusiastic about the award in the face of Canada's dissatisfaction. Lord Alverstone denied to the British Foreign Office and Elihu Root that he had made any political bargains with Americans. No matter, with the dispute out of the way, the goodwill of the United States in the western Atlantic and the Pacific enabled Sir John Fisher to concentrate his vessels in the North Sea.

The Continental hostility to the two countries seemed to foster the idea that the Anglo-Saxon race possessed individuality enough to warrant joint criticism, but much less was said about race after 1901. Our imperialism still made Englishmen say in 1903 that both nations had the same material interests and the same moral and intellectual ideals. Some continued to maintain that "the English-speaking people all over the world could maintain the peace of the world."

[1] Viscount Grey of Falloden, *Twenty-Five Years* (New York, 1925), II, 88; A. E. Duchesne, *Democracy and Empire* (2nd ed., London, 1917), 12; Gideon Murray (Viscount Elibank), *A Man's Life* (London, 1934), 132, 173–75, 188; Chamberlain quoted in Dennis, *op. cit.*, p. 129; cf. *P. Debs.*, 1899, 76: 126. Note in 1902 that work of Am. missionaries in the Deccan is instanced for imitation, *P. Debs.*, 114: 553. Swettenham, *Times*, Apr. 23, 1904, p. 16; Brooks in *Fort. Rev.*, Aug. 1901, considered politics and sentimentality as our two enemies in imperialism; cf. *Times*, Aug. 22, 1901; Mar. 29, 1902; R. H. Fitzgibbon, *Cuba and the United States, 1900–1935* (Menasha, Wis., 1935), 108–09; Lubbock, *Times*, Apr. 8, 1902. Note annual meeting of Chambers of Commerce, *Times*, Mar. 4, 1903; *P. Debs.*, 1903, 118: 497, 918. G. Smith, *Cont. Rev.*, 1899, 75: 621. In the *Proceedings of the Royal Colonial Institute* (London, 1870–1909, continued as *United Empire*) there were three items on U.S. before 1898.

[2] Sinclair, *Parl. Papers*, 1901, An. Ser. No. 2638, p. 129; cf. Foreman in *Natl. R.*, Aug. 1900 and Bradley Martin Jr., *19th Cent.*, 1900, 48: 393–406; *Blackwood*, June, 1902; *An. Register, 1904*, p. 443; *1905*, p. 458. American writers frequently complained in English journals about our colonial administration. A. S. Landor, *Gems of the East* (London, 1904), made voyage in 1902–03, had hope if there were better officials, and saw no reason for all the accusations directed against U.S. A. R. Colquhoun, *Greater America* (New York and London, 1904), 298, 299, 340–42; see also his *The Problem in China and British Policy* (London, 1900) and chaps. iv and v in *Mastery of the Pacific* (London, 1902). Note enthusiastic review of Price Collier's defense of British rule in India (*Times L.S.*, June 1, 1911, p. 210), *The West in the East: From an American Point of View.* H. F. Pringle, *Theodore Roosevelt, A Biography* (New York, 1932), 511; C. R. Enock, *America and England* (London, 1921), 223–25; J. A. Hobson, *Imperialism* (London, 1902), 78–85; see also Adolfe de Chambrun, *Le Pouvoir Exécutif aux États-Unis* (Paris, 1899). The *Sat. Rev.*, Nov. 9, 1901, p. 597, found in Roosevelt another proof that "There need be no divorce between the social reformer and the so-called imperialist." *P. Debs.*, 1902, 105: 1448, 1449; 106: 165, 527; 116: 214; 1904, 129: 15; 130: 218; 135: 1454–57; 1911, 28: 1287; 1912, 40: 523, 594. In 1903, only about 12% of traffic between Philippines and U.S. had been carried in American ships. Lyttleton, speech to Imp. S. Af. Assoc., *Times*, July 15, 1905.

[3] In Parliament (1899), Mr. Dillon thought Chamberlain's comparison of the Transvaal with Cuba was a libel on the U.S. Dilke, in addition, urged G.B. to initiate discussions of Clayton-Bulwer Treaty without consulting France. See *P. Debs.*, 1899, 66: 152; 67: 503; 77: 111, 439, 648–49, 677. Davitt aroused laughter by quoting the *Washington Post* as Am. opinion. Cf. G. H. Ryden, *Foreign*

102   AMERICA AND GREAT BRITAIN

Policy of the U.S. in Relation to Samoa (New Haven, Conn., 1933), 559. For Chamberlain, see *Times*, Jan. 30, Feb. 20, Nov. 30, Dec. 1, 2, 7, 9, 1899; and *Punch*, Dec. 13, 1899. McKinley's inaugural address got a cool reception. *Spec.* compared Roosevelt with Palmerston, Maxse of the *Natl. R.* considered him a dangerous Monroeist. In 1902 Roosevelt was thought to have hedged on everything but imperialism. Bowen, *19th Cent.*, May 1900; Ed. Dicey, *19th Cent.*, Dec. 1903, 885–902; *Natl. R.*, 1900, 35:547; 36:173; Brooks, *Atlantic M.*, 1901, 88:577–88; *Bookman*, 1903, 16:598–602; Wyndham, *Times*, Nov. 16, 1899; Devonshire, *Times*, Jan. 24, 1899; Ridley, *Times*, Jan. 26, 1899. The wild ovations for Dewey were considered sentimental weaknesses by the *Econ.*, Oct. 7, 1899. Arnold Haultain, *Goldwin Smith's Correspondence, 1846–1910* (New York, 1913), 321, 326, 331, 333, 364, 404, 421; Haultain, *Goldwin Smith, His Life and Opinions* (New York, 1914). Surprisingly little was said about Am. expansion which filled the North American continent!

⁴ Balfour, *Times*, Jan. 31, 1899. Dilke also referred to Laird Clowes's suggestion that the U.S. should ask G.B. to train some civil servants; for the improved relations after 1898 he gave credit to Pauncefote. S. Gynn and G. M. Tuckwell, *Life of the Rt. Hon. Sir Charles W. Dilke* (London, 1917–18), II, 503, 66–68. Clarke, *19th Cent.*, 1898, 44:186–95; Dicey, *Atlantic M.*, 1898, 82:441–45; Beresford, *Pall Mall M.*, July 1899, 18:370–83; *West. R.*, 1898, 150:168–70; Greenwood, *19th Cent.*, May 1898; "Diplomaticus," *Fort. R.*, May 1898; *Cont. R.*, 1899, 75:886–908; *Manch. G.*, Mar. 16, 1899; Sir Thomas Barclay, *Thirty Years, Anglo-French Reminiscences, 1876–1906* (London, 1914), 229–38, a member of the Mosely Educ. Commission who returned to Eng. to campaign for An.-Am. arbitration. Kipling, *D. Mail*, Jan. 17, 1899; White, *Natl. R.*, Jan. 1901. Also recall the 1896 pamphlet, *The Great Anglo-American War of 1900*, with a preface by Capt. Anson, R.N. Temple, *N. Am. Review*, 167: 306–16; *Brit. Weekly*, Sept. 25, 1898; *An American Response to Expressions of English Sympathy* (Anglo-Amer. Committee, New York, 1899).

⁵ Nevins, *White*, 220; Poet Laureate, *Times*, Nov. 7, 1901; Methodists, *D. Mail*, Sept. 6, 1901; Pretyman, *Times*, Oct. 16, 1901; Wilkinson, *Cont. R.*, 1900, 77: 793; Mahan in *Natl. R.*, Dec. 1901; *19th Cent.*, 1900, 48: 272–84; *Natl. R.*, 1900, 34: 818; *Fort. R.*, 1900, 73: 667. Morley's anti-Boer War speeches in 1900 were said to have damaged the Anglo-American accord.

⁶ *Campbell-Bannerman Papers*, Brit. Mus. Add. Mss., Vol. 41210, p. 175.

⁷ Chamberlain placed the American War before the Seven Years' War and was corrected by Sir William Harcourt. Chamberlain prided himself on his Am. knowledge, and frequently ran afoul of James Bryce whom he referred to on Am. matters as "The Professor"; Bryce countered, "My illustrious Pupil." *P. Debs.*, 1900, 78:837ff.; 79:138, 178, 1093; 86:133–34, 275–76, 571–72; 1901, 89:45; 92: 118; 99:994, 999, 1009, 1024ff. On payment of enemy's debts, see 1901, 98: 1147. *P. Debs.*, 1902, 101:424–25; 105:208, 370; 116:1283. Hammond, *Autobiography*, II, 425–26; Devonshire, *Times*, Nov. 19, 25, 1901. Note the amusing incident in 1902 (113:490–91) caused by Irish efforts to quote Roosevelt; Speaker ruled against it, and Mr. O'Brien cried: "I hope it will be noted in America that American opinion and Irish opinion are closured and gagged in this House." Dilke, in urging extension of Imperial Telegraphic Communication (1900, 83:983–84), described how we had recently cut cables. Col. Henderson (1854–1903) visited the battlefields of Virginia in 1883; his anonymous "Campaign of Fredericksburg"

(1886) led to his appointment at Sandhurst. See also Pierre Crabites, *Americans in the Egyptian Army* (London, 1938).

[8] Lord Charles Beresford, *The Break-Up of China* (London and New York, 1899), 98, 102–03; Tyler Dennett, *John Hay* (New York, 1934), 286. Chamberlain, *Times*, Jan. 19, 1899; cf. views at annual meeting of Assoc. of Chambers of Commerce, *Times*, Mar. 15, 1899; Gynn, *Dilke*, II, 504; Gwynn, *Spring-Rice*, I, 432–33, 449; A. S. Hershey reflects a similar Am. view in *International Law and Diplomacy of the Russo-Japanese War* (New York, 1906); *Brit. Doc.*, II, p. 199; Colquhoun, *Mastery of Pacific, passim;* Barrett, *Times*, Apr. 26, 27, 1899. *P. Debs.*, 1900, 81: 875, 887, 900. When England withdrew from the Samoan Archipelago in 1899 she demanded compensations from Germany not America, a result of Anglo-German competition for our friendship. The Samoan question had not increased Anglo-American coöperation.

[9] From the *Lansdowne Mss.* Cf. Spring-Rice (Gwynn, *op. cit.*, I, 453) who wrote to Mrs. Roosevelt, March 13, 1905, that one had to move very cautiously in admitting the necessity of a good understanding with the U.S.

[10] A. L. P. Dennis, *Anglo-Japanese Alliance* (Berkeley, Calif., 1923). *P. Debs.*, 1902, 102: 1246, 1279, 1287, 1309. A. Gordon Dewey, *The Dominions and Diplomacy: The Canadian Contribution* (London, 1929), II, 69–75; Gwynn, *Spring-Rice*, I, 483; II, 125, 199, 306–07; *An. Register, 1905,* p. 221; Chirol, *Times*, June 23, 1913. Karl Pearson held the view that British and American democracies were forcing the Asiatics back upon themselves. Note letter from George Williams and Lord Kinnaird (*Times*, July 14, 1905) which stated that it was mainly through Am. organizations that Y.M.C.A.'s were planted in many Japanese cities; an example used as a stimulus to British activity.

[11] *Lansdowne Mss. Coll.* Balfour's letter in original; Lansdowne's, in copy.

[12] M. W. Williams, *Anglo-American Isthmian Diplomacy: 1815–1915* (Washington, 1916); Latané, *Am. For. Pol.*, chap. xiii; for Mr. Norman's anxiety, see *P. Debs.*, 1900, 88: 841; also *P. Debs.*, 1899, 66: 152; 1900, 78: 922; 1902, 101: 87, 98, 99; *Spec.*, Oct. 26, 1901. The *Engineer* had urged the use of the Panama route, see *Engr.*, June 27, 1902.

[13] Based upon inquiries addressed to the Foreign Office.

[14] *P. Debs.*, 4th series, 1902, 101: 87; 116: 1242, 1258, 1280, 1286; 1902–03, 118: 26, 63, 1043ff., 1075, 1083; 1903, 126: 95–97, 107, 163–64, 127. Sir E. G. Clarke, *Story of My Life* (London, 1918), 319ff.; Pollock, speech to Lond. C. of C., *Times*, June 12, 1902; Macdonell, *Fort. R.*, April, 1903; the exec. committee of League of Liberals, Dec. 18, 1902, resolved against any aggression which might also endanger Am. friendship. The *Sat. Rev.*, one of few to support Government's stand, viewed Germany's presence in S. Am. as a balance. In December, 1902, reports were printed in London papers that Germany was recanting hostility shown during Sp.-Am. War. Mahan, *Natl. R.*, Feb. 1903, 871–89; Kipling, *Times*, Dec. 22, 1902; *Die Grosse Politik*, XVII: 242, 259, 262, 266; *Brit. and For. State Papers* (1901–02), XCV: 1081–82. Alfred Vagts, *Deutschland und die Vereinigten Staaten in der Weltpolitik* (New York, 1935), demonstrates that Germany had no aggressive designs in the New World. Dexter Perkins, *The Monroe Doctrine, 1867–1907* (Baltimore, 1937), esp. 328, 330, 343; also 172, 203, 205, 208, 217, 219, 236–40; one may express slight disappointment in such a specialized study that chap. iv, "McKinley's Administration and the Monroe Doctrine," does not have more on the British attitude. One may add that it does not seem safe to cover foreign presses,

unless with a special purpose, by citations of such papers in the journals of other countries. Historical and philosophical work on the Monroe Doctrine has been slighter in G.B. than on the Continent.

15 *Lansdowne Mss. Coll.; Brit. Doc.*, II, No. 199, p. 172; Balfour quoted in Hendricks, *Carnegie*, II, 180, and *Times*, Feb. 4, 1903; similar opinion of Lord C. Beresford. Cf. articles in *Empire Rev.* and *New Liberal* for March, 1902. For Crowe, see author's "British Diplomats and the Press," *Public Opinion Q.*, July, 1938, 435–41.

16 Long, *Times*, Dec. 19, 1902; cf. Beresford at Dublin, *Times*, May 22, 1903; Austen Chamberlain, *Times*, Feb. 2, 1903; June 29, 1903. *Lansdowne Mss. Coll.*, letter from Sir Montagu E. Ommanney, Permanent Under-Secretary. See Strachey, *Strachey*, 138. Gwynn, *Spring-Rice*, I, 211, 229, 399, 406, 414, 449, who kept reporting to Roosevelt, Hay, and Lodge German and Russian hostility. Similarity of ideals is probably illustrated by the British note to the signatories of Berlin Treaty, following and supplementing the American note on Jews in Rumania.

VI

PRELUDE TO SUCCESS

1904–1914

SO that the details discussed here may not obscure historical perspective, may one not say that the upshot of Anglo-American relations between 1904 and 1914 was that both countries suspected that England could rely on us in event of any world crisis? This implies reciprocal influences. But the issue certainly meant more to Great Britain than to us.

Our foreign policies, except in a few instances, hardly aroused what could be called "public opinion." [1] Continental opinion quoted in the British press gave pointed warnings of the American menace, and seemed very alive to the apparition of a new world power. Nor was Britain unaware of our desire to be heard in all parts of the world. These years also fostered the suspicion that our public opinion was unstable, and reflected itself in our diplomacy.

Sir Gilbert Parker declared in Parliament in 1905: "In the Sandwich Islands, Samoa, and Mexico, the United States had, to use an American expression, 'chiselled' us out of our position." Lord Curzon, who knew little about America, discussed "True Imperialism" in 1907 with an appeal to the duty of the Anglo-Saxon. To prove the general tendency towards an imperialistic destiny, he described our imperialism as following an inevitable course, perhaps even against a majority which had no military instinct and no spirit of aggrandizement. J. Ellis Barker, in a widely quoted article of 1907, asserted that our expansionism, because "business is business," was dangerous to the Empire. Although Sir Edward Grey looked favorably upon the coöperation of American financiers and British contractors in the Chinchow-Aigun Railway in 1910, the bilious *Saturday Review* cried, "The United States are working for the supremacy of the Pacific on lines which are as unfriendly to us as to

Japan." While defending England against harsh treatment of foreign trade, the Earl of Stanhope argued in the Lords in 1911:

> If the United States are going to deal . . . with the Hawaiian and Philippine Islands and drive out all other competing peoples, that surely is a Chinese wall if ever there were one.

In *Imperial America* (1914) J. M. Kennedy, a British journalist, warned England to beware of seductive America, and even suggested that trouble in South America might force England to issue a challenge; he condemned the contemporary arbitration movement as unrepresentative of the whole community and full of cant, because the only bond—language—had been debased by us.

In these later years the British press, if it said anything, still held that the Constitution was a most unsuitable basis for overseas expansion. The criticism against American "hustle" in colonial administration continued. To be sure, since the press argued that imperialism would strengthen the power of the Executive, difficulties might be overcome. Roosevelt's intervention into state politics to defeat Hearst led the *Saturday Review* to say:

> The limits set by the constitution upon Presidential power are daily demonstrated to be intolerable in a State which is rapidly expanding overseas.

No election after 1898 had been accepted as a repudiation of imperialism. In foreign policy Taft did not seem unlike Roosevelt, and when the Democrats under Wilson continued to make moves toward a treaty with Nicaragua, England had about decided that there was now a national policy which did not frown upon imperialistic diplomacy. When America assumed certain financial responsibility in Liberia, the English press hailed it as a significant step. Sir Harry Johnston, who was friendly with Roosevelt, gathered that the Foreign Office approved this intervention. The *Daily Mail*, slightly over-enthusiastic, heralded our approach to Liberia as epoch-making as the fall of Port Arthur. Nevertheless it was difficult for the press to square our tradition and idealism with imperialism, nor could it expect the Caribbean countries to overcome this logical obstacle.

It is not surprising that one of the very few American speeches to stir England was uttered by Theodore Roosevelt, fresh from shooting lions and a world-resounding pulpit tour, at the Guildhall, May 31, 1910.[2] Before he reached England, words had trickled in from Africa and Egypt. At the annual public meeting of the Society for the Propagation of the Gospel, the Archbishop of Canterbury said with pride:

Mr. Roosevelt had made no secret of what had been the impression upon his mind by the touch which he had been allowed to have with the missionary work in Africa . . .

In London, after reading his speech to Sir Edward Grey, who thought it would be small to tolerate the praise but not the criticisms, Roosevelt paid an amazing tribute to British policy, adding, however, that since Cromer had left Egypt, England's grasp had relaxed and her purpose had faltered. The day before the speech Roosevelt told the Earl of Warwick, "I'm going to make a speech that will set you folks thinking." He succeeded. What hurt was the charge of sentimentality in colonial administration. The Radicals were startled because they could not understand how an American Republican could preach an imperial gospel; actually the Radicals had by that time reconciled themselves to the incongruity, but not to its blunt, dramatic presentation on English soil by an amazing personality.

If the press was discreet, private conversation was not. "It was a novel as well as a bold thing to do," said the *Standard*. The *Spectator* went into a spiritual history of the race:

His speech is one of the greatest compliments ever paid to a people by a statesman of another country. He could not have made such a speech to a touchy, vain-glorious, or self-conscious race.

Although Ministerial journals found it slightly humiliating to British pride, part of the press decided that the speech would promote a stiffer Egyptian policy. The speech reverberated in the Commons. Grey was censured. Mr. Kettle said:

As for Mr. Roosevelt, he does not seem to me to be a person of very great importance, an unrivalled master of platitudes and attitudes, a sort of mixture of Tartuffe and Tartarin of Tarascon, who will very soon be forgotten.

Sir Henry Dalziel, who thought this foreign intervention a dangerous precedent, proclaimed that no Liberal paper supported Roosevelt, who had injured the British administration. Another Member
denied that Roosevelt had a right to speak, especially since there
were so many assassinations in America. But it was also said that
Roosevelt saw in three weeks what the Government had taken three
years to see. It is significant that this remarkable speech was on
imperialism.

Once the Panama Canal was acquired and on the way to completion, opinion held that our control over Central America was inevitable.[3] There were few outcries against this extension, and up
to the Tolls Controversy almost indifference to the canal. At the
Royal United Service Institution, November 6, 1907, A. R. Colquhoun declared that England had been unwise in withdrawing
her fleet from that region; Admiral Sir N. Bowden-Smith thought
otherwise. England did not watch carefully our work on the canal,
and the *Engineer* was not able to congratulate us upon the results
achieved in our first (*sic*) great experiment in railroad and canal
control. A few papers like the *Spectator*, at least up to 1910, argued
that America's armed control of the canal was the simplest solution, but the *Saturday Review* and *Scotsman* were not alone in suggesting that our control might throttle the British Empire. The
Economist (September 16, 1911) reminded us that to continue
our good work in Latin America confidence must be maintained and
the canal must benefit everyone. Mr. Shirley Benn counseled Parliament in 1912 to recognize the added importance of Jamaica as a
naval base, and to act immediately in order to avoid criticism after
the completion of the canal.

The achievement of constructing the canal was lost in hostility
over the Tolls question. The United States Government under
Taft maintained, in spite of the Hay-Pauncefote Treaty (Art. 3,
[1]), the right to exempt American coastwise shipping. Shippers
had now come out of their lethargy. British opinion regarded the
discrimination as a queer freak to be expected from the American
Government. Sir Edward Grey protested the measure, but we were
indisposed to arbitrate since no one had yet been injured by the
discrimination. L. Oppenheim argued in 1913 that the United

States must be willing to arbitrate. Bryce wrote to Roosevelt, January 14, 1913:

It is a real pleasure to hear from you that your position on the Panama Tolls question is what I had believed it would be. . . . I am personally anxious that there should be no misconception in Europe of the attitude of the United States people; for no people seems to me to have shown itself through its history more generally wishful to act fairly and rightly and observe its international obligations.

Suspicion of the Monroe Doctrine increased, papers recalled that they had predicted harsh treatment of the Hay-Pauncefote Treaty, and talked of "unctuous rectitude and cynical treachery." The Wilson administration in June 1914 repealed the provisions which exempted American shipping, to the great pleasure and relief of Britain. The failure of the British Government to display at the Panama Exhibition had aroused much discussion and was connected with this diplomatic controversy. In 1914, Sir Joseph Walton, who praised America's vindication of her honor, hoped that now England would give more attention to the exhibition at San Francisco and the One Hundred Years' Peace Celebration.

The canal was only one aspect of England's interest in our southward expansion about which she received constant warnings, especially after 1910.[4] The British press constantly preached that the Monroe Doctrine carried obligations. Britons paid as much attention to Elihu Root's early announcement, May 20, 1904, of the "Roosevelt corollary" as to Roosevelt's Congressional message the following December. The Dominican Republic was bankrupt, and Roosevelt concluded that we should act as receiver. British bondholders at first welcomed the intervention, partly because they were more interested in recovering past investments than in future exploitation. In 1904 and 1905 the Council of the Corporation of Foreign Bondholders hoped we would make defaulting South American countries pay their debts; but disappointment followed, and subsequent reports complained of our treatment of such defaulters as Guatemala, Panama, and Santo Domingo, and the activities of the American Government. The *Economist* and *Times* had been pleased to see Roosevelt assume this rôle in face of strong domestic opposition, but the *Times* declared, "There is no need . . . to offer high moral arguments for transactions of that kind." Quite correctly the *Saturday Review* observed of the "corollary":

> If this declaration was made with a view to sound public opinion on this side of the Atlantic, the Republican Government must be delighted at the reception given it.

The growing economic bonds between the two portions of the western hemisphere were not underestimated. The *Times* (November 22, 1906) concluded that Root

> . . . wants the intimate and fruitful commercial intercourse between North and South America in order to secure the economic, as well as the political, supremacy of the Monroe doctrine.

The *Times* was even optimistic enough to suppose that in time Latin American countries would realize that our police power could be used altruistically. The press late in 1909 declared that we must intervene in Nicaragua, and there were few objections to subsequent events there. In 1912 British opinion believed that we did not want to annex Cuba, but might have to, as explained by Sir Harry Johnston in a letter to the *Times*. However, Wilson's address to the Commercial Congress at Mobile, October 27, 1913, disquieted those financial circles interested in future investments as an undue extension of the Monroe Doctrine into the sphere of finance. England paid little attention to Pan-Americanism. Publicists and travelers warned England that South America should not belong to the United States alone. Lord Murray of Elibank, who disliked Wilson's Mexican policy, spent the year 1913 in South America seeking oil concessions for Messrs. S. Pearson and Son. Weetman Pearson (later Viscount Cowdray) withdrew a contract from the Colombian Government, November 24, 1913; he recorded at the time that "the American Government did not scruple to bring diplomatic pressure to bear upon Colombia to such an extent as to prevent the Colombian Government ratifying the contract it had made with us for the exploration of oil in that country." He discovered similar pressure in Costa Rica and Ecuador. Sir Harry Johnston objected to the abandonment of British claims in Central America, and in his *Common Sense in Foreign Policy*

(1913) he decided, "Treaties, in fact, only bind the polity of the United States as long as they are convenient." Sir Harry, who never could quite make up his mind about us, concluded that since we were friendly, England might gain by our influence. Once again this threatening extension of our power was used by Empire-builders to speed the confederation of the West Indian colonies, British Guiana, and Honduras. Very righteously, the *Economist* concluded (August 30, 1913),

> The economic operations of the American trusts are suspected of a political design which is absent from the purely commercial undertakings of British capitalists and merchants.

British opinion became more outspoken over Mexico, the story of which is necessarily incomplete.[5]

During these years it was announced as regularly as spring that American capitalists had an edge over competitors in Mexico. Mexico captured British attention when Wilson refused to recognize Huerta as President. The British did not find Huerta so distasteful, and Sir Lionel Carden, British Minister to Mexico, who was supporting British oil interests, advocated recognition. There was practically no approval of Wilson's Mexican policy in England. If it was condemned as amateurish, muddled, idealistic, impractical, and sentimental throughout 1913, it was condemned in 1914, surprisingly so for a sentimental policy, as injurious to British interests. No one minimized the task of subduing Mexico, and the journals which urged intervention expressed the hope that we would have adequate forces.

Some journals and writers predicted that America would annex Mexico. The *Spectator*, in November 1913, repeated that the only logical solution was annexation or a formal protectorate—or an entire reversal of a policy which was based on unworkable imperialism. It must be said that up to September 1913 the press advised patience to see whether Wilson's policy would work; after November irritation increased. We have the amusing spectacle of Ambassador Page instructing Sir Edward Grey, who had Egypt and India on his mind, in an elementary course in democracy which elevated the *principle* of our policy concerning Huerta. Grey, who was thought to be friendly to British oil interests, confessed he was impressed. Page decided that England had forgotten America's restoration of Cuba to the Cubans and our pledge to the Philippines; "They have," he said, "no idea of our notion of freeing men." (Actually Grey made concessions on Mexico in order to aid Wilson in settling the Panama dispute.) Englishmen had before them an image of the Standard Oil and Rockefeller. Barker wrote:

The United States have attacked Mexico for the flimsiest and most insufficient reasons. . . . Never in the history of the world has there been a more trumpery and a more ludicrous pretext for war.

Others argued that Wilson must deal effectively with Mexico or face the lapse of the Monroe Doctrine. By January the press had begun in full blast to urge British intervention, and soon Parliament was discussing the proposal, led in hostility to the American policy by Sir John Rees. Certainly very few Britons could conceive that delay would be effective and that anything short of force could remove Huerta. The *Manchester Guardian* (April 16) condemned us for encouraging revolution in a foreign country. The show of force on April 21 and the resignation of Huerta, July 15, did not make English journals enthusiastic over the ultimate solution. The feeling aroused by the Tolls discrimination undoubtedly conditioned the reception of Wilson's idealistic policy; the Congressional debates, filled with anti-British sentiment, put England in no mood to speak highly of America's diplomacy. Subsequent events were overshadowed by the World War.

Much vacuous vaporing characterized the subject of Anglo-American relations, but above all the belief grew that an Anglo-American alliance would be for the welfare of the world.[6] Chamberlain in 1905 found every intelligent Englishman convinced of England's absolute need of a good understanding, but as Spring-Rice added, most of them, not even the King, had better say so. Balfour in 1905 declared our isolation impossible. Carnegie told Roosevelt, August 27, 1906: "Never was there a British Cabinet so keenly favorable to peace and so anxious for coöperation with America, and especially with you; you have won their entire confidence." In spite of setbacks, many journals still looked to America to defend the principle of arbitration. Much was heard in 1908 and

1909 of a new species of "moral alliance," which was innocuous and vague enough. Others like Lord Grey and Lord Charles Beresford still talked of the similarity of ideals.

Temporary joint objectives improved intercourse and American influence. The Congo Reform Association drew much encouragement from its sister association in the States. Mr. Morel told the National Free Church Council in 1908 that the happy fact about the miserable Congo situation was Anglo-American coöperation. Grey in 1912 stressed mutual ideals when he reported that both countries had joined hands to blot out atrocities in the rubber region of Putumayo.

The press said little concerning our activities at the Algeciras Conference in 1906, a meeting of the Powers to solve the problem of the partitioning of North Africa. The *Spectator* observed, "President Roosevelt has again shown that he shares with our King the right to the title of pacificator." Lord Roberts looked upon the conference as demonstrating the converging sentiments of the two nations. Although Grey later told Roosevelt that American influence had not been used against France and England, the British feared our inexperience on such a knotty problem as Morocco, and our suggestion for joint French and Spanish control of Moroccan ports failed because of British opposition. Still less was said of America's rôle at the Hague Conference of 1907. Two episodes of unequal importance the same year afforded interesting side lights on the nature of public opinion. The British Governor of Jamaica wrote a foolish letter to Rear Admiral Davis for landing marines to help remove the débris of the earthquake. Strangely enough, panic almost seized the British press, it would seem, merely because Americans got there first and because the English were growing weary of our flair for showing off. Jesse Collings, who defended the Governor's action, regretted his resignation, which had been forced upon the Government. The second minor episode was the fact that Lord Leith was sorry that Bryce had not attended the opening of the Carnegie Institute because, according to Leith,

Those who have worked in the United States and in connection with the people of America are aware how sensitive they are, and how often it is that little things of this kind affect the public mind and grow from an acorn into an enormous tree of public opinion.

It was the Panama Canal and our fleet's round-the-world cruise in 1907, according to Roosevelt, which gave us our greatest international publicity before 1914. He said of the cruise:

The reception accorded to the fleet in Australia was wonderful, and it showed the fundamental community of feeling, between ourselves and the great Commonwealth of the South Seas.

The cruise was watched by the British populace and naval circles, but not so much as Roosevelt believed. The *Spectator* hailed the American fleet as "a perfectly new revelation of the formidable strength which the Republic can exert in any corner of the world." The London press, supported by Continental papers, did suggest that Australia might be swept into a Pan-American vortex. Strong British imperialists used Australia's reception to belabor British diplomacy in the Pacific for having brought about a sense of isolation in Australia and New Zealand. Thinking of their Japanese ally, part of the press viewed the cruise as ill timed. Claude M. MacDonald, British representative at Tokyo, reported that the reception at Tokyo was very enthusiastic: "There is not the least doubt but that the most excellent effect has been produced by this visit, and I know that Admiral Sperry and his officers leave her shores with a far higher opinion of Japan as a friend (or enemy) than when they first arrived." Thus the anxiety over our visit to Japan was quieted in official circles.

It cannot be said that the British public received much support from the course of arbitration in America. Some of the ups and downs of the arbitration treaties were correctly attributed to the Senate's unwillingness to lose any power. One senses that the British movement in 1911 for an Anglo-American treaty was somewhat ahead of the American movement and not very enthusiastic. Free Churches were in communication with American religious bodies; both Unionists and Liberals backed the proposal. Sir Edward Grey, who favored arbitration and something very close to a defensive alliance, declared that it was most certainly from our good faith that one would expect arbitration proposals. Part of the press believed that Taft put forward the proposal to distract attention from the real meaning of the Canadian reciprocity treaty. Earl

Winterton and Mr. Remnant cynically discussed arbitration and the Mexican situation at the same time. The American Senate so modified the treaty that Taft abandoned it. Nevertheless, there was no doubt that our desire to solve such problems affected England. This is perhaps more obvious in the field of international law. David Dudley Field laid the foundations of the International Association for the Reform and Codification of the Laws of Nations in the early seventies. English discussions became heated over our interpretation of the most-favored-nation clause. In 1905 and 1907 Parliament was told that we contended that a treaty right to most favored treatment did not entitle its possessor to participate in special privileges granted to others in return for reciprocal concessions. Because of this interpretation a prominent Unionist called us a "chartered libertine" in international politics. Lawyers urged the British armed services to imitate our manuals of the laws of war. From an early date we had favored the immunity of private property in naval warfare. As early as 1898 A. J. Balfour was inclined to think that Britain's national interests would gain by such a change, especially if so limited as to relieve commerce not attempting to run an effective blockade. Our attitude was called a legacy from the founding fathers in a secret memorandum prepared by G. S. Clarke, under the direction of the Prime Minister, for the Committee of Imperial Defence, May 1906. He added, "In recent years, however, the precept of Washington has fallen into oblivion," and quoted Mahan as maintaining that the abandonment of rights of maritime capture would reduce our navy's power. Further, England relied on our support of the doctrine that foodstuffs were not contraband unless destined for warlike uses. During the debates on the Naval Prize Bill in 1911, the Lord Chancellor disposed of the argument that we would not protest the stopping of food ships in event of war because we would consider ourselves bound by the decision of the proposed International Prize Court. To those who opposed the Prize Court Convention and the Declaration of London, Sir Edward Grey replied:

Does anybody believe . . . Americans would sign this Declaration if they thought that undue delay and interference was likely to be the probable effect of it?

Consent to the Declaration failed in the House of Lords. The academic interest in our views on international law became of vital importance during the World War.

It is now desirable to discuss two topics which were closely related to imperialism and foreign affairs: the impact of the United States in naval and military matters and as a factor in the development of Anglo-Saxon racial theories, about which a little has already been said.

One may confidently assume that through one channel or another, the military and naval officials of the United Kingdom knew all that was fundamentally necessary of the power and developments in our fighting forces. Even so, public discussion, particularly as it helped to form America's prestige abroad, should not be ignored. The information need not come from British attachés; indeed, as a friendly gesture, it has sometimes happened that the intelligence work of attachés has been decreased and put into other hands. The lessons of the Civil and Spanish-American wars were not entirely lost upon the English. Our move toward fighting fitness (plus some preaching by Roosevelt) was good material, even if not needed, for those Britons who preached greater defense and the honor of war. Articles on our armed forces became more numerous after 1898. Up to 1914 both personal and semi-official contacts were closer in the naval arm. Our armaments could not be disregarded after 1898 in fixing the defense policies of the Old World, and our naval expansion dealt a logical blow to the two-Power standard, the measuring stick for British naval needs. It was admitted now that America had become conscious of her sea power and that we should realize the need for a larger army and navy.

In general England decided that our military instinct was not strong.[7] In 1898 many professed surprise at our weakness in a struggle with a second-rate foe. The *Daily Mail* was one of the few papers to discover in us a keen and genuine military spirit. The war was, said Lecky,

. . . at least likely to have taught America a lesson which she had long neglected. It is that war is not a thing that can be extemporized, and that no nation, however great, is really secure which is not prepared

to defend herself both on land and sea in the first week after hostilities
have been declared.

Lord Wolseley decided that we were unprepared. Others concluded
that the war made us behave oddly. The wild ovations to Hobson,
on a "bussing tour in Kansas" as described by *Punch*, indicated that
we were not able to do brave deeds and forget how brave they
were. This different outlook on deeds of valor, and the national
enthusiasm to get at the enemy with preparatory strong words, did
not a little to upset the English during the World War, although
full tribute was paid to the essential bravery of the American
doughboys.

One of the Americans who influenced the British most strongly
was A. T. Mahan (1840–1914) whose views were more effective
abroad than at home.[8] Even the first full-length, eulogistic study
of him by the Englishman Charles C. Taylor did not take sufficient
notice of Mahan's influence in England. His writings caught the
British (and Continental) fancy at the right moment when appeals
were being made to the past to make the British more conscious
of the value of sea power. Mahan had close associations with Admiral Sir Bouverie Clark and Admiral Sir Cyprian Bridge, Gibson
Bowles, and Thursfield. The last-named said, "Mahan's opinions
govern the naval thought of the world." Sir John Laughton gave
thirty-two pages in the *Edinburgh Review* to Mahan's *Influence
of Sea Power upon History, 1660–1783*, which stimulated the
study of naval strategy. He popularized the words "sea power" in
England. His views were disseminated through the Royal United
Service Institution, magazine articles, reprints, and countless press
quotations. The British Government supplied his volumes for the
libraries of training ships. In a sense the British Navy League was
founded in 1893 to carry out his teaching. His books were used by
advocates of the two-Power standard and those who opposed elaborate coast defenses. Lord Wolseley, who also spoke frequently of
Robert E. Lee's generalship, wrote to Sir Frederick Maurice,
March 1897:

Mahan's books have done the country, and the Navy for that matter too, a world of good. It is a sad reflection that it has taken a Yankee

to wake up this generation of Englishmen to the meaning and importance of sea power.

Some of his most ardent admirers even attributed to him the popular resuscitation of the song "Rule, Britannia." Impressed by violent naval competition, Britons were even inclined to say with Admiral Sir Edward Seymour that "one great reason of that competition was the teaching contained in the writings of Captain Mahan." In his presidential address to the British Association, Sir Norman Lockyer paid a startling tribute to Mahan "the great teacher" as if to verify his warm appraisal of American education.

While advocating the institution of a General Staff the *Standard* (December 21, 1908) drew some lessons from him, and added, "It is no exaggeration to say that the publication of a new work by Captain Mahan is an event of international consequence." His articles on the German peril to British sea supremacy, first appearing in the *Daily Mail*, July 1910, were circulated in pamphlet form and aided in the controversy over the shipbuilding vote in one direction—toward a greater navy. His influence gained him an audience on other subjects and, as Maxse observed, his ideas on Imperial Federation made a great impression upon the English public. In July 1904 to the Imperial Federation Defence Committee, after a hearty tribute from Sir John Colomb, Mahan asserted that it would help the United States if the Empire were capable of united action. A few days later before an important meeting of Unionists, Joseph Chamberlain praised him as a true and sane imperialist who realized that the period was an epoch of aggregation, not segregation. The *Economist* observed quite truly:

Englishmen acknowledge, with a readiness which is for them a little unusual, the right of Captain Mahan to offer them counsel upon the conduct of their affairs.

Since America did not hide its information, the war of 1898 became more important in a technical sense than was expected.[9] Up to July not much was said of the American navy; by August the *Times* declared, ". . . never were the eternal principles of sea warfare more instructively illustrated." The war awakened the general public to the tremendous influence of naval victory or defeat upon the morale of a country. The Englishman might have begun to think the shores of the United States were immune from attack, but such was not clearly demonstrated in the press. As an authority, H. W. Wilson, has said, the conduct of the naval war was much criticized in England, particularly the timidity and caution of the Naval War Board and the organization of command. All this, however, turned British attention to her own board of strategy, the need for closer coöperation between the army and navy, efforts designed to make the marines an expeditionary force, measures to prevent leakage of information through the press, the use of electricity in warships, and the need of distilling and repair ships and colliers as adjuncts to the fleet. To England the war gave no definite answer as to the value of torpedo boats. Captain Philpotts declared that the only lesson was the absolute necessity of internal fittings which were made of non-inflammable material; Lord Beresford cited the use of provision ships ". . . as it is the first practical illustration of what can be done to enable a fleet to keep at sea." In Parliament Mr. Goschen, using American reports, showed how valuable were the services rendered by repair ships. Admiral Colomb in his "Lessons of the Spanish-American War" before the Royal United Service Institution, March 8, 1899, found additional support for his often-repeated principle: the futility of military preparations unless supported by an adequate naval force. In the controversy over strategy raised in the *Times*, one school of thought maintained that Mahan had exaggerated the importance of coast defense. Discussion had also been aroused over boilers, gunnery training, and the importance of coal supply. Although illustrations of our navy in action showed men of the highest type, the feeling seemed to exist that the personal factor was weak in the sense that the navy's personnel was too small in action and in reserve.

There has, of course, been an interchange of technical and administrative methods between the two nations.[10] The journal *Engineering* said in 1898:

As we have remarked on a previous occasion, there is so much in common between our own Navy and that of the United States, that anything which is of importance to one must necessarily be of interest to the other.

Journals were favorably impressed by the advantages secured by chiefs of technical departments who were able annually to issue unbiased reports; one editor was brave enough to suggest the idea for the British War Office. *Engineering* introduced in December 1898 the transactions of the American Society of Naval Architects and Marine Engineers because they were of wide interest to the British:

In the navigation of the great fresh water seas, and in the coasting traffic, both strictly protected, American ingenuity and fearlessness of design have been conspicuous, and in certain respects have afforded models on which we have moulded some of our own practice.

American yachting designs had been carefully studied and sometimes imitated; the races of 1885 and 1886, really trials between the British plank-on-edge type of cutter and the American type of broad light-draught sloop, led to the abandonment of the former.

Parliament was asked to observe that the "practical" Americans were actively experimenting with submarines. Admiral Field also reported:

Electric power is very largely adopted in the American Navy for working the turrets and all the other machinery, and I hope the Admiralty will in that respect follow the example of the United States.

An engineering controversy over the merits of the "tank" and "water-tube" boilers drew upon American experience; Mr. Arnold-Foster decided that we preferred the straight-tube Babcock & Wilcox boiler to the Belleville type which was the earliest water-tube boiler in general use in the British navy. J. H. Biles' paper on American naval construction at the Naval Architects, 1901, prompted Sir John Hopkins to emphasize the fact that we were always making improvements. Sir William White, a director of naval construction who admitted American influences, concluded in 1904 that American battleships were of really larger dimensions than British ships although the trial draught and displacement were less; he claimed that we were ahead in the production and use of nickel steel for forgings and castings. In 1906 Sir William declared that we stood next to Britain in warship-building capacity, but at a great distance. The same year the *Engineer* found no longer true the "axiom in this country that in the United States they are not very particular what a warship is so long as she 'whips creation' on paper." The British Naval Attaché wrote home in December 1907, commenting unfavorably on the low freeboard, open turrets, and submerged armor of the ships, and the great age of captains and admirals, in the American navy. The theory of the "all-big-gun single calibre armament," embodied in the British *Dreadnought* of 1906–07, which was one of the dramatic changes in British construction prior to 1914, benefited from the simultaneous working out of the plan in the United States.

It was very difficult to draw any clear-cut lessons from our naval organization.[11] Our efforts to meet new naval conditions brought about by the increasing mechanical complexity took the form of enabling engineers to qualify as "line" officers to the point of fusion of the two groups. In 1900 the *Engineer* viewed the plan a failure but urged the Admiralty to heed the "remarkable action taken by the United States." Pamphlets were also circulated which called attention to this reform. Mr. Allan expressed his satisfaction in Parliament in 1901 that the British navy had followed us to the extent that the engineer-in-chief had been given the relative rank of rear admiral; but he hoped it would also give higher rank and pay to chief engineers. At the close of 1902, based partly upon our experience, a profound change was made in the corps of officers. Instead of entering immediately upon their separate duties, officers received a common basis of training before being assigned to one of the three branches, officers, marines, and engineers. Under the new scheme engineers were no longer a civil branch, but became known as lieutenant or captain engineers. Mr. Haldane reported in 1903 the Admiralty's plan to secure the interchangeable officer, who was a great success in America. Although protests were made against making engineers jacks of all trades, the scheme of common entry and common training with subsequent specialization was retained.

The Earl of Selborne announced in 1901 the development of a much-needed school of naval strategy at Greenwich such as existed in the United States. Professor J. A. Ewing, Director of Naval Education, visited us in 1904 and returned convinced of our belief in education, the success of the amalgamation of executive and engineer branches, and the thoroughness of Annapolis. Several journals continued to urge that the whole cost of the education of junior officers be borne by the Admiralty as in the United States. Both countries in 1909 felt the need of strengthening and co-ordinating the thinking department of the naval service. Odious comparisons were being made in England which showed that American gunners practised more and shot more accurately; complaints were made in Parliament that by higher pay the American navy attracted British sailors with ten years' experience. The complaints persisted, but the Government persistently denied that the wage rates could be compared. Courtesy cruises were also effective in stimulating foreign attention to construction details.

The effect of the growth of our naval power upon England's ideal of sufficient naval protection is worth tracing in some detail.[12] American naval expansion, as compared with German development, aroused little anxiety. Viscount Wolseley went so far as to say in 1899:

> It would be of the greatest possible advantage to us that the American Navy should re-occupy the position it did, not as second to ourselves, but as our equals (Cheers).

Mr. Dillon in 1901 was aroused because Britain had encouraged us in a mad career of armaments, but, he added, since England could never build up to us, British statesmen would rue the day. By 1903 influential persons were advising a new conception of the two-Power standard.

Haldane, who dismissed Anglo-American naval rivalry, deemed it impossible to maintain the standard against our resources; nor did Sir Charles Dilke and Winston Churchill wish to count our navy in defining the British program. Using an argument often directed against Chamberlain's tariff proposals, Sir Charles declared:

> By interfering with the trade with the United States we are weakening one of our greatest Imperial securities in a general war. The people in this country had welcomed the increase of the fleet in the United States because in a general war she would be the protector of neutrals . . .

During discussions of the Naval Estimates between 1904 and 1909, especially the Liberals pointed out the wholly exceptional position of the United States. The pros and cons burst forth in full vigor in the Parliament of 1909. The Navy League wanted to include us in estimating requirements. Mr. Redmond, carrying on in the same vein as Mr. Dillon, declared that England and the Anglo-Japanese treaty ("which brought the American fleet round the world") had driven us to naval expansion. The Government was plagued with questions on this issue in spite of the fact that Mr. McKenna thought it "an academic question" because our navy was not involved in the definition of the two-Power standard. The big-navy men pointed out that hitherto Britain had not specifically included or excluded certain Powers from the calculations. It was insisted that the small-navy party relied on the possibilities of combinations, and that an Anglo-American naval war was not impossible. In the middle of the Easter holidays Winston Churchill revived the question by a letter which excluded the United States and which contradicted somewhat the Prime Minister. In a very hazy reply Asquith recalled that Earl Cawdor four years before had said the standard applied only to Europe, and that the United States was ruled out by distance. The opposition maintained that Britain's minimum navy had always meant equal to "the two next strongest Powers in the world." This "academic question" continued to be hotly debated the next year. Big-navy men reminded listeners that Mahan had solemnly warned that England's resolve was breaking in naval defence. Our navalism could be a useful weapon for larger estimates even though expenditures were directed against other countries. Sir Edward Grey clung to his limited standard, and in 1914, Churchill again justified the common sense of our exclusion. England had cast her lot amid the fortunes of the Old World Balance of Power in which the United States did not count directly, but we had destroyed a cherished tradition.

Obviously, England was not so much interested in our military arm. Wolseley may have praised our military volunteers, but as the Spanish war dragged on, British criticism became more outspoken.[13] "Since our own Crimean muddle," commented the *Economist* (June 24, 1899), "there has been no worse instance of military mismanagement than that displayed by the American War

Department in Cuba and the Philippines." This was the impression left upon the *Manchester Guardian* correspondent, J. B. Atkins, who hoped, in his *War in Cuba* (1899), that our failures would not stifle the English volunteer movement. Arthur Lee (later Lord Lee of Fareham), former British Military Attaché at Washington, held that the war offered good instruction for the Boer campaign. He thought the American army was the only one in the world which resembled the British army to any degree; he wanted Britain to get the same fine material as the American recruit by shorter terms of service and higher pay, better shooting and more rifle ranges, lighter mounted troop equipment, and a cavalry as well trained in scouting, horse mastership, and dismounted duties. Further, Lee hoped the Secretary of War would examine the privileges given to our army such as separate dining rooms, glasses and knives, and permission to wear plain clothes. Brodrick merely replied that the analogy did not hold, partly because we had a larger population to draw from. Wolseley also advocated a fair wage on the American plan. Lee continued his discussions in 1902 by telling the Royal Military Academy what pride he took in the fighting material of the American branch of the Anglo-Saxon race; in Parliament, however, he promised not to say anything rash about our army scandals.

America's plans for a peacetime reserve of officers and men were helpful philosophical arguments for Haldane's volunteer or territorial forces. In Parliament Mr. Drage wanted the volunteer movement to reach the schools, and arrangements as in America for school speeches about national heroes and patriotism on national festivals. Colonel Sir Howard Vincent, who praised West Point, could not persuade the Secretary of War to encourage thrift by leaving the soldier's pay to draw interest with the Government; but in a more detailed discussion, he concluded that the British soldier was about as well off. What was more important, he attributed our new willingness to enlist to an immense growth of military spirit rather than better pay.

To those who were convinced of the urgent necessity of far-reaching reformation in military administration, the *Times* suggested in 1903 a study of West Point. Lord Kitchener had advised the Australian and New Zealand governments to take West Point as a model for the military colleges they needed. The Secretary of War in 1905 believed that the time had come for England to establish an army school like West Point. It was Haldane, a civilian in charge of British war organization, who praised civilian Elihu Root's reorganization of our War Department and the establishment of a general staff; Root's reports, said Haldane, "are the very last word concerning the organization and place of an army in a democracy." In 1913 he concluded that the training of all officers, together with subsequent specialization, was better than the education at Sandhurst or Woolwich. But the British army felt no great need to follow our experience.

We may now turn from the concreteness of armed forces to the permeating nebulosity of Anglo-Saxonism which has been an important factor in world affairs and culture.[14] Because of the current noise over Teutonism and Slavism and the emphasis on diplomatic alliances based on political ideologies, we have almost ignored this underlying, racial catch-all which, whether a mere myth or not, continues to exert great influence upon the relations of the English-speaking peoples. "Blood is thicker than water," the theme song given wide circulation by the dramatic friendliness of British and American sailors in 1858 on the Pei-ho River near Peking, tends to obscure the checkered history and many silently accepted implications of this racial chauvinism.

It is in origin a British belief, which has responded sensitively to American influence, in the similarity and unity of a race which includes Americans, and which implies a spread of British prestige and institutions. No thorough history of the concept exists, and no one person or group became notorious, as in other race or pan-movements, by a philosophic exposition or cult-like support of this Pan-Anglian state of mind, partly, one suspects, because it was routine like brushing teeth in high society. Nor was it customary before uttering soul-stirring clichés, in spite of the new methods of comparative history and the principles of evolutionary philosophy, to study the intriguing differences of the distant branches of the Anglo-Saxon race (a term which did not come into wide use until about 1880), or the regional diversities of the United States. For convenience England had from the seventies onward adopted a doctrine of America's unity or unanimity (Lord Northcliffe: "What sheep!") which facilitated discussion of the American scene. Yet it is worth noting that those who had studied us, such as Sir Charles Dilke or Conan Doyle or Bryce, used phrases of Anglo-Saxonism, and those sympathetic with us felt especially free to lump "Americans" together as a compliment.

Up to about 1870 Britons preferred to stress the abnormality of Americans. After two formative decades, Anglo-Saxonism entered one phase of its luxuriant growth from 1896 to 1917. It helped to condition the nature and reception of America's impact. Too much emphasis on the unity of the Anglo-Saxon mind might have strengthened Britain against the infiltration of "foreign" influences, but this did not happen. We shall see that the strength of this racial concept was that, like the British peerage, it picked up helpful additions wherever possible: the community of language, ideals, tradition, institutions, morals, morale, ethos, righteous ethics, tolerant justice, humanitarianism, and even political aims.

This ideal of unity was not the hobby merely of *literati* or after-dinner orators whether American or British, or the peculiar devotion of men like Frederic Myers, Besant, W. T. Stead, or Conan Doyle, who played with supernatural phenomena. Perhaps the English held to the theory more than the Scotch, Welsh, or Irish. It seemed more powerful in England than in America, and keen observers from time to time warned England not to rely too heavily upon the sentimental tie of blood. But intelligent men of both countries encouraged one another. It was as much a convenient afterthought as a goal. Conservatives and Liberals alike gave lip service. Many sober Britons, who cannot always have been talking across the Atlantic or in irony, discussed us in these terms of race, and nearly everyone in the United Kingdom, then and now, has given expression to a corollary of the concept—that the welfare of the world depends on the union of the English-speaking peoples. The pull of the ineludible English basis of our civilization, many scholars admit, was a factor which governed our entrance into the World War. Our pro-Ally feeling was based somewhat upon class and educational divisions. Social contacts with cosmopolitan or upper-class Americans, groups more tempted to flaunt their English heritage, helped to keep this racial-caste theory alive.

Just as England began to realize that the seat of the race might be moving across the Atlantic, she began to learn that Americans were of doubtful breed. The presence of the Irish in America hurt the racial illusion; contacts with the mixed masses of American troops in 1917–1919 helped to shatter narrow racialism just as it was being repolished for Britain's new ally. The theory also rose and fell too frequently with the vicissitudes of Anglo-American diplomacy.

Just as the Continent was first responsible for using the term *Angli Saxones* before King Alfred's times, so Continental politics and opinion often employed the term and thereby have given it a semblance of truth by uniting England and the United States in discussions of imperialism, chauvinism, navalism, and now—democracy. The Continent produced such a sensational book as Edmond Demolins' *À quoi tient la supériorité des anglo-saxons* (1897). At the same time, the very desire of Germany to over-stress the cleavage between the two countries in order to find her own community with us has helped to keep Anglo-Saxons alert.

If racial ties had any meaning for the Empire, there was no sentimental reason for excluding the United States; to an extent, arguments for Imperial Federation (witness Earl Grey) were arguments for Anglo-Saxon Federation which might well lead to a Pax Britannica. Such proposals were numerous from 1898 onward. A racial concept devised for the Empire was so much the weaker if it did not provide for the United States.

Gladstone had spoken of what was "conventionally termed the Anglo-Saxon race" wherein the United States gave a Briton the sense of a common country.[15] But Sir Charles Dilke was the first important politician to identify completely modern America as an extension of the race. He wrote:

It is when the country [U.S.A.] is left that there rises in the mind an image that soars above all local prejudice—that of the America of the law-abiding, mighty people who are imposing English institutions on the world.

In the preface (which he considered his best piece of work) to *Greater Britain* (1866), he declared: "Through America, England is speaking to the world." In this "Greater Britain" he included "our Magna Graecia of the United States," a phrase borrowed from

Whitelaw Reid. (Although Reid believed "blood ties" had been over-worked, Senator Depew correctly predicted that Reid would use such phrases in England.) In the seventies, Robert Mackenzie, agent for the Westinghouse Brake Co. and publicist, looked to the day when members of the race, "recognizing their essential oneness, will be combined in a *Great Empire of the English.*" Seeley believed Greater Britain existed wherever there were Englishmen. We occupied a significant place in the thought of another historian, E. A. Freeman, whose lectures here nourished his idea of "everlasting ties of blood and speech" so long as he wasn't irked by Irishmen. An American was an American Englishman, and like Goldwin Smith, and later A. V. Dicey, he suggested a common citizenship, *sumpoliteia,* "a fellowship in civic rights." But he differed with Bryce in viewing an Imperial Federation as unintelligible, and with Chamberlain who in 1886 was raving about our Civil War as really a struggle for "Imperial Union." He wrote Bryce, December 16, 1886, his dislike for the terms "Imperial Federation" or "Federation of the British Empire":

Some say (as if it meant the same thing) a Federation of the English-speaking people. That indeed gets rid of the barbarians; but it implies the partnership of the United States, which will hardly be got for an "Imperial" concern . . .

Our imperialism invigorated Anglo-Saxonism in 1898, and common blood became a fashionable topic.[16] Those who disliked the ethnological chauvinism of the Continent (witness Dr. Charles Waldstein) tried to avoid pitfalls by erecting the vision of an "English-speaking Brotherhood." Yet whoever soft-pedaled race had to answer the Earl of Rosebery: "But whether you call it British or Anglo-Saxon, or whatever you call it, the fact is that the race is there and the sympathy of race is there." And Rosebery was willing to quote in a racial sense Canning's famous words about calling the New World into existence to redress the balance of the Old. Lord Cromer wished us good luck in our overseas adventures ". . . because I want the world to see that Anglo-Saxons can govern a decadent Latin race." Spring-Rice believed "The United States to be the real fortress of our race . . ."

By 1902 most of the frills had been added to Anglo-Saxonism.

Joseph Chamberlain, who covered all its philosophical content, declared that the two nations "can regard . . . questions of humanity from a different point of view from that of other nations, who hitherto have rejected all considerations of that kind as being purely sentimental." Lord Dufferin, who discovered identical "habits of mind," asserted, "We were certainly the only two nations that had an adequate conception of liberty and justice." Others quoted Carlyle to prove the two nations "are bound together by Heaven's Act of Parliament and the everlasting law of nature and of fact." Anthony Hope Hawkins added: "We are all Americans now. . . ." Lord Brassey once suggested we should act as a mandatory power in troubled China, but "The spontaneous sympathies of race will accomplish all we wish." No part of the press was free from this racial vocabulary.

Men like Salisbury, Bryce, the Earl of Onslow, Lord Ripon, Campbell-Bannerman, Sir Thomas Lipton, and A. J. Balfour each interpreted Anglo-Saxonism slightly differently, depending on what characteristics were to be added to the racial emphasis. Bryce and Salisbury might link us together as "living nations." Sir Edward Grey told Roosevelt in 1906: "I should say that some generations of freedom on both sides have evolved a type of man and mind that looks at things from a kindred point of view . . ." In a volume of 1905 prefaced by Earl Roberts and decorated with crossed flags, Major Stewart L. Murray sought to arouse British laborers to think racially so as to mold the two nations into a peace-persuading federation.

Protestant groups, especially Nonconformists, added the overtone of common Protestantism and evangelization to racialism. But the religious bond, perhaps partly because the Church of England in spite of its Pan-Anglican aims and Lambeth Conferences was not in closer contact with our "religious similarity," did not receive full expression except as implied in the phrase "common ideals." John Clifford thrilled to "The 'Alliance' and the universal establishment of the Kingdom of God!" Later, he feared that England had lost "the ethical and spiritual primacy [which] has passed to the Puritan Commonwealth." The eminent Hugh Price Hughes conceived of an Imperial Anglo-Saxon Federation in which Methodism would have a leading rôle. Mandell Creighton, historian and Bishop of

London, wrote on August 6, 1898: "The question of the future of the world is the existence of the Anglo-Saxon civilization on a religious basis." The British in 1896 had combined racialism, religion, and imperialism when they adopted the go-getting American watchword—"The Evangelization of the World in this Generation."

As might be expected from the history of other ardent nationalisms or racialisms, one of the most startling expressions of Anglo-Saxonism came from one of England's "frontiers" in the form of Cecil Rhodes's legacy. At the age of twenty-four, this South African imperialist had dreamed of the ultimate recovery of the United States as part of the Empire, and although a free trader, he would have made us realize the need for unity by a tariff war. Expressing some preference for our Constitution, he told Stead, "What an awful thought it was that if we had not lost America . . . the peace of the world would have been secured for all Eternity." He believed in Americans of "an elect race." Rhodes once envisaged a college under Professor Seeley to train people in the "English-speaking idea"; but ultimately this wish took shape in the Rhodes Scholarships to Oxford.

When population statistics were not satisfactory, the community of language and literature seemed more plausible, as it was to John Galsworthy.[17] The sales of English writers in America put a lyrical touch to the concept. England was sensitive to the divergence even here, but the gap might be closed, perhaps by the influence of American literature and movies on Great Britain. So long as our education emphasized English literature, and so long as Americans made a national shrine of Stratford-on-Avon, this part of the theory seemed based on fact.

Frederic Myers (1843–1901) once wrote:

> Ah, what imperial force of fate
> Links our race in high emprize!

Conan Doyle, who had supported Anglo-American amity when it was less fashionable, protested, as did others, against the term "Anglo-Saxon," and would have substituted "Anglo-Celtic" to appeal to the Irish. He dedicated his *White Company* (1890) "To the Hope of the Future, the Reunion of English-speaking Races . . ." In 1894 he wrote from America, "The center of gravity

of race is over here, and we have got to readjust ourselves." Sir
Mortimer Durand, a diplomat well read in American history, wrote
in *Helen Treveryan, or The Ruling Race* (1891), "I feel as proud
of the Stars and Stripes as I do of the Union Jack." "The outlook
of the New Yorker," said the dramatist William Archer, "is wider
than ours, but his standpoint is the same."

About 1900, H. G. Wells, and to a lesser degree Bertrand Russell, Pember Reeves, Webb, and Haldane, were "still clinging to
the dear belief that the English-speaking community might play
the leader and mediator towards a world commonweal." But G. K.
Chesterton, who always found the United States and Anglo-
American relations a most suitable subject for his stimulating paradoxes, wanted England to regard the United States with the fascination of a foreign country. This led him to distrust Wells's
model of the United States of the World. In 1911 Sir Bampfylde
Fuller proposed a "League of English Speech." Oscar Browning,
Strachey, Sir Edwin Arnold, Austin, John Davidson, Francis
Thompson, Kipling, and W. E. Henley all toyed with this racial
unity. The English imperial historian H. E. Egerton (1855–1927)
concluded his *Causes and Character of the American Revolution*
(1923) with a deep-rooted belief—"The splendid vision of an
Anglo-Saxon Brotherhood . . ." A. R. Wallace urged educa-
tionalists to teach it. John Masefield in 1916 would have fostered
it by a "big application of the idea of Rhodes Scholarships," and
with "some few scraps of autograph by famous English writers"
as thanks to Harvard and Yale for sending her sons to fight.

The war debts, naval competition, and the like up to about
1933 made us suspect as mongrels. Hitler aided in fortifying Anglo-
Saxonism with a super-structure foreshadowed in 1917, a union of
democracies for the preservation of a common civilization. The
strength of this appeal is shown by the haunting fear that should
the home of British culture and institutions grow weak and subservient, the unifying British basis of our nation would be dissipated. Thus, those Americans who consider themselves Anglo-
Saxons fear, as did Spring-Rice, that the United States could claim
to be Anglo-Saxon only so long as England remained great. This
brief survey shows that it is hardly possible that any new wine will
be poured into the bottle of Anglo-Saxonism. The drink is already

132 AMERICA AND GREAT BRITAIN

sufficiently intoxicating, and lights up everything from politics to scholarship. We seem to be approaching an epoch in which much of the nonsense of Anglo-Saxonism will disappear or become wisdom by the external pressure of ridiculous but powerful forces.

[1] Curzon, at Birmingham, *Times*, Dec. 12, and *Spec.*, Dec. 14, 1907; George Peel in *Friends of England* (London, 1905) mentioned the menace of aggressive America, but did not go deeply into the subject. Parker, *P. Debs.*, 1905, 143: 547; Stanhope, *P. Debs.*, Lords, 1911, 8: 605; Grey, *P. Debs.*, 1910, 17: 1388. Even the *Manch. G.* did not begrudge Am. intervention in Liberia. Sir Harry H. Johnston, *Story of My Life* (London, 1923), 408; Alex. Johnston, *Life and Letters of Sir Harry Johnston* (London, 1929), chap. xii. Johnston complained that the American Liberians had shown American traits and were too much given to politics; in outward behavior, "They are prudish to a truly American extent." He advised them to turn their backs on America. See his *Liberia* (London, 1906), I, 348, 354, 370.

[2] Archbishop, *Times*, Apr. 22, 1910. Cf. the World Missionary Conference, Edinburgh (*Times*, June 21, 1910) and report of Rev. F. B. Bridgman (Am.) from Natal. Seth Low did not want to leave the impression that the British Government was lukewarm or unfriendly to missions as a whole; the American Boards working in British territory had no complaint. G. S. Smalley, *Anglo-American Memoirs* (London, 1912), II, 368; *Punch*, June 8, 1910, p. 417. Grey said he never saw the speech—it was read to him; Grey, *Twenty-Five Years*, II, 92. *P. Debs.*, 1910, 17: 1111, 1129–31, 1140, 1147ff., 1158, 1369, 1372ff., 1375, 1386; 1911, 28: 1859. F. C. Penfield, *Present-Day Egypt* (New York, 1899), 314.

[3] C. M. Pepper's *Panama to Patagonia: The Isthmian Canal and the West Coast Countries of S. Am.* (London, 1907), an American account frequently recommended to English business men as a forecast of Am. influence. Colquhoun, *Times*, Nov. 7, 1907; Bryce, *Bryce Mss. Coll.*; see scathing article by R. B. Cunningham-Graham in *Sat. Rev.*, Oct. 26, 1912, 513–15; *Engr.*, Mar. 31, July 7, 1905; J. H. Latané, "The Panama Canal Act and the British Protest," *Amer. Journ. of Int. Law*, 1913, VII: 17–26; L. Oppenheim, *The Panama Canal Conflict between G.B. and the U.S.A.* (Cambridge, 1913); Sir H. E. Richards, *The Panama Canal Controversy* (Oxford and London, 1913); Arnold White, *Views of Vanoc* (2nd series, London, 1913); Hammond, *Autobiography*, II, 576; Benn, *P. Debs.*, Commons, 1912, 35: 1933–34. On the Panama Exposition, see *P. Debs.*, 1913, 56: 1246, 1773, 2063, 2330, 2503–05, 2661; 1914, 58: 1564ff.; 64: 94, 106ff., 1450–51; Hammond, *Autobiography*, II, 601–02. Lords Aberconway, Cowdray, and Rotherham were on committee urging government participation. Based in part upon inquiries to the Foreign Office.

[4] J. F. Rippy, "The British Bondholders and the Roosevelt Corollary of the Monroe Doctrine," *Pol. Sc. Q.*, June, 1934, xlix, No. 2, 195–206; J. A. Spender, *Weetman Pearson, First Viscount Cowdray, 1856–1927* (London, 1930), 210; see also 5, 7, 83, 190ff.; Pearson didn't think much of American achievements inasmuch as he had to finish the East River Tunnel, 1908. He said to Page, Jan. 1914, "Whatever the United States and Great Britain agree on the world must do." Hendricks, *Page*, I, 227. *An. Reg.*, 1913, 229, 463, 464; R. J. MacHugh in *Fort. Rev.*, April, 1914. Sir Harry Johnston, *Common Sense in Foreign Policy* (London, 1913), chap. vi.

⁵ Hendricks, *Page*, I, 148, 185–87, 188, 196, 204, 209, 211, 227, 270ff.; S. Nearing and J. Freeman, *Dollar Diplomacy, a study in American Imperialism* (New York, 1925), 87, 91. Haldane, *Times*, Nov. 29, 1913; *P. Debs.*, 1914, 59: 207, 1024; 61: 1502–03; 62: 110, 2106; 63: 904–05. I was naïve enough to be surprised at the great reluctance to discuss this episode in England, 1936–37.

⁶ Gwynn, *Spring-Rice*, I, 453. On Congo: see *Times*, Jan. 22, 1908, p. 17; Mar. 6, 1908; Feb. 9, 1909; *Stand.*, Dec. 29, 1906; Sir Charles Dilke (*Times*, Feb. 11, 1904) told the Aborigines' Protection Society to draw upon this American sentiment. Grey on Putumayo, *P. Debs.*, 1912, 14: 2355. The Atlantic Fisheries Award was viewed in September, 1910, as important because the procedure adapted in arbitration followed the more satisfactory precedent of the Bering Sea dispute rather than the Joint Commission of the Alaska Boundary. On Algeciras: see *Brit. Doc.*, III, 321; Vagts, *op. cit.*, II, chap. xvii. On Jamaica: see esp. *Natl. R.*, 1907, 48: 913, and *P. Debs.*, 1907, 170: 1356–59. Leith, *P. Debs.*, Lords, 1907, 173: 1363; 172: 1411–12.

Information on fleet cruise based partly upon inquiries addressed to the Foreign Office. See also, Roosevelt, *Autobiography* (New York, 1913), 542, 598; he also states British and German naval authorities did not believe the cruise was possible. At the 94th annual meeting of the Peace Society in 1910, Anglo-Saxon efforts were stressed, *Stand.*, May 25, 1910. A British-American mass meeting in favor of arbitration was held in Honolulu, July 9, 1911. Grey, *Times*, June 7, 1913; Lyon Playfair held the same views at an earlier date; Reid, *Playfair*, 364–65, 367. See *Spec.*, May 27, 1911, on Grey's endorsement of Monroe policy. The *Natl. R.*, April on, vigorously attacked the Treaty. Pirie, *P. Debs.*, 1910, 17: 1469; Winterton *et al.*, *P. Debs.*, 1911, 22: 1989–90, 2500–02; 23: 373, 872–73. Clark memorandum, *Campbell-Bannerman Mss.*, Brit. Mus. Add. Mss. 41213, pp. 143ff. *P. Debs.*, 1903, 119: 1478, 1484; 122: 723; 1905, 142: 13–14; 1907, 170: 631–32, 1417; 1911, Lords, 7: 408–09, 856; 10: 834, 845; Commons, 27: 869, 870, 879–80, 927.

⁷ *D. Mail*, Dec. 25, 1899; Lecky, *Memoir of W. E. H. Lecky*, 323; cf. Kipling's "America's Defenceless Coasts" in his *American Notes* and Steevens, *Land of the Dollar*, 42, 46. *Punch*, Feb. 1, 1899, 54–55; Nov. 5, 1902, 313; Lord Rosebery on volunteers, *Scots.*, Dec. 10, 1906. Americans who dislike this paragraph may joyously turn to the origin of the word "Mafeking." The last sentence in the paragraph is based upon interviews; for the purpose of national psychology it may be noted that Colonials sometimes were viewed as acting in the same way.

⁸ C. C. Taylor, *The Life of Admiral Mahan* (London, 1920), viii, 40, 42, 45ff., 61ff., 121, 133–34. Among his English acquaintances were Sir William Laird Clowes (naval ed. of *Times*), Sir Edmund Fremantle, T. G. Bowles, Lord Sydenham, *et al.* In press space devoted to Americans, Mahan would not be far behind Carnegie and Roosevelt. Note Bridge's art. on "Sea-Power" in 11th ed. of *Ency. Brit.*; W. L. Langer, *Diplomacy of Imperialism, 1890–1902* (New York, 1935), II, 415–23. Seymour, before China Assoc., *Times*, Nov. 13, 1902; also secy. of National Service League in same issue. Colomb, *Times*, July 7, 1904; Chamberlain, *Times*, July 9, 1904; *P. Debs.*, 1899, 66: 1143; Balfour, *Times*, Sept. 11, 1905; Sir F. Maurice and Sir George Arthur, *Life of Lord Wolseley* (London, 1924), 285; G. S. Clarke, *19th Cent.*, Feb. 1898; Lockyer, *Times*, Sept. 10, 1903; Seymour, *Times*, Mar. 17, 1904. Captain W. D. Puleston, *Mahan: The Life and Work of Captain Alfred Thayer Mahan, U.S.N.* (New Haven, 1939), 91, 106–10, 122, 145–47, 157, 277, 306, 338. David Hannay, "Naval Strategy," in 11th ed. of *Ency. Brit.*

⁹ H. W. Wilson, *The Downfall of Spain: Naval History of the Spanish-American War* (Boston, 1900), 425, 426, 430–38; Wilson makes a special point of disagreeing with the American criticism of Admiral Sampson. *P. Debs.*, 1898, 57:176; 62:877, 919; 1900, 79:1129, 1152, 1283; 86:256, 357. Beresford, *Break-Up of China*, 423–24; for illustrations see, *Illus. London News*, Apr. 30, and *Graphic* suppl., Apr. 30, May 14, June 11, 1898. Cf. Reuter, *op. cit.*, 108. A. S. Hurd, "American Fleet from an English Point of View," *Cassier's*, Oct. 1907, 32:468–70.

¹⁰ Adoption of armor belts of improved armor for cruisers came earlier in U.S., the *Brooklyn*, built in 1895, being so protected. Lt. C. Bellairs before R.U. Service Institution, *Times*, June 28, 1904. *Engineering*, Dec. 30, 1898, ed.; *Report on Shipping and Shipbuilding on the American Lakes, Ac. & P.*, 1900, xci; *P. Debs.*, 1900, 86:293–94, 307–08, 322; 1901, 99:750–51, 763; on boilers, *P. Debs.*, 1899, 74:1559, 1567, 1568; 1901, 91:987. Biles, *Times*, Mar. 28, 1901, p. 10, also held to the view that America led in yachting design. White, *Times*, Dec. 23, 29, 1904; *Eng.*, Dec. 21, 1906; see also Copley, *Taylor*, II, 274. *P. Debs.*, 1910, 17:843; 1911, 22:2470; *Punch*, Nov. 22, 1899, p. 247.

¹¹ Chief engineers in England got rank of lieutenant above 8 years seniority. On officer-engineer scheme, *Engr.*, Nov. 9, 16, 30, 1900; Nov. 29, 1901; cf. resolution favoring amalgamation by Assoc. of Headmasters, *Times*, Jan. 11, 1902; *P. Debs.*, 1900, 79:1147, 1251, 1258, 1294; 1901, 91:1010; 1902, 103:582, 1075; 1903, 119:917; 122:176; 126:167; 1906, 152:1351, 1462, 1481; 1908, 191:1702, 1707; see also Reports of the Douglas Commission; *Times*, Jan. 31, 1903; Brassey, *Times*, Mar. 12, 1901, also Oct. 3, 1901, p. 5; Ewing, *Times*, May 20, 1905; Selborne, *P. Debs.*, 1901, 97:239; Pay and conditions, *P. Debs.*, 1900, 87:822; 1903, 91:1038; 1907, 171:300; 178:1568; 1911, 23:21.

¹² Wolseley, *Stand.*, Mar. 16, 1899; Dilke, *Times*, June 4, 1903; Hurd, *The British Fleet* (Edinburgh and London, 1901), 62–63; Bellairs, *Times*, June 28, 1904, p. 12; Haldane, *Times*, Jan. 6, 1903; cf. *Times*, Jan. 18, 1905. Beresford's opponent in naval matters, Lord Fisher, wrote Dec. 27, 1910, "I was impressed by America. . . . They seem to know more of me in America than in my own land." In 1919, he wanted an alliance, deeming it insanity to build against the U.S. See Lucy, *Diary*, II, 331. *P. Debs.*, 1903, 122:714, 729; 1904, 130:1406, 1411, 1422; 1908, 185:361; 1909, 2:1111, 1112, 1113, 1530; 3:110; Craig said the Govt. included America up to December 17, 1908; *P. Debs.*, 1909, 4:183ff., 470–71, 626, 724–25; 5:1282, 1283, 1286, 1294, 1298–99, 1305; 8:908, 1784; 1910, 15:114, 221, 267–68, 372, 569, 576; 16:1220; 17:843; 19:701, 1885; 1911, 22:1860, 1881, 1884, 1953, 1979, 2513–14; 23:69–70, 131, 139; Lords, 1912, 12:312; Commons, 1914, 59:1926–27. References, unless noted, are to the Commons.

¹³ *Times*, Dec. 15, 1898; *D. Mail*, June 10, 14, July 6, 1898, which kept urging lessons from our use of the rapid-fire gun. Major F. R. Burnham, an American scout, was sent for by Lord Roberts. Major-General Sir Robert Baden-Powell went to the U.S. in 1903 to investigate American cavalry tactics. The military arm also had its courtesy visits, e. g., the Honourable Artillery Co. of London to the States in 1903. Such an event as the Bisley competition in rifle shooting, 1908, despite the ill feeling aroused by the conduct of participants, was seized as an opportunity to discuss the American rifle. Military details can be found by turning to the *Journal of the Royal United Service Institution*. Bigelow, *Manch. G.*, June 14, 1898; Sir

H. Vincent, *The United States Army* (London, 1905), pp. 8, 9, 11, 16; *P. Debs.*, 1899, 69:326; 1900, 80:1127; 1901, 91:141ff., 165; 94:76, 303; 96:236; 98:162; 1902, 105:228, 272, 370; 1905, 141:1214; 1914, 64:2123–25. Mr. Pirie (1899) reminded the military committee that the Americans had found during the war that the canteen system injured the health of the army. Haldane, *Times*, Sept. 1, 1913; Secy. of War, *Times*, Jan. 17, 1905; Lee, *Times*, Mar. 24, 1902.

[14] Anglo-Saxonism is not, for example, discussed in the volumes by C. E. Playne (but see her *Neuroses of the Nations*, New York, 1925, Pt. I, chap. iv; Pt. II, chap. v; and *Pre-War Mind in Britain*, London, 1928) or in the *Ency. of Soc. Sciences*. For a general account see Jacques Barzun's *Race: A Study in Modern Superstition* (New York, 1937). Homer Lea's widely read *Day of the Saxon* (New York, 1912) cannot be said to cover the subject; he contends U.S. is no longer Anglo-Saxon. *Twentieth Century American* (New York, 1908) by an Englishman, H. P. Robinson, who identifies the compelling racial urge of both countries to imperialism. Edmond Demolins, trans. by L. B. Lavigne, *Anglo-Saxon Superiority: To What It is Due* (1st Eng. ed., London, 1898) exhausted many editions. Edmund Gosse, "Isolation of the Anglo-Saxon Mind," *Cosmopolitan*, Nov. 1901, p. 47. Aline Gorren in preachy *Anglo-Saxons and Others* (London, 1900) unites both countries in a material progress based on a ready acceptance of toil and personal responsibility. B. R. Davenport, *Anglo-Saxons, Onward* (1899); B. G. Ambler, *Ballads of Greater Britain: Songs of an Anglo-Saxon* (1900). One of the lighter products of the Ghent Celebration was A. W. Holland's *The Real Atlantic Cable* (London, 1914) wherein language bond is emphasized, with blood and government following. This was not considered a racial peace by H. S. Perris in *Pax Britannica* (London, 1913), 297. J. R. Dos Passos, *The Anglo-Saxon Century* (2nd ed., New York, 1903) urged the removal of the only obstacle to the entente of the English-speaking peoples by the voluntary incorporation of Canada. Note John Fiske's vision of Anglo-Saxon federalism and J. K. Hosmer, *A Short History of Anglo-Saxon Freedom* (New York, 1890).

Racial discussion is avoided by G. Lowes Dickinson, *Appearances* (1914), 149–50, by viewing Am. as offshoot of Europe and an American as merely an average man of the total of Western civilization. C. A. Brooke-Cunningham, *Anglo-Saxon Unity and Other Essays* (London, 1925), emphasizes predominance of English speech in U.S. Hilaire Belloc's *The Contrast* (New York, 1924) carries out the thesis (pp. 15, 252) that the New World is wholly alien to the Old, citing Max Beerbohm and Cecil Chesterton as academic support. J. A. Spender, *Through English Eyes* (New York, 1928), 248, 296, and *Life, Journalism, and Politics* (New York, n.d.), II, 120, 122. About 1907 Viscount Esher discussed with Herman Hatzfeldt of the German Embassy their mutual interest in the contrasts of the two branches of the Anglo-Saxon race; see Brett, *Viscount Esher*, II, 258. Britons and Americans occasionally included Germany in their racial tradition.

Racial lore often throws off queer extremes such as the Anglo-Israelite theory which identifies the English-speaking peoples with the "ten tribes" of Israel. See an American book, M. L. Streator, *The Anglo-American Alliance in Prophecy, or the Promises of the Fathers* (London, 1900) inspired by two Englishmen, John Wilson's "Lectures on our Israelitish Origin," and Prof. J. B. Dimbleby. In England there had been a weekly the *Banner of Israel* and a monthly the *Covenant People*. Drawing upon British encouragement, the Anglo-Saxon Federation of

America was organized in 1928, affiliated with British-Israel World Federation of London, and published a journal in 1930 called *Anglo-Saxon Federation of America* (Haverhill, Mass.).
    See also J. D. Squires, *British Propaganda, etc.* and H. C. Peterson, *Propaganda for War: the Campaign against American Neutrality, 1914–1917* (Norman, Okla., 1939), 175–245. Note numerous Bishops on Lord Phillmore's unofficial mission to U.S., *D. Telegraph*, Jan. 25, 1937, the hysterical *Anglo-Saxony and Its Tradition* (New York, 1939) by the Englishman George Catlin, and plans of Lionel Curtis in *World Order (Civitas Dei)*, New York, 1939.
    [15] R. Mackenzie, *America, A History* (London, 1897), 567 and appendix; Gynn, *Dilke*, I, 66–68; according to a letter from Sternburg to Roosevelt in 1905, Dilke was interested in forming a London group, "Potentia," to create anti-German feeling in New York; see Vagts, *op. cit.*, 1860 n.3. Friedrich Brie, *Imperialistische Strömungen in der englischen Literatur* (2d ed., Halle, 1928), 154–55. Stephens, *Freeman*, II, 177–79; 346, 357, 383–384; Freeman, *Greater Greece and Great Britain and George Washington the Expander of England* (London, 1886), 103, 143; Freeman, *Lectures to American Audiences* (Philadelphia, 1882), 44, 54, 62, 169, and *Some Impressions of the U.S.* (London, 1883), 15–16.
    [16] Dos Passos, *op. cit.*, 56 n.1; Waldstein and Rosebery, *Times*, July 8, 1898; note also Rosebery's speech at Perth, *Times*, Oct. 24, 1898; Waldstein, *The Expansion of Western Ideals and the World's Peace* (New York, 1899), 16, 18, 107, 87ff., 157–58, 184; he also wrote *The English-speaking Brotherhood and the League of Nations* (Cambridge, 1919). Benjamin Kidd identifies Eng. and Am. liberalism and ideals in his *Principles of Western Civilization* (1902). Chamberlain, *P. Debs.*, 1898, 58: 1436; see also *Times*, May 14, Nov. 17, 1898; cf. Olney's memorandum to White, May 8, 1897, which was read by the whole British cabinet; Nevins, *White*, 124–25. Carnegie and Mahan preached much about race when in England. Dufferin, *Times*, Sept. 7, 1898, considered by Am. diplomats the most friendly speech to that date. Hawkins, *Times*, Dec. 12, 1898 and Pond, *Eccentricities*, 477ff.; Wauchope, *Scots.*, Nov. 19, 1898. John Clifford, *God's Greater Britain* (London, 1899), 184–85, 199; Clifford suffered some sarcasm for the "Doctor" given him by Bates College in 1883; Marchant, *Clifford*, 99, 229. Mrs. Creighton, *Life and Letters of Mandell Creighton* (London, 1904), II, 302; Strachey, *American Soundings, passim; Spec.*, Apr. 7, 1906; Austin, "The Old Land and the Young Land," *Times*, Nov. 25, 1899. Am. philanthropy in India proved to the *Daily Express* that "our cousins across the Atlantic are one with us in the larger affairs of life."
    Cromer quoted in Strachey, *Strachey*, 138; Brassey, *Times*, Sept. 24, 1900; Bryce, *Times*, Jan. 28, 1907; Balfour, *Manch. G.*, Jan. 31, 1899; Onslow, *Times*, May 4, 1899; *P. Debs.*, 1912, 41: 2355. Gwynn, *Spring-Rice*, I, 406, March 25, 1904, St. Petersburg; cf. letter of Rice to Lord Onslow, Sept. 23, 1915 (II, 306–07), "England now, and not the United States, is fighting for the cause of liberty. . . . The result is that the natural hegemony of the free English-speaking world falls to England. . . ." W. T. Stead, *The Last Will and Testament of Cecil John Rhodes* (London, 1902), 63–64, 99, 170; S. G. Millin, *Rhodes* (London, 1933), 172; Whyte, *Stead*, 207ff.; Hammond, *Autobiog.*, I, 222–24, 270; there was a scheme to found a society to work for the British Empire. Viscount Elibank, *Man's Life*, 150; Trevelyan, *Grey of Fallodon*, 114–16, 142–43.
    [17] F. W. H. Myers, *Collected Poems* (London, 1912), "A Letter from Newport"

(1871); see also *The Renewal of Youth and Other Poems* (1882) and "The Distress in Lancashire"; Myers visited U.S. in 1865 and was never out of touch with psychical research there. See esp. Brie, *op. cit.*, 212, 231. Doyle, *Times*, June 14, 1898; F. M. Thomas, ed., *Fifty Years of Fleet Street, being the life and recollections of Sir John R. Robinson* (London, 1904), 358–59. Sir Percy Sykes, *Sir Mortimer Durand* (London, 1926), 265–69; Nevins, *White*, 224. Wells, *Experiment in Autobiography*, 652; *Autobiography of G. K. Chesterton* (New York, 1936), 226–27 and *What I saw in America*, 15, 207, 254, 231. Lecky, *Lecky*, 361; S. D. Murray, *The Future Peace of the Anglo-Saxons* (London, 1905); Aleister Crowley, "Art in America," *English R.*, 1913, 15: 578–95. "To Thomas Bailey Aldrich," a poem by William Watson.

O. Bainbridge, *The Lesson of the Anglo-American Peace Centenary* (1914); for Wallace, see *ibid.*, 29. Grey, *Times*, Feb. 10, 1904; Harold Begbie, *Albert, Fourth Earl Grey* (London, 1917), 138–39. Stanley Lane-Poole, *Thirty Years of Colonial Government, Sir George Ferguson Bowen* (London, 1889), II, 453; see his paper before the Royal Colonial Institute, June 15, 1886. G. E. Boxall, *The Anglo-Saxon, a study in evolution* (London, 1902), a colonial viewpoint which finds the Am. political boss dominated by the Latin spirit. B. O. Flower, "Federation of the Anglo-Saxon Races," *Arena*, Aug. 1898, 223–38; Sinclair Kennedy, *The Pan-Angles: a consideration of the federation of the seven English-speaking nations* (London, 1914).

VII

THE AMERICAN PERIL

The superiority of the United States to England is ultimately as certain as the next eclipse.—ECONOMIST, March 8, 1851.
We may become a satrapy of the United States. . . .—VISCOUNT ESHER.

THE channels of trade, waves of economic prosperity, price levels, foreign investments, competition, and the like are fundamental to a study of influence abroad. The battles of industry and commerce are events likely to attract foreign attention. Britain produced excited responses to each change in our trade statistics, frequently out of all proportion to the ups and downs. British trade from 1901 to 1903 had not been good, but had improved sufficiently by 1905 to drown out the oratory of the tariff reformers. A recession in 1908 and 1909 gave Tariffism a brief respite. Perhaps, as some British scholars assert, nothing was wrong with the rate of growth of British exports in the two decades preceding the World War, a period of rising prices, but American and German commercial rivalry had grown very sharp, and Britain had seen challenged her supremacy in production and her share of the world's trade. The American invasion was an important change in the economic history of the world.[1]

The prophetic Stead went so far as to write the *Americanization of the World* (1902) in which he spoke of our emergence as "the greatest political, social, and commercial phenomenon of our time." But English opinion was unprepared for and startled by America's competition, especially as an exporter of manufactured goods. Actually, the factual material on the true nature of our industrial strength was inadequate before 1902, and the British imagination had difficulty grasping the rapidity of our growth. We helped to produce a fit of self-depreciation current in England at the turn of the century, a more receptive mentality, a desire to overhaul industry, and a blow to British complacency as effective as the German competition of the early nineties. The amount of free publicity for us was enormous, and the picture of a gloating and bragging America was painted more vividly. The editor of *Fielden's Magazine*, who discounted our competition but who advised "hustling," explained that America could not comprehend Britain's "lugubrious tirades unless these forbode our approaching doom." *Punch* ridiculed our bumptiousness in a poem "Morituri Salutant!"—

> What is the hope, then, for civilization?
> What is the cure for a century's tears?
> What—save the mighty American Nation?
> That is the obvious answer, three cheers!

An "invasion," through the press or otherwise, was stimulating, and the reception ranged from panic and hostility to the disarming view that England was proud of our triumphs.

It has been said frequently that Germany, because she was closer, better organized, and deliberately trying to undermine British supremacy, and in more direct competition with British industries, absorbed all British fears and attention. The United States was fully as much in mind as Germany in such a volume as A. Williamson's *British Industries and Foreign Competition* (1894). Benjamin Kidd, tainted with the American bogey, told the Royal Colonial Institute in 1903 that

The great danger with which British trade was threatened from the United States at the present time was not so much from an invasion of American manufactures, but it was that of our industries being drawn deeply into the organization of trade and production now proceeding outwards from the United States.

American competition pervaded the press between 1898 and 1903, and many papers of different platforms viewed us as Britain's greatest rival up to the World War. It seemed inconsistent to some to preach affection for us and slaughter for Continental nations for erecting barriers against British merchandise. Although not always sensible or representative, the *Saturday Review* was not alone when it cried in June, 1901:

The full force of the present American commercial concentration falls on us. What we have to do is by harder work, more scientific method, fiscal readjustment and imperial consolidation, to prevent the Americans getting so far ahead of us . . .

In a series conducted by the *Daily Express*, "Wake up, England!" American rivalry and methods were to the fore. Others recalled that Gladstone had written in 1879: ". . . it is the United States alone who, at a coming time, can and probably will wrest from us our commercial supremacy."

During the "Made in Germany" panic in 1896, level-headed experts had attempted to divert attention from the German threat to our formidable rivalry. Already in 1896 and 1897 our efforts to monopolize the cycle market forced England to look to her organization, distribution, and advertising. Secretary Gage's grandiose reports to President McKinley in 1898 contained ample material for reflection; total American exports for the first time had exceeded imports, and were increasing more rapidly than Britain's. Bryce informed audiences that America was driving out British trade, that we were developing lines of business which one might have expected England to hold. The Institute of Bankers was told in 1900 that American and German commercial power were directed against Britain. Reporting on its five years of existence, the *Daily Mail* (May 4, 1901) claimed as one of its public services that when American trusts were regarded by Britons as temporary expedients, it had foreseen them as permanent forms of commercial warfare;

At the risk of being thought unpatriotic this journal has persistently . . . called attention to the numberless blows administered to our commercial supremacy, chiefly by reason of the superior educational methods and strenuous life of the American and the German.

To meet the transatlantic commercial invader became a prime object of Northcliffe's paper. It suggested a process of amalgamations. In June 1901 it carried a series of articles by Fred A. McKenzie which became the sensational *American Invaders* (1902), in imitation of E. E. Williams' famous *Made in Germany* (1896). The *Westminster Gazette*, while not absurdly pessimistic, did admit:

It is a dangerous form of national conceit which assumes that the British product is so necessarily and obviously better than all others that none can stand against it.

Reflecting upon events since the publication of his book, Williams, like Lord Rosebery, Sir W. D. Pearson, Asquith, and the editor of the *Financial Half-Year*, concluded that the United States was the more powerful rival. Carnegie's utterances left some doubt as to Britain's industrial future. "We have reason to fear," said J. A. Hobson in the *Fortnightly* of March 1902, "less perhaps of Germany, though her competition will be serious, than from America." The *Scotsman* viewed the invasion of British industry by American capitalists as the most remarkable commercial development of 1902. Sir Alfred Bateman's apologetic memorandum for the Board of Trade convinced some observers that the last thirty years revealed us as the greatest threat, even though earlier memoranda had overlooked us. Blue books in 1903 put into circulation figures which showed that since 1890 the United States had increased exports to Britain from £97,000,000 to £127,000,000, while British exports to us had fallen from £29,000,000 to £19,000,000. Nevertheless, certain journals like the *Engineer* reported that British manufacturers smiled at American competition. Sir Christopher Furness, who sponsored a policy of combinations along the northeast coast, did not despair of British industry in his *American Invasion* (1902), even though excessive railroad rates and coal and iron royalties handicapped it. Inspired articles appeared in the financial press which urged Britons to keep their properties from American hands. Frequently it was but natural and necessary to condemn American products and methods, and the free publicity in the press.

Attention to American competition decreased after 1904, but along with the dangers of German rivalry it was discussed from time to time, usually in connection with the tariff reform movement, or a new American tariff, or the antics of an American combine. The movement of American securities homeward was taken to be irrefragable evidence of our growing wealth. Even though obsessed by fear of Germany, J. Ellis Barker distrusted our expansion and navy in his *Great and Greater Britain* (1914). Ambassador Page, that great friend of England who always beheld the vision of American leadership, was not far wrong when he expressed a well-worn view in 1914: "Our power, our adaptability, our potential wealth they never forget." Page even suggested that the governing class had an exaggerated admiration for the American people and something like contempt for the American Government; he added: "Economic envy may in the future play some part in our dealings. But this is not yet very active and is not at all organized." One may question whether our influence or the party lines were as clear as Page wrote in March 1914:

> The whole Liberal fight here is confessedly to bring this Kingdom, as far as they know how and dare try, up to the economic level and practice of the United States: that's their standard and aim.

This obvious exaggeration does, however, furnish a clue to pre-war history.

The United Kingdom observed that it was being passed in production in fundamental industries, primarily by the United States and Germany.[2] Great Britain produced 287,000,000 tons of coal in 1913, Germany, 190,000,000, and the United States, 500,000,000. During the years 1890 to 1894, the United States with 8,000,000 tons of pig iron a year easily surpassed the British output; by 1913, Great Britain produced 10,250,000 tons, Germany, 16,500,000, and the United States, 31,000,000. Germany and American steel production topped the British by 1894; in 1913, Britain produced 7,660,000 tons, Germany, 17,300,000, and the United States, 31,- 300,000. Looms in the cotton trade rose in Britain about 23 per cent between 1900 and 1913; those in the United States, about 50 per cent. Up to 1913 the challenge to the British wool industries was the larger share of foreign home markets being supplied by their own producers. Total American domestic and foreign exports to the United Kingdom increased from 1895 to 1901, and up to 1913 never went below the total for 1897. The average of our general exports for each 100 persons in the United Kingdom had been about £254 during the years 1880–1889; it had risen to £302 in the period 1898–1907. The percentage of manufactured products to the total exports had increased from 10.6 per cent in 1890 to 16.5 per cent in 1902. The average values of the exports of machinery of domestic produce during the years 1890–1894 were:

United Kingdom, 14.8 million pounds sterling; Germany, 3.3; the United States, 4.1; the averages during 1905–1908 were: British, 28.2; Germany, 18.7; and the United States, 21.7. The total export trade of the United States, as England's greatest rival, far surpassed Germany's between 1898 and 1909.

With added impetus during 1898 and 1899, the increasing value of American machinery exported to the United Kingdom caused profound agitation which had its effect upon British designs and methods. Iron and steel exports, including machinery, jumped from £500,000 in 1890 to £4,000,000 in 1899. Tariff reformers pointed their arguments with figures which showed that in a group of fifteen manufactures the British exports to protected foreign markets from 1895 to 1907 had increased 44 per cent, that of Germany and the United States, 125 and 500 per cent respectively; the same exports to identical markets in the British Empire gave the British an increase of 91 per cent while Germany and the United States showed an increase of 129 and 359 per cent. Between 1902 and 1913, according to Cole, British exports in iron and steel had risen in value by 88 per cent, those of Germany and America, by 116 and 277 per cent. Thus, in the battle for markets, we were becoming an important factor in British economic life.

By 1876 our machine-made boots and shoes had reached Birmingham; American shoemaking machinery which followed revolutionized technique. Competition by American shoes which were characterized by lightness, elegance, finish, and quarter and half sizes, had been steadily increasing, and was to be stopped only by using American methods and machinery or imitations. One of the features of the Shoe and Leather Fair in 1901 was American machinery in motion. The value of American boot imports had risen from £143,000 in April 1900 to £335,900 in April 1902; in 1902, 750,000 Britons were wearing American boots. Our ladies's shoes were fashionable, but with soles too poor to keep out winter dampness. American experts were at the disposal of those who bought shoe machinery, which sometimes produced strikes; by 1913 nearly 80 per cent of the manufacturing firms were clients of an American company whose hold had been started in 1900. To its much criticized leasing system must go some credit for developing the boot trade in the Midlands. In order to fight competition, dealers took pains to capitalize upon any example of poorly made goods; show windows carried graphic examples of shoddy, dilapidated American shoes and long-suffering, sturdy British footwear. At a congress of the Royal Sanitary Institute, July 1906, Americans were hailed as the chief offenders in leather adulteration.

Thanks to automatic machinery, we were able by 1897 to threaten Britain's overseas and home markets in bicycles. Single tube tires, wooden rims, and short mudguards did not catch the British fancy. Language differences were acutely shown by American catalogues sent over without changes in price or nomenclature. The collapse of this threat gave pleasure, but the British had learned more about automatic machinery. Possibly it was the unpleasant experience with American cycles which made England at the outset question the quality of our automobiles, and customers were sceptical of any car offered at prices lower than the British. But there were warnings as early as 1900 not to let the motor industry be led by America or France. Just as there had been attractive proposals to dump cycles at panic prices, so in 1907 there were rumors that British dealers had been tempted to dump American cars. The *Daily Express*, September 1913, invited British motor car makers to discuss how to meet our competition. Lord Montagu, after a visit, believed English makers or motorists had no idea of the magnitude of the American motor trade. In 1914 the London Traffic Branch of the Board of Trade said of the Manchester motor show:

The most marked change to be noted is the greater number and the improved quality of cheap British cars, a change which has been stimulated, and was indeed caused, by the pressure of American competition.

The import of American motor car parts increased from £18,333 in 1908 to £415,468 in 1912; the value of the finished American cars had risen from £96,291 to £762,909. Ford was the first to go abroad, and he began assembling at Manchester in 1911; sales jumped from 500 in 1911 to 8,000 in 1914.

The introduction of the Scott & Williams patent seamless machine in 1891, along with other inventions, suggested a new threat to Lancashire's textile supremacy. In 1899 and 1900 we consumed more cotton than Britain. Close contact with America's hosiery business, according to Professor Clapham, prompted "ruthless scrapping" of old-fashioned equipment and kept the industry up to date. American underwear displayed in such towns as Nottingham and Leicester illustrated the challenge. It was suggested that the needle-loom, invented by German weavers but developed in America, be investigated by ribbon makers. Our technical training in silk-dying and finishing also contributed somewhat to the British silk trade. Industrialization of the English silk trade became thorough only after the American market expanded in the twentieth century. In a general way cotton rings and speculation stimulated British efforts to develop imperial cotton supplies. Daniel Scully's gambles in 1904, even though a failure, encouraged the cultivation of cotton in Southern Nigeria, Sierra Leone, and Lagos. American reports of low production costs attracted deputations which advised slow adaptation of the Northrop automatic loom to the Lancashire trade. Although the superiority of American operatives was denied, many experts warned that the British cotton industry had not kept up to our efficiency.

American-made cars and engines on London's new subways aroused a lively controversy. The Central London Railway, opened formally in June 1900, and the Glasgow Corporation were criticized for buying American equipment. American companies were specially formed to develop English electrical railways. The response to American competition (treated in detail in later pages) was often curious. For example, the *Daily Mail* (December 27, 1900) carried an article: "American Furniture in England. A Further Indictment of the Trade Unions." This competition was chiefly in office furniture. In domestic furniture American designs were modified to suit English taste. The English disliked the scroll work "stuck on" to our furniture, and the glossier finish, and spoke of their furniture as "polished," ours as "varnished." Thus, from the petty matters of taste to the great stakes of national economic life, our competition was front-page news, especially the American octopus or trust.

Comments on the trusts were one illustration that our economic life was not so clearly understood as one might expect after decades of British investment.[3] Trusts and high tariffs fostered the opinion that America was reactionary, that it had killed individualism by allowing free rein to a few. It was even feared that the American millionaire, a type new to English soil, would have imitators. Both free traders and tariff reformers condemned our trusts, but both used them to serve their own purposes. The trusts did not elicit the full measure of anti-American hostility, but in a dramatic way they suggested as counter-measures the possibilities of collective organization and the necessity of revitalizing British industries which had lost some of their former individualistic confidence.

Both the Lancashire Cotton Investigation Commission in 1906 and the *Engineer* (which was one of the first journals to give prominence to the movement in the late nineties) complained that England had not paid sufficient attention to our trusts with their international ramifications, and to their terrible effect on trade and politics in America. Possibly William Clarke in a Fabian Society speech delivered in 1888 was the first to bring home the growth of our trusts; Clarke, like John Burns, William Mather, Henry Vivian, and others, was a friend of Henry Demarest Lloyd, and it was probably from this American reformer that he got the cue to watch American trusts. (Lloyd probably suggested to Stead his *Americanization of the World*.) In 1890 Alfred Marshall told the British Association that the success of our trusts had been brilliant but not solid. By 1900 England tried to improve its knowledge; in 1901 Lord Rosebery saw fit to suggest a course in the London School of Economics on the importance of American trusts. The Hon. Evelyn Hubbard, one of the directors of the Bank of England, delivered a lecture on "Trusts and Combines" in 1902 in which he observed that the tendency to monopolization differentiated American from British combines. A free-trade volume of 1903 stated for obvious polemical purposes, "These Trusts are lowering the tone of American commercial life to an extent which we in England can hardly believe." Professor Clapham feared that our methods of combination would prevail in England; Henry W. Macrosty in his widely quoted *Trust Movement in British Industry* (1907) hoped British capital would not adopt the grosser methods of political control. Might not labor, asked the *Manchester Guardian*, imitate these consolidations and start conflicts "on the scale of vastness which the American loves?"

From 1898 on there was a move toward the concentration of industry, following the form of combination more common in the

States than on the Continent. Such were the Bradford Dyers' Association, Ltd., the Calico Printers' Association, Ltd., and the Associated Portland Cement Manufacturers. The financial weakness of the Calico Printers in 1902 was described as "the natural result of unreasoning imitation of American methods." Many journals expressed joy in 1906 that the Lever Soap Trust, which was spoken of as the first large-scale attempt to introduce the American system, had shown signs of failure. The *Spectator* concluded hopefully that Britons revolted instinctively from anything like these American "exotics"; it also hoped the Whig spirit would enable Taft to battle the trusts. Alfred Mosely wanted a Roosevelt or a Hughes to check company-promoting in England. As in America, promoters outside the various firms had brought about the combinations. Our "big business" had been unfettered too long, but the increasing aggregation in England rather lessened her terms of reproach, especially since British organizations felt they were too hampered by legislative restrictions. Our example probably acted as leaven in the English policy of regulating too much. Professor W. Smart of Glasgow, James Bryce, and Sir R. Giffen considered our trust legislation suggestive but also a "warning." Later, in 1918, Alfred Marshall's bias against America's development (as compared with Germany's) had disappeared because he felt that our situation had improved. He never learnt much from English sources of the relation of law to monopoly, and he wrote to John Hilton, Secretary to the Committee on Trusts, that if new laws were to be devised, "I trust that nothing will be done of a far-reaching character without a careful study of the toilsome steps by which American expedients have been developed." The Federal Trade Act he viewed as a "master stroke of genius"; from our Federal Trade Commission he learned the "functions of a democratic government in regard to complex economic issues."

Had Britain not been confident about the unsoundness of our financial methods the inroads of American trusts would have been more threatening.[4] When by the middle of 1903 this weakness became apparent, many a panicky journalist wondered why he had not thought about it before. But this weakness could also be exaggerated. So thoroughly embedded were American oil interests that they aroused little opposition. News came frequently that the International Harvester Trust was swamping Australia and New Zealand. Charles Tyson Yerkes, notorious American promoter, outbid the Morgan interests and got control of London's railway service. Ohio C. Barker made a dramatic bid to capture the match trade by a deal with Bryant and May. It was later asserted that the Diamond Match Company, which in 1896 had built at Liverpool the then largest match factory, had improved the working conditions of English female laborers. The "menace" of the Steel Trust aroused even the most optimistic. Sir Christopher Furness was not panic-stricken, but he advised steel masters to imitate our encouragement of the inventive genius and the abolition of "rule-of-thumb" methods. *Punch* jingled about the "contest of Armour—the Cannae of meat." Americans were capturing the country trade as well as Smithfield. Renewed activities of the Beef Trust in England in 1907 proved the value of organization. The Departmental Commission (formed July 31, 1908) on combinations in the meat trade did not find that the agreement between the four American beef companies trading in Britain was yet a serious danger. The Beef Trust, the Committee found, made witnesses timid even in England;

> On the other hand there can be little doubt that the gossip of the market has a tendency to exaggerate the importance of any such combination as that of the American companies. They are foreigners; their managers are extremely competent men of business . . . their trade methods are both superior to those prevailing in this country and perhaps less influenced by dry considerations of sentiment.

Again in 1913 the Central Markets Committee of London expressed fear of the American firms in Smithfield.

Americans tried in 1902 to capture the British retail tobacco trade in a battle which struck at the everyday life of the masses and developed into a very nationalistic fracas. As a counter-stroke the Imperial Tobacco Company was formed by Player's, Ogden's, and Wills's in time to save some British firms from falling into American hands. Both groups indulged in amazing bonus offers to retail tobacconists. Campaigners who tried to organize tobacco retailers cried that our trust had made serfs of the dealers; at the same time retailers concluded that the British combination would soon use all the worst methods of the American Tobacco Company. Phillips' "Guinea Gold" advertisements depicted Uncle Sam kidnapping England and crushing workmen. (It should be noted that the International Seamen's Conference declared that the Morgan trusts would mean stronger fights against seamen's organizations.) The Imperial Tobacco Company appealed to patriotism to fight "the American system of Trust Monopoly and all that is implied therein." The trusts settled their differences and the bonus war ended. The *Daily Mail* declared,

If the Imperial Company has achieved a victory, it will have demonstrated that half the terrors of American competition vanish when competition is boldly faced.

American threats strengthened the appeals of such organizations as the "British Made League," the all-British shopping movement sponsored by the Union Jack Industries League, and the Imperial Industries Club. Still more disturbing was the threat to British shipping in the same year as the tobacco battle.[5]

America's overseas expansion demanded a large mercantile marine which England recognized as necessary and inevitable for American capital; but the readjustment, which meant a struggle for sea supremacy, kept Britons on edge. They professed to believe that native American shipbuilding was no advantage either to builders or owners; the press constantly argued that anything like a bounty or a subsidy bill, even if inevitable, was worthless. In spite of this optimism such steps were still regarded (without any apparent sense of contradiction) as harmful to British shipping. The Earl of Glasgow in his presidential address also told the Institution of Naval Architects in 1902 that

The great strides made in recent years in American shipyards were significant of the practical manner in which the subject had been taken up in that country, and British shipbuilders would do well to keep before them the need of constant thought and effort and of improved methods unhampered by custom or conventionality.

The executive committee of the Boilermakers' and Iron and Steel Shipbuilders' Society wanted to call a halt on the belittling of British workmen and methods.

American capital, backed by Morgan's plan to whip Atlantic shipping into a single unit, formed a "pool" which burst forth into the full light of public agitation in April 1902. "Morganeering" connoted a type of piracy directed against legitimate enterprise. While the Cunard Company remained aloof, such lines as the Leyland, Atlantic Transport, Dominion, and White Star fell into the traffic agreement. The episode added fuel to tariff reform and awakened the Government. The transfer of the Leyland Line in 1901 had already aroused a slight "scare," especially in Liverpool. The *Economist* said,

> To us the whole transaction savours far too strongly of the methods by which in the United States railways and other undertakings are dealt with, as if they were the property of the directors and the financial syndicates. . . . We should be sorry to see that system introduced here . . .

The chairman of Frederick Leyland and Company, Ltd. announced that "American capital was coming into the Atlantic trade to stay." Sir James Woodhouse the following year fanned the discussion in Parliament; although the press and the public may have exaggerated the combination (whose capital increased daily in the public imagination), he pointed out that "Americans are gradually capturing our industries . . ." On April 25, Gerald Balfour, President of the Board of Trade, who hesitated for a long time to answer questions about the deal, announced that an official inquiry would be premature. The event served to make more vital the work of the Select Committee on Steamship Subsidies.

Before this Committee, presided over by Evelyn Cecil, the chairman of Harland and Wolfe (Belfast) declared:

> We have seized the opportunity of making a friendly and profitable arrangement for all our interests, commercial and national, and even practical, as nothing can do so much to promote good relations between the two great Anglo-Saxon communities as the community of business interests.

Nor did the City appear alarmed. Opinion along the Clyde was divided because the British sold in a good market. Several papers advised their readers not to buy Morgan shares. Free trade would have to go, others added, if British shipping companies could not maintain themselves. Admiral Sir E. R. Fremantle asked, "What is the use of soldiers and sailors sacrificing their lives for a country so disposed?" The *Labour Leader* thought the deal would awaken those "who still believed in the patriotism of the capitalist or the investor." Continental opinion, particularly German, was widely quoted to show that the combine was regarded as a great blow to British shipping, and a great portion of British uneasiness was due to the fact that the German lines had made no dictated surrender to us. An agreement with the Government preserved the British character of the ships, but the whole episode had been impressive and humiliating. A subsidy for Cunard's was a direct outcome of the threat; W. R. Lawson added, "In the Cunard agreement we are committing ourselves to the principle of State ownership of commercial shipping." The episode also stimulated proposals for a fast service between England and Canada.

Although in later years England could not comprehend why we allowed our mercantile marine to fall into decay, American threats had not disappeared entirely. The Chamber of Shipping in 1903 protested our appropriation of the coasting trade between the Philippines and the Pacific coast. The rate war between the Houston and Prince lines between 1902 and 1905 enabled American industries to gain a foothold in South Africa. Earl Grey complained of the preferential rates from New York to South Africa, citing a twofold increase of American exports during 1901–03; "My noble friend, the Under-Secretary of State, said . . . that the Americans are very clever traders. I hope he will ponder over that statement." The Royal Commission on Shipping Rings, instituted in 1906, investigated the chief competitors, Germany and the United States, and came to the conclusion that its evidence did not warrant legislation copied from the Sherman anti-trust law; the minority report and some of the press would have preferred stronger measures. American shipping tonnage might not increase at an alarming pace, but American capital could work wonders.

England concluded that the trusts had caused a muddle which would ultimately harm our economic structure, and expected that the ranks of America's free traders would swell when trust profits were recognized. Up to 1914 England could not see that anyone had been able to curb the trusts; it believed that court decisions could not be effective against Standard Oil. But free traders went one step further—they believed that free trade alone could prevent price-raising.

Before turning to our competition in overseas and Imperial markets, it is essential to trace the very interesting and important rôle played by America in Britain's fiscal controversy which called attention to many aspects of America's life, and our relation to the Empire. American protectionist policies since the Civil War had been a nuisance closely watched; actually British exports to us rarely surpassed in value those of 1866. Various American tariffs, the McKinley, the Dingley, the Payne-Aldrich, and the Underwood bills which caused different degrees of hardship in different sections of Britain, accounted for varieties in the heritage of opinions respecting us, and changed the centers of British commercial interest in us. This American influence, which sometimes aroused Britain to beat our threat, left behind a bundle of misconceptions and harshness which ran through all classes of society. In the discussions renewed after the Boer War on tariff reform and preferential tariffs within the British Empire, we figured as much or more than Germany, as a threat or an example; hence, it is misleading to give too much emphasis to German competition and to the anti-German direction of British tariff reform. America's rivalry remained a bogey after the "Made in Germany" scare of 1896. If there had been an Anglo-American war, there would have been enough historical material to prove economic rivalry as a cause of the conflict. Looking at the problem in another way, the Continent disliked an American "peril," tariff, or expansion as much as a Pan-Britannic customs union, and a Continental anti-American customs union was a serious dream.

It is therefore not "obvious" that British tariff reform "had risen largely out of Anglo-German trade competition." [6] Protectionists themselves preferred to argue from our experience, and America was referred to as much as Germany or any other European country. Certainly this was true between 1900 and 1906. From 1897 to 1914 Germany gained no great favors in the British Empire, and yet the reform movement depended much upon the pressure on the colonial markets where America was making strong bids. Further, tariff reform was given a new birth by Chamberlain in the very years that the American example was being boomed, in the very months that America was looked upon as the greatest potential competitor, particularly in iron, steel, and the engineering trades.

One of the first to warn his countrymen to pay more attention to the United States, its mechanical ingenuity and universal education, was the prophetic free trader Richard Cobden, who said in 1835 what was being argued in 1900: "Our only chance of national prosperity lies in the timely remodelling of our system, so as to put it as nearly as possible upon an equality with the improved management of the Americans." Élie Halévy errs when he states ambiguously that only W. J. Ashley, a tariff reformer brought from Harvard in 1901 to help organize the Faculty of Commerce at the University of Birmingham, maintained (in his *Tariff Problems*, 1903) that the important question of the future was not Anglo-German rivalry so much as American competition with both countries. (Nor can one accept Halévy's statement concerning the fiscal controversy: "Inevitably the question was asked, why not follow the German example?") To be sure, Ashley was peculiarly alive to American developments, and his nine years at Harvard had buttressed his position as a valiant supporter of tariff reform. The promoters of Canadian-American reciprocity in 1911 seemed to him to be indifferent to the imperial connection.

The economic views of other Britons were modified by American experience. Just as an American trip had influenced Chamberlain's fiscal views, so Moreton Frewen's meetings with Reed, Cabot Lodge, and Blaine made him contemptuous of free trade, and Lyon Playfair learned of the effects of protection. After a visit of four months in 1875, primarily to study the problem of protection in a new country, Alfred Marshall probably became the first Englishman to know thoroughly the American case for protection. J. M. Keynes has said of Marshall:

The American trip made on him a great impression which coloured all his future work. He used to say that it was not so much what he actually learnt, as that he got to know what things he wanted to learn; that he was taught to see things in proportion; and that he was enabled to expect the coming supremacy of the United States, to know its causes and the directions it would take.

Although Marshall still remained a free trader, he contended that England had underrated the differences between the influences of foreign trade on an old and a new country, that Englishmen had refused unwisely to meet the arguments of Carey, the American protectionist. England by 1900 considered itself fairly well informed about American tariffs and competition, although Benjamin Kidd still felt the Old World had not yet grasped the intensity of our economic progress.

Both sides agreed that we were selfish in our tariffs. It became a question which side could best use American examples (which were repeated almost nauseously in 1903 and 1904) as a club. The founder of the United Empire Trade League, Sir Howard Vincent, who earlier had welcomed the stimulus of the McKinley tariff, planned to raise the fiscal question in 1901 because of our competition. Prominent leaders advocated protection for the iron and steel industry; Walter Long, a protectionist, quoted Schwab to show how dumping in England benefited Americans. Many trade groups, depending upon the potency of our competition, based their fiscal views on the present or future America. Mr. E. Parkes, M.P., told the Birmingham Chamber of Commerce, "Unless we adopted preferential tariffs, America was almost sure, when compelled to find outlets for her productions, to sweep our colonial markets from us." Chamberlain's speech of May 15, 1903, was directed primarily toward a scheme for coöperation with the colonies, but protectionist ideas were quickly connected with it in the hope of opening foreign markets and saving home markets. To drive home his arguments in Liverpool he described how British trade with Cuba suffered from American regulations, in Cardiff he outlined the effects of American dumping and tariffs on steel and the tin-plate industry. The annual average value of the export tin-plate trade to us before the McKinley tariff, 1887–90, had been £4,-278,667; between 1898 and 1901, the average value was only £806,600. This was a homely argument for the potency of a tariff, even though free traders pointed out that the Welsh secured other good markets. (Bonar Law even in 1908 willingly adduced America's bid for the tin-plate trade to Canada when appealing for fiscal reform.) A *Punch* cartoon, "An Eye for Effect," November 4, 1903, well illustrated the uses made of the American threats:

Balfour: "A'in't you made 'im too horrible?"
Chamberlain: "No fear! You can't make 'em too 'orrible!"

The tariff reformers made America a competitor worthy of
imitating and defeating, and America in their logic had to be surpassed or demoted by free traders. It was up to the free traders,
such as Harold Cox, Secretary of the Cobden Club, to prove that
England was not appalled by America's progress or its own deca-
dence. Opponents of Chamberlain up to 1904 avoided wherever
possible the references to America. Asquith admitted in 1905 that
no free trader had maintained that protection would harm a great
country. References to America became less numerous after 1907,
although Canadian-American tariff relations began then to figure
in all discussions. Once again, many Liberals were forced to paint
a picture of America which was less sanguine or worthy of imitation.
Inasmuch as Anglo-American friendship was fashionable, it was
considered effective dialectics to argue that the proposed tariff was
directed against us and was injurious to good feeling. Marshall
even wrote in 1904 that nothing so angered him as the action of
the Chamberlainites and their Canadian bodyguard in reviling the
United States as "foreigners."

Intelligent and useful comparison of the ends and means of the
financial structure of the two countries was difficult to make unchallenged.[7] Many declared such a comparison absurd because of
our large, internal, free-trade area; Morley advised, "Let us not
be deluded by references to America." While comparing the prosperity of free-trade England with protected Continental countries,
Lloyd George at Fulham, 1906, was interrupted by a voice, "What
about America?" His answer was most curious: "America has no
great landlords. The land there was free. I am now comparing
countries under similar conditions." Or Leonard Courtney drew
upon our internal experience to prove to the National Liberal Club
that protection was not needed for new industries. Only practical
politics governed the use of American examples. Reformers argued
—even with Cobden's biographer, Morley—that Cobden had not
foreseen the growth of American manufacturing. It was rather un-
convincing to be told by Mr. Harwood that "We in the North of
England are convinced that if the United States had adopted the
policy of free trade we should have had a very hard time of it."

Mr. Rea even suggested that protection had driven the "most highly specialized skill and capital of America" to British shores. Two things became clear, that the efficiency campaign of 1900 which boosted America carried over to the reform proposals, that England was uncertain about our attitude toward our own high protection.

The reform press also elevated America as a threat and a guide. Leaflets from the Birmingham Tariff Committee were filled with statistics and American lessons. One, "Your Wages in Danger," warned:

Have you ever thought of what is going to happen when the United States Steel and Iron Trusts start flooding this country with cheap iron and steel?

Chamberlain, impressed by our united defense, commercial unity, and constitution, constantly stressed American examples. He began his second fiscal campaign at Welbeck, August 4, 1904, with emphasis upon the benefits of our high protection, even to agricultural laborers. Lloyd George once declared that Chamberlain's men suffered from the "million mania of America." Bryce and others usually opposed Chamberlain by attributing our progress to character and resources. The *Scotsman* (January 15, 1903) even suggested that our emergency rebate on foreign coal was temporary free trade, "really the thin end of the wedge." In view of the reformers' predilections it was natural for Asquith to say that the Unionists' "campaign was started with an amount of clever engineering and skilful advertisement unknown outside America."

When America's finances rocked, the reformers had to pay for pointing to our prosperity. The *Westminster Gazette* (October 28, 1907) chuckled: "Altogether the United States hardly seems to be such a Paradise as Tariff Reformers are wont to picture." The reformers accused Mr. Runciman, Financial Secretary to the Treasury, of "foolish and mischievous" statements which attributed our financial crisis to protection. Free traders, who were doubtful whether even England could devise a "scientific tariff," seized upon the Payne-Aldrich tariff of 1909 as evidence of the pitfalls of tariff-making; reformers looked upon it as clear proof that we were not turning toward free trade. The bill brought no new horrors to England, but the possible trade complications suggested again the need for protection and weapons of retaliation. Balfour still insisted that protection enabled the trusts to dump, and thought free traders would be confused by German and American prosperity. Austen Chamberlain (usually suspicious of America's motives) was eager in 1910 to deliver England "from the grasp of the American beef trust." But he did add that the United States was "protectionist in a sense and with an exaggeration that no living man in this country has ever suggested."

The uproar of 1911 over the Canadian-American reciprocity treaty was also part of the fiscal discussion, but will be treated later. One of the important volumes of the year was free trader Geoffrey Drage's *Imperial Organization of Trade*, which repeated the well-worn opinions on our evil trusts, severe unemployment, friendship, and success which he attributed to "energy and tireless application to business." It was not quite clear whether the Democrats should be hailed as free traders, but the Radical press easily did so and welcomed Wilson's election as a blow to tariff reformers in England. The Liberals gloated over the lower rates of the Underwood tariff as an honest change of heart. But tariff reformers continued to refer to America and argued that our tariff by 1914 had moved closer to the English proposals.

What was the position of the United States in these proposals to overhaul Britain's fiscal policy? [8] Balfour, thinking of our "magnificent economic position," inaugurated the discussion in the Commons in May 1903 with a speech for preferential tariffs. We dominated the inaugural meeting of the Tariff Reform League, July 21, 1903. It was argued that a reduction in our tariff, achieved with or without pressure, would improve the Anglo-American community of interests. The problem of retaliation against us was very practical and difficult, and up to and including 1906 it was one of the chief obstacles for the reformers. Certainly the discussions in this direction tempered any anti-German bias of the tariff agitation. Asquith, Morley, Rosebery, Bryce, Churchill, and a host of others concluded that retaliation was aimed chiefly at us; further, it would not work because it would be applied chiefly against food and raw materials. A crowd singing "Rule, Britannia" interrupted Mr. Ritchie as he described its threat to Anglo-American cordiality.

Rosebery, who discussed our susceptibilities in such a way as to make his opponents appear like our enemies, did not believe we would quietly accept retaliation: "Why, they are the most pugnacious nation that exists!" Winston Churchill extended the argument:

The union of the Anglo-Saxon race was a great ideal, and if ever it was to be achieved it would be by increasing and not diminishing the friendly intercourse of trade.

Sir William Holland was of the startling opinion that Congress would permit certain states to impose an export duty on cotton in order to battle retaliation. Others suggested that retaliatory measures would stimulate American shipping subsidies. The reformers' principal contention was that we would give way if Britain were serious.

What was the nature of American opinion from which protectionists derived the most encouragement? [9] Since Honolulu had shut out British traders, Mr. Hunt suggested that America might be shown her mistake by British restrictions in the Fiji Islands;

I believe the Americans thought we were very foolish to render ourselves defenceless in the commercial struggle. . . . Was it not possible that some hon. Members opposite, if they took a tour through America and the Colonies, would also become firm believers in the policy of the ex-Colonial Secretary?

Earl Minto and the Imperial Tariff Committee reported that we feared Chamberlain's policy as of great consequence; protectionist journals assumed that this was a certain index of the need for change. To Carnegie a preferential tariff was "race imperialism" with the United States left out; when he reported that America would resent preferential tariffs, the *Times* censured him for not knowing his countrymen, and if he were correct, Balfour added, Americans were very unreasonable. American speakers frequently described to English audiences the pros and cons of protection. When standing for election as a free trader at Rochester (Kent) in 1903, Sir Harry Johnston described how ". . . it was the Americans who decided the issue. They had taken in hand the cement industry. . . . The Americans wanted Protection, to increase the value of British cement."

What were the supposed consequences of protection?[10] The trust menace and political corruption, which were easily associated with protection, were very effective arrows in the free-trade quiver. Men like Bryce, Rosebery, Runciman, and Asquith, and journals like the *Spectator* and *Daily Chronicle* constantly maintained that America's high tariffs had led to political evils. Winston Churchill predicted that a new party would arise in England similar to the Republican party, "rich, materialist, and secular"; he concluded from Roosevelt's failures that only a free-trade government could curb the trusts. R. B. Haldane told his constituents:

In other countries where tariffs were in operation politics had become matters of the most sordid self-interest. In the United States the best men served in the great State offices, but shrank from going into Congress because they did not like the constant lobbying of the big manufacturers and the trusts and the protected industries which battened by Protection at the expense of the nation and which used every influence to get the tariffs kept up or raised.

Others contended that protection had ruined American shipping. Our haggling over Cuban products led the *Manchester Guardian* (April 26, 1902) to say that never had there been "a more scandalous example of the political evils of Protection." The *Spectator* pointed to the "travesties of Colonial Empire that exist under Protection." Lord Cromer gave his views in a presidential address to the Unionist Free Trade Club in 1908:

The United States of America stand before us as an object-lesson of the demoralizing effect of protection on the political life of a country governed on democratic principles.

In a Cobden Club leaflet J. A. Hobson analyzed the bitter *Fruits of American Protection* (1907). Sir William Holland in 1909 could not but view America's tariff revision as farcical: "We are free from wolves now, and let us see that we remain so!" It was Austen Chamberlain's argument in the Debate on the Address, February 23, 1910, that such moderate duties as he proposed would not create trusts; it was our weak central power, not protection, which had preserved the trusts. Ramsay MacDonald had a pert answer for Chamberlain:

A bad political constitution is worked alongside of a bad economic constitution, and the result is that you have such places as Pittsburgh and the Steel Trust, the Beef Trust, and various other trusts.

Thus a great amount of contemporary American history became of vital importance to the British people. The picture of our high protection was perhaps blacker than ever painted by responsible American criticism.

Finally, the conditions and meaning of American prosperity and working-class life were vitally important in the fiscal discussions.[11] Chamberlain constantly preached that we had reached a higher standard of living; Sir Gilbert Parker said his protectionist colleagues "were challenged about wages, but wages were double what they were in this country." At least up to 1906 free traders had to combat the illusion that men in the Colonies and America were never out of work; this illusion had been used in organizing the labor branch of the Tariff Reform League. After a visit Mr. E. Parkes thought working conditions so much better that he wagered if any M.P. made a tour "he would find his conversion to some form of Protection would be complete before he came back." Balfour insisted that in spite of an immense immigrant labor problem our real wages were better, and that those who objected to fiscal reform were bound to explain how America could deal with the unemployed question more effectively. Tariff opponents merely pointed out that tariffs did not necessarily raise wages and demonstrated that our labor conditions were not improving. Relying on press reports in 1909, Snowden and Churchill showed that severe unemployment had fallen upon New York. But the country and Parliament were in doubt about American statistics which enabled Lloyd George to show that the higher cost of living ate up the increase in wages. This was important since in the campaign of 1909 predigested hints for free-trade speakers made a great fuss over New York's unemployment. One set of figures was derived from a printed appeal of an irresponsible and defunct charity bureau seeking donations from New Yorkers. Consul-General Bennett in New York had to deny that his report, which was eagerly seized upon by the Radical press, was capable of showing that the American laborer was worse off than the Briton. After a suspicious delay, the Board of Trade Inquiry into living costs in the States, begun February 1909, but not issued until 1911, rather silenced those who were glorifying our unhappiness. One M.P. slyly asked the Government how long it had known that wages in the States were 130 per cent higher than in the United Kingdom, and that real wages were 50 per cent better. This was ineffectively answered by appealing to our social chaos.

The fiscal problem made America's experience more vital, perhaps much more vital than Germany's internal career. America's stand, halfway along the road of closed economy, had been a threat to the British system. The experience of protectionist America, attracting new friends and upsetting old-timers, played a significant part in one of the greatest political issues which were faced by pre-War Britain.

We may turn briefly to overseas markets.[12] The press which regarded American imperialism with political sympathy nevertheless concluded that England would lose commercially in overseas markets. Trade began to follow the flag in Puerto Rico and the Philippines. British exports to the Philippines and Guam totaled in 1895, $1,995,854; in 1902, $3,905,376; in 1913, $4,718,000; American exports, excluding Guam, in the same years rose steadily from $119,000 to $5,251,000 to $25,360,646. The statistics for Cuba showed increasingly sharp competition, which the British Chambers of Commerce feared. Consul-General Carden, who advised a permanent form of government, explained that "Cuba's first year under American rule has been somewhat of a disappointment to Americans as to Cubans." But more favorable results later he did not resent.

The story of European markets belongs more properly to a history of Anglo-German trade rivalry. However, the United States passed the United Kingdom as an exporter to Germany in the decade 1891–1900. The yearly average share of imports to France during the decades 1880–1889 and 1896–1905 had been for the United Kingdom 13.5 and 12.7 per cent; for the United States, a rise from 8.3 to 10.7 per cent. During the same decades, the respective shares of Holland's imports were 25.2 to 12.8 per cent for Britain, 6.0 to 12.2 per cent for us; of Italy's imports, from

21.6 to 17.6 per cent, while our share rose from 4.8 to 11.9 per cent; of Belgium's imports, from 13.2 to 10.8 per cent while America's increased slightly from 11.1 to 11.4 per cent. To a degree during these years the United States had gained at British expense in various European countries. Consular dispatches, which received full press notice, emphasized our trade gains throughout the world.

American exports to China had increased 126 per cent from 1887 to 1897; consuls prepared British exporters in 1898 for inroads of American cotton, and iron and steel products. The Manchester Chamber of Commerce learned that between 1892 and 1899 American trade in sheeting had increased 197 per cent as compared with an English and Dutch increase of 6 per cent. The secretary of the Chamber in 1902 found no competition in the cotton goods market except the advance made by America in China. The war of 1898, observed the British vice-consul at San Francisco, 1901, made us realize that the Pacific Ocean trade should belong to us. The laying of the Manila cable was a harbinger of greater competition. From Tokyo, 1898, came the consular announcement, "The American invasion has only just commenced. . . . The tendency will be towards encroachment upon the trade hitherto belonging to Great Britain." The British Consul at Nagasaki warned the London Chamber of Commerce that our competition in Japan would be more formidable than Germany's. The British share of Japan's imports during the decades 1880–1889 and 1896–1905 fell from 42.2 to 21.9 per cent, while ours rose from 8.9 to 16.5 per cent.

Growing American competition in Latin America was reported, and such pressure aided the revamping of British trade methods which were often accused of tight credit, high prices, slow execution of orders, and poor adaptability. American competition was sharpest in the Central American region, but our exports to South America also had to be reckoned with, jumping from about one fourth of the British total in 1887–1891 to almost two thirds in 1912–1913. A special commissioner, Mr. T. Worthington, sent out to investigate trade prospects in South America, reported on Chile, 1898:

The advance in the import of American goods . . . is remarkable, and I think it may be taken for granted that wherever any American goods can be pushed in, no considerations of possible loss in the attempt will prevent their being given a full trial.

In Argentina, neat and light American machinery was delivered promptly, and our electrical equipment was sold as the most advanced. The British Consul-General for the Argentine Republic lamented in 1913 the unscrupulous methods and competition of our trusts. The British Minister in Venezuela anticipated America's competition as greater than Germany's; the acting Consul explained: "The Americans are taking a great hold on the Venezuelan market. They are not conservative and their business methods are quicker." Carden, often accused of being anti-American, warned British merchants to bestir themselves in Mexico. It was reported with glee in 1913 that Lord Cowdray's firm had secured oil concessions in Ecuador over American "monopolists." Although Britain held its own in South America up to 1914, the threatening American advance made Britons contemplate with misgivings the economic imperialism of her cousins.

The United States influenced Great Britain by way of the Empire.[13] America loomed larger than any other foreign nation as a commercial or emotional force in many portions of the Empire, especially in Canada. Quite significantly, Balfour told Lodge, October 9, 1903, that the Cabinet's opposition to Chamberlain's tariff policy was less important than the Alaskan boundary dispute. American pressure contributed much to the Imperial partnership now expressed by the Statute of Westminster. There were many signs to show that there was genuine, widespread alarm that the Americanization of the colonies or the "American peril" was growing at a rate dangerous to Imperial ties. Frequently in British thought, the United States and the Colonies were linked together, sometimes as similar "frontier influences" or comparable laboratories. But one should not be led to exaggerate Canada as an interpreter of American civilization to England.

By analogy with the attempted secession of our Southern States, some Englishmen began to wonder whether England would be as great without her colonies as with them. The result of the Civil War left America in a position to indulge in territorial extension. Sir Charles Bruce recalled:

While the motives that concentrated the policy of the founders of the [Royal] Colonial Institute were many, the dominant influence was the direct outcome of the consequences of the civil war in the United States.

To a great extent our political structure interested those who were concerned about Imperial problems. Lord Rosebery, whose tour of the world in 1882 gave a fillip to his own imperialism, wanted to open the House of Lords to colonial representatives on the lines of our Senate. As A. L. Burt has said, "The principle of Federation . . . had derived new vigour from its adoption in the United States Constitution . . ." In a land unspoiled by American history, books like Atherton's *The Conqueror* (1902) and F. S. Oliver's *Alexander Hamilton: an Essay on American Union* (1906) helped to stimulate Imperial thinking; the latter deliberately tried to show the necessity of Imperial federation, especially since the author found that the problems of eighteenth-century America and twentieth-century Empire "bear a startling likeness." One of Cecil Rhodes's cardinal doctrines was that the British Constitution was an absurd anachronism which should be remodeled on the American Union with federal, self-governing colonies as the constituent states. At the very extreme was W. T. Stead, who contended that "unless we can succeed in merging the British Empire in the English-speaking United States of the World, the disintegration of our Empire . . . is only a matter of time."

America was becoming the most potent trade rival of the British Empire. The value of our exports to the British Empire, including bullion and specie, increased between 1898 and 1901, and after ups and downs, finally reached a total of 270 million pounds sterling in 1912, or 110 million pounds more than in 1898. Between 1895 and 1907 American manufactured exports to the Empire increased at a faster rate than Britain's. However, Britain's total exports to British Australasia were satisfactory, and our increase from 1898 to 1901 was not yet strong enough to arouse agitation in England. American exports to New Zealand had jumped from £200,000 in 1896 to £1,000,000 in 1901 with locomotives, boots, and calicoes. The Premier of New Zealand in London in 1902 cited Treasurer Shaw's hope of transferring the sovereignty of the Pacific to America; "Did we not see in that a great danger? (Hear, hear.)" Our competition in agricultural machinery and motor cars was not pleasant. As a result of trade scares, special commissioners investigated Australia and New Zealand in 1905 and 1906. Although they believed our competition had been greatly exaggerated, the commissioners once again described the good services of our consuls, their push and adaptability. America's upward thrust in Africa was startling only between 1900 and 1903, and Englishmen attributed it as much to shipping rates as to American skill. However, Mr. Henry Birchenough, a special commissioner, declared in a Blue Book on South Africa, 1903: "America is undoubtedly our most formidable rival present and future."

The British West Indies fell more into the sweeping extension of American power. American and British exports (domestic) to the British West Indies (including Bermuda, the Bahamas, and British Guiana) increased together until 1913, when America pushed slightly to the front. In 1897 we had been viewed as the natural market for the West Indies; but as the Royal Commission (1909) on trade relations between Canada and the West Indies reported:

> The Commission of 1897 could not foresee . . . the acquisition of tropical possessions by the United States. . . . The geographical position of the West Indies Colonies must always tend to throw them under the influence of the fiscal system either of the United States or of the Dominion of Canada.

The reorganization of Cuba and the annexation of Puerto Rico were among the chief reasons for the steps taken to form a Confederation of the British West Indies with Canada. With the Indies facing severe competition in sugar there arose a cry for preferential tariffs; the British press began to report that the islands looked to America to escape ruin. It was not consoling for free traders to maintain that the islands would gravitate "naturally" to the United States. It was left for an Irishman, Mr. Dillon, to tell Parliament what was in the minds of many:

> I firmly believe that in a very short time all the West India Islands will go over to the United States. That will be the inevitable result of the war between Spain and the United States.

Britons began to take notice of the complaint that the Colonial Office had not paid enough attention to our expansion in the Caribbean area. Indeed, one usually finds that America was involved whenever a portion of the Empire declared that the Mother Country had neglected or restricted it. Efforts were made to improve transport facilities between Jamaica and England, between the West Indies and Canada. Some journals could find no reason why "Cuba should flourish whilst Jamaica languishes." Although the Commission found in Jamaica little fear of American retaliation, there was some dislike for preference with Canada because of the association of Jamaica's business community with American interests. As early as 1905 the British press began to suggest that the economic future of the West Indies depended upon the success of the Panama Canal. The American policy which secured the canal strengthened those persons who urged a united West Indies with a responsible government and a centralized procedure capable of handling such problems as the Panama Tolls. One senses a British feeling of inevitability respecting the relations between the West Indies and the United States.

America's influence upon the spirit, politics, and economic structure of Canada was fully comprehended by the British.[14] How real might have been the Canadian, or West Indian, or American threats of annexation cannot be discussed here; but there were enough conflicting reports in England to arouse attention and some suspicion whether Whitehall officials knew Canada's true sentiments respecting annexation. But just as the proximity to Japan was thought to cement the loyalty of Australia, so America was held to work similarly upon Canada. At the Colonial Conference in 1902, the First Lord of the Admiralty declared that, if independent, "The Dominion of Canada would have to frame its naval policy with a view to the navy of the United States." It was also thought that Canada, no matter what she might say at Colonial Conferences, would realize after observing our entrance into world affairs that she could not disregard the politics of Europe. England did not overlook the influx of American farmers into Western Canada; it might not be a threat, but it did suggest a lack of imperial organization to find Americans moving north while Englishmen poured into the States. At the annual London Celebration of Dominion Day, July 1, 1909, Lord Grey discounted fears of American emigration, and the Canadian Minister of Finance reassured his audience that the "American invasion" would have no adverse effects on national life. But as we have shown, the press urged England to wake up to the American-ization of Canada. Sir Wilfred Laurier said in London, May 1, 1907, "There was doubt expressed to him by some people in England lest the American citizen might Americanize and republicanize Canada. No such fear was to be entertained." When in England in 1911, he again was surprised to find that Englishmen feared the annexation of Canada. We shall see that our advocates of reciprocity who dropped veiled or unveiled hints of political union had got an unusually good press in England. But it was rather as the *Saturday Review* suggested in January 1909:

It is not likely that America can continue to supersede us economi-cally and commercially in Canada without Americanizing the Canadian in proportion.

Our inroads into the trade of British North America made us the only serious competitor. By 1913 our exports were almost three times greater than Britain's. Consequently, one might have anticipated that special commissioners in 1908 and 1912, impressed by our agres-siveness and the similarity of Canadian and American life, would issue the well-worn admonitions to British traders, and that others would complain of Britain's deficiency in consular and trade agents. Long before 1911 both free traders and tariff reformers watched the tariff squabbles between Canada and the United States. During the fiscal discussion of 1902 and 1903 the argument that economic union would lead to political union had already reached its hortatory maturity. The free traders naturally stressed the "inevitability" of closer commercial ties between us, and sometimes wondered whether in a preferential scheme any of the colonies could grant as much to Britain as would the United States. Reformers, if discreet, dared not go too far in magnifying American influences which suggested a weakening of the Empire and lukewarm loyalty; had there not been such patriotic restrictions, the pull of Canada toward us would have commanded more attention and very quickly would have de-generated into a panic.

Professor Ashley predicted before the London Chamber of Com-merce in 1903 that Canada would renew her agitation for a com-mercial union. When on a mission to Canada in 1905, W. A. S. Hewins, who aided the Conservative reformers, talked with Laurier;

"I suggested that if we adopt a tariff the United States of America might reduce theirs and quoted German views in support of this." The protectionist press in 1906 did not doubt that reciprocity would affect vitally the Imperial status, and would lead to political incorporation. A. D. Steele-Maitland described "a permeation of the whole of the Canadian business system with foreign methods, foreign capital, and foreign goods . . . without question at this moment the most serious existing menace to the Imperial connection." American capital, which frequently retained the guiding control of its investments, was more insidious than British capital which did not involve British influence. Up to 1911, the answer made to this was best expressed by Bonar Law:

I do not think there is a single Canadian who does not know that to increase the Dominion's development most rapidly, the best thing was to have a close commercial treaty with the United States.

At least the leaders of the Conservative party in the spring of 1910 had begun to appreciate the grave issues raised by Canadian-American negotiations. The cabled summaries, January 27, 1911, were more serious than many had anticipated.

These moves struck England in a tender spot, and probably inspired more public discussion of the United States than any other single event during this period.[15] With dramatic suddenness we had precipitated an Imperial problem into a strong party atmosphere and caused a new examination of American strength. Britain seemed equally uncertain about the true nature of Canadian and American opinions. Possibly a majority professed to believe that a commercial union would lead to a political union. Less and less did critics deny that Canada might gain from the reciprocity agreement. Bryce's *American Commonwealth* and his position as Ambassador at Washington during the negotiations of the treaty temporarily embarrassed his party. Lord Ampthill, the Earl of Stanhope, and others were worried about the following passage from this authoritative observer:

The material growth of Canada would probably be quickened by union, and the plan of a Commercial League or Customs Union which has lately been discussed, might, if carried out, lead to a political union.

Bryce's opponents felt that actually he had aided in planning a commercial union which, according to his texts from 1889 to 1909, might lead to political union—"indeed, it is hard to see how otherwise Canada would have her fair share in adjusting such tariff changes as might from time to time become necessary." Grey defended him by saying that if he had not behaved so well Canada might have wanted an Embassy in Washington. But it was necessary for Bryce in 1913 to drop the above and add:

> . . . the temper and feelings of her people, and the growth of a vigorous national sentiment among them, have not been making for their union with the far larger mass of the United States.

He had already written to Grey, January 27, 1911, that Pan-American propaganda or a freer exchange of commodities would not lead to closer political relations.

Canadian reciprocity was viewed as a momentous departure in the history of the British Empire because it would diminish the opportunities for preference within the Empire, deflect the food supply, injure British traders, and encourage Canada to develop "in accordance with considerations of geographic proximity." Government spokesmen relied on the inevitability of geographical factors as an excuse for having rejected Canadian offers. Others looked optimistically upon this agreement (which Balfour called "an Imperial disaster") as a step toward the confederation of the English-speaking peoples. Countless quotations from America were used recklessly by both sides; some to prove that the United States would become a free-trade country, that Taft and his advisers meant annexation, that the Canadian gains were doubtful. The *Manchester Guardian* declared:

> That a great blow has been struck at high tariffs in America is admitted, and English Protectionists are already rubbing their bruises in sympathy with their American friends.

Since papers like the *Daily Chronicle* hailed it as the "greatest single step towards Free Trade that has been taken in our generation," the defeat of the Canadian cabinet brought some grief to free traders and joy to the Imperialists. But the press did not minimize America's threat or influence, in language that was often inconvenient and impolitic. The seriousness of the situation, in spite of the *Standard's* charge, was generally appreciated in England. The whole controversy abounded in confusions of political and economic theories; there was unreality about much of the discussion which was obvious even before the Canadian Government rejected the treaty in September 1911. The political implications had been emphasized more in England than Americans understood. The defeat of reciprocity came as a tonic, and as a victory for the British flag. The *Scotsman* observed, "It is enough to say that the vote of Canada had fortified Imperial unity, and heightened at home the prospects of Tariff Reform." As Bonar Law put it, the episode was a "lesson" which had sunk into the minds and hearts of British people. The matter did not die down completely. The free-trade press looked complacently upon the Underwood Tariff as making those people appear foolish who had insisted that the demolition of the tariff wall would mean the end of Canada. A few very sanguine people remained to carry on the wishful thinking that a Canadian-American commercial understanding would lead to a vaster Customs Union of the English-speaking world. Very little had been said in England of American opposition to the reciprocity treaty, and little about America's shortsightedness which thus indirectly strengthened the Empire.

The "American Peril" was more than an academic question for the United Kingdom. The potential strength of America, and the increasing manifestations of it from the nineties onward, made a deep impression upon the thought and activities of Great Britain.

---

[1] G. D. H. Cole, *British Trade and Industry, Past and Future* (London, 1932); it is incorrect to say, as Nicholas Roosevelt has done in *America and England?* (New York, 1930), p. 51, that "only one prophetic voice" was raised to call attention to the significance of Am. growth, namely, Brooks Adams in his *New Empire* (1902). Adams's *American Economic Supremacy* (1900), expressing idea that England's mantle had fallen on us, was widely quoted in England. J. A. Hobson, "Approaching Abandonment of Free Trade," *Fort. R.*, 77: 435–36. A weekly trade review was started August 28, 1901, primarily to record Am. competition. E. E. Williams, "Made in Germany—Five Years Later," *Natl. R.*, Sept. 1901, 130–44; H. W. Wilson, *Fort. R.*, July 1901, 76–87; G. Gibbon, *West. R.*, 147: 310–16; Mark Warren, *ibid.*, Jan. 1899, 28–37; B. Taylor, *Fort. R.*, 1899, 71: 284ff.; *Natl. R.*, June 1899, 568–80; *Quart. R.*, 1902, 196: 228; Andrew Carnegie, "British Pessimism," *19th Cent.*, June 1901; Rosebery's speech at Edinburgh, *Times*, Nov. 3, 1902, citing Carnegie and attributing half of our success to education; *New Liberal R.*, March 1901; Bryce, *Times*, Jan. 11, Dec. 23, 1898. Only the title is significant in George Griffith's *The Lake of Gold; The Anglo-American Conquest*

of Europe (London, 1903). B. J. Hendricks, *Page*, I, 144, 152, 170, 217, 250; III, 34–37; Sir Edgar Speyer, *Times*, May 25, 1911; Hyndman, *Times*, Apr. 1, 1907. Notwithstanding the emphasis of the book, the reader will find the detailed bibliography in Ross S. J. Hoffman, *Great Britain and the German Trade Rivalry, 1875–1914* (Philadelphia, 1933) of value on the subject of Am. rivalry. Use has been made of such publications as the *Annual Register, Annual Statement of the Trade of the U.K., Statistical Abstracts* of the U.S. and U.K., the U.S. Daily and Monthly Consular and Trade Reports. Of the Commercial Reports, references will be made only to those cited; they are classified as Annual or Miscellaneous Series of Diplomatic and Consular Reports, and are to be found in the *Parl. Papers*.

For account of post-war years, see Ludwell Denny, *America Conquers Britain* (New York, 1930). J. H. Clapham's *Economic History of Modern Britain, Machines and National Rivalries 1887–1914* (vol. 3, Cambridge, 1938), *passim*, which just came to my attention, is probably the first general study to give proper attention to the Am. impact. But Professor Clapham (p. 37) tends to underestimate the discussion aroused by America and 1898 might well be substituted for 1903 (pp. 44, 45) as a date for the increased discussion by the British public.

² Cole, *op. cit.*, 106–08; J. Holt Schooling, *The British Trade Book* (London, 1908), 127. Values of Am. exports to U.K. of articles mfg. or partly mfg. (excluding articles of food, drink, or tobacco) were £10,279,669 in 1890, £21,317,471 in 1900. U.S. exported machinery (domestic and foreign produce) to U.K. in 1912 to value of £3,318,113; peak years were 1902, 1906, 1907, 1912, and 1913. According to *Parl. Papers*, 1903, cd. 1761, lxvii, iron and steel and manufactures thereof from U.S. to U.K. jumped from £594,418 in 1895 to £2,422,334 in 1897. Harold Cox, ed., *British Industries under Free Trade* (London, 1903), 235–52; William Page, ed., *Commerce and Industry, Table of Statistics for the British Empire from 1815* (London, 1919), II, 102; *British and Foreign Trade and Industry, P.P.*, 1909 (Cd. 4954), cii, p. 77. Mr. E. Swaysland made a special tour of U.S. on behalf of the Northamptonshire education committee to report on the shoe industry; he praised Am. labor. Am. shoe machines were said not to have been used to full capacity in Northampton. McKenzie, *op. cit.*, 47–61.

The International Cotton Congress at Zurich, 1904, bore witness to Old World interest and sense of danger in our habit of gambling in futures. For earlier discussion, J. P. Harris-Gastrell, *Report to the British Parliament on American Textile Industries, P.P.*, 1873, lxviii. One of the members of an informal commission of Lancashire spinners in 1904, Mr. T. M. Young, did not attribute high wages to the superiority of Am. worker, but to the exploitation of machinery. S. J. Chapman, *Work and Wages*, Pt. I, 171ff.; L. C. A. Knowles, *Econ. Development of British Overseas Empire* (London, 1924), 331; Clapham, *op. cit.*, 128; Montagu, *Times*, Sept. 18, 1912. Eng. mfgs. complained when Post Office in 1901 contracted for Am. equipment.

³ G. B. Shaw, ed., *Fabian Essays in Socialism* (London, 1889), 62–101; Lloyd, *Lloyd*, I, 75; *Report on U.S. Legislation affecting Trusts, Ac. & P.*, 1895 (C. 7641), No. 1, Commercial; Cox, *British Industries*, 107; A. Marshall, *Principles of Economics* (5th ed., London, 1907), App. A; Marshall bears witness to the development of Am. economic studies and thought. Kidd, *Principles of West. Civ.*, 404–73; Hubbard, *Times*, Feb. 20, 1902; Clapham, *Times*, Feb. 3, 1903; cf. G. Myers, *Am. Strikes Back*, 316–17, 326–27; U.S. Industrial Commission, *Industrial Combinations in Europe* (Washington, 1901), vol. xviii, pp. 7, 8, 23, 36.

[4] *Report of Committee upon Combination in the Meat Trade; Evidence, etc.,* P.P., 1909 (Cd. 4643, 4661), xv, p. 8; P. *Debs.,* 1908, 190:416, 436, 446; 192:853, 1496; 1910, 18:67, 79, 92; 1913, 54:795, 1654. The embargo on live cattle from S. Am. was viewed by opponents as increasing the danger of the American beef trust. For reports on cattle and meat trade in U.S., see *Ac. & P.,* 1897, lxxxviii, Mis. Ser. No. 403; 1899, xcvii, No. 481; 1900, xci, No. 537; 1902, ciii, No. 581; on cold storage, 1901, lxxx, No. 545.

[5] Glasgow, *Times,* Mar. 20, 1902; Bernhard Huldermann, *Albert Ballin* (London, 1922), chap. v; P. *Debs.,* 1902, 107:30, 426, 458ff., 462, 475, 477, 488ff.; 108:850; 112:1119–20; 113:228. Bryce warned against any hasty or impossible trust regulation. W. Wetherell, *Fort. R.,* 1902, 71:523. Mr. Pirie also suggested that harbor improvements in British ports should be borne chiefly, if not wholly, by the National Exchequer as was done in the States; see *Times,* July 4, 1902. Balfour, *Times,* Sept. 30, 1902. Note crusading novel for preferential tariffs inspired by the combine, S. J. Duncan, *The Imperialist* (London, 1904), 206–07, 399–407. Lawson, *Cont. R.,* Nov. 1902; Watts, *Times,* Feb. 18, 1905. Sir Thomas Sutherland hoped the Bd. of Trade would prevent any "Morgans" from making the Atlantic an American lake. Grey, *P. Deb.,* 1904, 138:395ff. *Report of the Royal Commission on shipping "rings,"* P.P., 1909, xlvii–xlviii; see esp., xlvii, pp. 6, 62–67; report contains interesting evidence of Am. competition.

[6] As held by Hoffman, *Anglo-German Trade Rivalry,* 285; see also 198–201, 259–61, 262; this excellent volume emphasizes the German threat although much of the material used actually discusses American competition, esp. from 1890 onwards. É. Halévy, *Hist. of Eng. People, 1895–1905,* 13, 126, 288, 303; Victor Bérard in *British Imperialism* (London, 1906), 200–04, emphasized the American threat. Cox, *British Industries under Free Trade,* 76, 107, 235–52, 333; also *American Progress and British Commerce* (London, 1902). B. Kidd, *Principles of West. Civil.,* relied much on Bryce; W. J. Ashley, ed., *British Industries* (London, 1903); P. *Debs.,* 1904, 129:906; 1906, 153:953ff., 1001ff., 1033; 157:1521–22. Parkes, *Times,* May 28, 1903; Chamberlain, *Times,* Oct. 28, Nov. 21, 23, 1903; Mar. 17, 1906, p. 8. P. *Debs.,* 1901, 90:41–42; 91:1100; Jeyes and How, *Vincent,* p. 222. *Political Writings of Richard Cobden* (London, 1867), I, 130; Wemyss Reid, *Memoirs and Correspondence of Lyon Playfair* (London, 1899), 371. J. M. Keynes, *Alfred Marshall, 1842–1924, a memoir* (London, 1924), 324, 362; in 1890, Marshall, under chairmanship of Lord Goschen, was active in promoting an economic society which imitated American Economic Association rather than an English "learned society" in that membership did not confer any sort of diploma. A. C. Pigou, ed., *Memorials of Alfred Marshall* (London, 1925), *passim.* Marshall could not agree with the conclusions of Prof. E. R. A. Seligman (of Columbia U.) whom the "Birmingham League and Ashley quote with such reverence." Marshall considered our economic literature, official and unofficial, as the best means of studying such things as price, transportation, etc. Anne Ashley, *W. J. Ashley* (London, 1932), 65, 69, 88, 102–03, 118; see his introd. to 1911 ed. of *Tariff Problems;* Ashley believed Ger. and Eng. were marked out to be friends in face of U.S. and Russia.

M. Frewen, *Melton Mowbray,* 181, 268–70; after one of his visits he read a paper to the Newcastle Farmers' Club on *American Competition* (2nd ed., London, 1885); he raised a clamor in Eng. by advocating trade in live cattle. Note description of dinner with Simon Cameron, John Bright, and Joe Chamberlain during which the latter revealed he had studied American tariff arguments. Hay called

Frewen an "argento-maniac" who hailed Bryan as the greatest personality since Lincoln. Cf. Lord Farrer (1819–1899) who understood American conditions, but never deviated from free trade principles or the gold standard.

[7] Only a few pertinent references can be given from a mass of speeches and literature. *P. Debs.*, 1904, 129:934, 623–33, 639; 1903, 123:196; 1905, 143:1468 where Mr. Moulton complains that G.B. has not shown anything like our industrial genius; 1906, 153:982; 1907, 172:1442; 174:891; 1911, 21:329, 393; 1913, 51:493; 52:310, 312, 1692–93; 1914, 58:678, 690–91, 719, 728; on sugar tax, 1901, 95:985, 991, 994, 1241. Drage's *Imp. Org. of Trade* (London, 1911), 239ff., 257ff., 313–20, 342; Morley, *Times*, Nov. 4, 1903, Jan. 20, 1904; Mosely, *Times*, Nov. 2, 1904; A. J. Low, *Protection in the U.S.* (London, 1904); Courtney, *Times*, Oct. 26, 1901; Lloyd George, *Times*, Jan. 1, 10, 1906; J. Chamberlain, *Times*, June 8, Oct. 7, 8, 9, Dec. 17, 1903; Jan. 16, Aug. 5, 1904; Feb. 2, 1905; Jan. 11, 1906; Bryce, *Times*, Oct. 9, 1903. Prof. W. A. S. Hewins argued in an Imperial Tariff Committee leaflet (1903) that Am. expansion meant we would soon use up all of our wheat. Asquith, *Times*, Jan. 5, 20, 1906; Hoffman, *op. cit.*, 262, "The agitation for tariff reform was a major issue in the election of 1906 and it centered national attention, perhaps as never before, on the German trade danger." Reformers did not single out Germany for discussion. Goschen, *Times*, Nov. 25, 1903; Balfour, *Times*, Nov. 18, 1909; on Runciman, *Scots.*, Nov. 20, 1907.

[8] *P. Debs.*, 1903, 123:192, 500, 544–45; 124:113; 1904, 129:662, 873, 928, 932, 939, 940, 946, 1047, 1079; 131:673; 1907, 169:802; 171:1270; Rosebery, *Manch. G.*, Nov. 26, 1903; Churchill, *Manch. G.*, June 17, 1904; Ritchie, *Times*, Oct. 10, 1903; Balfour, *P. Debs.*, 1903, 123:165; Boscawen, *Times*, Nov. 9, 1903; Tariff Reform League, *Times*, July 22, 1903; Brit. Assoc., *Times*, Sept. 16, 1903.

[9] *P. Debs.*, 1904, 129:747–48; 1905, 150:491ff., 530; 1907, 169:790ff.; 174:871, 893; 175:1224ff.; after a visit Lord Grimthorpe concluded that Americans felt dumping injured them more than it did England. Hendricks, *Carnegie*, 184, 189, 194; Carnegie cited Rosebery and the *Standard* in support. Harry Johnston, *My Life*, 400.

[10] Lord Playfair, who was frequently cited during the post-1900 fiscal discussion, had said at the passage of the McKinley tariff that if disaster and ruin did not follow, G.B. must reconsider her whole position and policy. It was rumored that Chamberlain had said it was Irish political organization, not Protection, which caused American corruption. Bryce, *P. Debs.*, 1902, 110:54; 1905, 143:1619ff., 1632ff., 1635–38; Churchill, *P. Debs.*, 1903, 123:194; 1904, 129:915; Austin Taylor, M.P., *Side-Lights on Protection: How the American Tariff has killed American Shipping* (London, 1905); Haldane, *Scots.*, Oct. 6, 1903; Cromer, *Times*, June 3, 1908; A. Chamberlain, *P. Debs.*, 1910, 14:221ff.; see also 257, 262, 263; 1909, 3:277; 10:927, 940, 960; 1911, 21:372, 505, 525.

[11] Perhaps with the exception of the U.S., Sir E. Grey thought the lot of workmen was more secure and more satisfactory under free trade. Balfour, *P. Debs.*, 1910, 14:403–04, 407. Mr. A. J. Sherwell (*ibid.*, 1909, 4:1488ff.) went into elaborate comparisons on unemployment to show that Earl Winterton, who had based his information on a pamphlet, was incorrect. Lloyd George rather held to the view that Protection caused the financial troubles of 1907; see *P. Debs.*, 1908, 193:686ff., 694; 1907, 174:878. Walter Long disputed Snowden's figures and cited *Am. Common.* to show our working class was better off. *Cost of Living in*

American Towns, P.P., 1911 (Cd. 5609), lxxxviii; vol. was fifth in a series; found labor dietary more liberal and varied, hours slightly shorter. *P. Debs.*, 1903, 123: 844, 910; 1904, 129: 959, 1042–43; 1906, 153: 1021ff.; 1907, 170: 637–38; 171: 472–73, 665; 180: 320–21; 1908, 185: 530; 186: 572; 189: 1622; 196: 1781; 1909, 1: 309–10; 2: 1224, 1625; 12: 1742, 1746, 1870, 1874, 1898, 1911, 1914; 1910, 14: 286, 390–01, 590; 15: 3; 1911, 21: 883; 24: 1357; 25: 15; 1912, 34: 99, 126, 137, 155–56, 783ff., 795, 814, 833, 851–53, 859.

¹² Cf. Hoffman, *op. cit.*, chaps. iv and v; Schooling, *op. cit.*, 421, 425; *Commercial Mission to S. America, Ac. & P.*, 1899 (c.–9100), xcvi, pp. 17, 18, 19, 28; *Foreign Trade Competition, etc., P.P.*, 1899 (c.–9078), xcvi, p. 97; also *P.P.*, 1901, lxxxiii, An. Ser. No. 2595; *Ac. & P.*, 1898, xciii, Mis. Ser. No. 455, pp. 4, 6, 10; *ibid.*, Mis. Ser. No. 442; in *Ac. & P.*, see 1897, xcvii, An. Ser. No. 1985; 1898 (c. 8648–116), xcix, An. Ser. No. 2094, p. 4; 1899, ciii, An. Ser. No. 2315, report by W. H. D. Haggard; 1914 (Cd. 7048–60), lxxxix, An. Ser. No. 5243; in *P.P.*, see An. Series of Commercial Reports, No. 2473, 1900, xciii, p. 3; No. 2647, 1901, lxxxv, pp. 4, 9; No. 2674, lxxxv, p. 36; No. 2825, 1902 (Cd. 786–129), cxi, pp. 3, 4; No. 2988, 1903 (Cd. 1386–65), lxxix, p. 21.

¹³ Sir Charles Bruce, *The Broad Stone of Empire* (London, 1910), I, 147, 154–58; A. L. Burt, *Imperial Architects* (Oxford, 1913), 152, 187–88; S. Low, *19th Cent.*, May, 1902; W. T. Stead, *Americanization*, Preface, 16, 20ff., 26; Beach, *P. Debs.*, 1904, 129: 687; Seddon, *Times*, June 18, 1902; Cockburn, reporting that Australia rejoiced to have U.S. in the Pacific, *Times*, July 22, 1905; *Conditions and Prospects of British Trade in Australia, P.P.*, 1907 (Cd. 3639), lvi, based partly on visit of 1905; for New Zealand, *P.P.*, 1908 (Cd. 3867), lxxiii, inspection made in 1906. *Commercial Mission to South Africa, etc., P.P.*, 1904 (Cd. 1844), lxi; Sir John Robinson, *Colonies and the Century* (London, 1899), 19.

Mr. Dillon, while discussing the Military Works Bill, 1899, objected to spending money on barracks at Bermuda, Jamaica, and Halifax. See *P. Debs.*, 1899, 73: 1367, 1368; 1901, 95: 953; 1902, 115: 283, 300, 325. Spencer, *Times*, Nov. 29, 1902, p. 12; "Imperialist" in *Fort. R.*, July, 1907, proposed to exchange them for Philippines. *Reports, etc., Royal Commission on West India, P.P.*, 1898 (Cd. 8655–57, 8669, 8799), l–li; *Proceedings of Conference relating to trade relations between the West Indies and Canada* (Barbados, 1908); *Report, etc., Royal Commission on trade relations between Canada and the West Indies, P.P.*, 1910 (Cd. 5639), xi, Pt. I, pp. 6, 21, 27; cf. the evidence taken in London, W. Indies, and Canada, Parts 2–4; evidence might suggest W. Indies were less fearful than Canada of the U.S. Louis S. Meikle, *Confederation of the British West Indies versus Annexation to the U.S. of A.* (London, 1912), regarding U.S. as a social enemy but a commercial friend. James R. Boose, *Memory Serving: being reminiscences of fifty years of the Royal Colonial Institute* (London, 1928), 195–96. Gideon Murray, *A United West Indies* (London, 1912); Sir H. H. Johnston, *Common Sense in Foreign Policy* (London, 1913), chap. vi, for a confederation; C. D. Mackellars, *Pleasure Pilgrim in S. Am.* (1908), have a care lest U.S. get Jamaica. On Newfoundland, see *P. Debs.*, 1907, 171: 495ff., 506ff., 526ff. London press generally in 1906 considered Newfoundland Convention a bad bargain. Gelber, *Anglo-Am. Friendship*, 162–63.

¹⁴ Our influence upon Canada had much to do with the formation or proposals of such organizations as the British Empire League (1894) and the British Empire Club (1906). Campbell-Bannerman and Sir R. Reid, while complaining against the huge military expenditures in 1901, protested against openly and avowedly tak-

ing Canada into account; *P. Debs.*, 1901, 93: 1576; 94: 835–36. Dewey, *Dominions and Diplomacy*, II, 334, 73ff., 332, 342–43; I, 30, 188–96; Thayer, *Hay*, II, 234; A. G. Bradley, *Canada in the Twentieth Century* (Westminster, 1903); W. A. S. Hewins, *Apologia of an Imperialist* (London, 1929), I, 144, 254, 263; Hewins explained to Balfour in Dec. 1908 the tariff machinery of France and U.S. Ashley, *Times*, Nov. 12, 1903; Laurier, *Times*, May 1, 1907, May 24, 1911. *Report on the Conditions and Prospects of British Trade in Canada, P.P.*, 1908 (Cd. 3868), lxxi, pp. 17, 26, 32–35, 36; cf. Cd. 6870 in 1913. Jacob Viner, *Canada's Balance of International Indebtedness, 1900–1913* (Cambridge, Mass., 1924), chap. xii; *P. Debs.*, 1902, 111: 1255–56; 1907, 169:902, 790ff.; 1910, 14:275 (Steele-Maitland); 19:1471, 1476, 1510–11.

15 In the reciprocity debates, Balfour found difficulty too in that U.S. held to old British view of fifty years past on favored-nation clause. Reciprocity aroused Mr. Hunt to ask whether we were not violating the Bagot-Rush treaty. *P. Debs.*, Lords, 1911, 7:20, 309, 316; 8:578, 595, 605–06; Commons, 21:57, 67–68, 71ff., 304ff., 316, 322, 323, 354, 363–68, 486, 513, 544ff., 1521; 22:13–16, 523–24, 1275, 1286–90; 23:584, 1036–37, 1046; 25:415, 570–71, 821–22; 26:1115–16; 29:1916–17; 30:682–88, 1247–48, 1942, 1948; Commons, 1912, 38:24–28, 166–67, 405. W. R. Lawson, in *Canada and the Empire* (1911), not underestimating Am. threat, counseled Imperial Federation; Bonar Law, *Times*, May 22, 1912; Bryce to Grey, in *Ac. & P.* (Cd. 5523), liii, p. 5; *Am. Common.* (1895), II, 528; (1913), p. 585.

VIII

BUSINESS NOT AS USUAL

BUSINESS and trade contacts facilitated the American impact. Such contacts, maintained by the governments, chambers of commerce, commercial advisers, agents, trade journals, exhibitions, and other obvious means, and aided by various channels already discussed, are among the strongest factors in the migration of national experience.[1] Yet as a caveat it is necessary to quote the *Economist*, December 31, 1910:

In view of the close connection between British and American commerce, we are apt to rely too much on second-hand knowledge of American affairs and opinions.

American-made products or artifacts in the United Kingdom affected the material interests of certain groups, and inspired qualitative judgments among the masses inasmuch as the products did not always lose the tag of foreign origin. American industries in Great Britain were an even stronger channel. American capital investments tended to become depersonalized and denationalized, but their very existence received publicity, certainly more publicity proportionately than similar American investments in Canada. British investments and trade in the United States suggested a knowledge of our economic life; six hundred million dollars worth of British-controlled enterprises in the United States (in July 1914) meant a direct contact with America's experience.

The significant but very elusive story of our industries and commercial ventures abroad is still shrouded in darkness. All the paraphernalia of that activity made a tangible impression and illustrated our technique more than capital investments which were made primarily for the exploitation of natural resources. Britons, after careful reflection, attributed much of their knowledge about us to our industrial representation abroad. No matter how great the conformity to national habits, an American plant never loses entirely its identity in the neighborhood. Sometimes its employees have very definite views respecting American characteristics. In addition, Britons were often sent to the United States for instruction. One may suggest, however, that the branch factory is often more secretive than the parent company in the States. But American merchandizing methods became better known when such firms as Singer Sewing Machine, Pittsburg Wire, Deering Harvester, and the National Cash Register companies found it desirable to extend their foreign sales organizations.

Group reactions cannot be completely explained by the trade statistics. Severe competition or invasions of the home market aroused interest in our methods. But the newer branches of industry (e. g., electrical and chemical engineering as compared with mechanical engineering) seemed more open to American suggestions, not always in direct relation to outstanding achievements. Capital watched the American scene more than did labor. The crisis of 1929, which forced many American branches to form public companies, stimulated additional British attention. Getting started takes longer than most American firms anticipate. Schemes which may be declining at home, such as door-to-door selling, may take on new life. The American Chamber of Commerce and the International Chamber of Commerce, and British organizations such as the Association of Chambers of Commerce and the Federation of British Industries have improved information service since the World War.

There were probably not more than a dozen firms of American origin, including banking houses, in England immediately after the Civil War.[2] According to a study made by Paul Dickens there were in 1929 about 389 American-owned factories, refineries, and merchandising branches in Great Britain. Another list of January 1937 noted about 236 American-owned branch plants or associated companies in the United Kingdom. American companies with British agents are of course more numerous. About 40 per cent of American manufacturing investments in Europe is centered in Great Britain, and automotive and rubber industries constitute the largest item in branch factory investment. Of the manufacturing investments established between 1860 and 1914 (either as American companies or foreign units), seventy were still in existence in 1932. In 1900 the total number of American branch factories could not have exceeded seventy-five. The impact would still be of major proportions even if much of the American experience were thrown overboard. Some American firms are proud of their English achievements, others are not. The failures would be as revealing for history as the successes. This is also true of British investments.

The unhappy memory of our repudiated states' debts lingered throughout the period; delinquencies of local governments in the seventies and eighties added more unhappiness; large holdings in the ups and downs of American railroads kept British capital awake. The purchase or profit of American investments was instrumental in forming many opinions about the United States.[3] Although our securities wandered abroad in many ways, most of them had been issued in American cities and were then used as collateral in London. What L. H. Jenks says of the early nineteenth century holds true to a surprising extent up to 1914:

America was so distant that so far as the ultimate British purchaser was concerned her securities could not well be differentiated.

Bank agents and promoters such as H. Osborne O'Hagan might do better, and their reports probably permeated through important minorities to increase the store of profitable knowledge. Two Americans started the *Financial News*, one of the first financial papers for the general public. American stocks inspired a Scottish bank clerk to send out thousands of leaflets which purported to give exclusive information on a coming rise in Erie Railroad stock; the rush to buy and the consequent rise netted him a large profit.

In 1838 the American market was definitely established in the London Stock Exchange; the first regular exchange of prices between London and New York began in August 1866. American bankers such as George Peabody, Joshua Bates, and Sam Ward had been familiar figures in England; many British financiers had cut their teeth in Wall Street. In raising money for American breweries and meat companies, O'Hagan made use of a new kind of security, certificates of indebtedness based on liquid assets; but it is remarkable that in his long career he used this procedure only once for an English company. The *Scotsman* might well remark that most people regretted they ever had anything to do with American breweries on any terms, a business that "had been conducted on the approved

Yankee principle of killing and being killed." Investment buying
had always been pushed by charming prospectuses, one of which the
Economist in 1905 picked out as glorifying "worthless" American
oil companies in Colorado. Many of the high-sounding mining companies promoted by Albert Grant came to grief; an American medical man selling "Florida Water" (a lotion) in Argentina got the
Argentine concessions with which Messrs. Baring Bros. and Co.
floated themselves into the "Baring crisis." A bulwark of British
credit, Overend, Burney and Co., failed in 1865 partly because of
the Atlantic and Great Western default. Warner, whose name was
a household word because of "Warner's Safe Cure" and "Warner's
Log Cabin Remedies," although a member of the New York Stock
Exchange, professed to know nothing about finances when he came
to London to form an English company. By skilful manipulation he
caught the "stags" and "bears" of the City in one of the biggest
"ramps" known for years. After a hectic career in Chicago, Whitaker
Wright came late in life to flash across London's financial skies. One
of the curious figures in the City was Sir J. H. Puleston, who built
up his Anglo-American reputation as one of the managers of Wells,
Fargo and Co.; he returned to England as head of the new London
office of McCulloch and Co., New York bankers, and became M.P.
for Devonport.

Companies like the American Mortgage Co. of Scotland, the
English Association of American Bond and Share Holders, and the
British Investment Trust had special interests in the United States
and reported upon conditions there. British land companies such as
the Capital Freehold Land and Investment Co., Ltd. controlled
millions of acres of American land. Seven British mortgage companies, with a capital of forty-five million dollars, were still operating in 1914. By 1913 British investments in the United States
amounted to more than one-third of the total outside the Empire;
probably the United States in 1899 furnished about one-half of
Britain's income from abroad. British investments in our future
amounted to 4,250 millions of dollars in 1914. Railway bonds,
which had always been considered highly speculative, made up most
of the European holdings at the outbreak of the World War. The
reports on British holdings by the American Dollars Securities Committee (1915–1919), which tried to protect the pound during the

war, showed that about 10 per cent of such securities were utility bonds and shares, and 13 per cent were issues of industrial companies. On all classes of investment, according to Lewis, Britain had perhaps done well with her money in our securities. The increasing American purchase of British securities from 1900 to 1914 was just as important as an influence and accounted for some of the misgivings of 1900–02 when American purchases ranged from Consols to English tobacco firms. As a broad cultural factor, it seems very possible that Britain was more interested in a comprehensive picture of our life when we were her debtor, but this is not clear-cut, partly because on *private* accounts America was still a debtor in 1936.

As basic to commercial importance, one must also consider the impression that America seemed to be outstripping England in invention.[4] Britons attributed this to systematic pursuit, proper rewards for labor's ingenuity and the inventors' rights, and sound patent laws which appealed to the Patent Law Reform Association and others who complained of England's expensive procedure and indifference. From 1896 there was a steady increase of patent applications or grants in England to American inventors. Between 1884 and 1908, residents in the United States had made 62,802 applications as compared with 52,730 from Germany. The boom years were 1898 and 1901 to 1904. Many American inventions were also "given away in England by the premature publication in America of the inventor's proceedings." Such news went abroad and was fatal to a future patent application in England. America's share of important discoveries and inventions had almost equaled England's during the period 1876–1900, and England was acutely aware that between 1901 and 1908 our share (second only to Germany) was almost three times as great as hers. By providing for the revocation of patents not worked in the United Kingdom, the Patents and Designs Act (1907) was said to have brought American factories to England.

Expositions, fairs, and celebrations also have international repercussions in many aspects of life and work.[5] They are sometimes dramatic summaries of achievements which stimulate the exchange of ideas, primarily, but not solely, in technology. Such exhibitions in the United States, perhaps not so influential as our exhibits on foreign soil, have brought congresses and special delegations which took the opportunity to make suggestions based upon American developments. Although Britain's first official participation in an international exhibition was at New York, 1853, our first notable impression was made at Philadelphia in 1876. Lowthian Bell made a detailed comparison of the iron industry, and added the important fact that Americans gladly showed British ironmasters about. If protection were given up, reported Isaac Watts, our textile industry would become a world competitor. W. W. Hulse demonstrated the superior ingenuity of our textile machinery; the Lord Provost of Glasgow suggested that British manufacturers might learn about the use of nickel and building and household ironmongery. Although earlier exhibits at London, Paris, and Vienna had produced some concern, many British visitors were deeply impressed by the more complete display of our machine tools. We were thought to be Britain's most powerful competitor in edge tools, the leader in substituting the emery wheel for planing machines, an influence on Canadian technique, and the new mecca for students of factory organization. When commenting on electric and telegraphic apparatus, Sir William Thomson praised our application of science to practice, more efficient patent laws, and willingness to adopt new ideas.

Partly because of high tariffs, Britons were lukewarm to the exhibitions at Chicago (1893) and that "outlandish place," St. Louis (1904). But the conferences which Chicago inaugurated, and St. Louis continued, served as contacts for many professional groups. British participation in these two fairs was thought to be politically necessary and significant. When describing the magnificence of the Chicago exhibition, Mr. William Emerson told British architects:

I only mention it to show what can be done by intelligent control, and I do not think we are behind our American cousins in either intelligence or capacity for design.

Lord Alverstone concluded that the British electrical industry did not half represent England there because the opinion had got about that Americans were far in advance, "which they were not." The Prince of Wales advised English manufacturers to realize the importance of the St. Louis show so that England could hold her own in our eyes. Relying upon his long experience with exhibitions, Sir William Henry Preece, Engineer-in-Chief to the Post Office, declared, "The way in which an American . . . deals with his business makes me ashamed of my countrymen." A furniture maker, whose American business had increased threefold since St. Louis, believed that we were not sufficiently well educated in high-class workmanship to do England any harm. Another exhibitor decided that our taste in glass products was most lamentable. Both expositions prompted Britons to credit us with having cheapened such displays by indiscriminate awards and side shows. In general, in spite of doubtful trade gains and suspicion that Americans were greater puffers, they impressed England with the great possibilities of American industry, and sometimes even culture.

The American exhibits in Great Britain, and also at Paris in the crucial year 1900, reached the consciousness of a greater portion of the British populace. Not much seems to have been made of our participation in the first great international exhibition at London, 1851, except as an opportunity for fraternal meetings, and discussions about a few ingenious processes and our "characteristic energy." One of the few things which received special attention was a meat biscuit from Texas. A Yorkshireman with business connections in the States, John Robinson Whitley, began his series of national exhibitions of arts, manufactures, and resources at Earl's Court on May 9, 1887, with America because he felt that Europe "already looks to the United States as the vanguard in the march of both material and moral progress . . ." This was the first American exhibition outside the United States. The press received this difficult private enterprise in good spirit and predicted that fantastic notions about us would be dissipated. In a dark moment, Whitley with some regret decided to use Buffalo Bill's Wild West and "local color" to strengthen the event. This no doubt helped to push attendance to 2,230,173, and resulted in the happy picture of Gladstone meeting Red Shirt, the Sioux Indian chief. Some critics saw in the fine arts section not only a skilful use of Parisian training but also a good promise for the future. Many of the paintings were selected to illustrate events in our history. The loan collection of American hunting trophies demonstrated the British sportsmen's knowledge and destruction of our West; the gardens reminded the English of their debt to native American trees and flowers. Apparently the working class was not so displeased as the artisans at the prospect of popularizing our manufacturing in England; the London Working Men's Association looked to this exhibit to promote friendliness among the laborers of both countries.

We exerted ourselves at Paris in 1900, where our exhibitors were double those from Great Britain. Although the British were not so exuberant as the Americans over this comprehensive evidence of progress, they were impressed and in a mood to ponder the lessons. It was a surprise to many, said Sir Albert Rollit, to witness the great progress of America and Germany in special machinery; Germany, we contended, had merely made excellent imitations. The Bethlehem Steel Corporation exhibit of high-speed tool steel contributed in a large degree to the development of that industry in England, even though a British juror decided that England was slow in profiting from us in general machinery. Another juror suggested that English toolmakers must educate their customers in the use of labor-saving devices and specialization. One British exhibitor, who declared the British felt small, pronounced the exhibit of harvesting machinery as "simply magnificent" and dispelling the fear that we wanted to copy from England, he sent his workmen and foremen to learn from American brains. Non-technical exhibits also had repercussions across the channel.

The press hailed the Glasgow International Exhibition (1901) which taught more about American labor-saving machinery; but the *Manchester Guardian* could not understand the furor since our exhibits were few.[6] The announcement of an American Exhibition at the Crystal Palace for the summer of 1902 came at the height of interest in us. "The hope of the Crystal Palace directors," it was announced, "is not only to appeal to the British trader but to arouse public interest in everything American, including the methods by which American commerce has been so vastly increased in the course of the last generation." The first reports were not very enthusiastic. No great impression was made by the Golden West and American Industries Exhibition at Earl's Court, May to October 1909, which offered as dramatic stimulants displays of the Red Man, Coney Island, and Chicago's Central Market. Buffalo Bill in 1887, 1892, and 1902 had already brought the West to the British public. Numerous special exhibitions, such as that of Business and Advertising from 1907 onwards, and of Gas and Electrical Appliances (Glasgow,

1911) made more fundamental impressions upon technical groups. In 1913 the London Chamber of Commerce exhibited samples of American hardware, hollow-ware, and tools which had found favor in the New Zealand market. The cultural effectiveness of the celebrations marking a hundred years of Anglo-American peace was marred by the outbreak of the World War.[7] An influential committee appealed for £50,000 to carry out the erection of monuments in Canada, England, and the United States, to establish an Anglo-American professorship and annual prizes for essays on Anglo-American relations. A general committee met in March 1913 to lay plans for an Anglo-American Exposition at White City, Shepherd's Bush. The Fine Arts Section brought for the first time to British attention 407 American canvases, with the artists classified according to their residence in France, England, or the United States. Meanwhile, in the face of strong opposition, the Government had decided not to exhibit at the Panama exhibition scheduled for San Francisco in 1915.[8] Sentiment, rather than knowledge, was exchanged at many other celebrations.

British opinion, which differed not so much according to social classes as to business groups, professed to see national differences in the means and ends of business which were often to America's discredit. Communists who desired weapons with which to cudgel the capitalistic system might well have used either conservative or radical British observations on our business and finance. Our hypertrophic business had clouded the outlook for a successful industrial democracy. While her pride as commercial leader, or such stereotypes as our speed, inefficient hustle, freebooting, or shoddiness, might condition her approach, she could not easily avoid the lessons, both good and bad, afforded by our growing economic system.[9] Eyes were turned as much to selling and distribution as they were to production.

One thing seemed clear—our excessive devotion to success. Even sympathetic journals concluded that an Englishman "rarely drives a bargain to the extreme point which an American regards as justifiable." "Broadly speaking," said the *Spectator* in criticizing Standard Oil, "the Englishman in his business relations never forgets the good old English maxim of 'Live and Let Live.'" Company promoting and corporation reports led many journals to observe that

Americans were unhampered by scruples which prevailed elsewhere. Making a distinction that was easily forgotten, the *Economist* declared in 1906:

We doubt if the general public, and even some financiers in the United States, fully recognize how deeply rooted is the distrust in this country not of the general honesty of the American people, but of the business methods of many of the great industrial undertakings.

An unethical atmosphere prevailed where a bankrupt might easily regain his position. E. L. Godkin, who, disillusioned by our imperialism and moral decline, returned to the English society he had repudiated in his youth, wrote January 22, 1902, "American methods are much more in favor over here than they once were, and the art of lying is much more popular." Our vital importance as a food basket and source of raw materials put a sinister aspect on any such episodes as wheat rings in Chicago or New York, or excessive cotton speculation.

During the progress of the Petroleum Bill through Parliament, Americans were regarded suspiciously; the statement was repeated everywhere that England was being made the dumping ground for oil of a dangerous, low flash-point which Americans would sell but not buy. A few fatal fires attributed to this oil made the East Londoners eloquent on the subject; "Death in the Lamp" was a current topic; whenever a baby was burnt there appeared a large picture of Rockefeller, or somebody else, described as an inhuman monster. Standard Oil, it was alleged, had flooded the Commons with literature and lobbied to prevent the raising of the flash-point—and it wasn't raised. On the happier side was Professor C. F. Chandler (1836–1925) who became known in England for his flash-point tests, his efforts to reduce lamp explosions, and his testimony to the House of Lords. Opinions got about in curious ways. In the City of London Court a woman sued an American contractor, who prided himself on speed, for damages from poisoning by gas; in repairing the street, the plaintiff's counsel argued, the American company had "hustled" so much with reckless men on piecework that the gas mains were punctured. The financial jugglings, intricate balance sheets, and fantastic extravagance of Whitaker Wright, a native with an American accent, easily misled some papers in 1903 and 1904 to label him an American. Curiously enough, the scandal over the American Marconi Company shares, which almost exclusively involved British leaders, was associated in many minds with American corruption or trickery. During the inquiry a series of questions turned upon a knowledge of American character:

Lord Cecil: "I am assuming that they are ordinary human beings." Mr. Booth: "They are extraordinary."

The circumstances surrounding the flotation of the Marconi shares, April 1912, induced Major Archer-Shee to get leave in 1914 to bring in a bill to control foreign companies.

The only representative of the American male species who could compete in drama or fiction with the American woman was the unloved American business man, almost always a millionaire capable of doing good and evil on a scale impossible elsewhere. Many believed that he was a new type. Laurence Oliphant's unprofitable financial encounter with an American prophet produced one of the first popular expositions of the unsavory doings of American financiers in *The Autobiography of a Joint-Stock Company* (1876). One of Sir Walter Besant's first novels, *The Golden Butterfly* (1876), centered about an American millionaire who lost fortunes quickly and entered English society with ease. Louis J. Jennings wrote *The Millionaire* (1883), which was said to have depicted the career of Jay Gould. American millionaires cropped up everywhere. Kipling genially described in "An Habitation Enforced" how an American tycoon and his wife completely merged into the life of a Sussex village. Another wooed in W. E. Norris's *Vittoria Victrix* (1911). Little wonder that the deputation from the New York Chamber of Commerce to England in 1901 was thought to be composed entirely of millionaires, with the inconvenient result of a flood of begging letters. The numerous jokes in *Punch* about American titans resembled a Marxian viewpoint. In an expansive mood, however, Lord Rosebery pointed to Carnegie as a lesson in thrift. As we have noted, men like Gladstone had been eager to know how wealth was accumulated in America, and the permanence of such fortunes. In spite of Carnegie's lavish charity, England came to no definite conclusions as to the self-dissipating features of American wealth, and never lost its amazement at the rapidity of accumulation.

It is difficult to find a good word concerning the financial structure of America. English observers usually maintained that our private and governmental finance violated all economic canons; almost unanimously they persistently advised deep-reaching reforms in our currency, taxing, and banking system. The *Glasgow Herald* declared, "American financiers and American finance are regarded by the average British business man with something approaching envious contempt." The press concluded that financial jugglery made our stocks dangerous for the British public. Without improvements in banking, England prior to 1914 could hardly believe that New York would ever challenge London as the money market of the world. A period of severe disillusionment followed 1902 for those English believers in an enchanted land which could ignore economic laws. The *Scotsman* added in 1903 that our financial methods were "of the extravagant order." W. R. Lawson in his *American Finance* (1906) warned that sinister speculation would be the future peril of the American people.[10]

The panic of 1907, which was expected for some time in informed circles, elicited the harshest criticisms and proposals for more centralized power or a central bank to cope with the currency crisis. The *Manchester Guardian* (November 12, 1907) said, "We shall not escape the influence of American commercial depression, though with us it should not come as a cataclysm." The Bank of England raised its rate to 7% in November, the highest since 1873. Sir Felix Schuster told the general meeting of the Union of London and Smith's Bank that an efficient banking system might have averted the depression of 1907, but added, like the *Labour Leader*, that abuse of capital always led to failure. Cecil F. Parr of Parr's Bank believed, however, that there was too much glib talk about the panic because the English banking system was no less rigid. Many journals believed with the *Economist* that "The financial crisis in America is really a moral crisis." Roosevelt's message to Congress in December left widespread disappointment. The repercussions of the panic were indicated by the *Saturday Review:*

The Americans cannot complain if their present financial embarrassment is the cause in Europe of a little secret chuckling, of a good deal of open head-shaking, and of some rather Pharisaical comparisons of business methods.

Despite the fact that England had been uneasy in 1901 over the placing of national issues in the States, or that Mr. Dillon might cry out: "When we were obliged to fall back on syndicates of American banks, on the Morgans and Steel Trusts, to take ten or fifteen millions of our loans, it ought to give us pause in our mad career," hope was retained because our finance was a crazy quilt. The Federal income tax in 1913 indicated some improvement in government finance; Schuster early in 1914 declared that the new tariff and banking acts would make us a more formidable competitor. Willy-nilly, the World War did the trick.

Attention may be turned to other aspects of American business.[11] In spite of some doubt about our business ethics, eighty-three British insurance companies were still operating in the United States in 1934. There had for a long time been an interchange of experience in the insurance world. The United States helped in the collection of comprehensive statistics on fire insurance and the cultivation of actuarial insurance. The non-forfeiture system, first introduced in the States and devised to benefit retiring policy-holders by the reserve value of their insurance, found its way into the United Kingdom. Britain was reminded dramatically of our insurance world by scandals which, according to the *Times* (October 13, 1905), should have convinced America of the need of imitating English management. The extravagant management of American life insurance offices had been no secret. An unfortunate beginning in London and a libel suit brought by the Equitable Life against the *Financial Times* were poor advertisements. During the fight in 1906 between the Mutual Insurance Co. of New York and the North British and Mercantile Co. for the British policy-holders of the former company, many uncomplimentary things were said about American business. Mr. M. R. Pryor, chairman, propounded theories at the meeting of the Sun Life Assurance on the advantages of a proprietary life office because America's mutual societies had a tendency to go astray. The *Times* commented: "It is well that the lessons arising out of the faults of American insurance management should be emphasized for our instruction here. . . ." Professing no desire to pit English methods against American, or to cause panic, the Earl of Onslow expressed anxiety, especially since the New York Life, Mutual, and Equitable had eighty thousand British policy-holders, and advised strict legislation. A Select Committee (Lords) on Life Insurance Companies was appointed May 1, 1906.

Mixed with genuine regret for the San Francisco earthquake was uneasiness over the great liabilities to be met by British fire insurance companies. That event also emphasized the seriousness of disasters in a vast continent and contributed to the general impression that sensational events on a large scale were always taking place. So successfully had these losses been met that there was a rush to insure with British firms. The catastrophe led the British to desire a stronger earthquake clause. During the discussion of the Assurance Companies Bill in 1909, it was viewed as an insult by Sir Henry King that a Member who was impressed by America's gigantic disasters should have wanted to know what funds were available for British policy-holders in British companies. While the National Insurance Bill was being argued in 1911, those who wished for greater centralization pointed out our interest in a federal control of insurance. Our business conditions and the hodge-podge of legislation were live issues whenever various Companies Acts, as in 1900 or 1908, were under discussion; whether the problems were "guinea-pig" directors or the grant of shares at a discount, British business tendencies were sufficiently analogous to warrant westward glances.

A "service" movement in business went from America to Great Britain, namely, the Rotary. Two business men of Manchester and London had seen the movement on a visit to America, and returned in 1911 to organize a mere get-together club in London, and another in Manchester the following year. The London Club was recognized as Number Two because by a stream of Irish-American influence on a commission basis, Dublin had been organized in March 1911. Clubs followed in Belfast, Glasgow, Edinburgh, Liverpool, and Birmingham. Perhaps naturally at first for any movement originating in America, British business and professional men were attracted to Rotary merely as a possible aid to business; this attitude soon died out, but not soon enough to prevent public quips. The organization, one member to each profession, was unusual for Britain. Perhaps the British clubs have become more light and the American a bit more serious. An American visit in 1914 gave Thomas Stephenson of Edinburgh, prominent in Rotary and editor of *Rotary Wheel*, ideas for the consolidation and extension of Rotary in Great Britain and

Ireland. After 1914, Rotary's offer of service in time of war, and Anglo-American friendship, did much to extend the movement.

In selling and merchandising, national peculiarities must be served—or modified. It did not help American salesmen to emphasize their nationality because it was generally agreed that our salesmanship was too high-powered. Any textbook in the art had to be considerably changed to meet British tastes. The more receptive attitude was neatly summed up in a recent review of *The Sales Strategy of John Patterson:*

A description in detail of American sales methods, at first alarming in intensity to European ideas, yet possibly applicable in small doses in the form of a tonic. These same methods, modified to suit national prejudices, have proved successful in every country.

Professor C. H. Oldham, who spoke at the British Association in 1913 on the "Scientific Study of Business Organization," testified to the pervasiveness of American business methods and textbooks;

At present we had to look to American business men and to American universities for guidance in this study. This position was unsatisfactory, for American business organization and practice differed in some important respects from British organization and practice.

Trade journals were brightened, and "system" or "efficiency" journals were imitated before 1914.

High-pressure salesmanship by mail, although much used by American firms in England, had not developed extensively in pre-1914 Britain. "Mail-order business" or "postal trade" received an impetus from American firms; likewise, in immediate pre-War years, installment buying or "hire purchase." Large firms about 1902 were beginning to remind Englishmen of their "little account" in American bill-collecting style. Penny markets and "universal providers" were not new to the English when F. W. Woolworth and Company Ltd. (1909) opened stores in Liverpool, Preston, and Manchester. At first they were regarded as social outcasts which tainted those who entered, and peculiarly American in cheap quality, but they progressed with energy and new display tricks. Reorganized as a public company in 1932, Woolworth's is still "American" to many people. A deputation of the retail trade in 1904 protested to the Postmaster General against the cash-on-delivery system as a movement to centralize trade, and cited American opposition to the system! Numerous trading houses observed that the proportion of office staff to workmen was higher in the States; this led to the plea that England must train scientific men to sell the products of industry. Some manufacturers took the hint that a little more show and finish, and neater packing for display had helped our goods, which were often inferior to British products. Our generous use of modern office equipment was frequently described. The first National Cash Registers were sold in England in 1885; progress was slow up to 1895 when sales mounted to 739 machines. Between 1900 and 1904, partly because of our stimulus, sales rose steadily. In the typewriter business British salesmen modified our methods to meet British taste. American devices, machinery, and appliances were always prominent at commercial exhibitions; such American exhibits formed half the show at London in 1912. Outstanding among American articles which had succeeded in England—automatic carpet sweepers, rocking chairs, the American "runabouts," etc.—were roll-top desks and letter-file cabinets. Card indexes, loose-leaf ledgers, and improved filing systems were making their way slowly by 1908.

Mr. Frank H. Cooper in 1901 had concluded, after observing a strategical site in Oxford Street, London, that an American could make a pile of money out of a modern store. Later, a man interested in Waring and Gillow's suggested to Gordon Selfridge a store run on American lines; Selfridge, recognized then as definitely American, began his "invasion," an experiment which the press hailed as worthy of close observation. London building authorities feared he was planning a skyscraper. His career carried "American business practice, theories, and ideals" to England. Although at first inclined to be contemptuous of British management, he later decided not to make his store too American. Its colossal size and organization were accepted as being based on American models, and such was the declaration of his first advertisements in 1909. The big store was to create the demand. Papers pounced upon circus-like methods which might ruin small shopkeepers; but from the beginning Mr. Selfridge avoided "shrieking" ads and claimed some credit for having added an aesthetic appeal to British advertising. Customers liked the store without compartments, the glass display cases, the bargain basement, "no tips," spending without the eagle eye of a floor walker, and the money-back guarantee. Mr. Selfridge has mentioned the desirability of combining American "zip" and "go" with English poise.

That ardent yachting competitor Sir Thomas Lipton may not have won the America's Cup from us, but he derived valuable business experience in America. At the age of fifteen he was working in a New York grocery store as an assistant.

It was run on up-to-date methods. These I studied keenly all the time I was employed there. I thought I could see subtle differences between shopkeeping in America as compared with the methods of the tradespeople in Glasgow. The wares offered, the food sold, might not be any better, but it seemed to me they were "shown" to fuller advantage, the assistants took a more personal interest in the customers they served; in short, there was an "atmosphere" in a New York shop . . . which seemed to me to invite trade and hold it.

Eager to apply his experience, he returned to buy a small provision shop in Glasgow; Lipton stores soon spread throughout the United Kingdom. He was one of the first Britons to realize the value of advertising; "During my travels in America I had observed that the firms that were making good were all regular advertisers." He always felt at home in America;

Probably this was owing to the fact that at the outset of my American associations I became a strong admirer of the spirit of genial combativeness which is so essential a feature of the average American man —of the "go-get-it" determination which stamps Americanism all the way through. I felt, rightly or wrongly, that I had in me a dash of the American character.

The influence described in these frank confessions also meant something to other business men.

Our competition aroused criticisms against the British Government and the Board of Trade for being indifferent and not so helpful to traders and investors as the American Government. Sir Charles Dilke was one of the first to direct attention to our consular service. In 1886 and again in 1896, the quality of our detailed consular reports had moved the Foreign Office to issue further instructions to the British consular service. The Chamber of Commerce's action in directing attention to the work of governmental commercial advisers in the States led to the appointment of a Departmental Committee of the Board of Trade to consider the whole question of commercial intelligence, and under pressure from American examples, the Board of Trade established a Commercial Intelligence Branch. The press, trade journals, and popular opinion constantly praised for imitation our consular service, the Bureau of Foreign Commerce, and timely reports on sudden developments of new or special branches of industry. The Commercial Intelligence Bureau in Eastcheap, established by Mr. Sell of *Commercial Intelligence*, with William Harper as first manager, followed the system of information for world-wide dealers which had been successfully worked by the Commercial Museum (Philadelphia) which had been commended by British trade agents. It was thought that various commercial bodies and chambers of commerce were functioning with great success in helping our advance to commercial supremacy. Through the American Embassy, the Executive Council of the Association of Chambers of Commerce inquired in January 1903 into the constitution, administration, and financial set-up of the chambers of commerce in this country. Various British agents advised an examination of sales methods, quicker delivery, better and cheaper packing, and a fuller line of samples to meet inroads of American agents in world markets. In a more general way men like Lord Brassey were telling the Association that British manufacturers who occupied themselves too much with production must follow America (and Germany) in paying more attention to distribution. British commercial efficiency profited by this forced attention.

We first made England realize the power of advertisement and, to a degree, the need for advertising specialists and experts.[12] Perhaps the growing responsiveness to business enterprise for its own sake, no matter how worthless the goods, also received some encouragement from us. Our influence helped to modify the feeling, which was noticeable at least up to the War, that it was bad taste to patronize a firm that advertised. Many prejudices and conditions modified our technique. Where it has failed or has been received with hostility, the social historian of national characteristics could gather instructive material. However, one finds many tributes and much amazement regarding the American flavor in advertising. An Englishman, C. H. Stirrup, drew upon American experience in his *Direct Advertising*:

The reader will find many references to American practice. I readily admit that some of these are not likely to be adapted in Great Britain within the near future; though who shall say that they will not be in the course of time? . . . Talk to some executives in the language of scientific selling and they quickly surmise, with disapproval, a trans-atlantic influence. Then comes their favorite argument: "American methods are out of place here. They don't pay."

No doubt some American campaigns, right in principle, were poorly conducted. H. D. Bradley of Pope and Bradley, London, has said:

Closely allied as are the people of the United States and Great Britain, it is absurd to imagine that one identical style of advertising copy is suitable in both countries. Such copy would lack atmosphere in phraseology and in mentality.

J. Morgan Richards, a dealer in proprietary remedies, which had to be widely advertised like canned goods and breakfast cereals, was responsible for innovations in English advertising from 1867 onward. In one campaign Artemus Ward's humor was used in the copy. He also used posters for wall space and devised the first sixteen-sheet double demy poster ever seen in England. After opposition he finally persuaded the *Illustrated London News* to insert an illustrative advertisement with blocks, and he was probably the first to engage a full advertisement column in a single issue of a London daily and a whole back page of several London weeklies. He was also active in the advertising club, The Sphinx. Richards and Mr. Barratt, according to Sir George Riddell, changed the face of English papers. After predictions of failure, English shops soon followed Selfridge in issuing daily full-page advertisements in several newspapers. Business catalogues, such as those sent out by the Westinghouse Company, were so prepared as to be read and preserved. An engineer added:

Some of the American catalogues are perfect models of a convenient and necessary handbook for engineers. One of them is used as a text-book in some of the technical schools.

Structural steelmakers imitated these.

Various business exhibitions, as at Olympia in 1910, reminded the press that advertising was more highly developed in America. At the time of the Bradford Exhibition (1904), it was intimated that that town had learned how to "boost" from America, and this municipal lesson was of practical importance. During a discussion of the Health Resorts Bill (1914), Herbert Samuel expressed the pious hope that competitive municipal advertisement would not flourish as with us. While the International Correspondence Schools sponsored a national movement in 1913 to promote efficiency and selling organizations, Thomas Russell, president of the Incorporated Society of Advertising Consultants, reported that efficient salesmanship had already enabled Americans almost to monopolize in England many articles which might just as well be English. England followed the progress of our laws which related to advertising. Bryce found that the National Society for Checking the Abuses of Public Advertising had inspired several organizations in America; but that body itself frequently justified its existence by the foreign activities of American advertisers such as the Chicago firm which in 1901 placed signboards on Dover Cliffs. In 1914 the Advertisers' Protection Society was interested in a law even wider in scope than ours on the net sales statements of publications. All in all, many varieties of publicity, which is fundamentally a democratizing or popularizing process affecting many aspects of human existence, have derived inspiration from America.

Efficiency and management also afford a good field of speculation for those interested in national characteristics.[13] As in selling and advertising, American books on the subject were viewed as helpful if "salted" down. American pressure had made many voices cry out for better management in British industries. Some suggested the remodeling of factories along American lines, a freer use of young men, and a greater scope of initiative and action for factory managers. Not much original British work had been done before the War, and some American books on efficiency remained unthumbed; nevertheless, our development of scientific management was sometimes imitated. Efficiency propaganda in Europe usually took the form of translations of American books which possibly penetrated Europe more than England. Partly because of labor's suspicion of American methods, British scientific management has developed rather in the direction of psychological research. This attitude probably had its origin in the conviction that our labor was exploited and disorganized, and annoyance with the "superior" American workman who was used as a spur. British labor closely watched the resolutions of the A.F. of L. which condemned F. W. Taylor's principles, and it remembered this hostility rather than any evidence of our acceptance of scientific management. Any application of Taylor's principles, primarily after 1914, had to be modified to fit English tradition and labor opposition. Output and time studies, piece or bonus rates were usually found undesirable. Even American time-clocks did not speed up production as anticipated. A hearty reception for American shop methods, reported from Nottingham as early as 1901, appeared unique to the *American Machinist*.

G. C. Allingham, who was among the first to present Taylor's and Galbraith's philosophy of work management to England, said in 1912 that "the system is perhaps not as widely known and as generally understood in this country as it might be." The system at Messrs. Vickers had some relation to Taylor's methods. The *Engineer* decided in 1913 that in spite of all that was written "little change is apparent in our methods." Americans in 1913 could not persuade a number of papers to start a crusade against the fallacy of restricting output. Outside of labor's ranks there was also some fear that scientific management would harm the energy, and ultimately the morale, of the workers. Probably A. D. and M. McKillop's *Efficiency Methods* (1917) was the first English book to link up the work of Taylor and other Americans. In the face of this tradition and in spite of great changes since 1914, the selection of Mr. Bedaux, efficiency expert, as guide for the Duke of Windsor's proposed social exploration of America was hardly calculated to please British labor.

Although it has already been shown that the status of American labor had been of great importance in the agitation for tariff reform, a fuller discussion is now in order.[14] There was not much rhyme or reason to the viewpoints on American labor. One notable opinion which grew more decisive from 1898 to 1910 was that American labor was not likely to produce any far-reaching social movements, and not even in the rank and file did American labor excite much articulate interest, perhaps much less than one might expect since the American lodestone was attracting hordes of British workers. Anglo-American labor contacts were feeble and often fruitless. At an earlier period, according to Professor Klingberg, "the British laborer and his champions," who argued for greater political influence and a better social and economic status, had drawn heavily upon Anglo-American anti-slavery agitation. Only weakly now did labor find any popular, democratic ideal in the States. Capitalists drew more encouragement from and made more use of reports on American labor—on the open shop movement, the freedom of output, and the superior working qualities of Americans who were not under the domination of economic fallacies which harmed their British comrades. Among those remaining in the British Isles one encountered a curious situation: labor held our working conditions to be worse than England's, and capital suggested that they were better. Thus indirectly, through the force of American competition, there were repercussions which ran deeply into the social life of the country.

A proposal was made in 1871 to unite the English Amalgamated Society of Engineers and Machinists (which insisted upon maintaining its own branches in America) with the International Union of Machinists and Blacksmiths in this country. An English coöperative society, headed by Thomas D. Lorral of Manchester, proposed in 1875 an arrangement of direct exchange between the society and the National Grange in America. Not much was achieved along such lines. Emma Patterson, who visited here about 1873, was impressed by the organization of women in sweated industries; she returned to England where she founded in 1874 the Women's Protective and Provident League. Inquiries addressed to Samuel Gompers, who was always trying to improve America's contact with Europe and to counteract European reports of our labor movement, showed how difficult it was abroad to understand the most simple facts of American labor. Gompers had corresponded with Ben Tillett, and out of it arose the plan for the British Trades Union Congress and the American Federation of Labor (frequently designated by the English as the American Convention of Labor) to exchange delegates every year. After being forced to explain several times that the mixture of nationalities retarded our trade union progress, the A.F. of L. representative, John Lloyd, invited the British Congress in 1894 to commence the fraternal exchanges. Gompers and P. J. McGuire were the first official American delegates at Cardiff in 1895. It is not noticeable that American delegates contributed much. In 1896 the Americans got little response for the idea of convening a bona fide trade union congress; in 1898, the American delegate reminded the Congress of the value of such exchanges, and added that the British needed a "commingling of Yankee dash." Our delegates in 1899 showed surprise that British unionists had not yet agreed on an eight-hour day, and in 1904 the Americans reminded their English colleagues of the importance of trade union labels which were adopted in England about 1893.

David Holmes (Chairman of the Parliamentary Committee) and John Burns came to Denver in 1894. Two British delegates reported in 1896 that they had been agreeably surprised by the orderly conduct of the A.F. of L. convention, and asked the Congress to base their code of rules on the American model, especially to secure the grouping arrangement. Some grumbling broke out the same year over the inadequate results of these junkets, but a motion to discontinue delegates was defeated. As early as 1893 Pete Curran (afterwards M.P. for Jarrow) submitted a resolution to the Congress:

> That this Congress instructs the Parliamentary Committee to draw up a basis of common agreement for the purpose of bringing all trade and Labour organizations into closer relationship on the lines of the American Labour Federation.

The principles embodied in the American organization were discussed in the years immediately following. The Miners' International Conference, meeting at London in 1901, invited American miners' associations to future international conferences; but it regretted that our miners were badly organized. From time to time American socialists lectured in Great Britain. Henry George and the no-rent theory had a good reception at the Trades Union Congress of 1882. Two Americans, Walter Vrooman and Charles A. Beard, worked out the scheme for the English labor college, Ruskin Hall, Oxford, with Dennis Hird as the first director. The British reception was cordial, but not much was achieved in the way of contacts. The college made efforts in 1900 to arouse labor's support for a convention of English-speaking peoples and a return gift of a labor college to America. Perhaps America had little to offer, but Sir George Livesey wrote of H. D. Lloyd's *Labour Copartnership* (1898):

It is strange that Englishmen should be indebted to an American for the best account of what is going on in their own country in the direction of copartnership.

Following a temporary isolation, American labor after 1904 again showed an interest in international labor relations.

Writing in 1912, H. M. Hyndman, English author and social democratic pioneer, described how distressed he was by our labor conditions.[15] Despite this he declared that American events were worthy of more attention from Britons. He quoted Adolphe Smith, Special Commissioner for the *Lancet*, to prove that Chicago had not improved since 1886; Hyndman added:

Things move so slowly indeed that the . . . analysis of American social and political affairs which I wrote more than a quarter of a century ago is absolutely correct to-day.

He suspected that our workers were better educated, trade and industrial figures were better, the standard of life was higher but not so high as claimed, capitalists were harsher, the personal equation between the employer and employed was less than in England, and that there was a sharp contrast between the nominal social and political equality and the actual position of American labor. Because of violence and the corruption of politics, American labor seemed forced to rely on "direct action." Hyndman, who decided that de Tocqueville and Bryce were inadequate on American history, wanted us to develop our own social literature; so far he felt that only Algie M. Simons, Markman's "Man with a Hoe," and Mrs. Charlotte Stetson Gilman had been widely read. Hyndman concluded, however, that "in no country in the world is it more true that the average of the Socialist army has improved in height, girth, depth, and stature than it is in America." Hyndman continued to hold to our Lewis H. Morgan's theories of primitive agrarian communism. Curran, who returned in 1901 impressed by our speed, told his listeners that socialism might advance more rapidly than in England, and disabused them of any illusions of a workers' paradise. Keir Hardie's visit in 1908 convinced him that American socialism was becoming more sane and potent. Having imbibed American popular philosophy in his youth, Thomas Burtt (1837–1922) the labor leader painted a picture of democracy free from mob violence. Ben Tillett was always amazed by the money complex and percentage ideas of our workmen and the jumping of social classes.

Tom Mann was not impressed by America's advantages in 1883 or 1913, but he did find a few kind words for the Trade Union Educational League. While agreeing with W. T. Colyer's *Americanism: a World Menace* (1922), Mann described how in the nineties British workmen hesitated to accept socialism because they were convinced that America flourished by giving free rein to all; he concluded:

> There is no earthly hope for the cure of economic and social troubles by following in the wake of America. And yet—and herein is the great lesson of this book—if we refuse to travel towards Communism, the only alternative is to become Americanized, with all that this involves.

One of the influential British interpreters of foreign labor problems was G. D. H. Cole who in his *World of Labour* (1913) set America apart, and intimated that the discussion of it was irrelevant and without lessons since conditions were so dissimilar. However, with special attention to the I.W.W., he observed:

> We are compelled to deal with the American Labour movement because it has, in fact, exercised a considerable influence in Great Britain. It was in America that the question of Industrial Unionism first came to the front, and it was from America that the earlier advocates of it in this country borrowed their ideas and arguments.

The violent destruction of instruments of production was "more in harmony with American methods,"—and evidently not for the land of the Luddites. Further, "In America, where industrial methods are always brutal, such acts [of violent sabotage] are often justified; but in a civilised country, certain canons of civilised warfare should be observed on both sides."

When writing for the post-War *Encyclopaedia of the Labour Movement*, Herman Finer reëchoed earlier British thought:

> The American worker has shown a disposition to strive for the shillings, and to sacrifice for them some of the general independence and social amenities of life.

Although British labor could not well divorce itself from the effect of American achievements and experiments, either along class or national lines, its enthusiasm was about that of an English conservative club of 1840. As a recent writer has suggested:

Frankly I do not see . . . who is going to put the gospel of American civilization into terms that will be, I shall not say acceptable, but even significant, to the emancipated British worker.

The economist Alfred Marshall observed that the individual counted for much more in American economic movements; "the Americans are the only great people," he added, "whose industrial temper is at all like that of the English, and yet even theirs is not very like."

Finer correctly observed that "The position of Labour in the United States of America has been represented by English capitalist newspapers as highly desirable." Domestic reasons had caused this. When all English trades complained that we surpassed them in getting results from machinery, and British workmen heard constantly that they were less educated and inferior to our workmen, the effect upon British industry cannot be minimized, but the chances for accurate descriptions of American life decreased. The Royal Commission on Labour (1891) devoted one volume to a report on the United States, one of the first attempts to deal with exhaustive American reports and materials. Foreign competition, John Burns asserted, was always being invoked, this time against the Factory Acts:

If we are within a measurable distance of losing our trade by factory legislation, as is said, in every industry where the Americans are our superiors, they are our superiors, not because of an invasion of the Factory Acts, but by employing men at a higher rate of wages than we pay them."

Mr. Caine, who spent six months in America investigating the reasons for our dangerous rivalry, concluded that "The whole question of competition with America rested on the improvement of the working people"; compared with conditions in England, the United States was "as heaven to hell." The *Westminster Gazette* advised employers to be certain they were offering similar inducements in hours, wages, and advancement. Supporters of the minimum or standard wage concluded that the bogey of foreign competition should not be allowed to stand in the way of higher wages; but comparisons, it was argued, were apt to be fallacious since American labor ran more machines. The *Scotsman* added in 1898:

The fact of the higher wages being paid in America without Trade Unions disposes in the most complete manner of the statement that Trade Unionism had raised wages at home.

Especially in 1899 and 1900 the press was agitated over the problem of American labor superiority.[16] Many assumed that our workmen would do twice as much work. Some attributed this new information to the fact that the engineering strike had caused British employers to make inquiries. Such information, often supported by American journals, soon reached the workers in the form of pressure to speed up work. G. N. Barnes, a famous labor leader who denied that the strike caused our inroads, declared that "low wage advocates and enemies of trade unionism have never failed to get access to the columns of British newspapers, and in so doing to give bold and more or less gratuitous advertisement to American and other rivals." He continued:

Centralisation and specialisation are, in short, giving an enormous advantage to American producers, and, inasmuch as they are entirely on the line of progress we would welcome them here.

Alfred Yarrow exclaimed in 1898, "I am greatly surprised at American methods of work and their results," implying that by contrast every American worked as hard as possible. The press hailed the return from the States of "Mabon" (Mr. W. Abraham, M.P.), a labor leader in South Wales—"The opponent of machinery has suddenly become its advocate." While Mr. Abraham found it necessary for the British workmen to struggle harder, he also added that capitalists must find modern machinery. He did not fail to describe us as crushed under a high tariff; he also decided that American comrades were setting a good example by fighting the trusts on conciliation boards and in arbitration courts. After a visit the editor of the *Leather Record* concluded that the chief evil was the National Union of Boot and Shoe Operatives, who restricted output; others went so far as to say that the best workers emigrated, that "the Trade Unions here were responsible to a great extent for the work turned out in America." The press hoped the Mosely Commission to the United States would convince British workmen that they suffered from economic delusions. Efforts were made to combat these criticisms without much success.

Many Americans were quoted to prove that we believed Britain's trade decline resulted from the unionists' curtailment of production. The Free Labour Association in annual congresses hearkened with cheers to America where the quick, go-ahead man was allowed to push forward, and resolved to ask Carnegie to publish pamphlets on the subject of free labor. At the Twelfth Annual Congress in 1904, a resolution was passed which expressed unqualified approval of the aims and objects of the National Association of Manufacturers and the Citizens' Industrial Association of America as "organizations potential for great public good." Yet English manufacturers perhaps did not draw the greatest possible encouragement from America's open shop movement. Arthur Lee thought that "There need be no pitched battles if the new American scheme of arbitration proves as successful in execution as it is brilliant in inception." Others also cited the General Conciliation Board in the States. Visitors to the English Electric Manufacturing Co. Ltd. at Preston and the Electric Railway and Tramway Carriage Co. Ltd. in 1901 decided that there was no need for the dismal, widespread predictions that English workmen would not submit to American practices in England. The textbooks of F. A. Walker (1840–1897), American economist, threatened the reign of Henry Fawcett at Oxford; Walker did more, for he dealt a decisive blow to the wage fund theory of wages and played a great part in the conception held by English students of the "place and functions of the employer in modern industrial economics." J. Lawrence, M.P., explained to the annual general meeting of the Linotype Company Ltd. in 1902 that probably the first great, new departure on American lines was about to be introduced with the approval of the union; the board had agreed that the principle of the maximum rate of wages could no longer be tolerated, and it claimed the right of paying a premium to good laborers. The "premium" system probably originated in America and first made its way to Scotland. Lord Brassey and others could not see that profit-sharing between labor and business had flourished with us.

Doubts about the actual status of American workers were not laid to rest.[17] The *Times* could not view with entire satisfaction the moral and material condition of workers whose lives were more precarious. Curran reported to the Liverpool Trades and Labour Council that artisans were as well off in England; Rev. John Wakeford, lecturing under the auspices of the Liverpool Fabian Society, demonstrated that our workers got little from a democratic constitution. Robert Blatchford, who didn't think highly of conditions in either country, was led to write *Dismal England* (1899) after reading a similar American investigation. Free trader John Morley, who knew little about our labor, provoked agreeable laughter at Arbroath when he pointed out that his opponents "will tell you the American worker is better off than you are." Yet one may conclude that the Board of Trade reports in 1911 on wages and the cost of living disposed of a current misconception: that our higher wages had been swallowed up by the high cost of living.

Although American unionism may have disappointed many Britons in its weak fight against trusts, nothing of union violence or the hard, aggressive tone of American socialism had been ignored. The steel strike of 1901 assumed importance in England because of the Taff Vail Railway case and some American opinion that Britain's steel trade decline had been due to the workers' usurpation of control. Generally, our strike had been viewed as useless and mischievous, and its collapse was accepted as the defeat of revolutionary unionism. The *Scotsman* said of the Pennsylvania coal strike of 1902:

> It has close resemblances to similar industrial struggles in this country, and its conclusion, whatever it may be, can scarcely fail of providing profitable lessons for both labour and for capital.

Not much came from efforts to get British support for our strike. But British delegates reported to the Congress in 1902 that at the present rate of progress American trade unionism would outstrip the British in influence and numbers.

The "direct action" of the I.W.W. had a stimulating effect upon the militant sections of British unions. James Larkin had founded the Irish Transport Workers' Union in 1908; in 1910 he had been joined by James Connolly, who brought from seven years of American experience the methods and phraseology of the Industrial

Workers of the World and a doctrine of fighting industrial unionism. Labor troubles in Ireland in 1913 brought the American example to the very doorsteps of England. The doctrine of Guild Socialism also, according to Cole, owed much to French syndicalism and American unionism. Britain had not been able to learn much from our labor legislation. The Royal Commission on trade disputes and trade combinations (1903) found our court decisions, especially in conspiracy cases, too conflicting to be used. Although the elaborate labor code of New York, particularly in such things as mechanics' liens, contained many items suggested for imitation, the most significant thing was that England saw with surprise that our courts, using the latent power of the Constitution, killed much needed labor legislation and turned the injunction into a strong weapon against labor. The Steunenberg case and the murder trial of Bill Haywood, chronicled fairly, said the *Labour Leader,* only by itself, added to the suspicion that very sinister elements had been interjected into the labor conflict. The *Spectator* blamed the faulty judicial system and State power; "the trial has been most distressing to those who, like ourselves, watch in the United States the daily progress of the greatest democratic experiment ever tried."

Great Britain was one of the European nations to establish a bureau of labor after the American model. The signing of the Fifty-four Hour Factory Bill by the Governor of Massachusetts in 1911 encouraged agitation for shorter hours in Lancashire factories even though opponents argued that American mills were sheltered by their protective tariffs. Trade union members who wanted payment of Members of Parliament kept combating the idea that "carpetbaggers" would be more numerous under such a system as existed at Washington. We had also been active in promoting an International May Day and an International Federation of Trade Unions.

That business was not as usual we shall see further in the next chapter.

¹ There is an interchange of data even where there is unrestricted British management of an American-owned factory. Information on this subject may be traced through commercial directories and the *Anglo-American Year Book.* Note an advertisement of the Lancashire Industrial Development Council: "Do you know the largest British Factory of American Origin is located in Lancashire?" Trafford Park, Manchester, was laid out with streets numbered consecutively, a new development about 1900. A prominent Am. firm discovered it could do little with high-

pressure and straight commissions, nor could it find salesmen with private cars. Frank A. Southard Jr., *American Industry in Europe* (Boston, 1931) is an excellent beginning which suggests how much further the history needs to be extended. The topic is distasteful to some Am. companies. The experience of the original managers or public relations men would be most illuminating. Southard (pp. xiii, xiv) finds that by 1900 there were 28 American-owned manufacturing plants in Europe; between 1900–1910, 50 more were added. In 1928 there were over 1300 companies in 28 countries. See also *American Branch Factories Abroad*, Sen. Doc., No. 258, 71st Cong., 3d Sess. (Washington, 1931), 29; same title, No. 120, 73d Cong., 2d Sess., 1933, Tables IIA and III. Technical contact may be close even where capital is distinct, as in the tinplate industry since 1933. Herbert Marshall, F. A. Southard Jr., and K. W. Taylor, *Canadian-American Industry: A Study in International Investment* (New Haven, 1936), lx, 3, 15, 19, 230, 242; the migration of the United Empire Loyalists, before any railways or branch factories, laid the basis for technical and cultural interchanges about which the authors are not primarily concerned.

[2] The American Chamber of Commerce in London has an enrollment of 700 (which includes British firms interested in the U.S.). Probably not more than 2,000 Am. business men are engaged in the U.K. There was an Am. C. of C. in Liverpool in 1801. Sir W. B. Forwood (*Recollections*, 1910, p. 81) mentions that he was president of an Am. C. of C. there in 1872 which was supported by dues levied on every bale of cotton imported into Liverpool. S. C. Johnson notes (*Emigration from U.K.*, p. 61) that in 1823 an Am. C. of C. was opened at 4 Coopers' Row, Liverpool, to persuade men to leave for North America. Contemporary press accounts (1907) estimated 2,000 Am. firms in London and 10,000 Am. business men —an exaggeration! The London C. of C. has for many years been in close touch with the New York C. of C.

C. W. Phelps, *Foreign Expansion of American Banks; American Branch Banking Abroad* (New York, 1927), 7–9, 133, 137, 139, 141, 149. International Banking Corp. in London, 1902; Empire Trust Co., 1913; of private firms, Harris, Forbes and Co. (N.Y.) estb. branch in London, 1913; Pynchon and Co. owned its London house, estb. about 1907; note also Morgan Grenfell and Co. partnership in London, 1910, predecessor being J. S. Morgan and Co. Oldest established foreign branch of an Am. commercial bank opened in one room, London, 1887, under control of Jarvis-Conkling Mortgage Trust Co.; in 1893 it came under management of N. Am. Trust Co., and expanded in 1912; the Guaranty Trust opened in 1897, the Farmers' Loan and Trust Co. in 1906. Private investment houses were less inclined to establish foreign branches, and private banking houses preferred the affiliate method. Consular agents reported we erred in centering mfg. operations in Birmingham in 1902 because of the strong hold of British manufactutrers on that city. The Scottish market perhaps more than the English credited Am. mfg. with quality and not mere cheapness.

List of Jan. 1937 of American-owned branch plants or associated companies may be analyzed as follows: Chemical, 23; Machinery, 23; Manufacturing, 22; Medicine and Cosmetics, 20; Electrical, 14; Office Supplies and Merchandising, 14; Auto and Body Equipment, 14; Engineering, 13; Food, 10; Phonograph and Radio, 7; Oil, 6; Home Equipment, 6; etc.

[3] L. H. Jenks, *The Migration of British Capital to 1875* (New York, 1927), 78, 80. A weekly publication, *Circular to Bankers*, praised Am. investments from

1832 to 1838. M. F. Jolliffe, *The United States as a Financial Center, 1919–1933* (Cardiff, 1935); W. F. Ford, "American Investments in England," *Cont. R.,* March 1902, 405–08; note interesting autobiography of Brit. promoter of many Am. undertakings, H. Osborne O'Hagan, *Leaves from My Life* (2 vols., London, 1929). Baring's banking house was excellently managed under Joshua Bates. Charles Duguid in *Story of the Stock Exchange* (London, 1901), 248–49, points out that while Cobden lost a small fortune in Ill. Central, W. H. Smith and Sir Peter Coats benefited greatly from "courageous" purchase of Am. r.r. securities in early sixties. At a meeting of London and New York Investment Corp., Mr. Fred. Walker reported that our financiers had not learned from the crisis of 1907, *Times,* Feb. 8, 1908; also report of Merchants' Trusts, *Times,* Feb. 29. In 1907 the Am. Investment Trust got court permission to extend its investments to Cuba and any possessions of the U.S. The excellent account by Cleona Lewis and K. T. Schlotterbeck, *America's Stake in Foreign Investments* (Washington, 1938), *passim,* does not probe into effects of Am. finance upon foreign life.

⁴ *Reports of the Comptroller-General of Patents* in *Parl. Papers; Ency. Brit.,* 11th ed., "Patents"; B. H. Thwaite, *The Cultivation of the Inventive Faculty; a lesson from the U.S.* (London, 1894) and *The American Invasion: or England's Commercial Danger and the Triumphal Progress of the U.S.* (London, 1902); *P. Debs.,* 1902, 109:95; 1907, 180:651. Pitirim A. Sorokin, *Social and Cultural Dynamics* (New York, 1937), II, 150–53; note also Mr. Boldyreff's analysis (II, 143) of space devoted to Americans in 9th ed. of *Ency. Brit.*

⁵ The influence of nineteenth and twentieth century expositions merits a synthetic study. Report of the Royal Commission for the Chicago Exhibition appears in *Journal of the Society of Arts,* 1893–94, 42:548–614. Except for agricultural machinery, Weetman Pearson found Chicago "far behind Leeds." Emerson in *Journ. RIBA,* Nov. 6, 1899, p. 11; Clapham, *Econ. Hist.,* III, 153–54. D. K. Clark, *Exhibited Machinery of 1862* [*South Kensington*] (London, n.d.), 117, 130, 238; William Whewell *et al., Lectures on the Results of the Exhibition* [*1851*] (London, 1852), delivered before the Society of Arts; 169, 262, 315, 320, 417. Charles Lowe, *Four National Exhibitions in London and their organizer* (London, 1892), 32, 40, 46, 70ff., 82ff., 107, 113; President Grévy suggested a similar Am. exhibit for Paris; about 1,078 Am. producers and manufacturers exhibited; Earl's Court was laid out in manner of Am. cities; 160 Am. artists exhibited. *Reports on the Philadelphia International Exhibitions of 1876* (3 vols., London, 1877, also *P.P.,* C.–1774), I, 27, 40, 91, 93, 97, 123, 153, 176, 216, 230, 232, 236, 271, 285; about 1% of the admissions were Europeans. *Report of H.M. Commissioners for Int. Exhib., St. Louis, 1904, P.P.,* 1906 (Cd. 2800), liv; *Report of Com. Gen. for U.S. to Paris, 1900,* Sen. Doc., No. 232, 56th Cong., 2d Sess., 1900–01, in v. 27–32; the govt. spent $1,397,500 at Paris. *Report of H.M. Commissioners for Paris Exhibition, P.P.,* 1901 (Cd. 629, 630), xxxi; Report of jurors, vol. 2, pp. 6, 10, 49, 50, and p. 134, for suggested lessons from U.S. Fisheries exhibit. *Report of Committee on participation of G. B. in International exhibitions, and evidence, P.P.,* 1908 (Cd. 3772, 3773), xlix, *passim;* Sir Alfred Bateman, chairman appointed by Bd. of Trade. G.B. spent public funds amounting to £40,462 at Philadelphia, £61,464 at Chicago, £128,000 at St. Louis.

⁶ The latest improvements in illustration introduced from the U.S. were seen at the International Press and Printing Exhibition at Crystal Palace, 1902. Mr. Ernest Schenk, chairman of the Crystal Palace Co., was aided by Mr. Henry Gilman;

English advisory committee included the Lord Mayor, Earl Grey, Earl of Crewe, Sir Douglas Fox, Sir Henry Irving, Viscount Duncannon, and Winston Churchill, names usually found on Anglo-American committees. Mr. Paul Cremieu-Javal was chairman of Earl's Court Exhibition, 1909.

[7] Before an influential meeting at the Mansion House, Asquith appealed for funds, declaring that Eng. took equal pride in our great men. The Duke of Teck outlined the aims. A monument to Washington and the purchase of Sulgrave Manor were discussed. H. S. Perris was secretary to the Brit. Committee. The *Scotsman* praised the celebrations and the Anglo-American professorship, but thought the interchange of scholars and editorial writers would have to wait the millennium. The sums desired were not raised in Great Britain. See *Illustrated Catalogue of the American Fine Art Section* (London, 1914), with introd. by Lewis Hind who says the American has dominated London, influenced Paris, and is creating a distinctive school in landscape; he called Redfield typically American in subjects and in treatment.

[8] Germany and G.B. had agreed not to participate officially. Asquith declared English merchants did not wish to exhibit. Note names on petition forwarded to Prime Minister, *Times*, Feb. 20, 1914.

[9] W. P. Wood, pres. of London Corn Assoc. at the Imperial Industries Club, *Times*, Feb. 18, 1904; *Measures for suppressing gambling in wheat contracts*, *Ac. & P.*, 1895 (C. 7645), No. 2, Commercial; *Report on Legislation in Regard to Gambling in "Options" and "Futures,"* *Ac. & P.* (Cd. 3863), cviii, supp. to Cd. 3280; Seton-Karr, *P. Debs.*, 1899, 66:1133ff.; E. E. Williams, *Sat. Rev.*, June 4, 1898, 738ff. *P. Debs.*, 1899, 68:854ff., 879, 891ff., 899–900; 1902, 108:537, 1014; 116:116, 1218; 1914, 63:316–19; 65:1170. For Gladstone, see Chauncey M. Depew, *My Memories of Eighty Years* (New York, 1922), 259, chap. xix. Kipling, *Actions and Reactions* (London, 1909); note millionaire in "Rita's" *Half a Truth* (1911); Duke of Manchester, *My Candid Recollections* (London, 1932), 88–89; Arnold Bennett, *The Loot of Cities* (London, 1905). Of the millionaires, Morgan had the best reception.

[10] W. R. Lawson, *American Finance* (Edinburgh, 1906), 1, 17; Schuster, *Times*, Jan. 23, 1908, Jan. 22, 1914; Parr, *Times*, Jan. 24, 1908; *P. Debs.*, 1913, 50:1310. Note Beresford's interest in 1902 in the fees paid by investors in the U.S.; *P. Debs.*, 1902, 112:274; also *P.P.*, Cd. 530, p. 157 of Appendix, and National Liberal Federation, *Times*, Feb. 28, 1903. To a slight degree some safe deposit banks were on Am. models. *Economist* suggested that British bankers might well imitate the American Bankers' Convention.

[11] Our pirating of "Made in Ireland" in 1911 encouraged British agitation for "fair goods under fair labels." Trade mark owners wanted change in Am. procedure for registration of trade marks. *Foreign Trade Competition, etc., Ac. & P.*, 1899 (C.–9078), XCVI; *U.S. Mon. Con. Rept.*, Jan. 1898, pp. iii–iv. *P. Debs.*, 1899, 66:324; 1900, 86:1122; 1901, 95:899; 98:387; 1902, 107:1083; 111:311, 315; 1905, 147:908; 1906, 154:1012ff.; 1907, 175:1078; 1909, Commons, 13:303; 1910, 17:27; 1911, 31:90.

Report of committee of Univ. of Chicago, *Rotary* (Chicago, 1934), 25, 37, 40. There are at present about 450 Rotary clubs in G.B. and Ireland. Review quoted from G. E. Milward, *Management Library, etc.* (1934), 17; H. G. Selfridge, "Selling Selfridge and Some Random Recollections of an American Merchant in London," *Sat. Eve. Post*, July 27, etc., 1935, and interview. Southard, *Am. Industry*, 123–26; Douglas Knoop, *American Business Enterprise* (Manchester,

1908), a Gartside report; Richards, *John Bull*, 211, on district messengers; Lewis, *America's Stake*, 110. Lipton was one of the first to introduce typewriters; Lipton, *Leaves from the Lipton Log* (London, 1931), 79–80, 95–96, 143ff. Fuller's (Am.) candy and cake stores struck public attention by daily-dressed, colorful windows. Am. plan of selling stamps in small books did not at first catch on, although suggested to Home Mails Dept. as early as 1901. Likewise, free "shoe-shining" to entice customers.

[12] Richards, *John Bull*, 41, 46, 49, 66, 68; he introduced the Am. cigarette into England (1877), and his poster of the "Old Quaker Smoker" became widely known; also proprietor of "Carter's Little Liver Pills" and owner of the *Academy*. Stirrup, *Direct Advertising* (London, 1924), suggests that an English jeweler would not circularize friends of engaged couples. Bradley quoted in Noble T. Praigg, ed., *Advertising and Selling* (London, 1923), 19th Int. Convention of Assoc. Advertising Clubs of the World, Atlantic City, June, 1923, p. 72; Eric Field (p. 205) found that only one bank in Eng. showed signs of modern salesmanship, namely, the Guaranty Trust Co. of N.Y.

[13] L. Urwick, E. Aston, and F. H. Cordukes, *Organizing a Sales Office* (London, 1928), 15, 18; Mr. Urwick is an Englishman greatly responsible for spread of Taylor's principles in England. Paul Devinat, *Scientific Management in Europe* (Geneva, 1927), 12–14, 22–23, 57, 83, 84, 127–63; Thiselton Mark, *Efficiency Ideals; a short study of the Principles of "Scientific Management"* (London, 1919), recommended beginning with study of volumes by Harrington Emerson, Taylor, Münsterberg, and H. L. Gantt; Mark had studied in U.S. in 1900 as a Gilchrist Scholar. H. G. T. Cannons, *Bibliography of Industrial Efficiency and Factory Management* (London, 1920); John Calder, "Cant of Efficiency," *Spec.*, 1905, 95:642. Am. books on management are kept prominently in view and treated fairly by G. E. Milward; see *Management Library, Subject Index* (London, 1934), and *Business Man's Guide to Management* (London, 1937). Copley, *Taylor*, II, 410; Bryce became interested in Taylor's scheme of efficiency. Allingham, in *Trans. of Jr. Inst. of Engineers*, 1912, 23: 38–74, 156–88. The Inst. of Mech. Engineers at St. Louis, 1904, thoroughly disagreed with Harrington Emerson's speech, "A Rational Basis for Wages."

[14] See *Workingman's Advocate*, June 10, 1871; *Miners' National Record* (Cleveland, Aug. 1875), No. 10, p. 164. W. J. Davis, *The British Trades Union Congress, History and Recollections* (London, 1910–1916), I, 111; II, 17, 71, 79, 90, 96, 102, 108, 114, 124, 151, 243–44, 256; G. D. H. Cole, *A Short History of the British Working Class Movement, 1789–1927* (vol. III, London, 1927), 73, 75, 152; Lewis L. Lorwin, *Labor and Internationalism* (New York, 1929), 39, 69–71, 105, chap. v. Halévy asserts (*Hist. Eng. People, Ep.*, p. 260) that the A.F. of L., not French syndicalism, provided British labor with a model for its annual Trades Union Congress. Keir Hardie, it may be noted, kept track of labor parties. Ben Tillett, *Memories and Reflections* (London, 1931), 216. Henry Lucy, *Diary*, II, 271; Caro Lloyd, *Henry Demarest Lloyd, 1847–1903: A Biography* (New York and London, 1912), II, chap. xviii, esp. 165, 181–83; F. J. Klingberg, "Harriet Beecher Stowe and Social Reform in England," *Amer. Hist. Rev.*, April 1938, 542–52. I wish to thank Mr. Edgar Cale for suggestions.

[15] H. M. Hyndman, *Further Reminiscences* (London, 1912), chap. xiv; Hyndman (p. 322) declared, "So little is known in Europe of the American movement that a leading French journal classed Eugene Debs with John Burns and Millerand

as a man who had abandoned the class for which he had striven." English papers were also hazy on the status of Am. labor leaders. The Countess of Warwick described Debs (*Discretions*, p. 128) as "one of the men who had courage to fight materialism in America. . . ." Tillett, *op. cit.*, 218, 220, 223–24, 227–28; Tom Mann, *Memoirs* (London, 1923), 319–21; cf. Lord Goschen quoted in Willson, *New Amer.*, p. 68n. H. B. Lees-Smith, ed., *Ency. of Lab. Movement* (London), III, 267, 268, 272; G. D. H. Cole, *World of Labour* (London, 1913), 95–96, 128. Harold E. Stearns, ed., *Civilization in the U.S.* (London, 1922), 469–89; Finer, in *Ency. Lab. Movement*, III, 266; Geoffrey Drage drew up report for the Royal Commission; see *P.P.*, 1892 (Cd. 6795x–xl), vol. 36, pt. 5. Burns, *P. Debs.*, 1899, 74:253. Mr. Souttor told Parl. that British laborer had better chance to succeed in U.S. than in Australia or Canada; see *P. Debs.*, 1899, 69:1515. Caine, *P. Debs.*, 1902, 101:202, with assertion that there was less drinking in the U.S.; G. N. Barnes, *Times Eng. Supp.*, Mar. 28, 1906, pp. 98, 100; B. Seebohm Rowntree declared Eng. working class families had much less food than poor families in Am. cities, *Times*, Aug. 21, 1902. Pigou, *Marshall*, 266.

¹⁶ *Proc. Mech. Eng.*, 1904, p. 958; also 1905, p. 8; *P. Debs.*, 1902, 107:458ff.; C. R. Enoch, *Farthest West*, 309; Lee, *Times*, Jan. 6, 1902; Free Lab. Assoc., *Times*, Oct. 21, 1902, Oct. 25, 1904; Yarrow, *D. Mail*, Jan. 11, 1898; Barnes, *Engr.*, May 19, 1899; Brassey, *19th Cent.*, June 1898; Lord Brassey's pamphlet, *The Comparative Efficiency of English and Foreign Labour* (London, 1904), and his introd. to the continuation of his earlier work by S. J. Chapman, *Foreign Competition, Work and Wages* (London, 1904), Pt. I, also pp. 28, 95. Chapman believed Am. were worked harder in iron and steel industries. F. A. Walker, *The Wages Question* (1876); W. J. Ashley, *Adjustment of Wages: A Study in the coal and iron industries of G.B. and Am.* (London, 1903), vii, 6.

¹⁷ *The Jungle* (1906) helped to explain to some Englishmen the reasons for the embittered nature of Am. labor. Mr. T. Burt's letter to miners, *Times*, Nov. 11, 1902. U.S. Dept. of Labor *Bulletin*, No. 15, Mar. 1898, pp. 197–219. *Brit. and Foreign Trade and Industry*, *P.P.*, 1903 (Cd. 1761), lxvii. *Royal Commission on trade disputes, etc.*, *P.P.*, 1906 (Cd. 2825–26), vol. 56. Trades Union Congress moved by a large majority in favor of arbitration treaty between the two countries, *Times*, Sept. 2, 6, 1902. Morley, *Times*, Jan. 6, 1906.

IX

THE INDUSTRIAL GIANT

OUR growth led to a severe British self-analysis which had spiritual as well as technical significance. Prosperity and competition, which perhaps are essential to cultural diffusion in an industrial civilization, enhanced the value of American experience. Differences in economic conditions and national outlooks made any change in industrial practice of slow and gradual tempo. The flood of American examples led to no dangerous over-imitation such as some have discovered in the post-1918 "rationalization" of German industry. The popular press, led by the *Times,* shouted in 1900 that British manufacturers did not know enough about American manufacturing; there was soon a surprising amount of technical information in non-technical papers. The *Manchester Guardian* sighed in May 1903: "We are all so much impressed nowadays by Americans and their methods. . . ."

One is struck by the details known of workshop organization, but much of the engineering discussion, particularly about locomotives, was brutally nationalistic. Hundreds began to cross the Atlantic on tours of inspection. The surprising American policy of exhibiting industrial methods and management aided in spreading knowledge. The invasion of American cycles and the engineering strike of 1897–98—caused partly by our influence—were proper preparations for the discussion of our experience. During that strike Alfred Marshall wrote to Edward Caird, Master of Balliol, that England was falling behind us and that she must be ready to avail herself of the new resources of production; if he were a workingman, he added, he could wish for no more hopeful conditions of life than those which he understood to prevail at the Carnegie works. Stereotyped technical ideas were associated with the word "American": rigid standardization of engineering designs and methods, ruthless scrapping of machinery, and of course, speed and often shoddiness. The following pages will illustrate how methods and products circulated, and will analyze the variety of opinions in different social classes and the economic foundations of many ideas that carried beyond industry and business.

Industrial contacts take place in many ways.[1] In the eighties Hiram Maxim, inventor of the Maxim gun, who was knighted in 1901, took his American experience to England; he declared, "At first my American tools were a little too much for the British workman. . . ." Englishmen learned to know the work of American engineers through the South African ventures of John Hays Hammond, Pope Yeatman, George Starr, Hal Tilghman, Robert Catlin, and many others. National jealousy was aroused when Hammond was made chief consulting engineer of Rhodes's interests. He was mainly responsible for persuading the British of the possibility of deep-level mining. Hamilton Smith (1840–1900) opened a consulting office at London in 1885, and his Exploration Company Ltd. became important in South African gold mining; he also introduced securities of American mining enterprises and helped to spread the use of our mining machinery and engineers in British possessions. Gardner Williams (1842–1922) was in charge of the De Beer diamond properties between 1887 and 1905, and was then succeeded by his son.

In planning his British ventures, George Westinghouse decided that alternating current, which Kelvin opposed, was sure to become the foundation for central-station development; that British railroads were mostly of the suburban type; that there should be great generating stations near coal mines, few central stations, and separate organizations to sell power to railroads. He had difficulty in impressing railroad managers with his air-brakes; but technical and sales forces were in England by 1872, and the Westinghouse Brake Company Ltd. was organized in 1881. In the works at King's Cross most of the machinery was American. In face of strong British competition, Westinghouse's devices proved most efficient in tests conducted by the Midland Railway in 1875. He saw England as an ideal field for extensive use and distribution of electricity, and organized his company in 1899. When he was bought out the British spokesman said: "Mr. Westinghouse's conception of what should be done was faultless. It was a misfortune that he was a quarter of a century ahead of his time. If Great Britain had accepted his advice countless millions of waste would have been saved." Westinghouse had told the third annual meeting of the British company: "Your company is entitled to the benefit of the additional experience which will . . . be acquired by your American partners." The building of the British Westinghouse Company—"counted among Westinghouse's mistakes"—at Trafford Park, Manchester, was dramatized as a speed record for British unionist workmen under American contractors. The speed records were hurled against other British unionists, and were spoken of as an American indictment of British trade methods. The building manager explained to the *Times* that he was not against unions, and that the success was due to good wages, good superintendents, and the newest mechanical devices. The President of the Manchester Association of Engineers in 1902 declared that the new methods of engineering at the works in Trafford Park were a matter of national interest. By 1904 English financial papers concluded that Westinghouse had built too large. The *Engineer* declared that those who exalted American manufacturing systems had overlooked some essential element: "national, psychological, what not."

During the engineers' strike, Alfred Yarrow came to study labor conditions; he also told our tool-makers of the excellent opportunity for exporting labor-saving machinery to England. His subsequent offer to pay three or four engineers to visit America was refused. In 1899 a leading English firm sent a special commission to study machine tools. In 1901 movements were afoot to send deputations of iron masters, engineers and workers. By that date nearly every important electrical engineer of municipalities or traction manufacturers had visited the States. Thus the time was ripe for Mr. Alfred Mosely's Industrial Commission, especially since the Educational Commission had been postponed because of the unsettled details of the Education Bill of 1902.[2]

Labor was not enthusiastic, for it realized that Mosely, who had been impressed by production statistics, more sober, energetic workmen, the general adoption of piecework and our higher wages, thought nothing could do more to spread his views than a deputation to America. The *Labour Leader* quibbled: "What will American Trade Unionists think of their British colleagues who thus come to them *in forma pauperis?*" Labor would have preferred an inquiry into distribution rather than production. Disclaiming any political animus, Mosely wanted his countrymen to note the superior organization of machinery, better education and living conditions, profit-sharing, and character records of employees. The *Economist* concluded (April 25, 1903):

> In the main, the tone of the reports is distinctly optimistic. The delegates have not returned with the idea so widely promulgated a year or two ago, that this country is a mere effete survival, destined to be devoured, in an industrial sense, by the lusty and assertive young Republic of the West.

The evidence was conflicting on drinking and gambling. Many delegates joined Mosely in believing that our labor-saving machinery was encouraged by the unions and welcomed by the masses, but they did not find much evidence of hustling. Some proposals to imitate Bishop Potter's National Civic Federation were put before various trade unions and supported by the press. One member contended that the National Cash Register Company (Dayton) set England a glorious example. The delegates were vague as to what should be imitated in English factories; perhaps what was suggested most frequently was the need for breaking barriers between employer and employee, better education, a few more labor-saving devices, heated workshops, more advertising, and a new spirit among employers. This very significant event did not receive the impartial attention it deserved, but the members had come into contact with a source of new ideas and methods that outlived press publicity.

The flow of other visitors was impressive.[3] The British Trades Union Congress sent two delegates to report independently of the Mosely Commission; they returned with the natural opinion that our workmen were no better and that English employers might increase their output if American methods were adopted. Both owners and miners investigated the problem of a sliding scale agreement and machine-mining rates. Mr. Parkes, president of the British Iron Trade Association and chairman of the special commission to inquire into our iron and steel industries, declared in 1902 that Britain needed cheaper transportation and production, undisputed shipping supremacy, and Imperial discussion. E. P. Martin, manager of the Dowlais Iron Works, profited from his American visits, and introduced labor-saving machinery wherever possible. Arthur Keen, J. Hartley Wicksteed, and members of Jessop & Sons also made important visits. The Government had thought it too expensive in 1904 to send a commercial mission. Twelve engineers visited in 1912 under the auspices of the International Exchange of Students.

Joint meetings and conferences also facilitated discussion—and kinship. Over two hundred American engineers visited England in 1900; the Institution of Mechanical Engineers made an American visit in 1904 which resulted in many papers on workshop methods. Sir William White, who confessed that Americans were a strange and touchy people, stressed the value of such visits. Lord Alverstone heralded Roosevelt and King Edward as peacemakers to the Society of Chemical Industry and some one hundred visiting Americans, July 1905. There was a joint summer meeting at Birmingham in 1910 with the American Society of Mechanical Engineers. The Duke of Devonshire and a committee of iron and steel men welcomed American delegates in 1911.

We acted as a great industrial stimulus.[4] "In these days," asserted Lord Rosebery, October 15, 1901, "we need to be inoculated with some of the nervous energy of the Americans!" The *Westminster Gazette* shivered at this outburst;

> The problem, if we are considering civilized life and not merely what is called commercial supremacy, is to find the mean between this American disease and the complacency which is fully convinced that old ways are best because they are old."

The press argued that England was behind in scientific organization, in the use of machinery, and the training of workers; in brief, England had relaxed. The *Times's* series on "The Crisis in British Industry" and "American Engineering Competition and Progress," both laden with American experience, won classical notoriety in 1900 and 1901. The *Times* preached that visitors to America were impressed by the indifference of British manufacturing "to the very real dangers which menace their industrial position." Actually, much industrial borrowing had taken place since 1885. Factory inspectors declared that America did things better, or referred to improvements that had come from imitation of American experience. The *Engineer* was properly cautious;

> In truth, it seems that we must adopt American mechanical engineering and metallurgical methods in their entirety or not at all; and this means little short of social revolution.

The one and only visit, that of 1896 with J. M. Barrie, had so impressed W. Robertson Nicoll that in the height of the panic in 1901 he cried out for our policies—"Fire out the fools," "Pay good men handsomely," make efficiency a watchword. Lawson in his *American Industrial Problems* (1903) did not fear Americans whose outlook was not cloudless, but he advised keenness, persistence, and thoroughness. With good spirit W. H. P. Greswell wrote the *United States and their Industries* (1899) for a school series in which he said:

> We must not be above taking a hint or two from them; and if we want to keep our place as manufacturers and traders, there is something we can learn from "Yankee notions" of all sorts.

The same thesis was advanced by John Foster Fraser's comprehensive *America at Work* (1903). In general, British visitors had been impressed. Only a few questioned the economic soundness of our incessant scrapping of machinery. Some decided that breadth and seriousness made our industrial success. Others, like Arthur Shadwell, adhered to the view that Germany, not America, should be used in comparisons. Sidney Low said of his *Industrial Efficiency* (1906), "What is here said is contrary to the popular opinion in England, which persists in regarding the Americans as a peculiarly tricky, dodgy set of persons, always on the lookout to take somebody in." Such opinion had been considerably modified because apparently we were outstripping Britain's efficiency.

Because of competition a meeting of the Institution of Civil Engineers centered about H. B. Molesworth's "American Workshop Methods in Steel Construction," January 1902, a paper which may be taken as typical of the desire to study American methods. The paper stressed standardization, specialization, and organization. The author had spent three months at the Pencoyd works of the American Bridge Company, and viewed our bridgework as equal or superior; he advised more systematic methods in the drawing office, and designing engineers for English works. The usual qualifications and additions were made by those present; one was that "In England only the best of American works were heard of." The president of the Institution of Mechanical Engineers, J. Hartley Wicksteed, did not find our works stereotyped,

> Nor are engineering designs and methods . . . confined to fixed types, such as we are apt to associate with the title "American"; and some tools of America, with which we are made most familiar through the columns of the engineering press, are not the type that finds most favor in the leading workshops which we visited.

A conference on "American Industrial Conditions and Competition," March 31, 1903, under the auspices of the British Iron Trade Association, was held in an atmosphere of the deepest pessimism. The general theme was that manufacturers displayed unwillingness to change and that American workmen were better. Enoch James added, "One obvious lesson to be learnt from America is that of listening to the man who knows." Others suggested that England should put her technical associations on a coördinated, business footing. England had not received many shocks any more stimulating.

By 1899 the United States clearly had taken Britain's place as a leading coal-producing country.[5] In 1900 the high price of Welsh coal and a severe decline in freight rates enabled American coal to get a foothold in regions about the Mediterranean, but British opinion was divided as to the seriousness of competition in Europe. In the Parliament of 1901 the Government discounted American competition and moved to add one shilling a ton to the coal tax; opponents exaggerated the threat to show that the tax was risky and something Americans would not use. While opposing the Miners (8 Hours) Bill, Sir Alfred Hickman quoted figures to show that we averaged 450 tons per miner in 1897, and the British, 297 tons; he believed the cheapness of American coal was due to machines which had now been installed in his own mines—but they were complete failures unless under-managers were at each machine. Northumberland miners were advised by their leaders to give more attention to American mining. Russell Rea added, "When Americans take up a business they generally carry it through." Strikes were broken by electrical "heading" machines brought from America. The suggestion made by Sir William Lewis at the International Engineering Congress at Glasgow, 1901, was heeded:

> There could be no doubt that British collieries would derive great benefit by following the American example and adopting electrical coal-getting machinery, especially in non-fiery mines.

Plans were also made to extend the scientific control of coal purchase based upon calorific value.

Careful study of American iron and steel production had become noticeable by 1887.[6] In the past Britain had taught America, and not all of the recent improvements were of strictly American origin; but England might have learned, said *Engineering*, "had we possessed the energy or humility to copy our American kinsmen." In 1903 Carnegie told the Institute that twenty-nine years earlier A. L. Halley, then engineer to Carnegie's works, had directed English attention to our development of the Bessemer process. By 1897 leading English firms were adding equipment which enabled them to follow American methods. The Institute that year acknowledged the rapid strides made in our blast-furnace practice. The competition was alarming, and Sir Lowthian Bell declared, "It was true we must prepare to meet American competition in our own country." There were also signs that the Germans were beginning to imitate America in making the best at the lowest price. A graphic proof of the harsh effects of this competition was a ragged deputation which waited on the Assessment Committee of the Merthyr Board of Guardians.

Part of the earliest work undertaken by the British Iron Trade Association was to report on American conditions: in 1876, the visit of W. S. Caine in 1893, and later Franklin Hilton, and in the presidential addresses of Alfred Baldwin, Sir John J. Jenkins, and William Jacks. But since no authoritative documents could be appealed to, an investigatory commission was appointed in 1901 under the chairmanship of Ebenezer Parkes. The report praised American workers for temperance and regularity, the advantages of publicity in the iron and machinery trades, the wider use of basic steel, and the interchange of information; but it denied British backwardness:

Probably no authorities have taken greater pains to inform themselves . . . as liable to be influenced by American competition, than those who have been concerned in the recent consolidations in South Wales. . . . Have they not been stimulated by what they saw and learned in the United States to take steps which implied a large amount of confidence in the future?

A mixer which blended the flow of several furnaces at the Carnegie works reached Barrow in 1889 and was in general use by 1908 in many leading concerns. The use of stamped steel had spread from the States, and steps were taken to improve Sheffield steel. In 1901 the chairman of Guest, Keen, and Co. Ltd. visited America to study the arrangements of the steel combine. Such firms as the Consett Iron Co. and Vaughn and Co. were being Americanized. Reports also attributed part of our advance to the fact that companies were managed by "industrial" not "commercial" men.

While men like J. S. Jeans spoke frequently of American competition, the impression grew that English manufacturers could make headway only if they adapted scientific methods and modern machinery. The Birmingham and Midland Institute was told that our coal and iron industry was almost perfect in development and arrangement. A Cumberland ironmaster concluded that England could learn from us in the use of university graduates and the smelting of iron ore. The *Report on the Iron and Steel Exhibits at the St. Louis Exhibition* proved that we had advertised well, the United Kingdom had not. Great interest was shown in the possibility of copying the subdivision of rolling mill work. Attention was also drawn to the rules of the American Foundrymen's Association for testing cast iron mechanically.

From 1850 onwards America made advances in the workshop which could not be overlooked by British engineers, in the interchangeable system of manufacturing, the turret, the protean cam, precision grinding machinery, process of milling, general use of working gauges, and scores of other devices and processes which were often designated "Yankee notions." [7] These exports of machinery and notions had affected the pace of industrial change in England. The British Commissioner to the Centennial Exhibition in 1876 rated American edge tools and miscellaneous hand tools above the exhibits of other countries. Charles Churchill and Co. Ltd., established in 1865, was perhaps the pioneer of the American machine-tool trade in Great Britain. In 1899 Alfred Herbert Ltd. was spoken of as a "firm who follow American methods of manufacture perhaps more closely than any other machine tool makers in this country." At the Stanley and National Show in 1898, the *Engineer*, which sometimes could not decide about the quality of our machinery, found that the firms which had closely followed our models in automatic tools had the best exhibits;

Is it possible that English manufacturers cannot find time to devote some attention to this class of machinery, and so offer battle to the increasing competition, or is it that they still profess to despise American methods? If the latter is the cause, they would do well to undeceive themselves by an inspection of American machines.

Nothing attracted more attention in 1898 and 1899 in mechanical engineering than the comparative merits of American and English machine tools. The success of the special American lathes for the manufacturing of bicycle parts had aided the introduction of other machines. Archibald Kendrick Jr. observed, however,

Between this country and America there is a difference of conditions, which manifests itself all through the design and construction of a machine, from the general features down to the smallest detail.

Before a conference of the Institution of Civil Engineers, Mr. Arthur Greenwood reported that Americans were more ingenious, but did not try to make so many varieties; he observed that the driving gear, originated by the American Sellars as a compromise between the screw and the rack, was being followed in England and Germany. Another engineer with American experience deemed it unfortunate that the English took their ideas of American machines from the lighter patterns, which were all that came to England.

A long controversy had been started in the pages of *Engineer* (1899) on the superiority of our machine tools. Some begrudged the praise for vertical lathes. James Vose, who stated that the Smith and Coventry keyway cutter had come from America, observed:

Up to now the principal differences in English and American methods have arisen from the fact that the American tool has had the castings, forgings, bar metal, etc., it had to deal with much more carefully prepared for it as regards softness, closeness to size, etc., while the English tool has always been expected to tackle anything which comes its way. . . . When the Americans decide that a change is advisable, though, they take it in hand at once.

The firm of Webster and Bennett, who admitted that there were antiquarians in the engineering trade, was located in Coventry in the midst of the district where many American machines were in use; it reported that as a younger firm it perhaps "felt the greater necessity of keeping thoroughly in touch with the best American . . . tool practice." A company which had been condemning our tools in the journal was buying more American than English machinery. Others doubted whether we really worked to micrometer gauges or tested our machines. Several managers believed that superiority consisted of specialization and in designing tools to produce work to samples. Mr. Hugh Campbell, who had started the controversy, replied to criticisms by showing that England could not touch our turret lathe or automatic gear-cutting machines, and that we had shown England what a milling cutter could do. The gist of the whole discussion was the need for freer adoption of machinery and plant, less complacent engineers, and labor's support to meet American competition.

Manchester was aroused by American tools which came in "with a lot of brag and bluff"; the Sheffield Technical School caused a flutter when it proposed to supplement its equipment with American-made tools. Joseph Horner found that American screw machines had no imitators until 1895; he viewed our designs apparent in high-speed drilling machines of English make, vertical boring mills, the housing of planing machines, and milling machines of vertical and planer type. England was told to grind all cutters mechanically, make use of electricity in driving machines, use compressed air for drills and hammers, and adopt our hoisting machines. Portable pneumatic tools, which were first generally used in America, were by 1903 arousing British labor's complaint against automatism. Sir Robert Hadfield, according to F. W. Taylor, acknowledged the Taylor process of hardening tool steel; but generally the English believed the discovery was an accident. After a visit to the Bethlehem works, Windsor Richards advised mechanical engineers to obtain more information "as to what was being done in America before arriving at the decision not to adopt these high-speed cutting tools." Since criticisms had been made of the endurance and stability of American machines, efforts were made to attract purchasers by using the term "Anglo-American" to indicate ingenious devices wedded to the greater durability of British tools. A minor result of the invasion was described by Walter Deakin:

> By a process of education, for which the American had been to a very large extent responsible, many engineers had condescended to consult the tool-maker as to methods of producing work, and that had induced tool-makers willingly to give more attention to these matters.

This was a useful vulgarization.

We were adding to the industrial pattern in other ways.[8] The advantage of standardization and specialization was illustrated by our competition. "In these matters," said Sir Benjamine Browne in 1900, "Americans see far more clearly than we do." Britons complained that because of lack of coöperation between civil engineers and makers of steel, engines, or bridges, their engineers did something different each time. Our practice of reducing the number of iron and steel sections was closely followed by British engineering committees. Sir William Preece reported that the British Association had been striving for years to introduce a standard screw gauge for small screws, and finally had to turn to Pratt and Whitney. We pointed to the necessity of standardization in the electrical industries. Preece organized a committee to act with Americans on the standards of light and illumination; a proposal came from America in 1912 for an international conference on photometric nomenclature and standards. To be goaded into standardization, essentially a leveling process which came naturally from a country of rapid expansion, by allegedly "individualistic" Americans, required some mental adjustment in England. Closely related was our specialization (often exaggerated by British writers) which the *Board of Trade Journal* considered in 1901:

> Probably in no other country in the world is the principle of division of labour carried out to a greater extent, or with greater success, than it is in the United States. That the results obtained justify the theory is too evident everywhere to be disputed.

In the manufacture of shoes, watches, firearms, and other articles our competition in foreign markets forced the adoption of American labor-saving devices. An official report on the tin-plate industry asked British manufacturers to inquire into devices for labor and fuel economy. Sir William Mather established the Castner-Kellner Company in 1895 to manufacture caustic soda and chlorine electrolytically, based partly upon the invention of Castner, an American. In 1900 when Professor Chandler of New York spoke to the Society of Chemical Industry, Jesse Collings said one object of the Society was to make England realize what they had to learn from us. The Industrial Alcohol Committee (1905) referred to our uses of absolute alcohol in arts and manufacturing; Asquith also saw the value of Mr. Mond's suggestion for similar legislation (passed in 1906) which allowed the use of denatured alcohol free from revenue taxes. But Sir William Tilden, discussing the chemical industry in 1913, observed that the experience of Germany and America "might . . . have been of greater service to our own manufacturers than appears to be the case." In 1901 an official report on our cement industry warned that it "does not appear to be receiving from British manufacturers the amount of attention it deserves." The chairman of the Associated Portland Cement Manufacturers reported that scientific development and labor-saving machinery would force Britain to follow. One of the largest firms in the combine, White and Company, had already started a battery of rotary kilns based on American patents. By 1911 the American dry process was extensively employed in England.

American foremen were in charge of nut and bolt factories, and several new tube factories which in 1904 were using our methods of butt and lap welding. Some persons disliked American printing machinery, which had been widely introduced during the strike of 1897-98, but over a long period our manufacturers had effected great changes in printing methods. American engines were not considered very satisfactory, but special efforts were being made in 1909 to meet our competition in water turbines. A visit to American and Canadian public works did not impress the President of the Local Government Board either as an engineer or sanitary reformer. In the following year, 1907, Professor Coker told the Institute of Sanitary Engineers to develop hydraulic laboratories, and referred to the equipment at Cornell University. American experiments with water-softeners were followed with interest. England seemed surprised at the extensive use of excavating machinery. By 1906 a steel bar for reinforced concrete was introduced. An instrument for comparing colors, already widely used in Europe and America, was new to England in 1909. The President of British Gas Industries, after a professional visit, noted with relief that British-made gas appliances gained by comparison with American products. The *Times* argued in 1912 that if American genius and methods had been successfully used in Britain to make sewing machines, the same might be done with typewriters. Experts concluded that much of our work in motor engineering, when studied and recast on solid lines by English engineers, was worth consideration. The Wrights in 1908 gave dramatic proof of our activity, and their English visit was said to have prompted the Prime Minister to take measures for improving the national organization of aëronautics.

The young electrical industry looked into American developments with less nationalistic eyes.[9] As a result of a visit in 1883, Sir William Mather "saw the possibilities of electricity," and secured the rights for manufacturing Edison's dynamo at the Salford Iron Works. Mather also bought for his factory the American machinery at the Paris Exhibition. Sir Ambrose Fleming, after an inspection of the Edison Central Station system in New York, reported that a public supply of electricity could become a profitable industry. English capital was constantly urged to copy our enthusiastic support of the infant. Factory inspectors in 1901 lamented that England in an age of electricity seemingly had to follow us. Many American-trained men were in British factories. On the opening of an engineering school at Cambridge devoted to the practical applications of electricity, the *Times* (February 3, 1900) said:

The . . . school may fairly be expected to supply men capable of holding their own against the element of American competition which, in this branch of applied science, has lately assumed very considerable proportions.

Dr. Edward Hopkinson told the Institution of Electrical Engineers that workmen were better in our more highly concentrated industry. An official report on the St. Louis Exhibition declared us

more responsive to new ideas. Our vast advertising of supply undertakings convinced some that an organized publicity campaign in
England would be profitable. A visit to electro-plating plants by the
manager of Messrs. Elkington brought new life to that famous concern. Investigators were sent to study our electric welding, and an
English company was floated; the promoter ruefully commented,
"We had not considered the enterprise of the American against the
want of enterprise of the Britisher. . . ." The *Times* concluded that

The electrical trade has suffered for the reason that it has had concentrated upon it, as a young industry, all the vigour of Continental
and American systems, with the consequence that firms possessed of
faulty conceptions of the science of commerce have been carried down
stream.

The hostility against American practice which had arisen when
British manufacturers could not supply generators and motors for
tramways had abated by 1905.

In 1879 two telephone companies had been formed in London to
exploit the inventions of Bell and Edison; disputes arose and the
two became the United Telephone Co., later, the National Telephone Co.[10] The scientist Sir Ambrose Fleming explained the Edison system at the Crystal Palace Exhibition in 1882. Developments
in telephonic communication were closely watched, and such was the
progress in America (and Canada) that our example was used as a
club to criticize the British telephone system. Mr. Frank W. Jones
reported to the annual meeting in 1901 of the Monte Video Telephone Co. Ltd. that he visited the States because changes there were
revolutionizing the business. A deputation from the London County
Council in the same year thought Lord Londonderry's apologetic
reference to the high cost of New York telephone service was unfair
because of the high wages and rents there. The "measured rate
service" was introduced into England in 1907. Major O'Meara's
candid investigation proved what could be learned in regard to
centralization. Those who were amazed by our rapid expansion opposed nationalization of the British system by declaring that it was
due to private management. As a result of official visits in 1911 the
Post Office introduced experimentally automatic telephone exchanges. General criticism in Parliament forced the Postmaster-

General to reply that our experience had been carefully studied in 1893, 1899, 1905, 1910, and 1911; "I have now two engineers with travelling scholarships living in the United States for the purpose of studying the method, the manufacture and use of telephonic plant." Up to the War many complained that Britain compared sadly with us in trunk service, speed, installation, low costs, and research.

There has been a comprehensive and historic interest in American railroads because of British domestic problems and investments.[11] One can find fluctuations in this interest caused by the spotted career of our railroad securities. The value of America's transportation experience was governed almost too much by commercial success or competition and the demands of pressure groups in the United Kingdom. The press had a surprising amount to say about our railroads which, particularly between 1896 and 1906, were linked with general engineering progress and competition. A newer type of transportation, electric traction, also added to this interest in technical America. The chairman of the Midland came looking for useful ideas in 1857. The general manager of the London and South Western line declared in 1902 that all knew American practice because "English railway general managers had been in the habit of going to America for more than fifteen years past." The Railway Research Bureau Service of the British railways also facilitated the interchange of ideas in a scientific way, especially by private monthly bulletins.

American locomotives, usually considered as rigidly standardized, furnished exciting competition between 1898 and 1903 and gave rise to a crusade against the product. The fact that American makers were able to meet an exigency on British lines aroused anxiety for markets where there was no natural preference for the British product. The fun may be said to have begun about 1840, when four American locomotives were ordered by the Birmingham and Gloucester (later a part of the Midland system) to pull the Licky incline. Early in 1899 the Midland, Great Northern, and Great Central bought American locomotives, partly, it was said, because of the engineering strike. Locomotives, with larger boiler and wider firebox, called "Atlantics" (because first used on our Atlantic Coast Line Railroad) first appeared on the Great Northern Railway in 1898. The first engine of the "Pacific" type (so-called because of its use on the Missouri Pacific), of long wheel base and great weight, ran on the Great Western in 1908. Relief was almost too obvious when the chairman of the Midland, Sir Ernest Paget, expressed dissatisfaction with the American engines. Reports had been issued, after misleading trials, which perplexed admirers of American engineering because they showed that the English product surpassed in fuel, oil, and repair costs. It was expected that these trials would lead to the abandonment of the "tin pots." But some of the press hoped that cheaper locomotives with British quality would be built.

The panic grew in 1900 when there were rumors that South Africa, the Sudan, the Uganda, India, and New Zealand bought our locomotives. Even a false report, such as purchases by the South African military director of railways, had a good effect upon British industry according to the *Westminster Gazette*. The editor of the *British and South African Export Gazette* complained that colonial officials quickly placed orders in America and then cried up their purchases. In order to make a strong case against Indian contracts for engines and railway materials, Sir Alfred Hickman had to abuse American products. His opposition extended to the building of the famous Gôktiek Viaduct by an American company; "The American record of bridge building was a very bad one and yet we went on buying American bridges." The Viaduct, 2,260 feet long and 320 feet high, for the Burman railways, was built by the Pennsylvania Steel Company at £15 a ton, to be erected in one year; the lowest English bid was over £26 a ton, to be completed in three years. The building of the Atbara Bridge had been another dramatic lesson. Could it be that the "idle brags of American engineers" (to use the *Standard's* phrase) were taking in the English? By 1905 bridge builders adopted more rational designs and details of plate-girder and riveted-truss construction.

Official correspondence had to be published respecting the comparative merits of locomotives in Egypt. The British needed too much time to execute orders, according to Cromer; "I am not competent to express any personal opinion as to the extent to which it would be possible or desirable to imitate the Americans in adopting the principle of standardization. . . ." Lord George Hamilton replied to Sir Alfred:

You seem to think that orders have only gone abroad because those who gave them did not understand their business. I wish that it were so. The competition we have to face is founded on something much more formidable and substantial. Chemical research, concentration of capital, thorough technical education, improved industrial organization have made in recent years greater advance in America than here . . .

Hamilton declared that every Indian engineer who visited America had been surprised by the progress and production there. The manager of the Eastern Bengal Railway, Lt. Col. W. V. Constable, recorded high respect for American methods and wanted to try larger wagons and bigger engines; he closed his report by saying,

I think many fair-minded men will agree with me that it is too often the case that other nations are too sceptical and critical of American notions . . .

However, the Indian and Egyptian trials were accepted in some quarters as vindicating the English. British engineers heeded American experience when building railroads in New South Wales or in West Africa, where conditions somewhat resembled those of our western states. The *Engineer* explained:

We repeat that Americans more fully understand what is wanted for railway service in a new and cheap country than we do, and that we ought not to be too proud to learn from them.

It was admitted that the American characteristics of improving and inventing had extended to the railroads.[12] The *Engineer* smugly observed that for no good reason England's railway reformers had taken the United States as the standard of excellence. But the *Westminster Gazette* (May 2, 1902) added:

Our British companies with their conservative methods and old-fashioned directors can very well bear a little stirring up by these volcanic Americans.

The *Times* explained that Americans spent freely for improvements and made loans terminable after forty years, while the English systems never had a cash balance, their debts were perpetual, and their capital was never written down. A committee of shareholders of the London and North Western composed of Mr. Burdett-Coutts, Lord Brassey, and others wanted the board to call a railway conference, and urged reforms based on our methods of handling traffic and detailed accounting systems (which some companies had already introduced). Lord Stalbridge, the chairman, spoke of the "great American wave" which passed over the country frightening everybody into fits. Earl Cawdor, chairman of the Great Western, complained in 1903 that directors had a great many of our examples hurled at their heads. The *Daily Mail* was displeased that Sir James Thompson of the Caledonian Railway should be loath to apply these lessons. It was announced in 1903 that its directors had for the first time sent three of their officers to investigate America. The general manager of the South Western praised the economic management of freight traffic. The Merchants' Trust declared that it preferred Pennsylvania Railroad stock to English railroad securities. Both Bryce and Sir Fortescue Flannery had demonstrated to Parliament in 1900 the importance of our development; the former wished to imitate safety devices, larger cars, and the manipulation of traffic.

Lt. Col. H. A. Yorke's report in 1903 was hailed almost with surprise to silence those who over-praised America. Yet Yorke, who urged no hasty adoption of automatic signaling and larger rolling stock, was impressed by American organization, particularly the separation of the traffic or commercial duties from the operating or working duties, a feature adopted to a degree by the North Eastern and the Great Northern. The general manager of the former had found that statistics greatly aided us; others thought we had avoided departmentalism. In 1905 the *Economist* wanted a central authority to control railroad rates, and still the traders, using American examples, wanted to know why transport costs could not be lower. In 1898 P. R. Simonds, who had written earlier about our railroads, thought British manufacturers could not compete with Americans as long as their haulage tariffs were based on the antiquated British railroad system. Faced with German and American rivalry, two nations which evidently enjoyed favorable railway transport, the British Iron and Trade Association unanimously requested a Select Committee in 1900 to consider railway nationalization. Sir William Acworth (1850–1925), who was very influential in the personal interchange of experience, had written *The Railway and the Traders* (1891), he explained later, to prove that English railways could not carry at American rates. Familiar with our statistical practice, he contended for new forms of British railway accounts, which were introduced in 1911; but only in 1920 did the ton-mile and passenger-mile statistical units become a requirement. England owed much to our efforts in securing cost data, and to cost accounting in the heavier industries.

American examples stimulated cheaper transport of merchandise and minerals by more careful loading, larger trucks and engines, better handling at goods termini, the discontinuance of superfluous trains, and the increased capacity of passenger coaches. English trucks were sometimes put on American tenders, to meet local tastes. Steel cars of an American type replaced wooden wagons on the Caledonian Railway in 1902. Much discussion arose over the benefits of the full-weather American cab which had found its way upon one or two English roads. Steps were taken to combine the end-door coach with the privacy of the old English pattern to make the corridor train. The *Engineering News* compared the English bull-headed rail with the American flat-bottom type to the disadvantage of the former. The arrangement made between the London and North Western and the Midland system for joint working and pooling of profits was borrowed from the States. Others were profoundly envious of the large annual mileage Americans were able to get out of locomotives. American ideas of comfort need not be imitated, said the *Times*, but punctuality might. At the British Association, Acworth described the attention given in American universities to the testing of locomotives and the progressive work done by various railway clubs in spreading knowledge of locomotive practice among engineers. The decision of the Supreme Court on the Hepburn Act (railway rates) was followed closely in England because of interest in a new railroad policy. After explaining how our railroads affected the price of English bread, the *Times* in 1912 declared that England had not paid sufficient attention to our railroads' assistance in developing industries in territories they served, to technical training, and the creation of reserve ability through apprenticeships. The period closed dramatically with the appointment in 1914 of an American, Henry W. Thornton, as general manager of the Great Eastern. This caused a stir, and the board was criticized for not training the men they needed.

The press gave the impression that the waste of life was staggering, and railroads were not easily excused.[13] Sir. H. A. Walker, later manager of the Southern Railway, thought America could not teach safety to England. *Punch* humorously recorded in 1904 that the North Eastern, following us, had created an accident claims department. The *Engineer* asserted:

We have heard it said that the American never cares to finish anything. He will take the greatest pains to construct splendid signals; but this accomplished, he is not particularly careful that the signals are worked.

But these criticisms did not prevent us from contributing to the agitation for railroad safety. The London and South Western planned in 1900 to introduce pneumatic signaling by an underground air-pipe. The Board of Trade was praised for studying our practice with a view to safeguarding life and limb. The automatic coupling prompted most of the discussion. The Bill for automatic couplings introduced in the Commons of 1899 by Mr. Ritchie would have caused an expenditure of £7,000,000 to refit existing stock. Although the Bill came from a visit of the Secretary of the Railway Department of the Board of Trade, the interest was of long standing. Railway men, truck owners, and workers had also sent investigating commissions. The President of the Board of Trade was convinced that the device did save human life, but he reported that the British companies naturally felt the system might work in America but not in Britain. The Bill was dropped, a grave step on the part of vested interests, it was said, in the face of America's example. The question arose from time to time in Parliaments up to 1914, always with our experience to the fore.

British public authorities were constantly reminded that America had not hampered the development of the new traction industry by piddling laws.[14] The Electric Powers Act in the session of 1900 had focused attention on the distribution schemes of other countries. The freedom which induced greater electrification of railways in America was one of the strongest arguments for change whenever special groups talked of legislation. H. F. Parshall observed that one of the chief differences between the two countries was that the Board of

Trade insisted upon the most expensive form of transmission system. Philip Dawson defended his paper on America's electric traction before the Institution of Mechanical Engineers in 1898 by saying,

The most important developments of electric traction in this country had been carried out on the lines of American practice, and had given the most satisfaction.

While others confirmed our advance, Mr. W. M. Morley added, "What were put forward as standards in American practice were not standards at all," because we changed with disturbing frequency. The past president of the Institution broadened the discussion:

Too many attempts had been made to persuade English engineers that what had been done so well and so successfully in America was the only thing that could be done anywhere else.

It was sometimes true, as Professor R. H. Smith asserted in his presidential address to the Civil and Mechanical Engineers' Society, that England was unwilling to learn, and he referred to "militantly British electrical engineers" who denied the value of our traction lessons.

A Glasgow Council's committee on tramways went twice to America and called to their aid H. F. Parshall, an engineer familiar with America. The Council wrangled over contracts in 1899; *Engineering* thought the Council would have been safe with Parshall, but possibly problems of electric traction were best solved on British lines. About 1897 Liverpool defeated a proposition to employ an American supervising expert for its street railways, but several companies had taken on American technical directors. Manchester, it was said, deliberately adopted the overhead trolley system because some American cities had found it cheaper and more adaptable than the conduit system. Yet Allan Baker's strong recommendation of the conduit system to the London County Council was based upon New York and Washington. Professor Kapp reported at the Royal Institution in 1908 that our engineers had set the standard in continuous current working. Pending complete electrification, American reports seemed to justify the policy of keeping local services distinct from main line traffic, one of electric, one of steam. Leeds bought cars from America; American firms planned lines in the neighborhood of

Newcastle in 1902, from Liverpool to Southport, from Liverpool
to Manchester. By 1902 one-half to two-thirds of the motors for
England's street cars were American; bid specifications were de-
manding our car trucks. Tramway exhibitions had been so successful
in America that they were imitated in England. One significant
aspect of our inroads was the ready acceptance of American standards
of pressure, general construction, types of motors and trucks, and
accessories, which showed what could be done by British engineers
in standardization which was, as Professor Ayrton explained, not
stagnation but only conservative radicalism.

London came under the spell of American activity.[15] The competitive aggressiveness of American capitalists taught the Government that London transit was inefficient. The press was agitated by
this struggle between Morgan and C. T. Yerkes, a fight which
originated or strengthened the plan of Parliamentary Committees to
ask for an absolute guarantee of capital, as had been promised by the
contending companies. Arbitration on the value of the American and
Ganz systems of electric traction for the Metropolitan and District
Railways, 1901, brought forth Yerkes and E. W. Rice as the principal figures who advocated the use of direct current. Yerkes, a
notorious American promoter, often pondered London's transit
problems. The London United Tramways, with Yerkes as chairman,
opened in the Hampton Court vicinity, April 2, 1903. Edgar Speyer
criticized Londoners for not coming forward with capital. Yerkes,
who commented on London's atrocious social conditions and his
ability to earn more money in America, suggested doing away with
the English mileage system, and advocated permanent commissions
as in New York and Boston; his American-built cars were dubbed
"Yerkes's Jerkers." Perhaps Yerkes's Underground Electric Railways Co. of London had not allowed sufficiently for differences between Chicago, New York, and London.

The London County Council had sent their officers in 1901 to report on our subways. The Royal Commission on London Traffic,
1903, made considerable use of American examples. The Commission delegated Sir David Barbour, Lord Ribblesdale, Sir John
Dickson-Poynder, and others to investigate, September through October, 1903. On the Advisory Board of Engineers was William Barclay Parsons, chief engineer of the Board of Rapid Transit Railroad

Commissioners of metropolitan New York. The investigators were pleased with independent railroad commissioners, and obtained valuable opinions "on the expediency of laying surface tramways in streets crowded with traffic." London, it was felt, was not up to New York. One commissioner thought the coöperation between private enterprises and the municipality might be imitated in England. New York examples brought no all-night tram service to London. In 1908 the general manager of the Great Western found the feature of New York's rapid transit system to be the great increase in travel caused by a differentiation of slow and fast services. H. F. Parshall came to England in 1894, associated with Dr. John Hopkinson; he became chairman of the Central London, the first traction system to use multiphase transmissions and rotary transformer conversion. With an American accent, training, and habits of action which he found at first somewhat out of place, Lord Ashfield, son of Henry Stanley of Detroit, became the general manager of the Metropolitan District Railway in London; prior to that he had been manager of electric railways in several American cities.

America during these years had begun to repay her industrial heritage. This necessitated on Britain's part a readjustment much more fundamental than any mere diplomatic revolution.

[1] Sir Hiram Maxim, *My Life* (London, 1915), 168, 169, 172; Lord Wolseley said upon trying the Maxim gun, "The Yankees beat all creation." *Auto. of J. H. Hammond*, I, *passim;* H. G. Prout, *Life of George Westinghouse* (London, 1922), 36, 62–66, 213, 264–66, 306–09, 328. The new works in 1900 of the English Electric Manufacturing Co., under Am. management, had buildings of the Yankee steel frame type. Eleanor C. Barnes, *Alfred Yarrow, His Life and Work* (London, 1923), 187; H. Smith in *Dict. Am. Biog.;* Pigou, *Marshall,* 398–99.

[2] It was reported that the Bd. of Trade bought 3,000 copies of the Report; one M.P. wanted it issued as a Parl. Paper. Sir E. H. Verney, *American Methods* (Edin. and London, 1904), 3; Holmshaw, *Times,* Nov. 22, 1902. *Mosely Industrial Commission to the U.S., Oct.–Dec., 1902; Reports of the Delegates* (Manchester, 1903).

[3] Frederic Manning, *Life of Sir William White* (London, 1923), 453, 454, 459; *P. Debs.,* 1904, 131:576–77; 136:992; *Proc. Mech. Eng.,* 1905, Pt. ii, p. 345; 1910, Pts. iii, iv, 855–928, 1002–08; F. W. Taylor's discussion on efficiency received few comments; see also *Proc.,* 1904, 533–937; 1905, 7–97. *Minutes of Civil Eng.,* 1900/01, cxlvi, Pt. iv, 133ff.; McKenzie, *Am. Invaders,* 68; Frank Foster, *Engineering in the U.S.* (1906), a report to the J. H. Gartside scholarship electors (estb. at Victoria University, Manchester, 1902, for study of commerce and industry in Germany, Switzerland, or U.S.). W. J. Ashley, *Adjustment of Wages,* vii, 133, 160–61.

[4] Rosebery, *Times,* Oct. 16, 1901; Claudius Clear (W. R. Nicoll), *Letters on*

Life (London, 1901), chap. ix; Nicoll kept in touch with Am. authors. Arthur Shadwell, *Industrial Efficiency: a comparative study of industrial life in England, Germany, and America* (London, 1906), I, chap. i; the *Daily Mail* used Shadwell to show the dangers of doing away with religion in Am. schools. J. F. Fraser, *America at Work* (London, 1903), 18, 32, 79, 95, 111, 127, 262; America's materialism prevented culture according to Fraser. Douglas Knoop, *American Business Enterprise* (Manchester, 1908), 96–97, a Gartside report. *Minutes Civ. Eng.*, 1901/02, cxlviii, Pt. II, 58–107; *Proc. Mech. Eng.*, 1904, pp. 953, 958; Iron Trade Conference, *Times*, Apr. 1, 1903. It is curious to note that Ashley said it was easier to obtain information on American conditions. In 1912 the *Times* urged a scheme such as our Civil Engineer's Appointments Board. Townsend, *Cont. R.*, 1902, 82: 564; Walter Ford on "Limits of the American Invasion," *Cont. R.*, 1902, 81: 787. The charge was frequently made that English constructors copied American ideas but with the essential features left out. Beginning Sept., 1901, *Engr.* had a special series devoted (p. 321) to "Iron Foundries and Foundry Practice in U.S." A. P. Loscher on workshop org., *Engr.*, Dec. 20, 1901, p. 633; Mark Twain, *Europe and Elsewhere* (New York and London, 1923), "Some National Stupidities" (written 1891–92), 175–85.

⁵ Sir James Joicey anticipated our strong competition. See *P. Debs.*, 1901, 89: 1370; 93: 471, 488, 506–08, 538, 545–46, 843–44; 94: 684, 699ff., 822; 95: 965; also 93: 822ff. *Report on Coal Mining in Illinois, 1898, Ac. & P.*, 1899, XCVII; *Report on the Coal Industry of the U.S., 1901, Ac. & P.*, 1903, LXXVI; also 1901, LXXX; 1902, CIII; 1905 (Cd. 2237–12), LXXXVI; 1906, CXXII. Sir Isaac Lowthian Bell, *Notes of a Visit to the Coal and Iron Mines of the U.S.* (London, 1886). Lewis, *Times*, Sept. 4, 1901. "An Electrical Heading Machine," *Trans. Inst. Mining Eng.*, 1903–04.

⁶ J. S. Jeans *et al.*, *American Industrial Conditions and Competition; Reports of the British Iron Trade Assoc.* (London, 1902), vi, ix, 1, 60–64, 85, 203, 231, 281, 323; Frank Popplewell, *Some Modern Conditions and Recent Developments in the Iron and Steel Production in America* (Manchester, 1906), a Gartside study; *Visit of the Iron and Steel Institute to the U.S.* (London, 1895); Victor S. Clark, *Hist. of Manufacturers in the U.S., 1860–1914* (Washington, 1928), 650. The president (1908) of the British Foundrymen's Assoc. did not regard Am. pig-iron specifications as applicable to Eng. Carnegie gave $65,000 to the Institute in 1901 for metallurgical research; he also discussed stock sales to employees. Jeans, *Engr.*, Dec. 19, 1902; McKenzie, *Am. Invaders*, 68–73; Clapham, *Econ. Hist.*, III, 151–56. On St. Louis exhib. see *Ac. & P.*, 1905 (Cd. 2237–7), LXXXVI; *Report on the Iron Ore Industry of the U.S., Ac. & P.*, 1902, CIII; *Report on Mining Industry of Colorado, Ac. & P.*, 1900, XCI. The Edison Ore and Milling Syndicate (formed 1898), supported by Sir Andrew Noble and others, was viewed as a step to defeat Am. competition. Tariff Commission in 1904 issued memorandum on iron and steel in U.S. and Ger.

⁷ Joseph W. Roe, *English and American Tool Builders* (New Haven, 1916), 102–04, 107–08, 140–41. Sir Joseph Whitworth (1803–1887) was impressed in 1873 by our use of automatic machinery and standardization; he and George Wallis wrote *The Industry of the U.S. in Machinery, Manufactures, and Useful and Ornamental Arts* (London, 1854). Possibly the system of "interchangeable manufacturing" was introduced into Eng. in making the Enfield rifle. G. H. Putnam, Am. publisher, once campaigned for Daniel Pidgeon, early importer of

Am. machinery and student of Am. affairs; Putnam, *Memories of a Publisher*, 277–78; Daniel Pidgeon, *An Engineer's Holiday* (London, 1882) and *Old-World Questions and New-World Answers* (London, 1884). Clarke, *op. cit.*, 173, 362; Kendrick on "American Planing Machines," *Proc. Mech. Eng.*, 1905, 57. Deakin, *ibid.*, 1901, 343–53; Richards, *ibid.*, July, 1903; Webster & Bennett, *Engr.*, Jan. 13, 1899; Vose, *Engr.*, Jan. 20, 1899; Campbell, *Engr.*, Dec. 30, 1898; F. B. Copley, *Frederick W. Taylor, Father of Scientific Management* (London, 1923), II, 86, 91. Details may be traced in *Machinery Market* (Arthur Wadham, ed.).

[8] Details may be found in *Chemical Trades Journal, Hardware Trade Journal*, and *Iron and Steel Trades Journal. P. Debs.*, 1904, 131:576–77; 1906, 159:622; Clarke, *op. cit.*, 767; *Report on the American Tin-plate Industry* . . . , *Ac. & P.*, 1897, LXXXVIII, Mis. Ser., No. 426, p. 7; *Report on the Zinc Industry in the U.S.*, *Ac. & P.*, 1901, LXXX; *Report on the Turpentine Industry in the U.S.*, *Ac. & P.*, 1906, CXXII; S. H. Higgins, *Dyeing in Germany and America* (Manchester, 1907), a Gartside study; *Report on the Cement Industry of the U.S.*, *Ac. & P.*, 1901, LXXX, p. 3; *Minutes Civ. Eng.*, 1900/01, CXLV, Pt. III, 44–173; Coker, *Times E.S.*, Mar. 6, 1907, p. 76; Burns, *Times*, May 21, 1906; Read, *Proc. Mech. Eng.*, 1903, p. 850.

[9] Details may be found in the *Electrician, Journ. Elec. Eng.*, and *The Electrical Review*. Mather, *Mather*, 16, 23–24; Sir Ambrose Fleming, *Memories of a Scientific Life* (London, 1934), 88. The Edison accumulator, described to the Inst. of Elec. Engineers in 1903, was still by 1912 not much used in England. On St. Louis Exhibition, see *P.P.*, 1905 (Cd. 2800), 54:350–51. Cf. two company reports (Electric Construction Co. Ltd. and Electric Power Storage Co. Ltd.) in *Times*, July 10, 1903. Hopkinson, *Am. Mach.*, Apr. 1900, p. xxi; Prof. Unwin on Niagara power stations, *Times*, Oct. 4, 1905. Factory Report in *P.P.* (cd. 668), 1901, X, p. 156. O'Hagan, *Leaves from My Life*, II, 195, 241–43.

[10] E. H. Johnson was Edison's representative in England. *P. Debs.*, 1898, 55: 1672; 1899, 73:June 20; 1902, 101:Jan. 27; 1911, 25:1367–68; 32:Dec. 13; 1912, 38:1043, 1585, 1615; 42:701; 1913, 52:594–98, 641; 1914, Commons, 64:720, 725, 729–30, 746, 757, 763, 775.

[11] McKenzie, *Am. Invaders*, 146ff.; *Times's* American Railway Number (London, 1912) issued in book form; *Proceedings of International Railway Congress Association, Washington, 1905* (Brussels, 1906); *Comparative Merits of British and American Locomotives in Egypt*, *P.P.*, 1902 (Cd. 1010), CIV, 6–9; Lord Hamilton cited in *Gôkteikiana, 1899–1901* (London, 1903), 5, ed. by R. F. Hunger; Hickman, *Times*, June 4, 1901; *P. Debs.*, 1901, 94:1026; 1912, 38:202. Lord Reay complained in 1909 that one hundred Am. engineers had been employed in ironworks in Central Provinces, India. W. R. S. Jones, *Proc. of Mech. Eng.*, 1900, pp. 577, 562, 573. Note career of the famous railway promoter, Sir Edward Watkin (1819–1901), who first visited U.S. in 1851, and who wrote *A Trip to the U.S. and Canada* (1852) and *Canada and the States, Recollections, 1851–1886* (1887). C. E. R. Sherrington, *Economics of Rail Transport in G.B.* (New York, 1928), I, 176–78, 203, 251; II, 15, 64, 317.

[12] W. V. Constable, *Report on the Railways of America* (London, 1902), 51; *P. Debs.*, 1899, 76:229, 250; 1900, 81:1292, 1298, 1310–11; 1901, 93:937–39; 94:1024ff.; 1912, 47:1630; 48:1066. The *Manch. G.* remarked slyly, March 2, 1914, "Under Thornton the Long Island Railroad is modernizing its signalling equipment. If he should plump for similar progress on the Great Eastern, Lord

Claude Hamilton will be presented with a fine opportunity." For H. A. Yorke see his *Railways, Report on Visit to America, 19th Sept. to Oct. 30, 1902, P.P.,* 1903, LX, 4, 6–8, 17; he believed our experience in "light railways" would be helpful. Note articles by a British railroad official in *Times E.S.* beginning Nov. 27, 1905. *Statist* in 1906 published a supp. on Am. r.r. *Reports on U.S. Railways, Ac. & P.,* 1905, Cd. 2237–38; *Minutes, Inst. of C.E.,* 1899/1900, cxlii, Pt. iv, 102–132; *Proc. M.E.,* 1901, pp. 1200, 1206; 1910, pp. 855–928. See also *Railway News.*

[13] Walker, *Times,* Oct. 18, 1902; *Proc. M.E.,* 1903, 899–912; *Minutes C.E.,* 1901/02, cxlvii, Pt. i, art. by J. L. Cridlan. It was asserted in Parl. that we had improved the bogie and the use of the self-acting brake. *P. Debs.,* 1899, 66: 1118, 1304–05, 1570ff.; 67: 647; 69: 661–62; 70: 1451, 1454–55, 1461, 1465; 1908, 186: 1568; 1909, Commons, 8: 1622, 1627–28, 1644.

[14] *P. Debs.,* 1903, 123: 54; Dawson *et al., Proc. M.E.,* 1898, 43–123; *ibid.,* 1902, 304ff.; Parshall, *ibid.,* 1910, p. 1216; *Jour. of E.E.,* 1900, 29: 297, 334. O'Hagan, *op. cit.,* I, 56. Earlier in the history of tramways an Am. engineer, G. F. Train, laid four or five tramways without Parliamentary authority; between Hanley and Burslem, in Bayswater Road, London; between Shepherd's Bush and Ealing, one at Birkenhead, and another in the Potteries.

[15] *Royal Commission on London Traffic, Reports, etc., P.P.,* 1906, 42: 6, 7, 630–31; *passim,* esp. paragraphs 403–1063 in vol. 40. Also report by F. W. Manners in *General Omnibus Company (London), Third Report, 1910, P.P.,* 1911, Cd. 5472, XXXIV. R. D. Blumenfeld, *All in a Lifetime* (London, 1931), 169; H. F. Parshall, *The Parshall Family* (London, 1915), 167–69. London tubes had hastily abandoned old type cars for premature Am. models. One innovation in London was the call, "Next station will be —."

X

POLITICAL PATTERNS

*Nothing can be more instructive than American experience if it be
discreetly used, nothing will be more misleading to one who tries to apply it without allowing for the differences of economic and social environment.*—JAMES BRYCE

AMERICA exerted no profound or revolutionary political influence upon Great Britain during these years.[1] Nevertheless it
will be instructive to examine what affected America's rôle as a political example, and to discover what use was made of our experience.
The outcome of the Civil War, according to Morley and others,
had been one of the strongest incentives for the extension of popular
government in England. Federalism as embodied in our history and
state system was of timely interest. England looked upon our political biology partly as illustration of axioms of political and social
science, partly as contemporary instruction or warning. Political
lessons were not clear because both sides of an argument usually discovered anything they wanted. This practice, however, depended
upon whether we had a good or bad name on foreign soil. One is
left with the impression that British opinion was not far removed
from our "radical" or "advanced" criticisms during the same years.
It emphasized, in a most convincing manner, political maladminis-
tration. Bryce attributed this to the fact that judgments were based
on Britain's conventional rather than actual standard. Surprisingly
little was heard of a brotherhood of democracies.

Bryce and his compatriots agreed on the political apathy of fas-
tidious minds, lax public management which relied on the ability of
every man to do anything, and the low tone of public life. British
opinion said little about insubordination or Wells's view that we
were ripe for a dictator. Bryce did not believe that we were jealous of
greatness; most Britons went further, for they discovered that we

worshipped greatness and "smartness," particularly in the capacity to earn money. Whether we were courageously consistent in carrying out political ideals, or were fickle, was not clear because England was uncertain about our goals. Nor was opinion generally so optimistic as Bryce on the strength and promptitude of our democracy, the law-abiding qualities of the people, the absence of struggles between the privileged and unprivileged, or that the New World had so managed as to have the "best security against . . . chronic Old World evils, even when her economic state shall have been less auspicious than it is now."

But what was very significant, Britons by the end of the nineteenth century saw a stable, conservative element in our democracy, so rigid that Tories, instead of confining attention to the failures of the American Commonwealth, now found positive values in our national career. It has not been sufficiently stressed that a large portion of serious opinion held to the view that our Constitution and institutions were undemocratic, less liberal than England's, and too inelastic to cope with new problems. During this period, those who supported the *status quo* usually profited most from allusions to America, and during the democratizing reforms from 1909 to the War, the Liberals frequently avoided the United States. Overseas migration does not necessarily liberate radical or progressive mental growth, and A. J. Toynbee in his recent *Study of History* has been one of the first to express in scholarly fashion the Englishman's growing suspicion that, fundamentally, America is old-fashioned. But out of a laboratory so vast came diverse instruction.

Lord Norton (1814–1905) wrote a pamphlet, "Europe Incapable of American Democracy"; twenty years later, in 1889, he sent the pamphlet to Lord Kimberley, the Liberal leader in the Lords, who agreed that any democratizing of the English system would make it more radical than ours unless our checks were also applied. The anti-democratic, comparative jurist Sir Henry Maine willingly looked to us for a lesson where the success of the Constitution, as he wrote in 1885, "and . . . of such American institutions as have succeeded, appears . . . to have arisen rather from skilfully applying the curb to popular impulses than from giving them rein." The arch-conservative publicist W. H. Mallock (1849–1923) was not infected by his subsidized visit of 1907, the fruits of which were lectures collected under the title, *A Critical Examination of Socialism*. Dicey observed quite correctly a tremendous change in attitude:

Respectable Englishmen are beginning to consider whether the Constitution of the United States may not afford means by which, under new democratic forms, may be preserved the political conservatism dear and habitual to the governing class of England.

Bryce could find very few achievements that were distinctly American, but "there is a thoroughness in embracing or working out certain political or social conceptions which is less common in England." By implication or practice, America might teach Europe to keep the judiciary out of politics, to improve the civil service, to maintain second chambers, to restrict legislatures' powers, the value of a rigid constitution, the advantages of direct legislation (an enthusiasm decreasing with later editions), and that the absence of an established church does not lessen the religious force in political or social reform. He suggested later that our system did not commend indirect election.

Even young Liberals, such as Leslie Stephen in the sixties, made the point that such was the difference between the two countries that the ugly results produced by American democracy would not follow in a democratic England. Gladstone fervently hoped the "spoils system" would never come to England. Lecky, who was peculiarly susceptible to America, observed in 1889 that Bryce's volumes made a great impression, especially on State government and the "machine," about which Englishmen knew little; he added:

I think the best judges over here believe that sooner or later something must be done to restrict the omnipotence of such a Parliament as we possess, and it can only be done by building on [America's] model.

After reading Rhodes's *History* in 1895, he wrote:

American books are much less read in England than they should be. They always interest me greatly, dealing as they do with the more advanced stages of the democracy to which we are coming.

His two gloomy volumes on *Democracy and Liberty* (1896, revised in 1899) deprecated the modern tendencies of democracy. For these volumes he followed Bryce's descriptions, although he believed that

Bryce minimized wherever possible the corruption of our courts and judges:

But no one . . . can follow American history without perceiving how frequently and seriously the democratic principle has undermined this first condition of true freedom and progress.

However, Lecky would have desired a written constitution to produce the stability he perceived in this country. In 1895 and later, Herbert Spencer anticipated a social crash because we tolerated the "smart man" and the financial tyranny of trusts. For a chapter on "Political Bias," Spencer once requested from an American friend "a supply of typical illustrations of the way in which your political machinery acts so ill—its failures in securing life, property, and equitable relations." A curious method of fact-finding! After a "most stimulating" two months' visit in 1904, John Morley, who foresaw America as the greatest power but one which exaggerated social difficulties by treading a democratic path, lamented the corruption of the Senate and the dangerous fatalism which pervaded our political affairs.

Henry George, thought of as very American in outlook, and frequently criticized solely on that ground, shocked British bourgeois complacency.[2] It was inevitable that "this wild man from California" —a State which affected England at many points—should be one of the long line of "Prophets" from across the ocean. His *Progress and Poverty*, which was first published in England in 1881 by Kegan, Paul and Company, who were sceptical about any American book on political economy, became a best seller. From his pilgrimage of 1883, presided over at the beginning by Labouchere, arose the English Land Restoration League, afterwards the English League for the Taxation of Land Values. His criticisms of rapacious landownership added impetus to the young Fabian Society and inspired British Socialism. He set George Bernard Shaw on the trail of political science, turned Philip Henry Wicksteed to economics, and influenced James Keir Hardie, the labor leader, and H. W. Massingham, Liberal publicist. The Irish Nationalist, Michael Davitt, who helped to contact Fenians in America, was further convinced by George of Ireland's need of a constitutional program joined to agrarian reform. The author of *Land Nationalization* (1882), Alfred Russell Wallace, who came lecturing in the eighties, may not have received his first inspiration from George, but he was encouraged by George's advocacy of the principle. Wallace also looked to America to lead as an ideal state despite the mockery of capitalism; Edward Bellamy's books first opened his eyes to the practicability of Socialism, and converted him about 1889 from land nationalization to Socialism. Graham Wallas, a leading Fabian, owed to William James's *Principles of Psychology* "the conscious desire to think psychologically" about his work as a political scientist, and he turned to the eastern States for much of his material.

Sidney Webb, economist and a Fabian, concluded his course of lectures on "The Actual Working of the American Constitution" at the London School of Economics, March 1899, by describing the weak points of municipal administration, our disbelief in government, and overweening conceit that every man was equally capable. For Mrs. Sidney Webb we proved that the rise of wages and improvement in industrial technique produced even greater inequalities of wealth and personal power. In the eighties Joseph Chamberlain had explained to her his desire to make life more pleasant for the majority; he thought of America:

Cultured persons complain that the society there is vulgar, less agreeable to the delicate tastes of delicately trained minds. But it is infinitely preferable to the ordinary worker.

Henry Labouchere also maintained a strong predilection for everything American; in 1883 he wrote to Chamberlain:

I was caught young and sent to America; there I imbibed the political views of the country, so that my Radicalism is not a joke but perfectly honest. . . . My opinion of most of the institutions of this country [England] is that of Americans—that they are utterly absurd and ridiculous.

He commended our education, would have patterned the House of Lords after the Senate, and approved of the American Constitution as an example for Ireland and England. Those who were "caught young" and sent to America from 1890 on were sometimes less enthusiastic.

Debates in Parliament about the United States were seldom full-dress discussions, but they turned attention to all phases of our life. Such Parliamentary references cut across party lines, pressure groups, geographical divisions, Government and Opposition. Comparatively, the Lords said about as much as the Commons; the Radicals, not much more than the Conservatives. The Irish considered themselves authoritative interpreters of America. Some of the attention was stimulated by the interest of special groups outside. Many members showed a desire to inquire into America's career because it was difficult to secure agreement on the nature of our experience. American and Colonial arguments and practice were frequently brought together, as in the debates on marriage legislation, sectarian teaching, local option, electric traction, and female suffrage. Of foreign countries, probably only Germany received as much attention. British government reports, travel, and, to an astounding degree, Bryce's *American Commonwealth* were the principal sources of information. Forty-two members specifically referred to information they gained as tourists.

A closer examination is now in order.[3] Agitation by the Liberal government for the reform and restriction of the House of Lords in 1907 produced many references to our political system. Many quoted from Bryce, a Liberal, to show the value of the Lords and two chambers, and that America believed England would soon need a veto power to protect the people against hasty representatives. A. J. Balfour did not want British institutions stereotyped and "petrified" as were those of America where an "immovable conservatism" prevailed. While contrasting our "extreme caution" with the Prime Minister's "reckless" proposals, Arthur Lee cited Alexander Hamilton's praise of the Lords, amid ironical cheers from the Nationalists; he found our lower house had less power than the Commons, "and yet it is far more representative of the people." The Attorney-General reminded Lee that there was no hereditary chamber in the United States. Prior to visiting us in 1886, Alfred Lyttleton wrote, "I expect nothing so I cannot be disappointed." In this Parliament he argued that America, where the able men shunned politics, best demonstrated the dangers of plutocracy. Morley, then Secretary of State for India, dissented, but Lyttleton insisted that

. . . the traditions of the best of American families is commercial ascendancy pushed to a very far extent. . . . I do not say that there is want of culture among those who take part in public life in America.

This echoed the Duke of Argyll's comment made in 1879:

Nothing makes one see the value of the independent territorial politicians of England more than residence in America, where as a rule the rich get rich too late for public life.

Others pointed out the dangers of single-chamber rule without a Supreme Court.

When the Lords turned down Lloyd George's budget of 1909, another struggle followed to confine the power of the upper house. Parliament was dissolved, and as a result of elections in January 1910, the Asquith Ministry had to rely upon Liberals, Irish Nationalists, and Labourites. The American note became strong in Parliament and outside.[4] An early conference of the two parties agreed that it might be useful, in addition to Dominion experience, to have President Butler of Columbia University give evidence on State constitutions, the referendum, and our methods of dealing with deadlocks between the two chambers. Opponents of the Liberal Ministry turned gleefully to American examples and analogies; they even began to suggest the value of the referendum. They pointed out how carefully we had protected our Constitution from change. Evelyn Cecil declared:

I cannot believe that the hon. Members who so glibly advocate the restriction of the Veto of the House of Lords . . . can have studied the history of the United States.

The Archbishop of Canterbury discovered throughout all the *American Commonwealth* a deep sense of the value of Britain's unwritten constitution. If Members were going to change the constitution, said Sir Frederick Banbury, who paid us a clever tribute, they should "frame an alternative that would keep the power in the hands of some Supreme Court that would compare with the Supreme Court in America."

Lord Ellenborough felt the referendum would save England from log-rolling, "the curse of the United States." Others quoted

Bryce to show our approval of the referendum. A week after receipt of a request from Grey, Bryce sent back, April 18, 1910, a report on our use of the referendum which was used primarily by speakers in the Lords debates, March 2, 1911. S. R. Honey, writing in 1912, blamed Bryce for confusing "referendum" with "submissions," and in the introduction to Honey's volume, J. St. Loe Strachey argued that in England only constitutional lawyers realized that we had used the referendum as a home-grown institution. For party purposes, Lord Rosebery observed: "I tremble when I think of the scorn of the United States when it witnesses our constitutional operations."

Election speeches juggled with many things. Opponents attacked the American gold which was supporting Lloyd George's ally, Mr. Redmond, who was said to have received £40,000 from the United States. This was a clever election trick which conveyed sinister meanings. Conservatives erected Redmond as a bogey with his pockets full of "Yankee Boodle." Page Croft opened his election campaign against the "Little England-American Alliance which for four years had misgoverned this country." Our support of the Irish cause aroused the future Earl of Birkenhead: "Let no one misunderstand its menace to our independence and greatness as a nation." Others wanted to know how many more Americans like Joseph Fels were contributing to Liberal free trade funds. Lloyd George tried to dispose of this issue in a demagogic appeal at Mile-End:

Now, what I should like to know is this. Since when have the British aristocracy started despising American dollars? (Laughter, and a voice, "Marlborough.") I see you understand me.

The Liberals, who did not want to submit a Parliament Bill to the people, so stressed the American aspects of the referendum that opponents could say the Liberals "disliked American methods." The Marquess of Salisbury criticized Viscount Haldane (during the Peoples Bill in the Lords) for making light of the classic example of the United States. The Liberals argued that our experience proved the referendum would not work, was too costly, and, judging from American voting papers, a "most misleading way of endeavouring to elicit the popular opinion" on complicated measures, even within small areas. The *British Weekly*, organ of Liberalism, concluded that it actually retarded progress.

As the discussion of the relationship of the Lords and Commons continued in 1911, American references gained in variety. Dr. Hillier read portions of the American Constitution to Parliament, and outlined its safeguards. Several Members painted the Senate as a greater bulwark of vested interests than the Lords. There was little agreement about our use of joint conferences between the Senate and the House. As a compromise, Sir Robert Finlay and Sir Frederick Banbury suggested a Supreme Court to determine what was a money bill, but Balfour correctly surmised that England would not tolerate the domination of any body of judges. Earl Fortescue cited Bryce, and the *Times* cited the career of Joe Cannon to show what dangers might arise if the Speaker were given political power. While one critic of the Lords pointed to us to outline the great difficulties should the Upper House retain power to interfere with finance, Mr. Neil Primrose found that the Commons really had the same power as the Convention which set up our Constitution. But the strongest appeal remained the same— that we were slow to change. Even Lord Curzon asked, "Were we to be less wise than America, less cautious than our Colonies?" This attitude was summed up by Harry Lawson: "If we had a tithe of the reverence for our Constitution that the Americans have, we should not attack it in this haphazard way."

Did all these references to us have anything more than academic importance? Actually, the Liberals never descended with any full-blown scheme for a new Second Chamber, and ultimately they relegated the reconstruction of the Lords to the future. The Opposition had managed to stress the value of a bicameral system while demonstrating that the Lords was as representative as any new-fangled Senate would be, and that it had much more prestige. The Liberal answers to the American examples were not very convincing. The direct effect is not obvious, but one may suspect that we were slightly helpful in restricting a greater departure from the *status quo*, that we served those who had never been considered the "natural allies" of our democracy.

That the United States had been a great factor in Canadian

federation, as much by pressure as by example, was still considered important.[5] As W. M. Whitelaw has said, "the success or failure of the American system to remain really federal will continue to have significance for these younger federations. . . ." In fact, British colonial affairs often involved American constitutional practice. This might be done with a mixture of enthusiasm and ardent hostility, as in the debates for the union of South Africa, 1909. The use of American precedents up to and beyond 1900 for Australian Federation elicited very little comment in England, even though Australia had turned from Canada's model to ours. Joseph Chamberlain thought that in general the Australian Constitution followed the American Constitution; Haldane disagreed because Australia retained the principle of responsible government. The Earl of Selborne viewed the Australian government as more flexible than ours, more akin to British instinct, and more democratic in providing for amendments.

Debates on Home Rule for Ireland naturally included the United States and its embodiment of federal principles.[6] A federalism which seemed to work in the United States apparently reconciled many Englishmen to a similar solution for Ireland. Carnegie preached a federal scheme in 1887 and 1888. Having become a warm admirer of our Constitution after 1878, Moreton Frewen said, "It was inevitable that I should apply these loose American analogies to the very mixed situation I found here." Through Sir Henry Maine Englishmen learned that Edward Phelps, the American Ambassador from 1885 to 1889, thought the Home Rule Bill showed a lack of experience in problems of federal and state power such as came constantly before the Supreme Court. When suggesting local self-government in 1902 on the lines of the American states, Mr. Whiteley and Mr. Pirie shrewdly linked this political device to the contemporary enthusiasm for our efficiency.

As the debate on the Parliament Bill encountered Home Rule in 1911, Frewen and Pirie, being largely Irish, wanted to see the American Constitution copied in the United Kingdom. Others, like Earl Grey and A. J. Balfour, repeated the traditional view that a solution for the Government of Ireland, possibly along American lines, would help Anglo-American relations. So frequently was this done that Austen Chamberlain wrote, "I think it unwise to lay stress on the American side of the case." In 1912 it was observed that the trend in the United States and Canada was toward closer federation. Walter Long, who argued that the Government preferred to rely upon the precedent of the South African union, did not believe, nor did Mackinder, that the American example was useful. Turning to our experience, others concluded that where there was concurrent legislation, State courts could not be trusted; hence, the Irish courts would lack zeal on Imperial Acts. Herbert Samuel replied by observing that since the Irish judges would be appointed, their approach would be significantly different. It was to be expected that again in 1912 a discussion of the Government of Ireland Bill would lead some to say that our states had too much power. Mr. Astor's project (reminiscent of his American background), ultimately rejected, for inserting the "due process of law" clause into the Bill, prompted Sir John Simon to observe that these words were not capable of interpretation, and not so satisfactory as the veto of the Imperial Parliament. John Ward did not want pundits on the bench to use this clause to thwart democratic legislation:

The injunctions, the obstacles placed by the Supreme Court in the way of ordinary labour action for the purpose of improving the conditions of the working people, form one of the most astounding features of American industrial life.

Nor did the Prime Minister, watching our behavior, so want to fetter the legislature. The tension in Ireland and the further discussion of the Bill in 1914 increased the interest in America's past. To Bonar Law, Ulster and America were not dissimilar, and the Americans, he concluded, were right in their rebellion. For others, the Scotland Bill seemed to follow the bad example of the Irish Bill, leaving to the Scottish Parliament all those things which might arise in the future. The reasoning was simple—Alexander Hamilton failed, our States retained the residuum of power, and the Civil War resulted. Thus the United States, which was characterized by Lord Charnwood as a "leading case" in the federal solution, could be made to serve almost any purpose.

By 1900 the laudatory estimates of the Senate by De Tocqueville and other European critics were no longer fully accepted in Great

Britain.[7] Bryce had shown that in advising or controlling the Executive the Senate might produce as many evils as benefits. As early as 1899 Members of Parliament were suggesting arguments much used later, that the American Senate, even though fettered by the Constitution and the Supreme Court, was less subservient than the House of Lords. Labourites were under no illusions: the Senate was a house of vested interests, scarcely to be preferred to the House of Lords. A cautious official report in 1908 found the Senate more powerful than the House of Representatives; Marriott viewed it as the strongest and most efficient of second chambers. But experience with the Senate's adventures in foreign affairs moved Britons to hope for a stronger Executive who retained the treaty-making power. Senator Lodge had to explain the power of the Senate (and our case for revising the Clayton-Bulwer Treaty) to Lord Lansdowne. The *Standard* in 1905 reported that we no longer admired the Senate; the *Saturday Review* spoke of it as "sharing in the general degeneration of Parliamentary institutions throughout the world." Lord Selborne said of the Senate's inquiry into the *Titanic* disaster, "If this . . . is taken as a precedent it is very difficult to say where we shall end." Another Member was undoubtedly over-enthusiastic:

We look perhaps with laudable jealousy . . . at the prompt action of the American Senate. They did not wait to investigate the law as to their capacity or their right to deal with certain people. The whole of England applauds them for doing it.

It was not thought desirable or necessary to circulate in England the results of this inquiry. However, Salisbury, who had admired the Senate and Supreme Court as early as 1885 as stabilizing factors, once said he frequently envied a state which had something like the Foreign Relations Committee of our Senate which could receive in secret "explanations which ministers would be only too glad to give." Several persons hoped for such a committee in England. Would August 1914 have been different had Swift Mac Neill's wish for our Senate's power over peace and war been fulfilled, or if Grey had followed Noel Buxton's suggestion for a Foreign Relations Committee?

America's experience was alluded to in establishing principles of taxation, most frequently in any agitation for broadening the basis of taxation.[8] Members pointed out that we had excellent laws on the taxation of land values; Andrew D. Provand added:

It was made a reproach to us that we would change our law for the American law of rating. Well, we should be much better off if we had the American law in regard to the taxation of cities, because then the full value of the land would be taxed, which it is not at the present moment.

Our system was based on the capital value of property; the English, on the annual value. The Conservatives met this thrust with several arguments, one being that there was terrible overcrowding in America. During the same Parliament Mr. George Whiteley opposed a Tithe-Rent-Charge Bill. Are not such measures, he asked, "an importation of the very worst form of American politics, and a system which smacks of 'the spoils for the victor'?" Opponents of a Land Values Bill in 1904 repeated that the New York system was very misleading.

The famous budget of 1909 brought forth reminders of the activities of Henry George, who was attacked as though he had numerous supporters in the Commons—so much so that Lloyd George had to say, "The idea of calling Henry George a Socialist!" Henry, not D. L. G., had been referred to as a "half-educated fanatic." Mr. Remnant, who violently opposed the land tax, quoted Keir Hardie's speech:

I remember the attempt made to capture the Scottish Labour party for the single-tax movement. Had it succeeded the Labour party would now have been what the single tax movement is, one of the most reactionary forces of our time.

Although Remnant added that the Liberals turned to Germany rather than New York, Mr. C. E. Hobhouse, Financial Secretary to the Treasury, declared, "The United States with all its protective tariffs, is going back to our Death Duties and Income Tax Duties, and Dividend Duties." Walter Long reminded the Secretary that the Income Tax had been declared unconstitutional. Lloyd George, in defending his budget, tried to use foreign examples, but he was interrupted when he suggested timidly that we had high licenses and special taxes such as income and death duties. Opponents of the Budget insisted that it would handicap Britain in her struggle with America for supremacy in the money market. Conservatives declared that the Government had put forward their report on America's taxation as "part of their defence for proposals to impose upon owners of land a special and crushing burden." The Attorney-General declared that the report was pertinent especially because it showed that we were able to distinguish between site and structure values. If Redmond was criticized in the elections of 1910 as a Dollar King, so was the American Joseph Fels, who was accused of making the land tax organization follow him and his money. Fels promised to duplicate up to £20,000 any sums contributed by others. Mr. Pretyman wrote, May 3, 1910:

> The Land Union welcomes the issue raised by Mr. Fels' letter, viz., whether British landowners, great and small, are to be taxed out of existence at the bidding of a foreign millionaire.

In addition to such criticisms, others argued that measures such as the Development and Road Bill would introduce "lobbying" of the American type into England.

England was indifferent and somewhat ignorant of our states' affairs, with the exception of New York, and for this reason was sometimes unable to comprehend our national policies. Her response to our municipal government was somewhat stronger but also curious.[9] W. T. Stead's "Satan's Invisible World Displayed, or Despairing Democracy: a study of Greater New York "(1898) was issued to show the Britons what would happen if they lost their municipal pride. Chicago also inspired Stead to reform it. Shaw suggested in 1901 that America should be farmed out to a European commission to reform local politics. "The condition of American cities," commented the *Spectator*, "is at present the opprobrium of Liberalism everywhere." "Municipal corruption," asserted the *Economist*, "has obtained its full height in America." When lecturing in England, Bryce frequently made comparative studies of municipal governments to our great disadvantage. While supporting the Local Government Bill in 1899, F. E. Smith said it followed the Report of the Royal Commission of 1894 which had recommended greater powers to various local bodies and had cited New York as a dangerous example of over-centralization. The failures of our city governments were used as weapons against municipal trading in England, and Lord Avebury warned that such practice might place British cities dangerously close to Tammany. The reports of the American Commission on Public Ownership and Operation which had visited England in 1906 were accepted by the *Manchester Guardian* as proving that we did not think English municipalization a failure, but that it would "break down in the less competent hands of American municipalities." Our example encouraged changes in modern fire-fighting equipment, up-to-date alarm systems, new instruction and drill classes for firemen, and improved ambulance service. Very few voices suggested that life in American cities was tolerable, even worth studying.

New York City, facing the Old World and receiving most of its attention, influenced the political approach to our other cities. The most optimistic might say with De Bary: "In its final outlook, New York, in all its worldly glory, is the embodiment of the supreme romance of life of the great western continent." But in some way Tammany became the "supreme romance" which England attributed to hurry, incurable optimism, a gold-rush atmosphere, and a tremendous zeal for working democratic institutions which reformers might emulate. San Francisco's graft hardly relieved the monotony of Tammany, which became a byword in England. When the *Globe* wished to criticize its opponents it only had to say,

Tammany methods having seated the London Progressives in office with a big majority, it was only consistent that the Tammany principle of "spoils to the victors" should have been given effect . . .

Lord Salisbury, Sir John Lubbock, and other Unionist leaders in 1898 dragged in Tammany corruption as a result which would follow the Progressive policy in London; Bryce stopped the comparisons by retorting that Tammany really proved the fatal effect of injecting national politics into purely municipal affairs. So detailed had been the reports about New York that opinion was easily aroused against our Mr. Croker, who retired to peace in Berkshire.

Very few scandals were overlooked. Our spoils system was the great *bête noire*.[10] Many a leading article proclaimed "Civil Service" as our principal need. In his *Pattern Nation* (1906), Sir Henry

Wrixon, relying on our unsavory affairs, demonstrated that a socialist autocracy "would be the lowest type of the spoils system"; Hobson, who read the evidence in another way, denied that our spoils system foreshadowed the official tyranny of socialism in England. The harshest thing Bonar Law could say about the Government in 1912 was that it had created a spoils system already rivaling ours, a comparison, evidently, that was understood by a large audience. English campaign methods appeared tame, but some politicians professed to see an increasing likeness to ours, particularly because of the tariff reformers and the suffragists. England began to realize that she might have lobbies of the American type in her own national life. The press disliked our constant political excitement, numerous elections, and overlapping of electoral areas as productive of nothing. Sir Michael Herbert told his Foreign Office that he was "disgusted and disheartened . . . everything in this country is subservient to politics; . . . really an Ambassador in Washington needs more than an ordinary stock of patience." The *Glasgow Herald* spoke of the puerilities of our federal and state elections. The national party conventions were incomprehensible "and a complete exposure of the fallacy of democracy." England had no desire to follow the practice of publishing campaign contributions even though the press could trace the canker of party funds in British politics. It is not surprising, therefore, granted this prevailing attitude, that the Royal Commission on electoral systems paid little attention to us. Yet as we approach 1914, more Britons believed that we were becoming self-critical and less tolerant of political dishonesty. Although startled by the waste of men, women, and wealth in New York, Sir Henry Jones, for example, professed to see an improvement between 1909 and 1912.

The Labour party discovered that the payment of members did not harm the composition of our Congress; others concluded that it fostered corruption and professional politicians.[11] Mr. Trevelyan, who cited Bryce as being impartial, referred to the Colonies, which were not so corrupt. Our pension expenditures could hardly be believed. England had viewed our resources as illimitable, consequently Roosevelt's conference on conservation was received as epoch-making, as evidence of new self-criticism, and as an inspiration for a colonial conference on the same problem. Our collections of data on social and labor questions were often cited as models. But during the Census Bill of 1900, the President of the Local Government Board remarked,

America has been often quoted, but I have reason to believe that the census returns in America are far less satisfactory than those in this country, and very often very much more inaccurate.

Our Government Printing Office was also cited as a model. But from such details it is desirable to turn to another matter: How common is the common law? [12]

The mighty bonds of legal traditions and the common law have been glorified. It was usually assumed that "the whole view of legal questions is similar in the two countries." There is a tendency, however, toward greater divergence, and the intercourse in legal ideas is probably less since 1918 than before. But we may well ask, what were the circumstances affecting this intercourse? How much did British lawyers consider and use America's legal development?

The visit of the Lord Chief Justice of England, Lord Coleridge, who acknowledged his debt to Webster, Hawthorne, and Longfellow, was the kind of dramatic event which served to illustrate the unity of the legal professions. Although he frequently viewed our problems as beyond him, he added that English lawyers quoted familiarly the Americans Kent, Story, Parsons, Duer, Philips, and Greenleaf. Lord Russell, who carried on his first journey letters of introduction from Parnell to Irish-Americans, visited us in 1883 and 1896. When in 1899 the International Law Association met for the first time on American soil, it was felt that a special tie existed between England and ourselves. Haldane had American correspondents, but he did not make his first visit until 1913 when he emphasized the legal traditions which united the Anglo-Saxon people. According to Bryce, the "imperishable tie" existed only through America's interest in England, and our legal arrangements, except perhaps in the easier passage between solicitor and advocate, were not calculated to commend imitation. The former Confederate Secretary of State, Judah P. Benjamin, whose *Treatise on the Law of Sale of Property* (1868) reached several editions in

England, achieved fame in his new home by influential arguments before the Privy Council and the Lords.

As early as 1895, in order to prevent divergence, Sir Frederick Pollock suggested (in America) that legal opinion might be exchanged between the leading judges of the two countries. The decision in 1911 that the Workmen's Compensation Act, modeled on the English Act, was unconstitutional showed how far apart two communities might be. Nor did legal students come to the States so frequently as medical students. Choate told the United Law Society in 1901 that ". . . there should be a great central University of law in London, in which men of both countries might become versed in all that was best in the tradition of the profession." Some journals hoped our cases and arguments would be cited more frequently. In 1894, after France and the United States had issued publications which kept abreast of foreign laws, Mr. Ilbert suggested to the Imperial Institute the need for a complete record of American (and British) legislation. It frequently had been necessary to cable America for a copy of a statute or a volume of State reports which could not be obtained in London.

In 1889, Lord Halsbury, L.C., spoke at length on the use of American experience:

We should treat with great respect the opinion of eminent American lawyers on points which arise before us, but the practice, which seems to be increasing, of quoting American decisions as authorities in the same way as if they were decisions of our own Courts is wrong. Among other things it involves an inquiry, which often is not an easy one, whether the law of *America* on the subject in which the point arises is the same as our own.[13]

A. McN. Munson, after studying case citations and textbook references in eleven thousand English cases, from the Judicature Act (1876) to 1914, found 251 references to American cases and 106 references to our textbooks, counting each case mentioned separately.[14] The citations, which were made by counsel more than the court, were often hazy about our geographical and political divisions. There were twenty-seven compliments and seventeen adverse criticisms. Two-fifths of the citations were in maritime law, twenty-five citations in international law and conflict of laws, with at least ten citations each in negligence, agency, real property, sales, marriage and divorce. England accepted from us, according to O. K. McMurray, the doctrine of riparian rights. Lord Lindley observed that the "older views of conspiracy have been beneficially modified" by American decisions. Lord Esher, who made the most citations (thirty), felt that while it was "interesting and profitable . . . to consider American cases," the practice was too academic to give ground for discussion. Almost one-half of the textbook references were to Story, Kent, and Parsons. The War somewhat increased the citations, but the *Journal of Comparative Legislation* thought the number "surprisingly small," and quoted Munson's conclusions "that the English courts are not getting so much help from American decisions as we would expect." American case law was by no means easily accessible to the English barrister, there being only one copy of the *Century Digest* in London. Possibly citations had increased because both Canadians and Australians "direct attention to the bearing of American cases upon knotty points before the Judicial Committee of the Privy Council," and because, the *Journal* added, conservative lawyers were giving up their insularity. Let us examine briefly a few English textbooks.[15]

The work of Story, who imported the theory of "comity" into Anglo-American law, helped to form the English conflict of laws. The first edition of A. V. Dicey and A. B. Keith's *Conflict of Laws* (1896) had notes supplied by John Bassett Moore. These were dropped in the second edition because Britons did not use them, and because the American market had been met by Beale's *Conflict of Laws*. Meritorious American books were beginning to destroy the British desire to appeal to both nations in books primarily designed for the English market. A volume published in Boston in 1859 by Francis Hilliard was the first book on the law of tort. W. T. S. Stallybrass in the seventh edition of Salmond's *Law of Torts* added references to American work, pointing out that Professor Bohlen's studies were not sufficiently known in England, and that we had made great contributions to the scientific study of the law of torts. Sir Mackenzie Chalmers in *Bills of Exchange* (8th ed., 1919) referred to the Negotiable Instruments Law (1897) of New York because "the cases decided on it will be useful to us."

T. W. Morgan in the 1933 edition of J. B. Porter's *Law of Insurance* let stand the abundant references to our decisions on problems which came before the British courts. Sir Thomas E. Scrutton as late as 1931 in *Charter Parties and Bills of Lading* discussed the Harter Act, February 1893, and its effect on English law.

But an opposite tendency is perhaps more noticeable. W. J. Byrne and A. D. Gibb in the fourth edition of Thomas Beven's *Negligence in Law* (1929) declared, "Mr. Beven indulged freely, and perhaps to modern ideas too freely, in references to American law. Most of these references have been cut out." H. A. Street in his *Treatise on the Doctrine of Ultra Vires* (1930) said, "American decisions have been omitted under instructions." In *Law Relating to Fire Insurance*, A. W. B. Welford and Otter-Barry found it impracticable to deal with our cases "owing to their number." Welford also made no such reference in his *Accident Insurance* (1923) because it was "impossible in England to keep pace with the cases" and the "growing divergence of principle." Sir Frederick Pollock, who had deprecated any divergence, wrote in the ninth edition of his *Principles of Contract* (1921):

> Learned Americans are still engaged from time to time in valiant efforts to reduce the common-law rules of contract, and the doctrine of consideration in particular, to strict logical consistency. That quest is . . . misconceived.

He said little in the tenth edition (1936) about the Restatement of the Law of Contract published in 1932 by the American Law Institute which was almost unknown in England; "A critical digest of this kind is remote from the needs of English lawyers."

Although the use of American law in the Empire is another story, there is the possibility, partly through such political analogies as drawn between us and Australia, that American law has thus crept into the British ken. Lawyers had feared that Australia would give too much implicit obedience to American cases, to the detriment of "the Commonwealth Constitution and the existence of the Imperial relations." The British expected a distinctive literature; it is not so clear that they expected a distinctive law.

Several influential voices stated that America offered valuable lessons in the teaching of law. As early as 1846 Lord Westbury drew attention to the evil results of the absence of a law school in England. Sir Geoffrey Butler credited Sir Frederick Pollock for calling British attention to the work done at the Harvard Law School. Sir Frederick declared: "The real monument to Maitland would be a School of Common Law in England worthy to stand beside that of Harvard." Although he advised no slavish imitation, A. V. Dicey thought law students might well be taught "to live in an atmosphere of legal thought." One of the Mosely Commissioners wanted such a school for London. The Law Society Conference at Liverpool, 1903, was told, "It was a great reproach . . . we were so far behind the United States and Europe." Sir Albert Rollit, president of the Law Society, described to a congress of law students the value of the inductive system of teaching and school associations. The Council and Legal Education Committee of the Law Society, which had been revising its procedure in 1903, now included lectures, classes, informal advice, and the inductive method successfully applied at Harvard. During the formation of the Society of Public Teachers of Law, December 1908, one piece of advice was to transplant American methods of teaching. Part of this attention was caused by Britain's belief in the strong social and political position of American lawyers, and to a lesser degree, that mere case-winning had not destroyed our interest in the scholarly aspects of law.

The press warned, however, that our State courts needed immediate reform.[16] The Thaw trial proved the demand for elevating the status and prestige of American judges. The weakness of our legal system, asserted Conan Doyle, had led to terrible results which would ruin our chance as an Utopia; Lord Alverstone, the Chief Justice, agreed, but added that England could learn from us in the treatment and reclamation of criminals. Wells could not understand our callousness toward abstract justice. Although some visitors expressed satisfaction with the arrangements of courts, defense of prisoners, and the appearance of juries, the press disliked thoroughly our judicial methods, especially elective judges. But David Dudley Field's simplifying work in 1847 on civil procedure, which united the courts of law and equity, was used twenty-five years later in English and Colonial reforms. The idea of a Domestic Relations Court appeared original enough to the *Man-*

chester Guardian, but difficult to work. In 1898, during the Criminal Evidence Bill, Sir Robert Reid and A. J. Balfour urged the adoption of the cross-examination which our experience favored, and the Attorney-General wanted to allow an accused person to give evidence in a criminal case. Sir Elliott Lees seized upon this support for legal changes:

> It is not an argument that carries any weight with me. I am not aware that either in the Colonies or in the United States is the law of the land as much respected by all classes, or that as much confidence is felt in the justice, as is the case in this country.

In general, the Act of 1898 moved closer to our practice.

The Federal courts, with the center of attention upon the Supreme Court, were less harshly treated. Bryce suggested that they gave England many positive lessons. Even the *Saturday Review* discovered in the Supreme Court something to be proud of. Lord Herschell spoke of its "high character for learning and ability"; Lord Macnaghten declared that one of its decisions made "a case of considerable authority." But Sir John Macdonell, a student of our legal practice who toyed with the Supreme Court as a model for a Supreme Court of the Empire, echoed a common view:

> English democracy murmurs at the intervention of the House of Lords; what should we think if nine old or elderly men, with neither coronets nor wigs, could set aside the most prized legislation of every session?

We may now select a few important topics to illustrate further the repercussion of our civic affairs. But first, a hint as to its variety. During the debates on the Sale of Food and Drugs Bill in 1899, a Member wanted our rules respecting margarine. Our restrictions on aliens were used to support immigration proposals and Alien Bills in Parliament, and the Aliens Act of 1905 was modeled to a degree upon our acts of 1882 and 1891. The American marine law which required instruction in the use of lifebelts gained recognition in 1906. A Member pointed out in 1913 that we had recently passed regulations he had urged upon Parliament, namely, that vessels of a certain size must carry three officers and a master. Laws compelling wireless installation on ships, and regulations for the patrolling of the Atlantic and information about derelicts indirectly affected the British position on these questions. Finally, several newspapers also wanted our law which prohibited the caging of native wild birds.

The intense interest in America's efforts to regulate drinking developed after the World War, but from an early date our career has been very important in British attempts to deal with the liquor problem.[17] Whether for good or evil, especially for our reputation, few subjects aroused as much attention to us, and uncertain, distorted evidence. Drinking habits and their regulation are indigenous, consequently one might expect that vested interests belittled us. Nor was our career strictly suitable for temperance or prohibition advocates who from about 1907 on preferred to turn to the Scandinavian countries. Fewer harsh things were said about Canada, but once again American and Colonial developments were linked together. The United Kingdom Alliance, the principal, fighting, political organization for total prohibition, was established in 1853, inspired partly by Maine's adoption of state prohibition. The Order of Good Templars entered England in 1868; about 1883 women's temperance unions followed. Our temperance lecturers circulated in England; anti-saloon leaguers toured under the auspices of the Free Churches. James Weston, a Yankee athlete, advertised what could be done without stimulants.

Between 1850 and 1890 temperance reformers undertook most of the American investigations; between 1890 and 1914 opponents of prohibition dominated. There were official reports in 1888, 1890, and 1894. The Royal Commission of 1896 received confusing evidence. Volumes published in the early nineties were still used as authorities as late as 1914. E. L. Fanshawe investigated because of the temperance issue in the General Election of 1892; without denying the possibilities of local veto, he concluded, as did his sponsor, Mr. W. Rathbone, and Professor J. Dove Wilson, that prohibition was a failure, and warned England not to legislate in advance of public opinion. In a joint volume, *The Temperance Problem and Social Reform* (1898), Arthur Sherwell and Joseph Rowntree (who favored the Gothenburg system) likewise attacked prohibition by pointing to us. Their lectures in the north of England prompted the Secretary of the English Temperance League to study America, for "If what Mr. Sherwell had stated respecting Maine was true, it would be very difficult to continue the advocacy of the strict veto and Prohibition." The honorary secretary of the United Kingdom Alliance testified to the Commission that Maine had not shaken his faith, but he thought it a grievous error to say that our measures could guide Britain. Dr. Norman Kerr, President of the Society for the Study of Inebriety, who drew upon his eighty visits, viewed Maine and compulsory temperance instruction a success. Unfortunately, many Members of Parliament rushed through the United States and Canada, and on their return posed as authorities.

The annual meeting of the Alliance understood what Sir Wilfred Lawson meant by his plea to break "the power of the British 'Tammany' which now ruled the country." Colonial and American churches at the Baptist World Congress (London, 1905) were urged to incite the United Kingdom to temperance. Comparative statistics on liquor consumption were usually misleading, but we apparently imbibed less. Some attributed this decrease to temperance legislation, which also aided our efficiency. The *Scotsman*, which frequently used us to discredit mild or bitter prohibition, expected such novelties as the breezy, "very American" Carry Nation, whose reception became very unpleasant. It added,

If the temperance extremists were open to reason, the example of Kansas would afford them a new example of the hopelessness of the attempt to compel people by legal enactment to become total abstainers.

While discussing the Liquor Traffic Local Veto (Scotland) Bill in 1898, Mr. Faithful Begg cast up our failures; a Member repudiated his figures because he had not mentioned that forty-two of the forty-six States had given the people a direct veto on the liquor traffic. Fuller discussion took place in Parliament in 1906. Mr. Whitaker explained the difficulty of enforcing laws of local option:

The enforcement of most laws in the United States by the local authorities was very lax. It was very frequently merely a question of backsheesh to officials. Municipal government in America, speaking generally, was rotten and corrupt. (Mr. O'Connor: "Shame!")

The Speaker told O'Connor, who considered us the great leader in democracy, that he could not rule out of order these comments.

Grey promised to supply more information, which he did in the *Report on Liquor Traffic Legislation of the United States* (1907). This report did not decide whether prohibition was a success in three states, but it viewed local option as effecting real prohibition, with the least friction, over the largest possible area. The Royal Commission on Whiskey (1908) did not follow the hint to set up a standard definition of spirits. It was very difficult to make sensible comparisons on the financial results of liquor taxation. But the fact that we did not compensate publicans who lost their licenses in veto districts, and the widespread inference that our liquor trade was taxed more highly, were of great consequence in numerous budget proposals which argued that the British trade could and should bear heavier taxation. The Maine plebiscite in 1911 aroused great interest. In general, those preferring the *status quo* in England and Scotland probably benefited most from allusions to America. A more exciting story began with our national prohibition.

If we were destined to occupy the British front page in lawlessness, it was only fair that Americans should contribute significantly to Britain's penal legislation and administration.[18] From the time of Mr. W. Crawford's exhaustive report in 1838 to the career of Sir Evelyn Ruggles-Brise, British prison reformers have responded to America's practice, and have watched our application of scientific experiment to the study of crime and criminals. Sir Evelyn declared at the Washington prison congress in 1910:

This coming of the Old World to the New to learn what lessons this new has to teach is a great historic fact, and may be an epoch in human thought and attitude towards the criminal.

To America belonged the credit for having started a movement for a permanent international association to study penal legislation, and the American origin of a conference which took place on English soil in 1872 evoked surprise. The Old World hesitated to admit that we had discovered anything new in the juvenile reformatory or indeterminate sentences embodied in the Elmira system.

The influence of Dr. Joseph Tuckerman in 1833, and American and Canadian visits in 1873, stimulated the English social reformer, Mary Carpenter. After a visit in 1869, Sir Michael Hicks Beach, who had thoroughly disliked Americans, concluded that

England had nothing to learn from us in prisons or workhouses. In 1884 Sir Howard Vincent, Director of Criminal Investigations in Scotland Yard, made a systematic study in Boston of deferred sentences; he advocated this experiment on his world tour to various Colonial governments, and made it the basis for his First Offenders' Act (1887). After another visit in 1904 he continued to stress the value of probation. Ruggles-Brise returned in 1897 to begin experiments for the rehabilitation of young prisoners. He reported carefully but not enthusiastically in 1899 on our development of the reformatory, parole, and probation. The State reformatories had caused misunderstanding in England; indeed, he added, "There is much . . . that is extravagant and to English ideas nearly approaching the ridiculous." This was fully demonstrated in the debates on the Prisons Bill (1898), which was designed to give flexibility to prison control and more power to deal with individual cases. John Dillon and John Burns reported that many prisoners at Elmira had been reformed; Mr. Davitt explained further:

All the sarcastic comments upon the alleged proposals to convert prisons into hotels, and about English prisons becoming American Elmiras, is simply subordinating a question of high social interest to the ends of mere bantering and irresponsible criticism.

J. E. Redmond found that our convict establishments were designed to improve prisoners; "the whole spirit of the American system is more humane than the system here." He urged communal dining, better food, and more visiting hours. While Burns did not desire anything so comfortable as the Denver prison, he wanted the parole and medical men on prison boards.

Interest increased after 1900. The Howard Association continually referred to our practice, and pressed for the parole system as the most needed reform in British methods. It also advised the further adoption of the probation of young offenders, and reported a wide acceptance of its pamphlet "Methods of Penal Administration in the United States." We influenced the principles of the Borstal scheme (formally started in 1902) which made provisions for juvenile adults in a penal reformatory, and the introduction of salaried probation officers in the Probation of Offenders Act (1907).

By the Prevention of Crime Act (1908) two American methods were more widely applied—the education and reformation of young offenders and the legalization of the indeterminate sentence. The Home Office secured detailed information on probation by 1910; Ruggles-Brise praised more in 1911 than in 1899. The chairman of the Prison Commissioners for Scotland in 1911, W. G. Scott, viewed our practice superior in four points (to which British opinion moved cautiously): a wider use of probation, conditional liberation, the extension of the reformatory system, and more highly developed prison industries. Cecil Leeson based much of his *Probation System* (1914) upon American practice.

The idea of juvenile courts had started in Massachusetts in 1869, spread to the British Colonies, particularly South Australia, and then to England. In 1902 the Scottish Branch of the National Society for the Prevention of Cruelty to Children acknowledged our leadership in the protection of children, and, with the Society for Reform of School Discipline, recommended separate courts. European attention was drawn formally to the children's courts and probation by a representative of the Howard Association at the Budapest Congress in 1905. The State Children's Association's plea to the Home Secretary demanded the American probation officer, but the press remained lukewarm to these suggestions. The Children's Act (1908) definitely established children's courts. Lord Reay and others also had incorporated provisions which restricted the sale of tobacco to children. Parliament in 1914 was urged by our examples to extend such courts and the use of special magistrates.

Our female suffrage movement penetrated both sides of the struggle in Great Britain without, however, altering vitally the course of events.[19] Our contacts with the suffragists grew closer down to 1914. In the late eighties, even those Englishmen who did not directly oppose female suffrage, said Mr. McCarthy, viewed "the forward movement in America as something altogether noisy, shrieking, grotesque and ridiculous," such as the American woman who came to London wearing trousers. English writers also dwelt upon the hold of "free love" upon the American public. The interest in suffrage had at least one effect—it drew English attention to states which otherwise were ignored. Both sides for different reasons played up American corruption. One found that evil was not curbed by the female vote, the other, that corruption was much less in suffrage states. Mrs. Pankhurst expected great things from us even though our suffragists had yet to become practical politicians. Mrs. Fenwick Miller, reporting on the International Congress at Washington, 1902, praised the American woman's ability to arrange conferences, and advised imitating annual meetings where suffrage delegates could give district reports. But our influence came rather by instilling strength or despair.

Our experiment with women's enfranchisement was not sufficient, declared Mr. R. Whitehead to Parliament in 1907, to use to advantage, nor did women who had the privilege use the vote. Mr. Massie added:

The advocates of woman suffrage were very careful to avoid saying much about the United States. The influence of women was very powerful there, and yet only four States gave the full franchise to women, and those were mushroom States in the West, Ohio, Colorado, Wyoming, and Utah.

The International Woman Suffrage Alliance, which originated in America in 1888, held a convention at London in 1909 where our progress was reviewed. A lively press correspondence was under way. Lord Cromer spoke as though only the least advanced states were committed to the female vote. Mrs. Humphry Ward's letters in 1907 and 1909 hurt the suffragettes and aroused a flood of protests. She wrote, "In America, I believe, as soon as the women's suffrage movement became dangerous, the common sense of the community practically put an end to it." She and the Women's National Anti-Suffrage League professed to be encouraged by our failure. Israel Zangwill, slightly bored, reminded both sides that England was not concerned about American women. Sylvia Pankhurst, who once thought of becoming an American citizen in spite of our appalling social conditions, visited America in 1910 when our sympathy for the English movement was at its height; she needed such support, for stormy years were ahead.

While debating Parliamentary Franchise in 1910, Balfour could not find that we had advanced social legislation any faster than England. The victory of female suffrage in California in 1911 gave some hope; Mr. Lansbury went so far as to say that women had purified politics in "The great United States which is one of the bugbears and bogeys of our opponents." The anti-suffragists, closely watching the first women's vote in Illinois in 1914, made the rather foolish observation that the votes seemed equally divided between the parties. The Earl of Selborne, in a very important speech which forwarded the cause, quoted our example:

You will find from that experience that the fears entertained by the conscientious opponents of this measure have not been realized. You will find also that that intense sense of injustice under which so many women labour in this country has been removed, and removed without danger to the state.

Viscount St. Aldwyn and Lord Charnwood denied this reasoning; Charnwood asserted that the American examples (California, etc.) were from

. . . crude, unsettled, undeveloped communities where laws are not made in order that they may be kept and where great influence still attaches to the outworn catchwords which did duty well enough in the infancy of democracy.

But possibly, in this instance, we encouraged change.

The British response to various elections and political personalities has been intimated before. England thought little about the possibility of a third party, nor did it view our career as a struggle between Jeffersonian and Hamiltonian principles. The press usually condemned our system of presidential elections and tenure, and the interval between national elections and a new Congress. England apparently could talk more easily about the principles, personalities, and chances of the Republican party. Jules Cambon, French Ambassador at Washington, observed discerningly, June 1901: ". . . The Republican party which governs is the party of the rich, the most susceptible to the seductions of English society. . . . England recognizes these weaknesses and plays upon them with art." This also suggests an important American influence upon the opinions and myth-making of the seducers. No love was lost for Bryan, but his reputation improved after his English visit in 1910. Except for silver and Tammany, a few Liberals would have favored his election in 1900. But it is worth noting that Alfred Marshall, who called himself a bimetallist, opposed the "excrescences" which English bimetallists had borrowed from American silver men. Most of our presidential elections were lost in domestic preoccupation. McKinley appeared evasive. The election of 1904 was passed over in almost complete silence and was not taken as hostile to British interests. Taft's treatment of the Canal Tolls made England almost willing to see a Democratic President. The three-cornered struggle was too complicated to be followed; what interest there was centered upon Taft and Roosevelt. The campaigning of 1912 proved to the *Manchester Guardian* "how backward America is in some of the elements of social civilization." English critics also frequently accepted the Irish "boss" as the typical representative (and deficiency) of American politicians.

Of all the character analyses made by Britons, that of Roosevelt deserves most space. "Teddy" expanded as did the nation, and interested England in the President's office and American personality, as Lord Lansdowne said, more than anyone since Lincoln. The British imagination could grasp this personality, which some wit described as a combination of Gladstone, Rhodes, Beresford, John Burns, and Kaiser Wilhelm. His African trip made him in spirit a fox-hunter. His speeches and books, composed of "half-truths written in large texts" (*Times*), interpreted Americanism to the English. "To a peculiar degree," observed the *Westminster Gazette* in 1910, "he embodies the characteristics of the American people." Was it not William Watson who wrote:

> . . . Nay, thou art more:
> Thou art her fiery pulse, her conquering will;
> Thou art America, dauntless Theodore.

Although England was quite uncertain about this "opportunist's" achievements, H. G. Wells considered him the measuring standard for the constructive world of the new century.

We have thus seen the foreign repercussions of America's political rôle. Perhaps our middle-class government during these years helped to reassure Britain of the bases of freedom and prosperity, of slow, but inevitable, progress.

---

[1] Bryce, *Am. Common.* (1891), chaps. xciii–xcv and 1888 ed., III, 583. U.S. had journals of pol. science when the subject was still unrepresented among Brit.

periodicals. W. S. Childe-Pemberton, *Life of Lord Norton, 1814–1905: statesman and philanthropist* (London, 1909), 277; Lane-Poole, *Bowen*, I, letter of Nov. 22, 1875; 9th Duke of Argyll, *Passages from the Past* (London, 1907) and Dowager Duchess of Argyll, ed., *George Douglas, Eighth Duke of Argyll* (London, 1906) where the Duke records his unexpected delight with the New World. Sir Henry Maine, *Popular Government* (New York, 1886), p. xi; Andrew D. White (*Autobiography*, New York, 1905, II, 403, 397) urged Maine to stress the popularity of the veto power as shown by its extension to items of supply bills in state legislation.

W. H. Mallock, insignificant "First Impressions of America," *Outlook*, 86: 462–67; Maitland, *Stephen*, 172. Lecky, *Lecky*, 215, 268, 281; at first a moderate Liberal but elected to Parl. as a Unionist in 1895. Lord Macaulay in 1857 believed Jeffersonian politics could exist "without causing any fatal calamity" so long as there was free land. Another historian, Lord Acton (1834–1902) seems to have picked up his Am. views mostly by travel; "Lord Acton's American Diaries," *Fort. R.*, 1921, vols. 110, 111. Lecky, *Dem. and Liberty* (1896), I, 64, 94, 100, 105, 112. David Duncan, *Life and Letters of Herbert Spencer* (London, 1908), 160, 137. Carnegie, *Triumphant Democracy*, 471; Ogden, *Godkin*, I, 11–12, 113–14, 201, 212; II, 6–15. Morley, *Scots.*, Jan. 19, 20, 1905; *Recollections* (London, 1917), II, 105. Non-Radical papers denied his analogy between our race problem and yellow question in S. Africa. Morley, who was unconvinced by Walt Whitman, recalled that he left Am. in 1868 without making rash statements.

² L. F. Post, *The Prophet of San Francisco: Henry George* (New York, 1930), *passim*. The Duke of Argyll, who treated George with scorn, believed he knew only frontier conditions. His audiences were very hostile in Cambridge and Oxford. See E. G. Fitzgibbon, *Essence of Progress and Poverty, extracted from the American of Henry George, and done into and dealt with in plain English* (London, 1884). Lucy Masterman, *Mary Gladstone (Mrs. Drew), Her Diaries and Letters* (London, 1930), 306–07; C. H. Herford, *Philip Henry Wicksteed* (London, 1931), 197–98, 205–06, 211–12; A. R. Wallace, *My Life* (London, 1905), II, 194, 199, 259, 266–68. Wallace says few Eng. socialists knew Bellamy's *Equality* (1897), sequel to *Looking Backward*. Graham Wallas, *Human Nature in Politics* (London, 1908), Pref., 3, 243; at Harvard in 1910; dedicated *The Great Society* (1914) to Walter Lippmann. Mrs. Sidney Webb, *My Apprenticeship* (London, 1926), 7, 9, 124, 392; A. G. Thorold, *Life of Henry Labouchere* (New York, 1913), 42, 226, 237–38, 531–33. Englishmen at times may have thought David Lloyd George resembled an Am. politician; he studied Lincoln and our election methods. But one may question Hendrick's statement that he drew more inspiration from us than any other prominent Briton; B. J. Hendricks, *W. H. Page*, III, 22; J. Hugh Edwards, *D. Lloyd George* (New York, 1929), I, 45–49.

Author has deposited at Library of Congress a "Selected Bibliography of British Government Reports relating to U.S., 1895–1914." I am now preparing a critical bibliography and history of foreign government reports and investigatory commissions relating to U.S.

³ Argyll, *Passages from the Past*, II, 438; F. Harrison, *George Washington and other American Addresses* (London, 1901), 22–23; E. Lyttleton, *Alfred Lyttleton* (London, 1917), 155; Sir Francis Powell urged members to "devote their time and industry to a study of that most interesting Constitution." *P. Debs.*, 1907, 176: 933, 970, 999, 1162ff., 1176, 1186, 1221, 1236–37, 1246ff.

⁴ S. R. Honey, *The Referendum among the English: A manual of "Submissions to the People"* in the American States (London, 1912), pp. v–xiii, xx; H. W. V. Temperley, *Senates and Upper Chambers* (London, 1910), 33–34, accepted Am. example as condemning any unicameral system. *P. Debs.*, Commons, 1910, 15:1491; 16:943, 1275, 1286, 1290; Lords, 5:159, 235–36; 6:890, 971, 975; 1911, Lords, 7:255, 269, 713; 8:873, 1070–71; 9:212, 218, 268–69; Commons, 21:1815; 23:1306, 1841; 24:279, 299, 338, 341, 718, 764, 1164, 1411, 1485, 1486, 1507–08, 1650, 1658, 1668, 1817, 1823, 1847, 1867; 25:450, 917, 1223ff. Mr. Hamar Greenwood (29:1455) said our Senate was corrupt because small, therefore, keep the Commons large. Cuba, Bulgaria, Switzerland, and U.S. were reported; see *Reports Respecting the Institution known as the Referendum, P.P.*, 1911, Cd. 5522, LXIII. Austen Chamberlain, *Politics from Inside* (New Haven, 1937), 191, 194.

⁵ Haldane, *P. Debs.*, 1900, 83:98–99, 52; also Lords, 85:11–14. Erling Hunt, *American Precedents in Australian Federation* (New York, 1930), 253, 15–21, 37–38, 45, 100, 118, 167, 179, 184, 254–56. The Australians probably knew as much about Am. institutions and history as the British without quite so much first-hand knowledge of governmental practice. W. B. Munro, *American Influences on Canadian Government* (Toronto, 1929), a brief survey. Essays by W. M. Whitelaw and C. W. DeKiewiet in Conyers Read, ed., *Constitution Reconsidered* (1938).

⁶ Frewen, *Melton Mowbray*, 252–59; Hendricks, *Carnegie*, I, 321ff.; Rt. Hon. Lord George Hamilton, *Parliamentary Reminiscences and Reflections 1886–1906* (London, 1912), 211ff. *P. Debs.*, 1902, 101:631, 635; 1911, 24:1411; 1912, Lords, 13:500, 564–65, 742; Commons, 34:58, 199, 1459–60, 1902, 2135, 2148; 46:611ff., 635–36, 2082, 2085–90, 2220, 2230, 2233, 2266. Astor's amendment was lost 197 to 299. In 1913 when opposing Plural Voting Bill, the Earl of Ancaster cited Am. checks on the popular vote; Lords, 14:July 24. J. A. M. Macdonald and Lord Charnwood, *The Federal Solution* (London, 1914), Pt. II, 51–68; A. Chamberlain, *op. cit.*, 279–82. *P. Debs.*, 1913, 53:1487–88, 1553–54 (Franchise and Registration Bill); 1914, 60:93–94, 98, 132, 914, 1239, 1660, 1734; 61:1759; 62:1486.

⁷ "Memoir of Henry Cabot Lodge," *Proceedings LVIII, Mass. Hist. Soc.*, April 1925, 336–67. Salisbury, *P. Debs.*, 1899, 66:26; before Constitutional Club, *Times*, Dec. 17, 1898. *P. Debs.*, 1902, 110:718–19; 1913, 53:403–06, 456; 1914, 64:103; *Treatment of International Questions by Parliaments in European Countries, the U.S., and Japan, P.P.*, 1912–13, Cd. 6102, LXVIII. *P. Debs.*, 1899, 66:775; 1900, 82:1124–25; 1902, 114:647; on voting and rules of order see *P.P.*, 1902, Cd. 907, CIV and Cd. 909, CIV; *Reports respecting the Composition and Functions of the Second or Upper Chamber in Foreign States, P.P.*, 1908, Cd. 3824, LXXXVII; also Cd. 4252 on limitations of debate. On *Titanic*, 1912, Lords, 11:852, 854–56; Commons, 37:778, 859, 1091–93, 1513, 1838; 41:2038. A member wanted an absolute Committee of Rules to allot time for individual bills; another reported that the cast-iron rule on debate made our Congressmen oratorical rather than argumentative.

⁸ *P. Debs.*, 1899, 66:522ff.; 539, 548, 554, 571, 578; 73:823; 1904, 131:872; 1909, Commons, 4:998; 6:75, 84–87, 93, 174, 193–94, 206–09, 273, 343; 562; 10:927, 966; 11:2393; 12:2079, 2100; 1910, 18:1409, 1453; 1914, 63:1774; 64:2024, 2035; on stamp duty, 1909, 11:632–38; see also *Taxation of Land Values in New York, Boston, San Francisco, and Cleveland, P.P.*, 1909, Cd.

4578, LXXXI; also Cd. 4750, LXXI, Pt. 2; *P.P.*, 1908, LXXXVIII, on testamentary bequests. On Fels, *P. Debs.*, 1910, 17:514–15; 1911, 21:932; *Times*, May 3, 4, 1910; Aug. 15, 1912.

⁹ *P. Debs.*, 1899, 67:370, 1207; 1907, 171:1801. Shaw, *Lab. Lead.*, Apr. 20, 1901; Lord Avebury, *On Municipal and National Trading* (London, 1906), 122; Avebury, *Scots.*, Jan. 22, 1903; Sir A. T. Griffith-Boscawen, *Memories* (London, 1925), 97ff.; Roof Roofer .(i. e. Rufus Randell) did not exhaust the theme or the amusing possibilities of an *American Politician in England* (London, 1898); *Report on the Fire Department of Boston, Mass., Ac. & P.*, 1899, No. 472, Mis. Series, XCVII; De Bary, *Land of Promise*, 25.

¹⁰ Hobson, *Crisis of Liberalism*, 151; Harmsworth, *19th Cent.*, Aug. 1900; A. H. Crosfield, *Manch. G.*, Jan. 24, 1910; for Royal Commission, see *Reports, etc., P.P.*, 1910, Cd. 5163, 5352, XXVI; *Application of Principle of Proportional Representation, etc., Ac. & P.*, 1907, LXXXVII, says little about U.S. except surprise that P.R. is not more used. Lord Charnwood (*P. Debs.*, Lords, 1913, 17:54) wanted to inquire into our legislation on regulation of party funds. Herbert quoted in Lord Newton, *Lansdowne*, 262–63. H. J. W. Hetherington, *Life and Letters of Sir Henry Jones* (London, 1924), 99, 113, 223, 228.

¹¹ *P. Debs.*, 1900, 80:498, 507; 1907, 173:236; 174:390–91; 1911, 24:690; 29:1391, 1394, 1400, 1440–41, 1449, 1453, 1630, 1650, 1669; 1914, 61:1161–62; *Report of His Majesty's Representatives Abroad respecting Payment of Members of Foreign Parliaments, Ac. & P.*, 1911, Cd. 5714, LXIII. A national park on the style of Yellowstone had been frequently suggested.

¹² E. A. Jones, *American Members of the Inns of Court* (London, 1924), useful for earlier period; E. H. Coleridge, *Coleridge*, II, 325–27, 334; Charlton Yarnall, ed., *Forty Years of Friendship: as recorded in the Correspondence of John Duke Lord Coleridge and Ellis Yarnall, 1856–1895* (London, 1911); R. Barry O'Brien, *The Life of Lord Russell of Killowen* (London, 1902), chap. x. Choate talked about Supreme Court before Social and Political Education League, *Times*, May 14, 1903. Between 1865 and 1914, U.S. participated in 38 multipartite administrative treaties which to a degree brought Am. experience and law to British attention. In this sense, the subject has not been studied. But see H. Rieff, *The United States and International Administrative Unions* (*International Conciliation*, No. 332, New York, 1937). Possibly the career of Benjamin, who entered Sir Charles Pollock's office, led Eng. judges to look westward; H. H. Hagan, "Judah P. Benjamin," *Am. Law Rev.*, 1914, 48:382–84. Note visit of Am. Bar Assoc. to Eng. in 1924; also T. Burton, *Lawyers on Holiday* (London, 1930).

¹³ *Law Reports*, 1889, 42, Ch. Div. at p. 330. In Munson's study noted below, Lord Halsbury made 10 Am. citations. It is instructive to add here Sir Francis H. Jeune who in 1893 referred to the opinion of Shaw, C.J., in *Farwell v. Boston and W.R.R. Corp.* (1842), 4 Metc. (Mass.), 49, as "the most complete exposition of what constitutes common employment" and a decision "which, no doubt, materially influenced the House of Lords."

¹⁴ In *Am. Law. Rev.*, 1914, 48:559–69. Marshall received most of the compliments; Lord Macnaghten classed Mr. Justice Holmes with Maitland. Similar quantitative studies should be made for Canada and other parts of the Empire. *Journ. of Comparative Legislation*, 1915, XV:58–59.

¹⁵ Pollock, *Expansion of the Common Law* (London, 1904), 19–20. See *Norrington v. Wright*, 115 U.S. 89, 206; also Cockburn, C.J. in *Scaramanga v. Stamp*

(1880), 5 C.P.D. at p. 303, C.A. "Judicial Appeal in the Commonwealth," *Journ.
Comp. Legis.*, 1908, IX: 269–80; W. Harrison Moore, "The Australian Common-
wealth Constitution, 1901–02," *ibid.*, V. Note cases *Rex* v. *Bamford*, 1901 and
Wollaston v. *Rex*. Butler, *Living Age*, July 30, 1921, 255–60; W. P. Groser,
Mosely Educ. Report, 174–97; Dicey, *Cont. R.*, 1899, 76: 742; Rollit, *Times*,
Jan. 14, 1903.

¹⁶ Munson, *op. cit.*, 48: 564; Bridgewater, *Journ. Comp. Legis.*, 1903, 5: 507–08;
Macdonell, *19th Cent.*, Aug. 1901. *P. Debs.*, 1898, 56: 978, 1006, 1016, 1017,
1063–65, 1262; 58: 275; 59: 743; 60: 679. 1899, 74: July 17; 1902, 101: 1285;
1911, 24: 2136; 29: 691; 1913, 53: 52–53; 55: 1280; 1914, 59: 966, 993; 63:
581, 655–56, 672. *Report on Immigration into the U.S., Ac. & P.*, 1906, CXXII,
No. 655, Mis. Ser.; *Report on Purchase and Holding of Lands by Aliens, Ac. & P.*,
1902, CIII, No. 567, Mis. Ser. Our more elaborate indexes for wills were also cited
for imitation.

¹⁷ Guy Hayler, *The Master Method, an enquiry into the Liquor Problem in
America* (Newcastle-on-Tyne, 1901), 15; Dean of Durham said the volume showed
the benefits accruing in certain states. E. L. Fanshawe, *Liquor Legislation in the
U.S. and Canada* (London, 1893); *Royal Commission on liquor licensing laws:
1896, Précis of evidence, etc.*, P.P., 1899 (Cd. 9076, 9379), 35: 96–98. *Record of
Proceedings, Baptist Congress*, 257, 267; records the influence of J. B. Gough, Neal
Dow, Francis Murphy, Frances Willard and others. *Report on Liquor Traffic Legislation in U.S., Ac. & P.*, 1907, LXXXVII, Mis. Series, No. 657; but see previous
report, Mis. Series, No. 324. Birkenhead, *Frederick Edwin, Earl of Birkenhead*
(London, 1933–35), I, 186–87, and *My American Visit* (1918) and *America
Revisited* (1924). Earl Winterton's *Pre-War* (London, 1932), 117ff.; he concluded
that Tammany Hall prepared way for contemporary gangster. *P. Debs.*, 1899,
70: 1231–35, 1237, 1250; 71: 152; 1900, 81: 472, 489; 1902, 101: 202; 1905,
145: 1037–38, 1041, 1078; 1906, 155: 1246–49, 1258, 1263; 157: 644; 1908, 191:
958; 192: 216; 194: 969, 978, 981–83, 994–45, 1009, 1384ff.; 1909, Commons,
4: 1006–07.

¹⁸ Crawford, appointed under Prison Act, came back an ardent supporter of the
solitary system; his *Report on Penitentiaries* (1838) and papers by Mr. Russell
reached Parliament and were widely discussed. Major A. G. F. Griffiths ("Prisons,"
11th ed. *Ency. Brit.*) says basis of cellular confinement remained obscure in Eng.
until revived by Am. practice. Ruggles-Brise, *Prison Reform at Home and Abroad*
(London, 1924), *The English Prison System* (London, 1921); Dr. Adolf Lenz,
*Die anglo-amerikanische Reformbewegung im Strafrecht; Eine Darstellung ihres
Einflusses auf die kontinentale Rechtsentwicklung* (Stuttgart, 1908); S. H. Jeyes
and F. D. How, *Life of Sir Howard Vincent* (London, 1912), 153, 199; Lady Victoria Hicks Beach, *Life of Sir M. H. Beach* (London, 1932), I, 22ff. *P. Debs.*,
1898, 55: 1166–67, 1179, 1193, 1198ff., 1202–04; 56: 102–04; 60: 450–51, 458–
59, 478; 63: 807; 1906, 157: 1101–02; 1914, Lords, 17: 252–54; Commons,
61: 213, 226.

Report of Chairman of Commissioners of Prisons, etc., P.P., 1899, XLIII, 3, 7,
8–14; on prison labor, see P.P., 1894, XC, p. 16; *Report by Sir E. Ruggles-Brise
on the Proceedings of the Eighth International Penitentiary Congress, Wash.,
1910*, P.P., 1911 (Cd. 5593), XXXIX, 2, 6, 12, and *passim; Memorandum, etc.*,
P.P., 1907 (Cd. 3401), LXVIII; *Report, etc.* (by W. G. Scott), P.P., 1911
(Cd. 5640), XXXIX, 26; *Report of Committee on Probation of Offenders Act,*

1907, P.P., 1910 (Cd. 5002), XLV; Capt. A. St. John of Penal Reform League gave most of the favorable Am. evidence. L. F. Schmeckebier, *International Organizations in which the U.S. Participates* (Washington, 1935), 13–26; E. C. Wines proposed intern. congress as suggested by Sollohub; U.S. represented at all intern. congresses, but did not contribute money to Commission until 1897.

A commission to investigate prisons for the French Govt. ultimately led to De Tocqueville's famous *Democracy in America!*

[19] Sylvia Pankhurst, *The Suffragette Movement* (London, 1931), 347–50; Justin McCarthy, *Reminiscences* (London, 1899), II, 270, 274–78; Joseph Fels assisted the movement in England. The National Union of Woman Suffrage Societies read with glee a resolution from Am. colleagues protesting against the "attitude of the British Government as opposed to those Liberal and democratic traditions which they and we alike inherit." *West. G.*, Oct. 8, 1913. *P. Debs.*, 1907, 170:1104, 1106, 1113, 1138, 1140, 1155; 1910, 19:63, 257, 283, 1333; 1911, 25:770; 1913, 52:1759, 1763; 1914, Lords, 16:16, 26, 36, 76, 94–95, 105. But note that in 1914 session, the Lord Bishop of London gave witness to Am. women's efforts to pass legislation to protect young girls; Lords, 16:22; 15:111ff.

XI

THE UNITED STATES AND EDUCATION

NO Briton will boast that America is treated comprehensively in any sphere of his school system. Spasmodic political fascination has not been strong enough to make up for the disbelief in the educative and cultural value of American civilization. But Britain's interest in our education has been deeper than many realize, and in time that may promote a reconsideration of the position of American studies. One of the most significant steps in West European culture will have been taken when Britain admits them into her system *on their own merits* as subjects of knowledge and world history.

A very slow change, recognizable by 1900 and gaining momentum since 1918, has brought this issue to some importance. Bluntly stated, the current British effort (Lord Spencer called it a "movement") to improve their understanding of American history and literature rests upon the conception of a common destiny which somehow close Anglo-American coöperation must preserve. There have been Britons, sometimes inspired by itinerant Americans or financial assistance, who advised a sounder study of our culture. Not much came of the various efforts before 1914 to improve Anglo-American contacts via education.[1] The *Times* in 1901 praised Choate's suggestion of exchanging schoolboys; in 1905 Mrs. Bertrand Russell outlined to the Society of American Women in London the advantages of annual scholarships for our women at Oxford and Cambridge. One American thought the time ripe for an Anglo-American university with a constant interchange of students. The London County Council in 1904 agreed to extend the scheme of correspondence between London and American students to non-provided schools. A movement began in 1909, under the Vice-Chancellor of Sheffield, to promote "grand tours" to the New World; but English undergraduates could not escape their exams.

The Central Bureau for the International Exchange of Students opened in 1910, partly to promote intimate knowledge of our "needs, progress, and potentialities" to increase Britons' "efficiency as citizens." During the first year, forty students took a three months' educational tour.

The Rhodes Scholarships increased Oxford's personal contacts with American students. But it may be suggested that these scholars who mold opinions, form numerous friendships, and modify the academic program, have not made Oxford, as compared with Cambridge (which also has American students), peculiarly alive to American civilization. The *Spectator* said, however, "Mr. Rhodes's bequest is a most striking beginning in the work of creating a 'union of hearts' in the Anglo-Saxon world." These scholars who represented new ideals of education would bring fresh, healthful blood to Oxford and, continued the *Times,* would lose themselves in an atmosphere "less vulgarized by absorption in luxury and athleticism." The *Saturday Review* asked: "Was this New World coming in to restore or to upset the balance of the Old?" Earl Grey wanted our racial imperialism and generosity to bring English students to America. The Americans were thought alert and versatile, but not thorough. At first the feeling of both nationalities was mainly one of curiosity, but an Oxford don wrote in 1914 that our students encouraged steadiness and work. In *Zuleika Dobson* (1911)—the beautiful heroine who wrecked Oxford one might have expected to be an American—Max Beerbohm made his classic Duke observe that the Rhodes Scholars "are a noble, rather than a comfortable, element in the social life of the University." By 1914 it was also a troublesome question whether Cambridge should be expected to compete against our athletes. The centralization of all these scholars increased their corporate spirit and made them recognizable, but possibly it decreased the breadth of their influence upon England. However, the snappy scholar who made his professor watch the clock, as depicted by *Punch* (November 19, 1902) in an "Oxford of the Future," could not but have some spiritual significance. American demands modified Oxford's curriculum, and extended instruction for the degree of Bachelor of Civil Law and the degree of Doctor of Philosophy. According to Vice-Chancellor A. D. Lindsay,

The research degrees were instituted before the war to meet a demand at first created by the Rhodes Scholars. . . . The growth of honour schools in America is creating a much greater demand for reseach facilities from our American Rhodes Scholars.

In turn the migration of these students to England has sanctified British university appeals for American money.

Between 1925 and 1939 at least 2,558 students over fifteen came from the British Isles (excluding the Irish Free State) to study in the United States.[2] Based upon total populations, the Irish Free State sent more than three times as many students as England; Scotland or Northern Ireland, twice as many as England; and England, more than Wales. (By the turn of the century there were complaints that too many colonial students went to the United States.) Since 1925 over three hundred Commonwealth Fund Fellows, supplied with Harkness money, have taken graduate work here. Sir Walter R. Buchanan-Riddell, the chairman, declared:

Former Fellows can visualize American problems and American difficulties from a basis of personal knowledge and thus help to dissipate ignorance and mitigate misunderstanding on the part of others who have not had their good fortune.

The Fund avoided the mistake of dumping all such scholars into one university, or of sending all to a few universities like the Henry Fund operating between Oxford-Cambridge, Harvard-Yale. About one-half of the Fellows have studied liberal arts (including economics), and about one-half, the sciences. Many of the Fellows who were neutral before embarkation have developed a sensitiveness to America. Some became over-stimulated by the reception given them and developed an itch to remain in America or to return as soon as possible. In the boom period preceding 1929, this tendency was strong and would have decreased the Fellows' influence in England. One-half of the Fellows came from Oxford and Cambridge. Applicants for Rhodes scholarships have been twenty times more numerous. This American experience does not help their career immediately since employers, except possibly in architecture, are not yet impressed by the American sojourn. Recently the fellowships have been extended to civil servants. The University Grants Committee declared:

The institution of the Commonwealth Fund Fellowships is a conspicuous recognition of the value derived from a period of postgraduate study abroad. Additional endowments for this purpose would be of great advantage to the Universities.

Between 1920 and 1937, the Rockefeller Foundation and the International Education Board brought 171 British students to the United States; seventy-five in the social sciences, forty-eight in the natural sciences (including agriculture), twenty-eight in the medical sciences, fifteen in nursing and public health, and five in the humanities. The Brooks-Bryce Foundation tried to stimulate Anglo-American studies by awards at Yale and Oxford and in private schools. The British Joint Committee for Interchange of Teachers, working within the English-speaking Union, since its inception in 1924, arranged fifty-nine exchanges of teachers, mostly women in elementary and secondary education.[3] Traveling scholarships in honor of Walter Hines Page enabled British teachers to come westward. A group of American private schools, since Father Sill's scheme was launched in 1928, received some seventy English public school boys, while Americans went to famous English schools. The American University Union, which is used primarily by Americans in London, also facilitates intercourse in Anglo-American educational circles. The exchange teachers mentioned above may not be the most influential group in England, but they serve as a channel of information; it must be noted, however, that fifty per cent of the Americans did not believe they were effective in this sense while in England. Many felt that America "usually represented something very humorous or wildly adventurous to the British students." In addition to the usual results of travel, the British exchanges' response to our education may be described as moderately favorable; a handful returned with a spirit of innovation. Nearly all thought the movies harmed British ideas about us.

Lacking detailed material on the American attitudes of pre-War British school children, we may turn briefly to a survey completed during 1936 and 1937 in the age group thirteen to sixteen, keeping in mind that the cinema, and perhaps a few other channels, have brought America closer home.[4] One is soon put on the defensive trying to moderate student views on our racketeering, excessive devotion to sports, wealth, tremendous speed, and all the dangers of giantism. This defensive must be taken up more speedily within the gates of the public schools and more quickly in England than in Scotland or Wales. These students relied upon the following sources in the order named to give them most of their ideas about us: the cinema (six times stronger than the next channel), newspapers, school books and training, teachers, American stories and fiction, American tourists, magazines, home training and discussion, speeches, imagination, English travelers, radio, etc. One may criticize the insertion of "imagination," but it is probably underrated in the tabulation. Typical American products also served to form opinion. The radio will no doubt soon extend its influence.

The following statements were agreed to or strongly agreed to by a large majority of the students (an * indicates strong agreement):

*1. American moving-pictures give a true picture of American life.
*2. The U.S. should join the League of Nations.
*3. It is easier to acquire wealth in the U.S. than in Great Britain.
4. I want to learn more about the U.S.
*5. The union of the English-speaking peoples would safeguard the welfare of the world.
6. There is more difference between Scotland and England than between Canada and the U.S.
*7. The U.S. would join Great Britain in any future war.
*8. Americans are boastful.
*9. The Negro is badly treated in the U.S.
*10. Americans speak very poor English.
*11. All Americans use slang.
*12. American-made products never have the quality of British-made products.
*13. I can tell when a moving-picture comes from America.
14. Great Britain should not have to pay her War Debts to the United States.
15. Americans are good sportsmen.
*16. Americans carry speed to excess.

The following statements were disagreed with by a large majority of the students (an * indicates strong disagreement):

*a1. The U.S. is more democratic than England.
a2. Britain has to fear American competition.

*a3. There are many art museums in the U.S.
a4. Americans think and act in the same way we do.
a5. Justice is effective in the U.S.

Opinion was well divided on the following statements:

b1. British newspapers should print more news about the U.S.
b2. I am more interested in the U.S. than in Europe.
b3. England can learn more from Europe than from the U.S.

Many of these results warrant serious reflection. Answers to statement 1 showed that for many the story and action were the only interest, and that no intimate connection was made between the film and American life. While by no means decisive, the sentiment on statement b2 was remarkable. Most of the "agreements" to statement 6 came from Scotland and Wales. Answers to 10 and 11 did not prevent the use of Americanisms. These opinions, like similar pre-War ones, would govern America's influence.

Still unrecorded in histories of education is the surprising amount of attention to American education, especially between 1898 and 1904, which was a factor in the reconsideration of British educational administration, teaching, and theory.[5] This existed in widely different groups and institutions, commanded a good press led by the *Times, Daily Mail,* and *Manchester Guardian,* and developed with the refreshing idea that something constructive could be learned from this experimental laboratory. England rather decided America's economic expansion depended partly upon the educational system. A national system well integrated from kindergarten to university, and our strong conviction in the value of education excited special notice. Perhaps the enthusiasm and system rather than its product or methods attracted Britain, for it was felt that while we overspent on equipment we trained for livelihood, not character or cultured scholarship. But, at least in verbiage, we received more attention and tributes than any Continental nation.

This interest was not new in 1898. The report in 1865 on the United States and Canada by James Fraser, later Bishop of Manchester, had done for elementary education what the Mosely Commission did for secondary education in 1903. J. J. Findlay reported in 1894 for the Royal Commission on Secondary Education that our high schools did not deserve the epithet "irreligious," and cited

Fraser as having been more willing to accept sectarian education since he had visited American schools. According to Sir Philip Magnus, the Royal Commission of 1881 had been deeply influenced by the study of technical education abroad. Studies had been made of our summer schools by 1887, and the World's Fair at Chicago in 1893 brought British teachers into contact with the child-study movement which resulted in the formation at Edinburgh of the British Child-Study Association (1894) and also the Childhood Society, and prepared the way for the influence of men like G. Stanley Hall and Earl Barnes. P. G. Craigie, while investigating agricultural colleges and experimental stations in 1893, was impressed by the great practical energy being devoted to the spread of knowledge; he stressed the value of the "demonstration plot," but the opinion persisted that there was excessive duplication of effort. Non-academic travelers, such as W. H. Russell in 1882 and G. W. Steevens in 1897, were apt to belittle our education.

The work of the Royal Commission on Secondary Education in 1894, a report on agricultural colleges in 1895, a special report of the Commissioner of Education in 1897, another on commercial education in 1899, very important special studies in 1902, an analysis of domestic science in 1905, and the evidence given on agricultural education in England and Wales in 1908 are the principal official documents.[6] As a close observer of the United States, Sir Michael Sadler, General Editor of the Special Educational Reports (1902), explained:

> For many reasons, and not least on account of the close relations between the English-speaking peoples, American education has always been a subject of special interest to English students. Of recent years this interest has rapidly increased, and the educational methods and experiments in the United States are watched by many English teachers and students with a marked degree of sympathy and attention.

Sir Michael praised our belief in education and individuality, escape from non-essentials, and reliance on technical and university training; he criticized the lack of intellectual discipline and too many short cuts. The volumes he edited were linked to the contemporary trade "panic," and left the impression that our education was to make the efficient man, a view acceptable to the *Saturday Review*.

Miss Alice Ravenhill, who investigated at the request of several organizations, found that the increasing attention to health which had resulted from a Report of the Inter-Departmental Committee on Physical Deterioration made timely her discussion of domestic science which she would have imitated. Although contributing to the stock of facts, the official reports followed rather than led public discussion. There was no desire to run too fast, consequently, there was official anxiety over the scope of the Mosely Education Commission,[7] and some fear among the commissioners that English opinion might whip them if they advised imitation.

Alfred Mosely, who became interested by his contacts with American engineers in South Africa, appreciated the broader aspects of our education. His industrial and educational commissions were important milestones in Anglo-American contacts. Sir Michael Sadler and Sir Philip Hartog were among those he consulted. Sir Philip writes:

Mr. Mosely was immensely impressed by what he had seen of education in America. He felt that England had many lessons to learn from America in this matter.

Mosely, like Sir Thomas Lipton, thought the American boy better trained for life's struggle. He even went so far as to say that the Education Act of 1902 had "been worked out on lines somewhat similar to those followed in the United States." Part of the press wanted the Commission to inquire into comparative cost; the *Times* asked it to look over normal schools, and predicted that it would find a harder working youngster. Professor Ayrton, the physicist, suggested an inquiry into methods of science teaching to "assist the committee of the British Association." The Commission partly fulfilled a plan on foot in 1901 to inquire into commercial and technical education; behind that had been Mosely, Lord Reay, Sir Joshua Fitch, Sir A. L. Jones, Dr. W. Garnett, Sidney Webb, and Graham Wallas. The subjects placed before it were: the development of individuality in primary schools, social and intellectual effects of the wide distribution of secondary education, the effect of specific instruction in business methods and applied science, and current opinion as to the value of professional and technical university instruction as preparation for business careers.

The Commissioners differed but marked our eagerness and liberality, the close contact between school and community, and the nationalizing and utilitarian purpose of our system, and mentioned the need of imitating organization and coördination. The report meant to Sir William Anson that England needed secondary schools coördinated with elementary schools and a new faith in education, to Lord Reay it showed the secondary rôle of examinations. Conferences such as those arranged by the Sanitary Institute, the King Alfred School Society, and the National Federation of Head Teachers' Associations used the report for various purposes: warnings not to exaggerate the value of technical education, the lack of culture in our teacher training, and praise for the "accredited schools" system. Both the personal contact and press notices were helpful, but the members hardly agreed with Mosely that England lagged behind us a generation.

In 1900 Carnegie paid some British professors to visit Canadian and American universities. Canon Francis Holland, before founding the Baker-Street Church of England High School, made an exploratory visit. British Westinghouse chose men from public schools and universities for training in its Pittsburgh works; such groups (one was called the "Holy Forty") brought home valuable experience. Mosely's scheme for sending five hundred teachers in 1906 was described as an "eye-opener" by the *Times*. Between September and December 1908, over one thousand American and Canadian teachers visited England. The Gilchrist Educational Trust pioneered by sending teachers "to make reports which the Trustees hope may contribute something valuable to the solution of secondary education problems in England." One of them, Miss S. A. Burstall, recalled:

This American visit wrought a profound change in me . . . it strengthened my instinctive belief in education, and showed me how to carry out this if the opportunity ever occurred.

The president urged the Manchester Association of Engineers to visit our educational exhibit (which had been moved from the Paris Exhibition) as an education in itself; it prompted Sir John Gorst to say that we were "distinctly in favor of general education." American school books were sometimes considered more practical.

Some Britons would have imitated our Federal Bureau of Education which had encouraged the comparative study of the science and systems of education.

Our expansion gave a general shock to educational policies.[8] Joseph Chamberlain, when campaigning for a university at Birmingham, found in all our social classes an enthusiasm for education and specialized training which Britain would have to imitate, an opinion also held by Sir Philip Magnus. Lord Reay at University College urged England to "take a leaf out of the book of that great republic . . . and establish a national system" unspoiled by creed or class. On being installed Lord Rector of Glasgow University, November 1900, Lord Rosebery (who spoke, Englishmen thought, like an American) declared:

The Germans are alarmed at the development of American commerce, and we are alarmed at both. At any rate, both in Germany and the United States, you see a systematic devotion to commercial, and technical, and scientific training.

Earl Grey, presiding at a conference of trade unions to secure popular support for scientific education in the north of England, praised these American allusions by Chamberlain and Rosebery. Sir Thomas Lipton claimed "it would be a good thing to send every English boy to America when he is seventeen, and keep him there for several years." Leaders like Haldane, Rollit, McKenna, Salisbury, and G. W. Balfour warned that England must meet our technical and scientific training with increased expenditures. Our better system of secondary education, Asquith and Sir H. Fowler added, supported inroads into British commerce. In his presidential address to the British Association in 1903, Sir Norman Lockyer preached that England needed state-aided funds to compete with our private endowments, a scientific council, and greater willingness to use trained youths. Sir Michael Sadler observed in 1912:

This temper of mind, the spirit of the pioneer, was far commoner in the United States and in Canada than in Europe, but its stronger infection had caught hold of the younger England and would have an influence in English education.

The press generally praised this spirit. After drawing attention to the work being done in higher commercial education at the Universities of Pennsylvania, Chicago, and California, the *Times* (September 12, 1901) continued:

It takes one's breath away, and makes the mouths of educational enthusiasts in England water, to see the rapidity and decision with which important movements are thought of and carried out by Americans.

The *Times* also held that our examples would be more profitable than German ones, namely, the close connection between academic and industrial life, consolidation, secondary agricultural schools as links with the university, manual training, and the like. "There is no country in the world," averred Miss Burstall, "so helpful to a student or worker in English education as is America." The National Association of Education Officers reported,

North America is a land prolific in educational experiments . . . and fortunately the predominance of the Anglo-Saxon race makes the national outlook sufficiently resemble our own to render comparison valuable.

Those who stressed the coöperative system of education found our system most helpful for English experimenters. So far little had been said of the cultural achievements of America's education, but even the above opinions did not go unchallenged. Some saw no reason for decrying Britain's public schools, others could not find superior education or skill among our lower classes. But shocks such as outlined above were important.

References to American education widened the basis of discussion too much to suit most officials. This began in Parliament in 1901 and 1902 during debates on an important Education Bill which dealt with school administration.[9] Sir John Gorst, Vice-President of the Board of Education, reiterated his view that the "unphilosophical and practical Americans" did not attempt specialization until a comparatively late age, and that our Paris exhibit had shaken France's belief in her own system of early specialization. Mr. Mather added illuminating details:

You find under the American system all classes of the community mingling together. . . . That is precisely the plan that we advocate on this side of the House, and which many hon. Members on the opposite side desire to see carried out and adopted in England. But to do this you must adopt the American authority which is a universal school board in every city of the country.

Sir William Harcourt regretted that Earl Percy professed "not to know what the American system was," that we were "very difficult to deal with." Others cited Massachusetts in the hope that the Government would propose stronger and more democratic measures. Bryce felt in 1902 that schools in the hands of the people could repair any deficiencies in methods. Sir Charles Dilke lamented that a system such as ours or Australia's was "past praying for." In the Lords, the Bishop of Newcastle, who related commercial prosperity to education, explained that he had learned from his three visits the value of one authority to coördinate education, that efficient education did not demand an authority elected *ad hoc*, and that municipal rivalry was a wholesome thing. The controversial Act, which aimed at coördination, gave state money to denominational education and abolished *ad hoc* elections.

Our business training was closely followed. It helped the founders of the London School of Economics and Political Science in 1895. Our example aided discussions for the University of Liverpool, and for specialized faculties of commerce in the northern universities. Provisions for separate commercial schools for youths seventeen to eighteen, on Boston and New York models, were urged for English cities. While presenting the London Chamber of Commerce prizes in its commercial education scheme in 1901, Mr. Alexander Ritchie explained that England paid America (and Germany) a high compliment by imitation. But the stir over commercial education, prompted largely by our competition, did not satisfy everyone as a legitimate interest; it was as though we were pulling education to one side. England might give the profession of public accounting to America, but we raised it to a cultural position in higher education. Nevertheless, Haldane could point out that we were endowing universities rather than hospitals or churches. The *Scotsman* declared:

> If we are to succeed in the industrial struggle we must learn from our kinsmen across the Atlantic to set a higher estimate on the gifts that commerce requires.

There were also efforts to draw fully upon our experience and "phenomenal progress" in technical and scientific education.[10] Silvanus Thompson on his first visit in 1884 discovered our rapid expansion of technical education and gained valuable guidance for spreading such education in England. Lord Playfair told the Old World in 1885 to watch our great advance in joining science to administrative offices. An abbreviated list of those who drew strong and favorable arguments from our progress is impressive: R. B. Haldane, A. Acland, Bonar Law, Norman Lockyer, Alfred Yarrow, William White, William Ramsay, J. J. Thomson, W. E. Ayrton, William Preece, William Dyke, A. W. Rücker, Joseph Dimsdale, J. J. Welch, and John Perry. All organizations like the Association of Technical Institutions and the British Association were informed of our activity. Apparently there was a strong tendency to view our developments as more applicable than the Continent's. Charges of superficiality and sensational press reports were set against these tributes, but larger donations, closer business contacts, better equipment, and so forth, began to characterize Britain's technical education.

Sir J. Wolfe Barry, president of the Association of Technical Institutions, preached in 1903 that manufacturers must be convinced of the value of training; further,

We desired to see in this country what was so observable in America —namely, that almost every one was a mechanic and knew something of applied science.

Under such stimulus, correspondence was submitted to the Manchester Chamber of Commerce which showed the advantages gained by us through utilizing university graduates. Under the auspices of the British Association, a large deputation loaded with American facts waited on the Prime Minister to urge larger funds for higher education. The next year, 1905, Lord Mountmorres, Director of the Institute of Tropical Research, praised our government's work in scientific research. Before a meeting at the Technical College, Sunderland, to secure a chair of metallurgy and fuel to benefit Durham, Dr. W. A. Bone predicted that our specialized schools would dominate world markets in iron and steel. Sir Norman Lockyer, who often spoke of needing American "push" to develop science, in 1905 reminded the inaugural meeting of the British Science Guild, a group rising in the atmosphere of American examples, of our numerous state-aided universities.

Manual training was discussed at several conferences. With the aid of Sir William Mather, impressed by his American travel, and Professor C. M. Woodward of St. Louis, the Manchester Technical School established in 1895 the first manual training school on American lines. Our experience seemed to justify outside work by technical teachers and the elevation of manual training to an integral part of the school system. After a visit the Principal of the Smithwick Technical School decided on the utility of the combined trade school and workshop. Associations heard about the benefits of advisory boards of employers and employees for each section of a technical school and well-equipped part-time trade schools. Post-graduate instruction was of special interest because of proposals in London in 1903 for a central technological institute. At a conference the same year which discussed the training of engineers, some advocated the "sandwich system" (part study, part work) as used by us. Several agreed with Professor W. E. Dalby, who investigated at the request of Mr. Yarrow, that our courses were more practical than Germany's or Switzerland's. The address on transatlantic engineering schools by R. M. Walmsley before the Institution of Electrical Engineers in 1904 originated from problems facing the Northampton Institute (Clerkenwell), and the fact that American schools were giving matriculation exams in London on the suspicion that their training was more attractive; Walmsley wanted better equipment and systematic factory visits. Several listeners, including Professors H. E. Armstrong and W. C. Unwin, thought our college experience merely showed England what not to do; but the discussion indicated that somehow our engineering progress must be accounted for. It will be recalled that the press cried "Educate, Educate!" that even the unfriendly *Saturday Review* upbraided England for letting us outstrip her in scientific matters. The *Engineer*, which sometimes argued almost mystically that our education had nothing to do with progress, became whimsical in 1905:

Our own manufacturing engineers are very reticent folk, not at all given to boasting, and Press representatives who have gone to the United States have come back mightily impressed by the first sight of operations which they had never seen in this country. Persons competent to form an opinion of value have arrived at quite different conclusions.

The panic over technical education, and consequently the exaggerated use of America's examples, had subsided by 1910. Most of the professional journals had become critical by 1908, scathing by 1912. But the furor had stimulated liberalizing improvements and expansion in technical and scientific instruction.

We have already seen how much those who wanted a well-integrated national system turned to our elementary and secondary education.[11] In this respect, the criticisms were more severe, the attention much less general, and the conclusions very conflicting. Jesse Collings (1831–1920), Joseph Chamberlain's close friend who helped to form the National Education League (1868) for free and non-sectarian elementary education, derived some encouragement from us. Speaking of efforts to unite all social classes in the elementary schools, the President of the Board of Education said in 1911, "I only wish it could be done . . . here as well as it is done in America." The adoption of the kindergarten as part of our educational philosophy was held to be of great significance for England. The tendency to standardize pupils was a warning, but Miss Burstall added, "We need to liberalize and enfranchise our elementary education as they have done during the last generation." (She would also have imitated our gymnasiums, personal hygiene for female students, school health programs, library technique, and better textbooks and stratification of subjects in the curriculum.) She used her American experience at Manchester in 1900–01 to start housewifery and secretarial courses (with touch-typing) in the high schools. Although some urged American high schools for England, the National Association of Education Officers declared the system wasteful. Professor Armstrong told the Association of Public School Science Masters that a state-directed system would inevitably make Britain as mediocre as America. Certain schools, such as Bedales at Petersfield, have been especially susceptible to American methods. The Dalton Plan, it may be noted, spread from the County School at Streatham in 1920.

Safely proud in the possession of Oxford and Cambridge, little attention was given to the non-technical training of American universities.[12] The English author George Birkbeck Hill (1835–1903) declared in 1893, "Harvard strides while our Universities crawl." Sir William Tennant Gairdner said little about medicine after a visit in 1891 (he chose rather to write "Impressions about America for My Children"), but he did regard the vast expenditure for the university and hospital of Johns Hopkins "as depriving them of the right of being, or becoming models for us in Europe." But some sought hints from the freedom and scope of the colleges, and the elective system. R. K. Risk sent forth his volume on our universities in 1908 because of Scottish university reform, but since we were not scholarly, the reformers would hardly draw "special lessons from these complex institutions." In 1912 both Haldane and Bryce pointed out the rapid strides made by us as compared with England, but the latter questioned our academic standards. The *Times* offered no tributes, although it argued that English universities should be as quick to admit and amend faults, and to minimize the examination system. The *Daily Express* proclaimed:

We present the case against the "higher education" which still holds obstinate sway in twentieth century England, in spite of the lessons taught—if we would only learn them—by our alert and progressive rivals in Germany and America.

The British also observed our ability to attract colonial students. L. T. Hobhouse and Graham Wallas described a growth in America of the authority of methodically and specially instructed thought on social and political questions which was not without repercussions in English sociology. Professor John Rhŷs commended for imitation our devotion to ethnology. Everyone envied America's collegiate philanthropy. The sabbatical year, at first scoffed at as a "rest-cure" typical of hectic America, has since 1918 been approved in principle by British universities. Many journals amused themselves, sometimes brutally, with the pedantic pretense of American scholarship and freakish courses. About the hordes of graduates, *Punch* asked,

When everybody's somebody,
Then who is anybody?

An interest in summer schools, manifested as early as 1887, continued throughout this period. An interdepartmental committee appointed by the Home Office described the success of the Summer
Vacation School and Children's Recreation School at the Passmore
Edwards Settlement, schemes which had been borrowed from us
by Mrs. Humphry Ward in 1902, followed by the Bishop of
Hereford at Hereford. Mrs. Ward declared:

> The energy and the resources of the American settlements had
> much to teach them. They had been wholly instrumental in the or-
> ganization of vacation schools which we in England had only just
> started. Americans too had done more to influence the municipal life
> of the great cities for good than we had in this country. (Hear, hear.)

Our training in patriotism impressed others. Lord Kelvin complimented several American universities for making students better
citizens; the Conference of National Federation of Head Teachers' Association cheered Rev. John Watson for saying, "I should
like to see the national flag raised every morning above the schools
of the people, as in the United States." Lord Stanley of Alderly
wanted our ceremonial saluting, but it was more elaborate than
anything desired by the Earl of Meath, who specialized in such
matters.

English coeducationalists nearly always appealed to our experience, hence much depended upon our progress. This led to curious
exaggeration and glib reports which often underestimated American opposition to coeducation. Britons were told that the system
could be imitated, and would refine the boys without hurting the
girls. But Dr. C. W. Saleeby and Frederic Harrison contended
that it harmed the best girls. It was also said that the "gentle,
give-and-take style," which made our high schools lower than the
English sixth form, did not inspire imitation. Sir Joshua Fitch also
warned that opinion had turned against female teachers, but the
Spectator hailed the schoolmarm as a "standing rebuke to the
popular misconception of the American woman as a selfish bird-
of-paradise."

American ideals of peace and equality held a large place in the life of James Hirst Hollowell, who took an active part in the movement for secular control of education. He rejoiced to tell England that a secular educational system had the Bible in the schools and an atmosphere of ethical and Christian spirit.[13] Ardent Nonconformists quoted ours as a happy solution of the religious problem. In Parliament in 1902, Humphreys-Owen and Lloyd George, somewhat to the distress of Bryce, cited American and Colonial hostility to sectarian teaching; D. L. G. declared:

In America they had tried to settle this difficult problem, and he thought that in the United States religion was much more prosperous than here, from the point of view that they taught the children in the schools, not dogmas, but religion which they could understand.

Sir Francis Powell expressed the typical rejoinder: "the conditions there were not such" as to encourage imitation. Bryce posed the question in 1904:

In Protestant Germany the children got Protestant instruction. Had that made them as devoted to Christianity as were the children of the Protestant United States, where no denominational instruction was given?

The strongest answer to such a question was illustrated by the Bishop of Liverpool's letter to his rural deans on the Education Bill in 1906:

The third reason for asking for organized opposition to the Bill is that it will weaken our national Christianity, and will in time bring about the same deterioration of character which the best men in the United States and in New South Wales are deploring today.

Even though certain societies such as the Northern Counties Education League and the Liberation Society might use America in their propaganda, the nature of the religious problem in the British schools was such that little could be achieved by such references, especially since important organs like the *Times* deemed our moral teaching inadequate without a religious basis, and still others clouded the whole issue by attributing all our evils to the lack of religious training in schools.

Our efforts to teach temperance had at the outset influenced similar steps in the United Kingdom, namely, the Band of Hope and the Church of England Temperance Society. And our example was a persuasive factor in 1909 when the Board of Education issued a syllabus of temperance teaching for optional use in elementary schools. The United Kingdom Alliance frequently pointed out that the "system of national instruction in scientific temperance is well worthy of the consideration of the British people." A petition on physical deterioration, signed by fifteen thousand medical practitioners and presented to Lord Londonderry, concluded that physical hygiene, especially as related to the effects of alcohol, was more completely dealt with by us. This illusion was destroyed by influential observers who showed that dogmatic, inaccurate, almost fanatical teaching had entered our schools in this way.

At a conference on school hygiene, Lord Reay commended for imitation frequent meetings between teachers, parents, and children: others advocated the education of teachers in the laws of health. Our steps aided legislation in 1907 which provided medical inspection for elementary schools.

Professor Haddon told the British Association that England should also educate students and the community by museums. Surprisingly enough, it was suggested that we better understood the educational value of the English language and how to teach it; alarm was even expressed that American methods might be adopted in teaching English literature. However, at the first meeting of the English Association, Sidney Lee declared that in advanced English scholarship, the United States, Germany, and France surpassed England. Professor G. G. Ramsay even dared to say in his inaugural address to the Classical Association of Scotland in 1902, "The subject in which the greatest advance was being made in the secondary schools of America was . . . the classics." But the conception of America as the home of fake degrees persisted throughout the period. Charles Garnett lost his libel action against the *Christian Herald* which labeled American degrees as bogus or shoddy. The "National University of Chicago" was accused in 1897 of dispensing suspicious degrees in Manchester, London, and Preston.

Thus we have seen that our repercussions in education have been very diverse and often important.

It is also pertinent and very revealing to study the British use of American history.[14] Our historians in writing Old World history do not feel compelled to explain that they write to serve no domestic party; English historians, wherever they touch any phase of American history, feel that such denials are appropriate and necessary. This has made American history a political lesson, a sort of moral tale of Sandford and Merton which apparently has no dramatic or literary fascination. This attitude, which arises partly from distrust of American history as a discipline, means that England will look first to political, then social, then cultural America. The Senate of Cambridge University in 1866, on Washington's Birthday, rejected by a vote of 105 to 75 Henry Yates Thompson's offer to endow a lectureship to be appointed by the President and Fellows of Harvard on "The History, Literature, and Institutions of the United States." The reasons given were Harvard's Unitarianism and an unwillingness to feed our "self-conceit."

One of those who had voted for the lectureship was Charles Kingsley, who felt that our history was significant for England. As Regius Professor of Modern History at Cambridge, he tried to deliver an impartial series of lectures about us in 1862. He had altered his violent abolitionist sentiments (expressed in *Two Years Ago*), and wrote, "I could not help finding out, when I came to read up, that the North had exaggerated the case against the South infamously." The struggle might be a blessing by breaking up "an insolent and aggressive republic of rogues." The Civil War merely increased E. A. Freeman's interest in his *History of Federal Government* (1863); he did not feel that American history was necessary for England, but he expressed his delight with any volume which treated it as part of English history. Yet Freeman complained that England always recalled the French 1789 and never the American 1789. Edward Dicey wrote in 1898:

Many years ago, when I first visited the United States, I gave utterance in writing to the apparent paradox that in order to understand England it was necessary to study America.

It was always Bryce's contention that Britain could profit more than any other country by America's experience. His *American Commonwealth* so satisfied the British that it discouraged further research into American history. Much to the distress of his English admirers, George Otto Trevelyan (1838–1928) at the age of fifty-nine left unfinished his *Life of Charles James Fox* to write the *American Revolution*, which appeared between 1899 and 1914, unread in England, but a gesture appreciated by Americans. He contended that the conduct of Fox and other British statesmen could not be understood without knowing transatlantic events. Apparently at the suggestion of H. A. L. Fisher in 1910, Oxford established lectures on the United States which were given by J. F. Rhodes in 1912, C. F. Adams in 1913, and by A. T. Hadley in 1914. Under the revealing title *Trans-Atlantic Historical Solidarity* (1913), Adams began his lectures in an elementary fashion.

The Sulgrave Manor Board administers the Sir George Watson Chair of American History, Literature, and Institutions endowed in 1919. Sir Francis Tripple brought the idea to Watson, who wrote to the Duke of Connaught, President of the Anglo-American Society, that ignorance was the principal stumbling block:

> In spite of the brotherhood of arms during the war, there is still a call for much discriminating labour to banish this prejudice. . . . It is necessary to generate a new interest in America and make America and its life and thought better and more universally known and understood in this country.

Viscount Bryce gave the first lecture, June 27, 1921. That October two regular courses of weekly lectures were begun at University College, London, covering the period from 1783 onward. In the summer, along with the opening of the Institute of Historical Research, came the first Anglo-American Historical Conference. English money endowed a chair of American history at Oxford in 1922. When suggesting a chair in American Studies to supplement American history at Oxford, Dr. Flexner described to Mr. Eastman the potency of such studies among future British leaders. A few years later an American gift enabled the University of London to organize the Commonwealth Fund Chair. There is also a permanent lectureship in American history at St. Andrew's. Cambridge in 1939 appointed as Professor of Political Science D. W. Brogan, who is a well-known student of American affairs. Six of the sixteen universities in the United Kingdom offer American history as an honors course: Oxford, Aberystwyth, London, Bristol, St. Andrew's, and Birmingham. Of course such institutions as the London School of Economics may also inject American material into their courses. Because of the examination system it is difficult to institute formal courses in the great public schools, but steps have been taken at Bembridge and Westminster. Mr. Plimsoll, the reformer, reminded Americans in 1895 that none of the thirty-two books used in British elementary schools made unkind references to our part in the American Revolution; but instruction stopped at 1783. Many books now in use are distinctly out of date, and committees are working on suitable textbooks. One university library had not more than fifteen books relating to American history. A committee of the Anglo-American Conference of Historians in 1926 reported difficulty in obtaining our historical writings and government documents.

A. F. Pollard advised Britons in his Watson lectures, *Factors in American History* (1925), to study us as much as we do them, and described our history as revealing the course of universal history and social evolution with material sufficient to provide good historical training. British and American history provided a mirror of truth for both nations because of the startling theory "The more they change, the more they grow alike." Pollard explained:

In the whole range of our differences of opinion, whether on matters like blockade, freedom of the seas, right of search, continuous voyage, the limit of territorial waters, or on problems like union and secession, the treatment of native races, the government of dependencies, there is hardly a British precedent to which America has not appealed, nor an American principle which Great Britain has not invoked.

Galsworthy expressed a desire "to unriddle the significance and sense of America." Arthur Bryant, who analyzed a strange collection of our big-wigs in his *American Ideal* (1936), held that Englishmen could learn more from our history than from that of any other country. H. G. Wells, however, told the author he preferred a meaningful world history of mankind; any "increased study of the events of the separate history of America . . . would only produce irritation which would be accentuated by the common language so long as British and American people could imagine no common goal in the future." The Professor of American History at London, H. Hale Bellott, has argued wisely that "a demand merely for the addition, because of its present impact upon us, of the history of the United States . . . is as intellectually unsatisfying as it is educationally unsound." Nevertheless, America has one toe inside the academic door.

¹ H. J. Darton-Fraser, *A Handbook on Foreign Study* (Edinburgh, 1909), under authority of Students' Representative Council, omitted U.S. Andrew Macphail, *Essays in Fallacy* (London, 1910), 147–48; Sidney Ball, "Oxford's Opinion of the Rhodes Scholars," *Amer. Oxonian*, Apr. 1914.

² Buchanan-Riddell in *Directory of Commonwealth Fund Fellows, 1934*; statistics on students based upon figures communicated by the Immigration and Naturalization Service, U.S. Dept. of Labor, Washington. An estimate of 1904 found about 2,673 foreign students in the U.S. A sketchy survey made in 1923 showed students from G.B. and the Empire concentrated in liberal arts, dentistry, education, engineering, graduate work in arts and sciences, medicine, law, etc., in about the order named.

Babbitt, until very recently, seemed to be the source of many impressions held by the Commonwealth candidates. A hand-picked selection of their impressions (E. B. Reed, ed., *Commonwealth Fund Fellows and Their Impressions of America,* N.Y., 1932) reveals very receptive frame of mind, keen response to American scenery, particularly the West, and a few minor, personal revolutions. Cf. Eric Linklater's *Juan in America* (1931). The *Report of the University Grants Committee, 1929–30 to 1934–35,* 46n. Other fellowships such as the Choate, Procter, Mills, Sidgwick, and International Fellowships of the National Association of University Women account for a few more British students in the U.S. Communications from the Rockefeller Foundation. One of the results of the Rockefeller and Commonwealth grants is E. M. Hugh-Jones and E. A. Radice, *An American Experiment* (London, 1936). Sir Arthur Steele-Maitland wrote *The New America* (London, 1934) with Rockefeller funds. On Brooks Foundation see, *Aspects of Anglo-American Relations* (New Haven, 1928) and *Anglo-American Prize Essays* (London, 1925, etc.). Also W. G. Lyddon, *British War Missions to the U.S., 1914–1918* (London, 1937), 54–56.

³ *Reports of the English-speaking Union, 1922–*; unpublished minutes, etc. Note special committee on Interchange of Schoolmasters from 1929 onward. In 1927 the *Times* offered a reciprocal press fellowship for work in England. Details may be found in author's articles, "British Teachers and the United States," *School and Society,* June 12, 1937, 821–26, and "Survey of Interchange Teachers," *Landmark,* Aug. 1937, 397–400.

⁴ For details and finer measurements, see author's article, "American Attitudes of British School Children," *School and Society,* Dec. 25, 1937, 838–40. See answers to similar questions in Am., *American Observer,* Mar. 14, Apr. 4, 1938.

⁵ K. Stevens, *Encyclopaedia of Education* (1921), "Child-Study"; *Ac. & P.,* 1895 (C.–7699), CIII; *P.P.,* 1895, XLVIII, 385ff.; Major Craigie's evidence before the *Agriculture Education Committee,* 1908 (Cd. 4207), XXI, Pt. ii, 474; M. Vivian Hughes, *A London Home in the Nineties* (N.Y., 1937).

⁶ *Royal Commission on secondary education: 1894, Reports, etc.,* P.P., 1895, XLVIII, XLIX; see also *Royal Commission on elementary education acts: 1886,*

Reports, etc., P.P., 1888 (Cd. 5485ii–85iv), XXXVI; *Report on Agricultural Colleges and Experiment Stations of U.S.A., Ac. & P.,* 1895 (C.–7699), CIII; also in 1895, see *P.P.,* 1895 (C. 7711), CIII, 505; *Reports of Commissioners of Education: Special Reports, Ac. & P.,* 1897, XXV; *Report on Commercial Education in the U.S., Ac. & P.,* 1899, XCVII; see also *Report on Education in Chicago, Ac. & P.,* 1900, XCI; *Special Reports on Educational Subjects,* P.P., 1902, XXVIII, XXIX (or vols. 10 and 11 of the *Reports*). Also vol. 15 of the *Special Reports* for Ravenhill's observations or *P.P.,* 1905 (Cd. 2498), XXVI; *Report on the Chicago Summer Vacation Schools, Ac. & P.* (Cd. 2237–1), LXXXVI. *Agricultural Education in England and Wales, Reports, etc., P.P.,* 1908 (Cd. 4207), XXI, Pt. II; U.S. and New Zealand are examples most frequently used; Major Craigie declared U.S. could not be used as an example.

[7] Interviews with George Mosely, Sir Philip Hartog, Sir Michael Sadler, and others. Mosely, *Times,* May 14, 1903; Sir Charles Elliott on Am. engineers in S. Africa, *Sat. Rev.,* Sept. 30, 1905, 424; Ayrton, at British Assoc., *Times,* Sept. 17, 1903, preceded by Professor Marshall Ward who opposed those impressed by our realistic "nature study" which he thought a catch-word. *Education* praised the report and added that discipline was less strenuous. Opinion of National Union of Teachers approximated Anson's. *Report of the Mosely Educational Commission to the U.S. of A., Oct.–Dec. 1903* (London, 1904). Almost agreement that there were too many female teachers. Mr. Harry Coward, president of the N.U. of T., voiced the greatest enthusiasm. A. Edmund Spender, *Random Notes on the Mosely Education Commission* (reprinted from *Western Morning News,* 1903).

S. A. Burstall, *Retrospect and Prospect; Sixty Years of Women's Education* (London, 1933), 109–10, 113–16; also *Impressions of American Education in 1908* (London, 1909), 294. Some Gilchrist productions are M. H. Page, *Graded Schools in America* and Alice Zimmern, *Education in America.* W. Fellows and J. B. Elwell, *Report on Education in U.S. and Canada* (Leicestershire Educ. Committee, 1907), were not deceived by glorious syllabuses. See also J. Hollowell, *American School System* (Northern Counties Education League, 1902).

[8] Lord Reay and Haldane asked Gertrude Atherton about Am. educ. Reay, *Times,* July 30, Aug. 5, 1901; Rosebery, *Times,* Nov. 17, 1900; Lockyer, *Times,* Sept. 10, 11, 1903; Lipton, *West. G.,* May 13, 1901; Sadler, *Times,* July 24, 1912; Burstall, *Impressions,* 1; J. H. Whitehouse, *Education* (London, 1935), 204, 212; Natl. Assoc. of Educ. Officers, *Education in relation to Industry; A Report on technical schools in Canada and U.S.A.* (Leeds, 1912).

[9] *P. Debs.,* 1901, 90: 670, 674; 94: 653ff.; 96: 1201, 1404, 1425, 1429, 1437; 98: 1015; 1902, 107: 660, 670, 682, 704, 753; 108: 588; 113: 361, 365–66, 369; 115: 527, 1243ff.; 116: 19. B. Willson, *The New America: a study of the imperial republic* (London, 1903), 212, 233.

[10] W. E. Dalby, "Education of Engineers," *Proceedings of the Institution of Mechanical Engineers* (London, April, 1903), 281–349; L. E. Mather, ed., *The Rt. Hon. Sir William Mather* (London, 1925), 16–24, 103–25, 193–99. Note also Mather's introduction to T. C. Horsfall's "Reforms Needed in our Educational System" and the preface to C. W. Eliot's *Education for Efficiency; an Address* (n.p., 1905) which he wanted circulated in G.B. J. S. and H. G. Thompson, *Silvanus Phillips Thompson* (London, 1920), 50–51, 120–23. Sir J. N. Lockyer, *Education and National Progress* (London, 1906), introd. by R. B. Haldane,

passim. W. P. Groser, on the Mosely Commission, wrote *Education and Industrial Success* (1904) at the request of the Parliamentary Industry Committee because he adumbrated "so strong a case for reform." R. M. Walmsley, "Transatlantic Engineering Schools," *Proc. Inst. of Elec. Eng.*, Feb. 1904, XXXIII, 364–471. Burstall, *Impressions*, 299; an account presented to the Salford Education Committee, E. S. A. Robson, *Report of a Visit to American Educational Institutions* (London, 1905), 46, 109, 165–66, covered 38 institutions and held engineering success due to schools; Mosely *Report*, 26–37, 40–63, 174–97, 198–210, 344–50, 359; *P. Debs.*, 1914, 62: 81.

¹¹ Collings wrote in 1872 "An Outline of the American School System; with remarks on the establishment of common schools in England." H. T. Mark, *Individuality and the Moral Aim in American Education* (London, 1901), a Gilchrist report; Burstall, *Impressions*, 290–97, *Retrospect*, 148, 181–84. C. W. Kimmins and Belle Rennie, *The Triumph of the Dalton Plan* (London, n.d.).

¹² Lucy Crump, ed., *Letters of G. B. Hill* (London, 1906), 212; Hill, *Harvard College by an Oxonian* (N.Y., 1894), 316. G. A. Gibson, *Life of Sir William Tennant Gairdner* (Glasgow, 1912), 296; Gairdner did, however, write a sketch of O. W. Holmes in the *Brit. Med. Journ.*, 1894, II, 948–49. Fitch, vol. 10 of *Special Education Reports*, chap. 1; R. E. Hughes, *Schools at Home and Abroad* (London, 1902); after a two months' visit, Percy Gardner wrote "Impressions of American Universities," *19th Cent.*, Jan. 1899, 102–12; Rhŷs, in Mosely *Report*, 310–29; R. K. Risk, *America at College: as seen by a Scots Graduate* (Glasgow, 1908), 1–2, 212. Grant, *Special Educ. Reports*, Vol. XI, Pt. 2, 85ff.; A. G. Bowden-Smith, *An English Student's Wander-Year in Am.* (London, 1910), 79.

¹³ William Evans and W. Claridge, *James Hirst Hollowell and the movement for civic control in Education* (Manchester, 1911), 60, 65; for a similar view, to combat the legends of Sydney Smith, see Gibson, *Gairdner*, 308; *P. Debs.*, 1902, 113: 361, 365–66, 369; 115:527; 1904, 131:1078; 1908, 197:430; 1909, Commons, 2:997. Bishop of Liverpool, *Times*, Apr. 23, 1906; H. T. Mark, *Special Educational Reports*, X, chap. 2; T. C. Horsfall began as early as 1893 to show evil results of secular education in U.S. Francis Gasquet, *Times*, Feb. 13, 1906; cf. *Proceedings of the First International Moral Education Congress, 1908* (London, 1908), 25–26, 32, 50–51, 58. The advantages of a special museum instructor were presented by an Am. to the annual Conference of Museums Association, Ipswich, July 1908. Ramsay, *Times*, Dec. 1, 1902. *U.S. Dept. of State, G.B.*, Vol. 191, No. 320.

¹⁴ M. F. Thorpe, *Charles Kingsley, 1819–1875* (Princeton, 1937), 150; F. W. Maitland, *The Life and Letters of Leslie Stephen* (London, 1906), 176–77. E. A. Freeman's ominous title was *History of Federal Government, from the Foundation of the Achaian League to the Disruption of the U.S.* (London, 1863); W. R. W. Stephens, *Life and Letters of E. A. Freeman* (London, 1895), II, 231, 324, 410; Freeman, "Impressions of America," *Fort. R.*, XXXVIII (1882), 133–55, 323–46. Bryce, *The Study of American History* (Cambridge, 1921), 37, 39, 47; G. M. Trevelyan, *Sir George Otto Trevelyan* (London, 1932), 132, 137, 138–42. Dicey, *19th Cent.*, XLIV (1898), 490; A. F. Pollard, *Factors in American History* (Cambridge, 1925), vi, 50, 295, 306, 310. John Galsworthy, *Addresses in America, 1919* (New York, 1919), 45; Pollard, *Times*, Dec. 6, 1919; Arthur Bryant, *The American Ideal* (London, 1936), analyzes Lincoln, Jefferson, Emerson, Whitman,

298 AMERICA AND GREAT BRITAIN

T. Roosevelt, Alan Seeger, Vachel Lindsay, and Walter Hines Page! Robert McElroy, *American History as an International Study* (Oxford, 1926); Bellott, "The Place of American History in English Education," *History*, March 1937, p. 334; C. W. Ackerman, *George Eastman* (Boston, 1930), 485. Armstrong College (Newcastle) and Manchester have sometimes given courses in Am. history. Note correspondence started by Sir Josiah Stamp, *Times*, June 25, 1937.

XII

AMERICA AND LITERATURE

AT this point one must quote the outworn observation, 1820 vintage, by Sydney Smith (who lost money in American investments):

> In the four quarters of the globe, who reads an American book? or goes to an American play? or looks at an American picture or statue?

But through the decades our fiction and non-fiction have permeated British thought.[1] They have affected writers and also the community; although often unsatisfactory or uninspiring, these writings have at least set Britons to wonder about our mental habits and tastes. Perhaps American books have never been the primary source of information for the majority, and not so important as the press or hearsay. It is significant, but not surprising, that much of our literature did not appeal to Britain, or frequently that it appealed too much; nor is it strange that the reception differed among various social classes.

Our exports of books to the United Kingdam rose steadily from 1902 to 1913. G. Haven Putnam's father about 1841 was one of the first American publishers to go to London. In 1903 there were in London at least ten firms which imported American books. Douglass, the Edinburgh publisher, sold successfully his series of American stories. Jonathan Cape pioneered by opening a New York contact office; Heinemann's connection with Doubleday was useful, but possibly Unwin's house did more to fill the market with American books. Heinemann had on his first list in 1890 Harold Frederic and Alexander Brown's *Genesis of the United States;* his prospectus for the new "Dollar Library of American Fiction" hailed the great increase of American authors. Macmillan, an important and comprehensive publisher, did not necessarily stock in England its American imprints. The Oxford University Press opened an

American branch in 1896 and the Amen House agency for our university press books in 1909. An American School and College Textbook Agency opened in London in 1902. During one week in 1901, twenty out of sixty publications issued were by American writers. Much of our technical output began to supersede German writings.

Our books were often poorly advertised, and inadequate announcements made it difficult for even an enthusiast to locate such books. Although our reference works and encyclopaedias were not generally known in trade circles or libraries, our steady encroachment upon the *Encyclopaedia Britannica* illustrated the gravitating pull of increasing numbers of overseas subscribers (three times as many by the fourteenth edition) and, perhaps, a growing recognition of American scholarship. The ninth edition was sold in impressive quantities in England by using our sales techniques. In this edition, in preparation from about 1873 to 1889, approximately thirty Americans wrote on subjects not pertaining to strictly American developments. For the eleventh edition, with A. T. Hadley as an associate editor, in preparation from 1903 to 1910, about seventy Americans contributed on general subjects. The American tone became complete in the fourteenth edition from "Air-Conditioning" to the end.

The flood of American books, especially in 1905, reminded the British how much they disliked our copyright law.[2] The printing trade constantly protested a law which forced British authors to print their books in the States—a process by which additional Americanisms crept in. Our competition in medical, psychological, sociological, and economic writings prompted the Parliamentary Committee of the Labour Congress to ask the Board of Trade to apply the Patents and Designs Act of 1907 to copyright; others suggested a Pan-Anglican Copyright Union. Our reinforced act of 1909 was received as a direct discrimination against England. Although Sir Henry Craik asked Parliament in 1911, "How many American authors could be printed here with any prospect of a large sale?" Mr. Joynson-Hicks, who wanted to compel such printing, showed that American books were gaining popularity. Copyright procedure, however, did not increase America's influence to any great extent. American publishing did come in for a share of attention in the battle between the *Times* and the British Publishers' Association which the *Times* insisted was like an American book trust.

Booksellers, who are very conservative, usually objected to an American imprint which, publishers assert, often at the outset reduces orders about 80 per cent. In addition to general suspicions about textbooks or scientific and scholarly works, they pretend to dislike the format, flat-back covers, deep gutters in the binding, poor editing, and even the smell of American glue. Like the pre-War *Engineer,* many found "annoying features" in textbooks which were wholly theoretical and crammed with mathematics, or "wholly practical and filled to overflowing with descriptive matter reminiscent of the catalogues from which they draw their origin." A prominent Midland bookseller will take no American books by reasoning that an English firm with its own imprint, if it expected sales, would print them in the United Kingdom. Booksellers were ready to believe that our books, taking into account market differences, were easier to sell in Scotland.[3] In pre-War years only Harvard or Yale professors carried any prestige. Further, since Americans had no history and little civilization, how could they be expected to write about either? Yet an Englishman observed in 1908:

> What is really strange is that educational authorities have been prepared to accept and to utilize in English schools many American educational books carrying American forms of speech and American spelling.

The London County Council in 1925 approved a children's series, but teachers soon complained that students disturbed them with the spelling of "gray," "odor," and "color"; the publisher set up plates with English spelling. Publishers on their part complain that schools develop no literary or historical background which would arouse interest in American books. Although many publishers feel that suspicion has not abated much since 1914, more assert that an American book now gets the attention it merits.

Material abounds for the study of early American history in England, but the general reader, and even the research student, must be affected by the breadth, quantity, and availability of books relating to the United States.[4] British libraries leave much to be desired in this respect. The British Museum has most of the necessary

302   AMERICA AND GREAT BRITAIN

books, but some in the Reading Room have been out of date. The American collection at the Institute of Historical Research, formed by a gift of G. L. Beer's books and the Manton Marble Collection of early government reports (about one thousand volumes and five hundred pamphlets) presented by Lady Conway in 1922, and augmented in 1926 by an American government donation of 226 volumes of diplomatic correspondence and Senate documents, constitutes one of the best research collections. Professor Graham Wallas made an extensive collection relating to our political problems for the British Library of Political and Economic Science at the London School of Economics, and during 1898 Mr. and Mrs. Sidney Webb, at the request of the Library's trustees, obtained, in addition to standard works, a large number of official reports bearing upon public administration. The Carnegie Endowment for International Peace presented a collection numbering 2,500 books and pamphlets to University College (London) in 1920. Other special institutions with restricted membership and a few club libraries have enough volumes for well-read gentlemen, but the rest of London, apart from circulating libraries which are loaded with many sensational American books, is not well served. Universities and public schools are not overstocked with American history or literature. Municipal libraries do not fill the gap. Manchester had seventeen volumes on America in the reference room; the Sheffield reference catalogue contained sixty items, mostly pamphlets from our Department of Labor and iron and steel reports; the selection at Birmingham may be called representative if not adequate. County libraries serving rural areas have less demand for American books.

Records of library circulation do not justify more than a few general observations. Librarians usually insist that American novels are read as novels rather than as reflections upon our life. Exposé books had a large following. The cinema increased the circulation of Merriam's *Chicago* in the expectation that something was to be said about urban wild life. Books by S. E. Forman, J. T. Adams, Mencken, Kreymborg, Untermeyer, Fosdick, Cadman, Corey, Soule, Mumford, Stoddard, Breasted, Dewey, and Van Loon were withdrawn frequently in Manchester and Sheffield. At Manchester, Mitchell's *Gone with the Wind* was becoming as much used as Upton Sinclair or Sinclair Lewis; Whittier, Lincoln, Emerson, and Bryce's *Commonwealth* were still in demand. At least 60 per cent of the librarians concluded that our historical writings and attractive volumes on science were satisfactory, but that sociological treatises raised complex problems which did not interest England. Wales and Scotland, more than England, read our evangelical books and sermons. British radicals know America's proletarian literature.

The New-Old World relationship teased writers as one may see in Henry James (1843–1916), the American novelist.[5] Had James been weaker he would have been an occult émigré. By his own career, which in miniature marked an epoch in transatlantic cultural relations, by the application of his genius which was drawn by an almost dangerous, monomaniacal absorption in the subtle interplay of the Americano-European legend, he was something of a prophet of America's impact abroad. James preferred to discuss the Old World impact upon Americans, but the reverse process was never absent. Rebecca West has asked:

Why had he continued to write about Americans in Europe long after their common motive and their individual adventures had ceased to excite his wonder or his sympathy?

Because, as he adumbrated in *W. W. Story* (1903), he was still drawn to the relation of America to Europe ("treatable, but in too many lights"), and he could not have been completely satisfied that even his excellent pages, especially since our influence was given a secondary rôle, had "done" the complex subject.

From 1876 to 1888, years of "monstrous and unattenuated contrast," James wrote his international novels with almost Old World surprise at the primitive, flitting inroads of Americans. A critic of his adds: "In Europe Americans stood out and offered possibilities to the novelist much more than in America. Life quickened into drama." It is difficult to believe, however, that this was all that captivated James, whose novels would have become insufferably artificial. Because the first surprise had worn off, James did not turn again to the international theme until the new century, when America's invasion purported to be of greater significance. At first James had found the Continent uncongenial and turned to England, a move which in view of his own background produced more subtleties. James once wrote that the two countries should "cultivate with talent, a common destiny." Yet England looked upon him as an American who correctly interpreted us. This may have been presumptuous because James found the American consciousness "the more touching the more primitive we make it." [6] He tried to sense how the American, "incredibly unaware of life," would appear in Europe. He endowed his characters with a delicacy which nurtured considerate relations with others, witness Ralph Touchett, Dosson, Christopher Newman, and Adam Verver, and in this he probably departed from Old World opinion. But the continental antics of his American girl which made "Daisy-Millerism" a by-word conformed more to this opinion. Although James wrote, January 18, 1879, about the second part of *International Episode*, "It is an entirely new sensation for them (the people here) to be (at all delicately) *ironized* or satirized, from the American point of view and they don't relish it," [7] he looked upon the Anglo-American world "as a big Anglo-Saxon total destined to such an amount of melting together that an insistence on their differences becomes more and more idle and pedantic." [8] The directing force of that "melting together" was to be England not America. He died a British citizen and his last completed work, *The Sense of the Past*, described a young American, heir to an old London house, who became completely enveloped in the past!

Although England apparently expected our literature to be of a new species, it was always somewhat puzzled by it. Professor Woodberry suggested in 1903 that England sought to identify American talent by its exceptional variations—Harte, Twain, Whitman, or Joaquin Miller, but he might as well have added Longfellow or Mr. Dooley, Emerson or A. T. Mahan.[9] The British realized that it was difficult for the two countries to agree about our literature; some thought it a miracle that the language unity had been maintained. Taste diverged in strange fashion. Frequently, Britons were more curious than we about certain American literary figures. There was also the dubious view (put forward again recently by Townsend Scudder's study of Emerson) which sanctified British judgment because the Atlantic Ocean gave perspective.

The heritage of earlier literary links carried on into our period. George Ticknor was a wealthy pioneer of transatlantic culture.

Stead concluded in 1902 that Franklin was the first American to have a vogue, then Cooper, Emerson, Motley, and Longfellow, and later, John Bright's favorite poet, Whittier. In 1890 Froude said that it was Emerson, whose influence had been steady, who had convinced him he did not belong to the Church of England. During the nineteenth century many popular American works were first published in England. But Franklin's *Autobiography* and Thoreau's *Walden* did not get into popular English reprints of "classics" until about 1900. Our writers were occasionally honored by memorial exhibitions. American humorists such as C. G. Leland (Hans Breitmann), Clark (Max Adeler), Locke (Petroleum V. Nasby), and Browne (Artemus Ward) flourished from 1860 to 1880 and broke down the resistance to Americanisms. Leland also promoted the Gypsy Lore Society in England. Twain's influence extended more markedly into the first decades of the new century; Dooley's comments, which must have been difficult for the English to comprehend, spread in syndicate fashion across prominent papers. Sir Walter Raleigh in 1915 spoke of George Ade as the greatest living American writer. The British public seemed peculiarly eager to read anything which promised to be funny even though it remained a mystery. J. A. Hobson wrote: "Hardly any American ought to be taken quite so seriously as most English readers take Mark Twain or Mr. Dooley." (And one might add the *New Yorker*.) Popular children's books, which often conveyed exotic glimpses of a romantic country, were sometimes denounced as "unrestrained and superficial" because "a good deal of ugliness goes with the American comic standard in these matters."

English reviewers were charged with unfairness. They certainly noted monotonously the origin of a book, sufficiently expressed as "American," "too American," or "very American." [10] There were constant, almost snobbish pleas in technical reviews not to let this origin frighten readers. The regular book critic of the *Daily Mail* reported in November, 1900 that he was criticized for using his column on behalf of American authors;

Such criticism . . . does not arise from lack of literary generosity, but is instigated by the prevailing point of view that English readers are not interested in the remote affairs of the book world in America.

Time and competition made these objectors admit the need for such attention. Chalmers Roberts observed:

In my immediate experience, the books of Miss Wilkins, of Miss Glasgow, and of Mr. Norris have had the best receptions, both from critics and buyers. I could astonish American readers with a list of names unappreciated in England.

P. A. Vaile, who had bitterly denounced us, declared in 1907 that the American novel was gaining in England because of its vitality. In 1910 Gertrude Atherton thought that Mrs. Wiggin was one of the very few who had "held on" in England. Miss Atherton, who went to London to make a reputation which America would have to acknowledge, spread native lore in her popular *Patience Sparhawk, American Wives and English Husbands, Californians,* and *Senator North;* her novel about Alexander Hamilton, *The Conqueror,* figured in Imperial federation discussion. "John Oliver Hobbes" (Pearl Craigie), daughter of the prominent London-American J. Morgan Richards, won a position in literary circles, satirized our labor-saving machines, and delineated a clever American *demi-mondaine.* By complimentary press correspondence, G. W. Smalley paved the way for Edith Wharton; Poultney Bigelow gained the proper sort of social recognition. Americans had to recognize Stephen Crane partly because of the resounding British success of *The Red Badge of Courage.* With A. S. Hardy's *His Daughter First* (1903) before him, a *Times* reviewer suggested timidly that we now produced novels full of promise and health, fiction which viewed with detachment the ordinary life of the average man and woman. The *Times* also decided that one could no longer talk glibly about America's literature. But Edward Garnett's evaluation of our fiction in the two decades preceding 1914 was typical when he found that it was characterized by exaggeration, a presentation and glorification of "standardized" morals, manners, and social ambition.

Mrs. A. Gilchrist and William Michael Rossetti appointed themselves Whitman missionaries in England.[11] There was an ardent Whitman coterie at Bolton (Lancashire) which celebrated his birthday with speeches and songs. While reading Whitman at Cambridge in 1868–69, "a profound change," which minimized the importance of opinions and ideas, came over the poet Edward Carpenter (1844–1929) who visited Whitman in 1877 and 1884. In 1883 Thoreau's *Walden* nearly paralyzed him; "What sort of line my life would have taken if Thoreau had come to me earlier, I cannot tell. It is certain there would have been a considerable difference." Carpenter continued to spread the study of Whitman, who had also influenced Margaret Bondfield. Robert, First Earl of Lytton, heartily disliked Whitman and American humorists.

H. G. Wells, who was amused in his early days by the Wild West of Cooper and Reid, recalled the early eighties:

It seems improbable that I did not then encounter the opposition of Socialism and individualism, but oddly enough I cannot recall having thought at all about Socialism until I read Henry George at Midhurst.

Lord Snell was stimulated by Emerson and Henry George, and later by the romance of our West. Asquith's first impressions of America came from *Martin Chuzzlewit* and *Uncle Tom's Cabin*, later from Uncle Remus and Edith Wharton. This statesman, who seems to have read much American fiction, once observed the unredeemed odiousness of some characters in books sent to a friend: "One feels almost thankful that they could not have been created or have existed anywhere but in America." One wonders whether Lord Rosebery, who praised Owen Wister's *Lady Baltimore* as brilliant, was serious when he told Henry James that his ideal of a happy life was that in Cambridge, Massachusetts, living like Longfellow. Viscount Esher, who thought Wister and Roberts wrote about a new race, recorded, "What freshness there is in these stories from the new world." Ford Madox Ford's reading illustrated the steady flow of our fiction; in his youth, the redskins of Cooper and Reid, then the West of Boone and Bowie, the mining camps of Bret Harte, then, "last of all the Wild West of Buffalo Bill which took place in the Earl's Court Exhibition in the West End of London. Those twain had met." The *Times* mourned the passing of Bret Harte, who had helped to open British eyes to our West. For the girls, as Mrs. Maxwell Armfield noted, Harper's *Young People* and *St. Nicholas*, L. M. Alcott, and the "Katy" series surpassed any English writings. G. K. Chesterton testified to the saturation of English children with *Huckleberry Finn* and

Little Women; on his own part he could read the *Autocrat of the Breakfast Table,* but not O. Henry, without thinking about American origins. The diplomat Lord Howard of Penrith chose Twain's volumes as conveniently representing America.

We may now inquire into the influence of the American language.[12] Ruskin wrote significantly in 1871:

> You have felt, doubtless, at least those of you who have been brought up in any habit of reverence, that every time when in this letter I have used an American expression, or aught like one, there came upon you a sense of sudden wrong—the darting through you of acute cold. I meant you to feel that: for it is the essential function of America to make us feel like that.

Americanisms, he thought, resulted from a penchant for degradation. The adoption of a word or expression *may* illustrate that American ideas or manners have made their way into British life; at least it demonstrates that we have found a poignant language adequate to express many aspects of modern Western civilization. Up to the fourth edition (1936) of his *American Language* H. L. Mencken thought the differences between English and American would continue to increase; he now states:

> The Englishman, of late, has yielded so much to American example, in vocabulary, in idiom, in spelling and even in pronunciation, that what he speaks promises to become, on some not too remote tomorrow, a kind of dialect of American, just as the language spoken by the American was once a dialect of English.

The force of greater numbers is as strong as the talkie in modifying this common heritage.

The alarm against Americanisms has a long history. Many glossaries to aid English comprehension followed the first one by Rev. Jonathan Boucher in 1800. Sir William Craigie concluded that the invasion began in earnest in 1820; Mencken, in 1913. Eric Partridge decided that Americanisms were not popular until after 1918. H. W. and F. G. Fowler in their *King's English* (1906) treated them as foreign words; they disliked both details and the general tone of this language, an attitude which might conceivably hinder the fluent exchange of ideas. The *Athenaeum,* however, thought in 1898 that American books did not need footnote explanations for such words as "cops," "to swing," etc., because British readers of current fiction knew enough already. English frequenters of American bars in the West End of London were speaking a jargon in 1900 that was scarcely American or English. An Englishman ironically suggested that American should be taught, and that our local humor books should be translated to "provide suitable employment for a number of indigenous men of letters whose original compositions are no longer required owing to the superior merit and more popular style of their American competitors."

Herbert W. Horwill, in his *Dictionary of American Usage* (1935), a work begun in 1902, has said:

Usages that to-day are peculiar to America are to-morrow adopted by English writers and speakers, *frequently without the least suspicion of their transatlantic origin*. [My italics.]

In addition many miss the meaning of our racy speech, retranslate slang terms, and imply that our idioms are merely slang. Professor Weekley, who discussed our development of the preposition as in "up against it," wrote in 1930, "There is to Englishmen such an attractiveness in American idiom that very slight contact with it is quickly reflected." Prime Minister Chamberlain spoke of himself as a "go-getter for peace." Probably about one thousand Americanisms are being used by English writers. A brief list of American usages which are naturalized or being naturalized reflects some of our influence: caucus, Tammany, graft, bucket shop, crook, get away with, pull (influence), buncombe, to stump, rally; hard-boiled, frame-up, beat it (make off); feature (give prominence to), dance hall, float, balconies, stage (a deliberate organization of incident); cereal (breakfast food), fudge, layer cake, kitchen cabinet, popcorn, nut sundae; bellboy, jaywalker, blow in from somewhere; highbrow, money to burn, happening, bromide, cover (in journalism), cub (reporter), editorial, yellow, write up; to fire (dismiss), to be a back number, cut (reduction), bargain counter, filing cabinet, proposition, get there, get on to, hold up (delay), hustle, scab; boom, conservative (estimate), department store, publicity (for advertising), up against, sob-stuff, ready-to-wear, junk, bank on (rely on), wildcat (scheme), can (tin), shape (condition), stay put, mixer (said of a person), pussyfoot (temperance advocate, from Pussyfoot Johnson who stirred up resentment in 1919), upper crust.

Many of these usages came into England before 1914, particularly those in the category of business. *Punch* and others noted in the nineties our influence on the press—"There is a more conversational, almost a slangy tone about it." Slang might even be worked into advertisements, and fun made of our efforts to reform spelling! Lever Brothers cried out

> Uncle Sam may spell Soap *Sope*, But
> John Bull spells it *Sunlight*.

Our Department of Commerce urged the American sales promoter in England "to use British English in his sales drive." Ambassador Choate, who shocked English society with his Americanisms, irritated Lady Frances Balfour by describing her father as "in good shape." It was important that language differences were something of which all classes were aware, even if an unintelligible Cockney asks sneeringly about our movie slang. The American woman, usually called the "Fair American," always spoke with a nasal (*sic*) accent: "Guess, Popp, you'd better jump into your boiled shirt. There goes the hash hammer"; or on entering Venice by train, "Waal, I guess this is where the Adriatic slops over!" *Punch* even imagined "the prim people of the United States never use the word 'leg.'"

The shock of cold shivers Ruskin described attracted attention, but also warned of a different mental approach, and frequently set up a resistance to contamination which restricted both our language and the experience expressed by it. Unfortunately, too many Britons think of American speech only as "Sez you!" or "Oh yeah!" Many have felt that the approximately common language is not an unmixed blessing. Wales and Scotland appeared less perturbed by Americanisms. Because of its underworld flavor, parents complained of our language which was considered a true reflection of our morality. There also exists a mental quirk which can account for the varieties of speech of Lancashire, Yorkshire, the Cockney, and the Scotch, but not the American in general, or Brooklyn, or

Chicago, or Mississippi in particular. Such invasion of language as has taken place proves the power of the cinema, press, and business, not the connivance of British literary masters.

British books on the United States are much used throughout this volume as records of the American impact upon individuals and as reflections on our significance.[13] The influence of pure and simple travel books may be easily exaggerated. One does not find that many whose careers fell within the years from 1895 to the present were much affected by these potboilers. Such books enlightened (?) us more than Britons, and were more eagerly read by us. Their force declined rapidly with the improvement of other channels of information. J. L. Mesick, who analyzed earlier travels, concluded that they "seem to have depended little on one another." Travel tales, which outnumbered serious studies in contrast to our writings on British life, rarely mentioned anything which struck commentators as suitable for careful attention or imitation. As early as the 1820's the literary war began between those who favored or assailed America with analyses which contained many interesting gaps of information. Conan Doyle thought no country had ever been so maligned by the traveling Briton, but the fundamental question here is not about hostility but intelligence. That travel literature was marked by unreality and naïve surprise; very little was said in many words. These reporters were misled by a tendency to inform America rather than their own public; hence, not many were so enduring as Bryce or De Tocqueville, who wrote for their compatriots. After hasty assimilation many of them seemed impelled by a carminative frenzy which demanded verbal expression, excitement that must be killed by writing a book. It is therefore necessary to go beyond travel books.

Gladstone once told Chauncey Depew that no one since De Tocqueville had written a good history of the United States, and that an Englishman, free from bias, would on the whole better understand the task than an American.[14] Nor was Gladstone evidently aware of Bryce's interest when he wrote, November 15, 1883, to the Chief Justice of England, Lord Coleridge, who had just returned from a visit during which he was the first foreigner to sit with the Supreme Court *in banc:*

I think you have rendered a public service by your excursion to America. . . . I wish the two countries to be married at all points, and you have married them at one important and vital point, namely in their legal profession. I should have liked to ask you, was it not after all tremendous? And, have you done or thought anything, or do you see your way, as to getting some competent person to study and then write upon the social state of America? which is almost a sealed book to us, while even of its material condition we are but roughly and loosely informed.

Gladstone, who feared that England was losing sight of America and her progress, said he always advised young politicians to study our political history. Thus the time was ripe for James Bryce.

The preëminence of Bryce's *American Commonwealth* as a source of information is bewildering; probably no nation has relied so exclusively upon one book to learn about another country. And yet this volume, designed especially for British needs, took on so much more rapidly in America that the author, more British than English, was surprised. Up to 1914 about nine thousand copies were sold in Britain.[15] Bryce's complaint that those who cited our experiments to the Old World neglected facts is illustrated by many examples in this book. Curiously, Bryce's hostility to Britain's policy in South Africa inspired some of his political opponents to say, "The book is an arsenal where English enemies of the United States find weapons ready to hand."

Let us turn briefly to other British books.[16] Some of these tried to profit by the sort of interest expressed by Sir Walter Raleigh, "I want to hear about America, and whether it's really as awful as they say." Some, like G. W. Steevens's *Land of the Dollar* (1897), which first appeared in the *Daily Mail*, could not escape the Mormons or the Pacific Coast, which was still held by H. A. Vachell, a novelist, to be a *terra incognita* for Englishmen. The dramatist Archer, who had visited twenty years before, wrote in 1900:

It has been literally the dream of my life to revisit the United States. . . . What the land of Cooper and Mayne Reid was to my boyish fancy, the land of Washington and Lincoln, Hawthorne and Emerson, is to my adult thoughts.

One reason for the visit was to see how America's feeling towards England had been changed by the war of 1898. In his *Land of Contrasts* (3rd ed., 1902) J. F. Muirhead, a Scotchman, proposed to find instruction, but concluded, like other sober travelers, that generalizations and short-term views were dangerous. G. B. Hill, who visited in 1893 and 1896, expressed a deeper fascination:

What I have been for many years eager to study is your New England States. There are four great cradles of Liberty—Greece, Holland, England, and New England.

Such motivation was illustrated by T. P. O'Connor, journalist and parliamentarian, who returned from his first visit in 1881 a blind, enthusiastic lover of everything American; in 1890 he became more critical, and in 1906, everything seemed like an earthquake.

There were others, like De Bary who came to recover from a breakdown, who justified their books by exalting America as a supreme object lesson in the social world even though there was an impassable gulf between the two countries. Beckles Willson put it another way in 1903: "Indeed, for the first time in her history, America shows a united front to the world which it were disingenuous for us not to acknowledge." A. Maurice Low, whose comments on America were widely quoted in England, concluded in 1908 that there was no reason to talk about our literature or art; in 1909 he struck upon the conservatism and idealism of this nation and regional differences without flattering democracy. A New Zealander wrote *Yankee: America's Peril* because Englishmen had been too kind; even the *Saturday Review* decided that a nation so depicted could not last. T. R. Burlford was one of those who wrote because "Americans are systematically undermining British influence and British institutions at home and abroad." "Rita," after two months undisturbed by our interviewers, was puzzled by our diversity, and out-Trolloped Trollope. She was at ease when she regarded America as the very antithesis of England; the trip which seemed such a great effort led her to conclude: "We do differ, and I think always will. There are racial prejudices on both sides to combat, and complete understanding is impossible." The poet and journalist, T. W. H. Crosland (1868–1924), who satirized our millionaires, humorists, actors, beautiful women who were not beautiful, *et al.*, echoed Sydney Smith in his *Abounding American* (1907): "Can anyone point to anything in the world that America is accomplishing which is purely and simply calculated to serve the highest interests of the human race?"

No one would deny the effect of an American visit as hinted by Arnold Bennett; but its meaning would be of less importance to readers since only eight weeks went into the production of *Those United States* (1912) which did not explain Bennett or America. The poet Rupert Brooke could not avoid previous "impressions," the widely different views of his friends, or the American invasion of London music halls—"a very definite taste of a jerking, vital, *bizarre*, 'rag-time' civilization"; he departed into rather fresh paths by noting our excellence in fish, architecture, jokes, drinks, and children's clothes. With Henry James's interpretation (which J. A. Hobson found useless) ringing in his ears, H. G. Wells came looking for the American Vision, the America thirty years hence, and gathered ample sociological food for thought and increased optimism for the world's future.[17] What William James anticipated as *"the* medicinal book about America," others pronounced false and superficial. Although the conclusions of a British Tory and a British Socialist may sound the same to our ears, there is this difference with Wells, that he took seriously the American venture, letting it pour into his thought, so much so that he often talks of having been Americanized. As if in one of his fantastic romances, he discovered that the New World gave an Englishman valuable perspective. This reflected a new attitude toward America as a laboratory for thought.

These few comments intimate the background, origins, and results of the writers' visits. Their observations, more than the political utterances of the governing class, emphasized the distinctness of the two nations. How else could a travel book be exciting? For the most part the books were aimless. But one is constantly reminded of an attitude expressed by Shelley: "Nay, start not at the word! America!"

America has in one way or another often crossed the lives of British writers.[18] Although by 1900 Frank Harris, who spoke like an American, no longer felt himself confined to American scenes or characters, his biographers say of this stormy petrel in English journalism: "America . . . nurtured him with raw Western life, college years and opportunities enough for the bombastic and intense individuality to grow." In 1907 he visited the United States for the sole purpose of studying the Haymarket tragedy, around which he wrote *The Bomb*. Far removed from Harris was "Ian Maclaren" (John Watson, 1850–1917), Scottish author and divine, who found "something in the atmosphere of America that was eminently congenial"; he died in Iowa while on a lecture tour. The biographer and critic Sir Leslie Stephen, who read American history in his student days at Cambridge, met Lowell at a critical period of his life. His pamphlet, "The *Times* on the American War," first brought him prominence. His English friends detected after his visits of 1863 and 1866, made purely for political reasons, an accent and an outwardly Americanized man. He wrote to Lowell, January 1, 1864:

> As the one-eyed is king among the blind, my three months in the United States is regarded as an unlimited field of experience to which my weaker brethren reverentially appeal.

He planned an essay on the United States about which Maitland says, "I gather that, had it been written, we might now be saying that it stood between Tocqueville and Bryce." Although one of the first Englishmen to analyze American humor, he sensibly abandoned the larger project, but the idea carried on to Bryce, whom he introduced to Lowell in 1870.

America was a sensuous experience for Rudyard Kipling who once contemplated settling permanently in Vermont. In 1892 he married an American whose brother collaborated in writing *Naulahka*. He gained from us his earliest impressions of temperance and popular government; Bret Harte affected his technique; America conditioned his thoughts about race imperialism. Conan Doyle, like Besant, confessed to the romance of America, and did not hesitate to use American backgrounds for his stories. Herbert Spencer was touched by American aid for the completion of his Synthetic Philosophy. Carlyle, Browning, and Tennyson were said to have been appreciated first in the States. We accepted George Meredith as a poet, and American approval aided the run of his novels. When he wasn't annoyed by pirated editions, Ruskin, who numbered Emerson, Lowell, and Norton among his instructors, admitted America's heartier understanding. W. E. Henley (1848–1903) in the late eighties achieved a poet's reputation more quickly and widely in the United States. Louisa Alcott and Henry James were the two profound literary influences upon Frank Swinnerton. Anthony Hope Hawkins ventured an American trip in 1897 "led by curiosity and the hope of gain." Frances Hodgson Burnett enriched her experience by a long stay in Tennessee; in 1899 she wrote from Kent: "One seems to need them both—America for mental stimulation, and England for quietness and rest." The Scotchman Robert Barr, founder of the *Idler Magazine*, made ample use of his American background, giving the local color of business hustle in such novels as *A Chicago Princess*, *The Woman Wins* (1897), and *The Victors* (1901). American setting and color may be found in R. D. Blackmore's *Erema* (1877), Kennedy's *A Man Adrift* (1899), S. R. Lysaght's *The Marplot* (1893), the western novels of Ridgwell Cullum, who returned to England in 1904, R. L. Stevenson and Lloyd Osbourne's *The Wreckers* (1892) which depicted shady finances, in novels by H. A. Vachell, Gwendolen Overton, A. H. Paterson, Frederick J. Niven, Sir A. T. Quiller-Couch, and E. Phillips Oppenheim. It was the West and high society which most fascinated the British. After 1914 the sweep for material and inspiration became broader.

William James commented on brother Henry's projected visit to the States:

It appears that what you crave is millions of just such shocks, and that a new lease of artistic life, with the lamp of genius fed by the oil of twentieth-century American life, is to be the end and aim of the voyage. . . . All my stingy doubts wither and are replaced by enthusiasm that you are still so young-feeling, receptive and hungry for more raw material and experience.

This function of America is significant, and perhaps typical, but the resultant book, like so many others similarly inspired, was one of "omissions, silences, vacancies." What Carlyle wrote to Emerson in 1872—"There is something huge, painful, almost appalling to me in that wild Western World of yours"—brilliantly described America's growing importance for Britain's literary consciousness.

[1] F. M. Bicknell, "Yankee in British Fiction," *Outlook*, 1910, 96:632–39; B. Bissell, *The American Indian in English Literature of the Eighteenth Century* (New York, 1925); William B. Cairnes, *British Criticism of American Writings, 1783–1833* (2 vols., Univ. of Wisconsin Studies in Language and Literature, Madison, Wis., 1918–22). It behooves students of literature to make synthetic studies of Am. literature abroad.

[2] *P. Debs.*, Commons, 1911, 23:2615, 2634; 29:2614, 2180–83, 2177; see also *Minutes of Evidence taken before the Law of Copyright Committee, P.P.*, 1910 (cd. 5051), XXI.

[3] Possibly the Empire is more receptive to Am. books, S. Africa perhaps more than Australia. One firm in the 1920's sold five times as many Am. business books in Germany as in England; four times as many in Holland and the Scandinavian countries. Robinson, *Twentieth Century American*, 223; G. H. Putnam, *Memories of a Publisher* (New York, 1923), 59, 234; *U.S. Monthly Consular Report*, Aug. 1908, No. 335, pp. 182–92.

[4] Cf. R. A. Rye, *The Student's Guide to the Libraries of London* (London, 1927), 39–40, 253–54, 298–99; at the South-Eastern Agricultural College, Wye, Kent, there are 3,500 volumes, 100 of them referring to Am. agriculture. Teachers' libraries in various cities have Am. pedagogical volumes. Lord Lee of Fareham has formed a nucleus of a library in Cheltenham College to be known as the Roosevelt Library; Ambassador Houghton drew up a list of Am. books which were presented to Coleg Harlech, an adult residential college in South Wales. Escott, *National Links*, p. 225, could not have had in mind the modern circulating libraries when he said they form "a healthy link between the reading public on both Atlantic shores." A small exhibition at the Sheffield Library in 1936 described Oliver Wendell Holmes as "having a conservative strain unusual in an American." A workers' educational class in this city was studying Am. literature.

[5] *Complete Novels and Tales of Henry James* (35 vols., London, 1921–23); E. L. Cary, *The Novels of Henry James* (New York, 1905), 75, 78; Van Wyck Brooks, *The Pilgrimage of Henry James* (New York, 1925), 65, 105, 106, 109, 119; C. P. Kelley, *The Early Development of Henry James* (Urbana, Ill., 1930), 264–65; note the European impact upon Gertrude Wentworth in *The Europeans* and Isabel Archer in *Portrait of a Lady*. Contemporary agitation is expressed in *The Ambassadors* (1903) and *The Outcry* (1911); in the latter an Am. millionaire tries to secure an Old World masterpiece. An adroit Am. adventuress gets an English baronet in *Siege of London* (1883); in *Princess Casamassima* (1866), another of doubtful qualities hobnobs with Socialists; in *Wings of a Dove*, an heiress cannot entice an Englishman to spend her money. Cf. L. F. Austin's *Points of View* (London, 1906), 151, 210ff.

[6] James, *W. W. Story*, 6; Story's statue of George Peabody is in London; see *Complete Novels*, pref. to vol. XVI, p. xix; also pref. to *The Reverberator* and *Lady Barbarina* (prefaces begun about 1908).

[7] Brooks, *op. cit.*, 105.

[8] Percy Lubbock, ed., *The Letters of Henry James* (2 vols., London, 1920), I, 143, 426.

[9] G. E. Woodberry, *America in Literature* (London, 1903), 239–40; Townsend Scudder, *The Lonely Wayfaring Man; Emerson and some Englishmen* (New York, 1936); I. R. Brussel, *Anglo-American First Editions, West to East* (London, 1936); Mencken, *Am. Language*, 224; F. J. H. Darton, "Children's Books" in *Ency. of Education* (1921); for earlier period see Darton's *Children's Books in England* (Cambridge, 1932), 224–39; J. A. Hobson, *Modern Outlook* (1910), 201. Stephen Leacock in *19th Cent.*, 1914, 76:456. Raleigh, *Letters*, II, 416.

[10] Daniel Chaucer in *Transatlantic Review*, March 1924; P. A. Vaile, *Wake Up, England* (London, 1907), 88; Roberts, "American Books in England," *World's Work*, Oct. 1904, 8:5431; Atherton, "The American Novel in England," *Bookman*, Feb. 1910, 633–37 and *Adventures of a Novelist, passim*. Edward Garnett, *Friday Nights; Literary Criticisms and Appreciations* (New York, 1922), 259; Richards, *Life of John Oliver Hobbes* (*Pearl Craigie*) (London, 1911).

[11] E. Pennell, *Joseph Pennell*, I, 119; Edward Carpenter, *My Days and Dreams, Being Autobiographical Notes* (London, 1916), 64, 87, 88, 116, 167, 250; M. A. Hamilton, *Margaret Bondfield* (London, 1924), 52–53; Lady Betty Balfour, *Personal and Literary Letters of Robert, First Earl of Lytton* (London, 1906), II, 369–74; H. G. Wells, *Experiment in Autobiography* (New York, 1934), I, 78, 168, 179; Desmond MacCarthy, ed., *H.H.A. Letters* (2nd series, London, 1934), 23; M. V. Brett, ed., *Journals and Letters of Reginald, Viscount Esher* (London, 1934), I, 30, 384; Lord Snell, *Men, Movements, and Myself* (London, 1936), 45, 58, 225; Snell's first visit to U.S. in 1919 made him optimistic. G. K. Chesterton, *What I Saw in America* (New York, 1923), 83, 204; F. M. Ford, ed., *Transatlantic Stories* (London, 1926), p. viii; when Ford says Middle Westishness pervades the world he means the boredom of no more lands to discover. Harold Blodgett, *Walt Whitman in England* (New York, 1934, Cornell Studies in English, vol. XXIV). See Charles Marriott's *Love with Honour* (1902).

A survey of 200 Britons who traveled to U.S. showed that only 50 had ever read many Am. books; 25 put literature as primary source of information. Most quoted during 1898–1914 were probably Lincoln, Whittier, Lowell, Dooley, and Mahan. In general, Britons questioned seem to have depended on the following authors in the order named: Sinclair Lewis, Alcott, Twain, Sinclair, Emerson, J. T. Adams, Harte, Dreiser, Cooper, Stowe, Ferber, London, J. Lincoln, Whitman, Robert Chambers, George Gibbs, Wiggin, Atherton, Cather, Porter, Churchill, Wharton, (Mitchell), Wilkins, Norris, Canfield, Melville, Mary Johnstone. Book sales might suggest a different rating.

[12] Much historical work remains to be done on American language abroad. H. L. Mencken, *The American Language: An Inquiry Into the Development of English in the United States* (4th ed., New York, 1936), vi, 3–49, 84, 223–319. Mencken says (p. 28) the "sect of British Americophils is small and feeble, though it shows a few respectable names." According to him (p. 45), William Archer, a Scotsman, launched in 1899 the revolutionary theory that the Am. language had merit. Among those more favorable to our language have been Robert Bridges, Wyndham Lewis, Virginia Woolf, and Sir John Fraser. Strachey says (*American Soundings*, 213) of Mencken: "The real trouble and misunderstanding begin when his books are offered for the perusal of the British public. They in their ignorance, and especially as the source of communication is American, think that the extracts are significant and even typical. The ordinary Englishman has little standard of comparisons in things American." Eric Partridge, *Slang Today and Yesterday*

(London, 1933), 229, 239, 288, 292, 299–303, 310. He estimates Canadian slang to be about 80 per cent American, Australian, 25 per cent. J. Redding Ware, *Passing English of the Victorian Era* (New York, 1909); Hamil Grant, *Two Sides of the Atlantic* (London, 1917), 175–76; Horwill, *A Dictionary of American Usage* (Oxford, 1935), Lady Balfour, *Ne Obliviscaris* (London, 1930), II, 388–89. Jokes about Americanisms, abating slightly after 1905, always find a good audience.

[13] Only about 10 per cent of the Britons questioned mentioned travel books as a source of ideas about the U.S. E. D. Adams, "The Point of View of the British Traveller in America," *Pol. Sc. Q.*, June 1914, refutes charges of persistent hostility and malice between 1810 and 1860. J. L. Mesick, *The English Traveller in America, 1785–1835* (New York, 1922) noted travel over the same regions, little discussion of home life or political system; Mesick claims study is valuable for the contributions to our knowledge of Am. conditions, and does not examine what influence the volumes may have had in England. This is also the approach of Allan Nevins, *American Social History as recorded by British Travellers* (New York, 1923). G. H. Payne, *England: Her Treatment of America* (New York, 1931) is a polemic against an Anglo-Am. alliance. He says (p. xii), "It is begging the question to say it is a minority that represents the anti-American feeling in England"; he identifies, much too simply, this attitude with the ruling minority, but his distinction between Scotch, Welsh, and English is sound. J. G. Brooks, *As Others See Us* (New York, 1908); Collinson Owen, *The American Illusion* (London, 1929), v. Having fed on travel books, Alan Raleigh produced clichés in *Real America* (London, 1913); Mrs. Alec Tweedie, however, deliberately avoided reading any such books, and visits in 1900, 1904, and 1912 left her adoring oysters, women, grapefruit, roses, rivers, elevators, quaint ways, and hospitality—*America as I saw it or America Revisited* (London, 1913). Note Margaret Halsey, *With Malice Toward Some* (New York, 1938), an Am. on England, and an indirect product of the exchange system of teachers!

[14] Henry Lucy, *Diary*, II, 60; E. H. Coleridge, *Life and Correspondence of Lord Coleridge* (London, 1904), II, 336; Coleridge recorded that in 1856 (I, 283) the *Federalist* was almost unprocurable in England, but that Gladstone had read and praised it; see also meeting of Rosebery, Carnegie, and Gladstone, July 1882, Hendricks, *Carnegie*, I, 258–59.

[15] Information supplied by Macmillan Co. Ltd., London; interview, Lady Bryce. Bryce first visited U.S. in 1870; Henry Sidgwick, S. A. Brooke, A. V. Dicey, and W. Robertson were especially interested in its composition. W. E. Lingelbach, "American Democracy and European Interpreters," *Penna. Mag. of Hist. and Biog.*, Jan. 1937, 17. Bryce as Ambassador was not certain whether we would object to a title; Choate advised him to wait; see *Campbell-Bannerman Papers*, British Museum Add. Mss., vol. 41211, 1906, pp. 360–63. Bryce's chapter, "Temper of the West" (written 1887), sometimes cited as close to Turner's thesis, suggests the U.S. as "frontier" influence on Old World. In letter, Feb. 22, 1895, he agreed with Roosevelt that frontier life affected modern Am. character. (*Bryce Mss. Coll.*; cf. Godkin and J. S. Mill in Ogden, *Godkin*, II, 42–43.) Bryce, *Social Institutions of the U.S.* (London, 1891), 270; A. and E. M. S. Sidgwick, *Henry Sidgwick* (London, 1906), 102, 454, 567. Cecil Chesterton's *History of the United States* (New York, 1919), conceived in 1914, was designed for English readers; interesting, but based upon slight research. Robert C. Brooks, ed., *Bryce's "American Commonwealth": Fiftieth Anniversary* (New York, 1939).

320 AMERICA AND GREAT BRITAIN

¹⁶ William Archer intended merely to study the Am. stage, instead he wrote the impressions of eight weeks in *America To-day* (London, 1900); the visit was important inasmuch as "Anglo-American patriotism," which had been a youthful dream, was buttressed by fuller knowledge which made him a frequent interpreter of this country as a "creation of the Anglo-Saxon spirit." See C. Archer, *William Archer: Life, Works, and Friendships* (New Haven, 1931), 235–36. W. H. Russell's *Hesperothen* (London, 1882), written on a hasty trip with L. and N. W. Railway officials and the Duke of Sutherland, was still read in the nineties. Vachell, *Sport and Life on the Pacific Coast* (London, 1900), devoted much space to the Western woman. Dean S. R. Hole, *A Little Tour in America* (London, 1895), 16–19; J. F. Muirhead, *Land of Contrasts* (London, 1900); David Macrae, *America Revisited* (Glasgow, 1908), acute observations on race and Mormons. Lady Raleigh, ed., *Letters of Sir Walter Raleigh, 1879–1922* (New York, 1926), II, 335.

Wanderlust produced E. H. L. Watson's *A Conversational Tour in America* (London, 1914) and William Winget's *A Tour in America* (Torquay, 1904). T. C. Porter's *Impressions of America* (London, 1899), travel blurb for the Far West. A. G. Bowden-Smith, *An English Student's Wander-Year in America* (London, 1910). Beckles Willson, *New America* (London, 1903); T. P. O'Connor, series "America Revisited" begun in *P.T.O.*, one of his papers, Nov. 17, 1906. Lucy Crump, ed., *Letters of G. B. Hill* (London, 1906), 212, 221, 224, 252; Hill was captivated by the career of W. L. Garrison. Richard De Bary, *The Land of Promise: an account of the material and spiritual unity of America* (London, 1908), shows some understanding of frontier influences. Hare Booth's superficial *Glimpses of Our Kith and Kin* (London, 1896) indicates that he considered the visit a tremendous undertaking. General impression left on Charles Whibley (*American Sketches*, Edinburgh, 1908) was the sadness of an *old* country which did not know how to live. A. M. Low, *America at Home* (London, 1908), *The American People: a study in national psychology* (London, 1909). "A Year Amongst the Americans," *Times*, Dec. 1907–Jan. 1908. Rita (Mrs. Desmond Humphreys), *America—Through English Eyes* (London, 1911) said (p. 11), "There is a sort of social insanity in the U.S. that sets the rest of the world agape"; but she did predict great things. Note influence of her contacts with Americans at the Lyceum Club in *Recollections of a Literary Life* (London, 1936).

Curious hodge-podge in A. M. B. Meakin, *What America is Doing: Letters from the New World* (Edinburgh, 1911); J. A. Hobson, *A Modern Outlook: studies of English and American tendencies* (London, 1910), married an Am. Reprints from the *Times*, Alexander Francis, *Americans: an Impression* (1909); six chapters on education, four on race and nationality, and five on social conditions. T. R. Burlford, *American Hatred and British Folly* (London, 1911), also wrote *Gruesome America*, *Britannia's Awakening*, and *Facts for American and Irish Liars*. P. A. Vaile, *Yankee: America's Peril* (London, 1909), vii, viii. Louis Kight, *An Englishman in America* (London, 1907), a novel. Arnold Bennett, *Those United States* (London 1912), devotes space to Am. child; note also items on millionaires and N.Y. press in his *Loot of Cities* (London, 1905). W. Sorley Brown, *The Life and Genius of T. W. H. Crosland* (London, 1928), 200ff. Rupert Brooke, *Letters from America* (London, 1916), visit in 1913, preface by Henry James. Note remarkable coincidence between many of these travel books and article by one who had not visited us, W. L. George, "What America Must Be Like," *Everybody's*, May 1913, 28: 658–66.

[17] Interview. Wells, *The Future in America: a Search after Realities* (New York, 1906), also *An Englishman Looks at the World* (London, 1914). Wells devoted several pages to J. Morgan Richards, Am. business man in London, as typical of the Am. who is insensible to the state as an aspect of his personal life.

[18] A. L. Tobin and Elmer Gertz, *Frank Harris: A Study in Black and White* (Chicago, 1931), 29, 143, 154, 216, 221; Sir W. Robertson Nicoll, *"Ian Maclaren": Life of Rev. John Watson* (London, 1908), 199; F. W. Maitland, *Leslie Stephen* (London, 1906), *passim*. Kipling, *American Notes* (Boston, 1899), *Letters of Travel: 1892–1913* (London, 1920); *Captains Courageous* (1897) which portrays a millionaire and New England fishermen. George Meredith, *Letters of George Meredith* (London, 1912), II, 633; Henry James, ed., *The Letters of William James* (London, 1920), II, 195; see also II, 147, 278, 308; *Swinnerton: An Autobiography* (Garden City, N.Y., 1936), 31, 326.

XIII

PLEASURE OR SOMETHING

THE British stage, which was strongly affected by Americanizing influences, brought our viewpoints, local color, caricatures, and types to Great Britain. It stimulated discussions not only about taste and drama but about our entire social structure. As contrasted with the present, the stage, at least up to about 1909, held the position now maintained by the American film, but without ever penetrating to the masses. Today, very few Britons conclude that they get much of their American impedimenta from the stage. But the nature of contacts and professional interchanges, probably as much eastward as westward, remains much the same as it was during 1898–1914. If historians had more fully exploited the regional responses to American drama and to the detailed changes made in the adaptations of American plays, the literature of national psychology would be much richer. It seems clear, however, that national differences appeared more acutely on the stage. Our permanent conquest of the stage was not taken seriously, but the persistent inroads of actors and plays could not be overlooked. The predominant conclusion about our drama summed up its influence as pointing to naughty liveliness, virile rawness, as pandering to sensationalism and vulgarity. Yet there was sufficient belief in the merging of national tastes to give credence to the rumor that Carnegie was planning to endow an Anglo-American theatre.

The commerce between the English and American stage grew to vast dimensions after the late eighties.[1] In the first quarter of the nineteenth century Cooper's *Pilot* had been dramatized at the Adelphi in such a way as to give to the Yankee *dramatis personae* all the odious characteristics originally given to the English. The stage was often as chauvinistic as mechanical engineers. Edward Sothern was scarcely regarded as an American—not so Kate Bateman in October 1863, and Joseph Jefferson in 1865. Dion Boucicault acquired Asley's Amphitheatre in 1862 to show England that comfort and ventilation could be as good as in New York's Winter Garden. In the seventies came John Sleeper Clarke, Edwin Booth, John E. Owens, Charles B. Thorne, Stuart Robson, Mrs. John Wood, and a host of others. Clarke was so successful that he settled in England, where he managed several theatres, preceding the Bancrofts at the Haymarket. Owens was not recognized at his own worth because the "dialect play" was not then understood in England—"applesass" was not English. Ada Rehan, John Drew, Paul Arthur, Nat Goodwin, Annie Russell, and others were received without national bias. Indeed, H. G. Hibbert maintained that it was the English-born Richard Mansfield who raised the first outcry about English prejudice because he was not received at his American valuation. The acceptance of our dramatic verdicts has always been very hesitating. But the way was prepared, sometimes by men like Charles Matthews, the "entertainer," for New World favorites.

Part of the Americanizing of the English stage and music hall, reaching something of a climax by 1886, had been the enthusiasm for American artistes, ballet dancers, freak-fashionists, variety shows, comedies, step-dancers, tumblers, and eccentrics. Augustin Daly began his visits in the eighties, and flew the Stars and Stripes over his own theatre; he filled the stage with adapted farces from the French and German, more innocent, asserted Hibbert, than the later "Criterion comedy," and American adaptations which retained all the improprieties and set a nasty fashion. One of these, he added, was Bronson Howard's *Saratoga*, adapted to English circumstances as *Brighton*. A period closed with the appearance of Ada Rehan at Daly's in 1886. The first fresh surprise was over.

William Archer claimed that down to 1895 Miss Mary Anderson was the only American "star" of first magnitude to win a place in England's theatrical world. About the first entirely American play, with an important cast, was also Charles Frohman's first great success, *Secret Service*, with William Gillette, whom England discovered as a star. American personality came to be a big factor in London. The poet of the Sierras, Joaquin Miller, might invade drawing rooms in top boots, but it was difficult to predict the reception of American personality upon the stage.

The press discussed theatrical invasions in 1898, 1901–02, 1907, and 1910.[2] Our theatre expanded into England about the same moment that economic competition aroused new interest. During the five years ending December 31, 1897, the total number of American dramatic pieces in London was twenty-seven, nine of which were produced during 1896. And yet Daniel Frohman thought the press was kind while the public remained indifferent. The *Daily Telegraph* commented in 1898:

There was a wail the other day about the American invasion. Let them come, these capital comedians, and the more the merrier, if they take some of our star-gazing actors and actresses off their stilts.

In a lecture on municipal theatres in 1902, Sidney Lee observed,

The London stage was falling in a most strange fashion under the sway of the American capitalist. He was now controlling as many as eight London theatres.

Apparently making the most of the interest aroused by the Spanish-American War, three American companies were acting in London by April 1898, while a play of American origin was being staged at St. James's. The *Daily Mail*, December 4, 1901, hinted that the outcry was raised because of our go-ahead methods. By 1907 the *Daily Express* concluded that the Americanizing process would go no further.

Greeted by the *Daily Mail* as an invader bearing yellow drama of syndicate quality came Charles Frohman who, according to his American biographers, "revolutionized the economics of the British stage; invested it with life, energy, action; established a whole new relation between actor and producer." He produced in London between 1892 and 1915 about 125 pieces, giving England some typical American dramas—*The Great Divide, Brewster's Millions, Alias Jimmy Valentine,* and *The Dictator.* He felt that the English theatre had dignity not possible in American theatrical production, and the Duke of York's Theatre, the lobby filled with pictures of American stars, became his pride. He was the principal American importer of the Gaiety shows; his first American female star was Annie Russell in Bret Harte's story *Sue.* He spent a fortune upon Barrie's suggestion of a Repertory Theatre. The more he crossed the Atlantic—and he was sometimes called "to-and-Frohman"—the more he liked to think the two audiences were becoming one. But, he observed,

An English audience sitting before an American play hears mention of West Twenty-Third Street or Washington Square, and while it is wondering just where and what these localities are an important incident in the dramatic action slips by unnoticed.

There were drawbacks greater and more subtle than geography, as his long experience would have illustrated.

The necessity of modifying American productions often decreased the strength of the impression.[3] The *Daily Mail* confidently hoped that George Alexander would treat the virile *Conquerors* with the artistic restraint and good taste needed to make it acceptable to English audiences. When interest in divorce legislation was high, Langdon Mitchell's comedy, *The New York Idea* (1907), used a London program which explained that this drama was in the realm of possibility; the *Westminster Gazette* decided it was "sheer nonsense, and surely no picture of life even under the most fantastic divorce codes!" Adaptations even went so far as to transplant James A. Hearne's *Shore Acres* to Cornwall, leaving a few details such as turkeys and Santa Claus; unfortunately, the *Times* did not think Cornwall would be as sentimental as America. Cosmo Hamilton, who believed that he was the only author to adapt an American play into an English atmosphere, translated the colloquialisms and scene of Thomas Buchanan's *A Woman's Way*. A language difficulty was overcome by giving farces such as Clyde Fitch's *The Truth* an English setting, but at some sacrifice to reality because, at least on the stage, English and American characteristics were not always interchangeable. In 1898 the critic in the *Academy* belittled American plays; *Too Much Johnson* elicited a shrewd remark: "The commonplace French story has acquired a quaint exoticism in coming to us *via* New York."

In 1900 Samuel Smith (Flintshire) introduced a resolution in the Commons which denounced the demoralizing character of recent plays, citing American imitations of *Lord Quex* and particularly an American adaptation of the French play *Zaza;* Smith agreed with *The Era,* which he quoted:

It is a great grief to us to find American actors and actresses taking part in such a disgraceful libel of their own calling.

In addition, Smith recalled William Archer's opinion of the *Belle of New York:* "What was it but one long glorification of the vulgarest order of debauchery?" Smith explained, however, that he "traveled in America for months, and never saw a lady appear as they often do in London." As affecting diffusion, anthropologists might say, this Parliamentary episode illustrated the type of resistance frequently caused by cultural habits being similar to the new elements.

It was Daniel Frohman's opinion that Bronson Howard's *The Henrietta* failed because the audience was unfamiliar with the type and took the humor seriously; the same thing happened to Henry Miller in *The Great Divide.*[4] He could not understand the success of *Mrs. Wiggs of the Cabbage Patch*—unless it offered a caricature of rural character which Britons considered the real American; the *Scotsman,* predicting its success, commented, "How far it is to be regarded as an international caricature one can hardly say." Frohman suggested, "American plays that represent social people of good standing brought to the Englishman no sense of reality." Among the American successes which failed in England were *The Lion and the Mouse* and *Paid in Full;* the former, after an enthusiastic first night, fell flat because the English were not able to comprehend that a judge could be disgraced and debarred by a political "ring." Even an audience prepared for anything from America needed dramatic reality not too far removed from conditions they understood. Even though the press thought the part played in unmistakable English fashion, *Brewster's Millions* failed because the British took it as a business proposition and could not believe that the young man spent his inherited millions. Charles Frohman successfully tried upon the British public the unctuous American humor of William Collier in *The Dictator,* which succeeded, added *M.A.P.,* in spite of its New Yorkism. The *Times* criticized *The Girl,* an American sketch by Edward Peple, in these terms:

Perhaps the clowning would have been more tolerable had there been any attempt *to portray the characters as American.* The assertion of the program that the scene is in New York is supported by the mention of dollars and the use of "guns." [My italics.]

This suggests that there were few successes and more failures proportionately of mixed teams of American and English players in American pieces or adaptations than of American companies playing American pieces. Difficulties of language and race called for undiluted Americanism.

The *Manchester Guardian,* Feb. 28, 1910, carried London news: "America must be an odd place. *The Climax,* produced tonight at the Comedy, has been played with great success on the other side." A year later, speaking of *A Fool There Was,* the same paper declared:

A certain part of the London theatrical public is becoming so Americanized that possibly it may be taken in by this rather nauseous and artistically quite contemptible sensation-mongering.

The word "American" was so closely identified with "shoddy" even in entertainment circles that Mrs. Harriet Day (professionally known as O Hana San) brought an unsuccessful libel suit against the *Times* for having permitted Harold Child (who once passed three days in New York) to say that a sketch of hers, *A Vision of Japan,* given at the London Hippodrome, July, 1911, was "a bad American imitation." [5] Mr. Child contended that the whistling and music were American, that the sketch smacked of the Pacific coast, displayed an American flag, and threw revealing, moving lights on the lady's figure, a stage trick brought from America by Loie Fuller.

Beginning in 1898 a run that lasted until 1902, *The Belle of New York* became a theatrical event of importance. [6] Earlier musical comedies brought over by Minnie Palmer, Patti Rosa, and others were "adapted" to the English stage, usually with only an American star or two. This was the first musical comedy, wholly American in locale, characterization, authorship, and interpretation, thrown upon a London audience. The chorus girls were not so lethargic as the Gaiety girls, they possessed *le diable du corps;* Hibbert declared, "It sounded the death knell of the lymphatic show lady." All the chorus work and pictorial achievements influenced future English choruses (but not enough to blot out differences). The *Academy* greeted its noise (others recalled *Adonis* as an extravaganza of the wildest sort) by saying it was "pervaded by a characteristically American flavour which ought to prove agreeable to the frivolous-minded public." Archer called it a "profligate orgy." In 1901 a *Westminster Gazette* critic described the chorus in *The Fortune Teller* as having the "beauty and loveliness which I fear must be regarded as peculiar to the American companies." Americans in London declared the ballet *New York* by Newham Davis to be inaccurate and insulting.

George Bernard Shaw found the noisy, farcical comedy *Never Again* (1897) aggressively American with horseplay that seemed silly to an English audience:

> The truth is, all this knockabout stuff, these coarse pleasantries about women's petticoats, Katzenjammer, and so forth, belong not to American civilization, but to American barbarism.[7]

The *Academy* could not imagine that *The Heart of Maryland* had been an American success; "American invention exhausts itself in mechanical pursuits; it has none left for the stage." Shaw hoped Frohman had done a good turn by putting the fool's cap on an American's head since it might make the Briton see his own puerile heroism and bunkum. In addition, according to Shaw, American melodrama proved that the routine of melodrama and farcical comedy was not an art but an industry, and that our industrial skill (which might offer a lesson to English managers) produced smarter, better-drilled companies which worked harder and wasted less time.

So far as Londoners were concerned, declared Daniel Frohman,

> The American feminine rôle in Clyde Fitch's *The Woman in the Case* was pleasing because it aroused their derision against the woman. She was thought to be an American type.

In 1906 H. E. Brookfield and Cosmo Hamilton's *Belle of Mayfair* at the Vaudeville Theatre, London, brought Leslie Stuart's "Why do they call me a Gibson girl?" sung by a Swedish-American, Camille Clifford, to pave the way for a Gibson Girl craze that lasted in England until the War—in music-hall sketches, plays, advertisements, and society. Clifford, who married a noble scion, was skyrocketed into a leading rôle. Hicks and Hamilton's *The Catch of the Season* had also used Gibson Girls, and Hicks did not have to fume at the American flapper, who had not yet reached musical comedy. The American wife of T. P. O'Connor wrote *A Lady from Texas* (played by Kitty Cheatham, who had married an Englishman) in 1901 which capitalized upon the great interest in American girls; Clement Scott predicted that this rough, unsophisticated child of nature, who talked rapidly and dressed loudly, would not harm English society. The girls in R. C. Carlton's productions, *The Undercurrent*, *The American Heiress*, and *The Dollar Princess* were what the British thought they should be. *An American Citizen*, the hero forced to marry and renounce citizenship in order to get a fortune, followed *The Cowboy and the Lady* at the Duke of York, July 1899. *The Girl from Up There* (1901) was attractive without any lyrical qualities. Many importations in 1909 did not call for serious attention, not even *The Chorus Girl*. One of the hits of 1911 was *Baby Mine*, which an English audience could comfortably regard as chiefly satirizing the American woman's distaste for motherhood.

Plays on American Indians in 1907, such as W. C. deMille's *Strongheart* and Donald McLaren's *Last of His Race*, fell flat while American farces such as the *Earl of Pawtucket* and *Divorçons* romped to success. But the glories of the romantic West were constantly offered to the London public, as if taste were being stimulated by the new-born cinema. The sentimental domestic melodrama of "great heart interest," *The Three of Us* (1908), laid in an American mining camp, the 170 performances of *A White Man* (1908), produced in America as *The Squaw Man*, and the 1912 quota of *The Cowboy and the Girl*, *The Cowboy Jury*, and *The Cowpuncher* brought the frontier to London. Other local color was conveyed in *Way Down East* (eight performances in 1908), and George Ade's *College Widow* (more than thirty performances in the same year). In 1912 Charles Klein's *Find the Woman* explained the New York policemen's "third degree," and critics wondered how Eugene Walter's *The Easiest Way* got past the censors. By 1914 a wholly American production, *Adèle*, invaded the home of English musical comedy, The Gaiety, and it was not so noisy or breathless as London anticipated. The greatest success of the same year combined New York English and Yiddish to produce *Potash and Perlmutter*.

One of the fathers of American minstrelsy, T. D. Rice, visited England in 1836 with the famous song, "Jump, Jim Crow!" which produced Jim Crow hats, pipes, and knick-knacks. Christy Minstrels followed. For years London supported two minstrel troupes, Moore & Burgess and the Mohawks, which instilled audiences with Negro melodies. "Pony" Moore convinced schools and parents of the high tone of his performances; even Queen Victoria saw a traveling troupe. Along with the Haverley Minstrels came Eugene Stratton, who achieved fame as the "Whistling Coon." Americans showed England how to accommodate the one-act play to music halls and to curtail the "vocal comedians." Belasco also contributed to the stock in trade of stage managers. By 1905 one-third of the music-hall performers were Americans.

Buffalo Bill's "Wild West" in 1887 helped to set the pace at Earl's Court for "colossal spectacular undertakings." Inspired by the exuberance of friendship, Boxing Day, December 26, 1898, found the theatres concentrating on entwined flags. At the Alhambra Miss Heloise Titcombe entertained with dances, closing her number by waving the Union Jack and the Stars and Stripes to the melodious, intermingling tunes of "Yankee Doodle" and "God Save the Queen." Barnum & Bailey repeated a water spectacle of the American victory at Santiago. A pair of American ladies who gave "lecture-recitals" seemed original in 1898. Burton Holmes's "travelogues" were considered novel. The American Comedy Four, who introduced a wild antic in the middle of a straight number at the Empire in 1901, were spoken of as "typical American artists." With the purchase of the Princess Theatre in 1900, B. F. Keith planned to give London continuous vaudeville. In 1907 an American took charge of the amusements at Crystal Palace. Drawing on his experience at Coney Island, F. McClellan went over to help at Earl's Court during the coronation of George V because English exhibitions and summer resorts were not jolly enough. At

Olympia in 1909 a new diversion was held on the American Roller Rink—a fancy-dress carnival of an idealized farmyard. In 1913 *Hullo, Ragtime* had a pair of Americans, one singing, one playing the piano and vocalizing—already a familiar combination in London. Thus, the entertainment world tasted of pleasures from beyond the sea.

The profession of dramatists and actors included many who were familiar with the United States and sometimes painfully aware of its moods.[8] An American triumph was desirable even though it might not be rated highly in London. Sir Henry Irving (1838-1905) has been hailed as one of the important contributors to Anglo-American understanding. In 1871 Irving joined with the American H. L. Bateman, who took over the Lyceum Theatre; in 1883 he made his first American tour. The American invasion of the stage he looked upon as a stimulant to English brains and energy. Henry Arthur Jones, who first toured in 1885, was always more popular here than in England. He watched closely our theatrical progress; he approved of the endeavors of Professor Baker and others to bind together literature and drama. He said in 1906 at Harvard:

When I was in America last autumn after an absence of twenty years, I could not help feeling that I was in the presence of immense forces that are gradually shifting the foundations, and changing the drift of American civilization. . . . I could not help dreading that in a few generations the centre and seat of whatever curious system of Anglo-American civilization may then be current, will be irrevocably fixed on this side of the Atlantic.

America's power had reached to the dramatic consciousness of England. Although thinking of a common drama as a strong international link, Jones felt that there were numerous and obvious reasons against the wholesale importations of American plays. In addition, our drama and theatrical trusts played a part in the British movement for a national theatre. The failure of the American National Theatre offered some "very puzzling and thorny questions to the promoters of the English scheme." Jones concluded that it taught them to avoid a huge theatre, and to secure popular support and a wide repertory.

Mrs. Clement Scott held that the American trips of Edward Sothern and Fred Leslie became the turning points of their careers. "Dundreary" Sothern "might have remained a stock actor at Weymouth or Birmingham all his life had he not visited America which developed [his] latent humor." Leslie was great before the trip, "but the study of American humour suggested to him exactly the things that were to him most humorous." At the age of fifty-eight Clement Scott wrote on "Why Do I Go to America?"

> I go . . . because I do not believe that the stage of America is tied to the skirts or the shoestrings of Society. I go to study a young, vigorous, and healthy art.

Seymour Hicks (sometimes called "Stealmore Bricks") declared that he was not the only one who indulged in the innocent task of transplanting witty lines to England. In 1903 at the Gaiety he introduced the first American tramp character in the revival of *Jack Shepherd;* an American song, "Her Golden Hair Was Hanging Down Her Back," later helped his vogue in England. His wife in the old *Shop Girl* sang "Louisiana Loo," Leslie Stuart's first London success. Therefore, in many devious ways one can suspect the working of American influences.

American music, which has been heard and hummed in the British Isles, elicited opinions regarding our taste.[9] Judging from the sale of sheet music, piano rolls, and phonograph records, many American songs became popular hits; from 1919 to 1933, eleven of the sixteen most popular songs were of American origin. At least up to the World War, our technical skill in reproducing music, and since then our expansion into the world of jazz and dancing entertainment, have spread our lighter musical compositions. Less lively songs have been used in British schools, but except for a few Southern melodies, no definite images were created in the children's minds. John Philip Sousa's tunes commanded an audience made greater by piracies; in addition he infected the British Army's bands with stirring marches and, sad critics added, with devilish devices for making variety cat-calls. Sousa's concerts were popular in England; but the *Westminster Gazette* concluded that his selections proved that English audiences had better taste. The piracies of our tunes were so considerable that a public meeting under the auspices of the Musical Defence League was held in 1904 to extend the protection which British composers enjoyed here. Evidence before the Copyright Committee in 1909 showed that American music rolls had greater sales by having no copyright protection. Isidore Witmark, publisher of the popular Daddy Long-Legs Fun Songs, came to London in 1901 with new ideas for revolutionizing the music publishing trade.

Along with music went dance creations. Some of the first Anglo-American balls in 1900 and 1901 were not only for charity but for introducing more lively steps into the prosaic style of the English ballroom. At first ragtime tunes were played surreptitiously in London restaurants, but by October 1912, 250,000 copies of "Alexander's Rag-Time Band" had been sold in England. With the dawn of 1913 the ragtime craze was in full blast and left its mark on the plethora of revues that year. Discussion became public and heated over the merits of substituting our dances. An American experiment with the waltz, the Boston, although bitterly assailed, had rejuvenated the English dance. Some American variations of the "Rag" had names with unfortunate zoölogical implications: "Bunny Hug" and "Turkey Trot." A "Peeress" complained: "I need not describe the various horrors of American and South American negroid origin." Oscar Browning added: "Why does our English society persist in copying the worst features of American society instead of learning from the best?" The *Times* observed:

> Another influence which has reached the ball room is the subtle permeation of all our way of life by the American sense of the dignity of hustle.

Oscar Hammerstein's abortive efforts to bring additional opera to London began at his massive London Opera House, November 13, 1911. His venture was not favored, and the *Times* decided that his courage and enthusiasm had been "very inadequately realized." His opera struck the public as a commercial venture rather than as a cultural achievement, and our influence continued to be the "Turkey Trot." For serious artists the verdict of American audiences or critics was not sufficient. The nature of musical appreciation was illustrated in a homely way in the divorce proceedings of a Philadelphian, D. S. Bispham, who endeavored before the Rt.

Hon. Sir Francis Jeune to establish his English domicile; Jeune agreed:

> Having adopted music as a profession, it was quite obvious that his natural home was in England, the centre of the musical world, and that his visits to the U.S.A. were merely for professional purposes.

The radio has only just begun to be an important factor in bringing America to the notice of the British public.[10] Re-broadcasts or short-wave broadcasts have so far been more important in this respect than any English domestic program. The spread of American jazz and spirituals, of speakers and viewpoints, may soon become more discernible in the British Isles. But in the radio world America has been more interested in England, the ratio of westward broadcasts being 100 to 2 eastward in 1930, 100 to 31 in 1936. A new series of short-wave broadcasts, "America Speaks," inaugurated February 1938, tried to exploit more fully this channel in presenting American viewpoints to the British public. Although radio's effect is still limited, Britons do not seem to pick up stereotyped ideas or personalities from it.

British cartoons relating to us have not influenced many people, but in all their moods they helped to fix a few symbols—the cigar-smoking, black-hatted tourist, the eagle, the dollar mark, Uncle Sam and Columbia. The long, loose-limbed Uncle Sam subsequently became rotund. It cannot be known how much of America was portrayed in the pictures and drawings exported to Great Britain; the number of such items increased in 1902 (1,300), but the peak year in value was in 1911 (£39,111). *Punch* between 1898 and 1914 carried about seventy-five drawings relating to America or Anglo-American relations. Stock Americans may linger long after their usefulness, but British portrayals did not diverge greatly from our contemporary cartoons.

No great social force of recent decades has left so little available history as the youthful motion picture, consequently, not much can be said about the flood of American films, and the resultant stimulation to new ideas, appetites, and lands which captivated the British from 1907 to 1914, and increasingly thereafter. Even in its infancy the American film carried stereotypes to England—cowboys, Indians, desperate lovers, and desperadoes, and presented entertainment in a guise which increased the desire to know more about sensational America, sometimes with shocks to British decorum. The films carried to a less sophisticated audience a product which could be accepted as American since it was made by Americans and patronized by them. Breaking upon a mass of people slightly unconscious of America, the cinema began to form a background of popular knowledge. But Hollywood's victory in Britain suggested a similarity of national tastes. If films have been nothing more than a vehicle of emotional outlet, and have juggled with the realities of American life, that fact assumes tremendous significance when films are exported.[11] Some suspect that America's influence and contributions might have been stronger and more healthful without her world-wide celluloid conquest. Even before the expansion of the industry in 1907, Parliament discussed obscene exhibitions which came from the States. Hall Caine referred to mutoscope exhibitions at Earl's Court, Hampstead Heath, and elsewhere, and urged the Home Secretary to investigate. Already "undressing" pictures (predecessor of the "strip tease" exported to London in 1937!) were popular; one of them, "Searching a Pretty Girl," represented a room in the New York Custom House. Our pictures at the outset represented a slightly lower form of civilization than had been seen on the British stage. But there were no organized outcries as when America invaded the stage, and criticism had not yet the facile expression of the established dramatic critic. By 1912 the upper classes began to realize that American products might be suggested unwittingly to British buyers. Through the cinema America affected public morals and sentiment.

One of the few sources for the cumulative effect of early American movies is found in the reports of the Commission of Inquiry instituted by the National Council of Public Morals in 1916–17.[12] America fed the theatres' sudden demands in 1908, and they had got used to it. Since more than 90 per cent (pre-1914 estimates were 60 to 75 per cent) of the films shown in British picture houses were American, it was difficult to raise England's standards without our improvement. The Report hesitated to estimate the influence of the films.

Abundant evidence has been presented to the Commission that there is room for much improvement in many of the film stories. The continual harping on incidents of marital infidelity in films, *mainly of American origin,* is unworthy of the magnificent opportunity offered of introducing dramatic stories of real merit. [My italics.]

First had come the "home dramas," then by 1910 films of cowboys and ranch life which dominated until 1912. Speaking of a weekly audience in 1914 of about 7,000,000, in approximately 4,500 movie theatres, the Report continued:

The cowboy and Indian films, which are immensely popular with school children, have merits peculiarly their own. They are crude, but they represent a lower standard of civilization, and appeal so directly to the primitive instincts and emotions that their position is secure.

A London exhibitor thought it would not be desirable to reduce the "Westerners" since they showed regional life. Cowboys and Indians were everywhere—even on the streets of London at 3 A. M.!

The Report added:

The good detective story will always be popular with the normal schoolboy, but the typical American "crook" films, dealing exclusively with crime, do not meet the demand in a satisfactory way.

The censors had trouble with these films because they showed how thievery could be accomplished. The British Board of Censors also made a distinction between "crime" stories and cowboys' "costume" crime, which were not viewed as harmful. The managing director of the Transatlantic Film Co. Ltd. declared that the two publics had similar tastes, and that we sent only a few undesirable films. The Chairman then remarked that female undress "is taken less notice of in America than here because it comes into the cinemas so much." One examiner explained that Americans enjoyed films "based on the idea of a man who loses his soul"; another did not like pictures of employers (frequently Americans) who made advances to poor typists seeking work. In the spread of Americanisms, the silent captions (more easily altered than the sound film) played a part. One of the Board observed:

The sub-titles of the American films I consider a serious evil. The grammar and the spelling and the language are deplorable, but the task of correcting them was not imposed upon us, and we do not take it upon ourselves to deal with it.

John Kay reported that school teachers found the film had increased the children's vocabulary "notably by American slang phrases."

As with newspapers and periodicals, it was not thought desirable that American films should flood the colonies. Sir Evelyn Wrench in 1914 described the efforts made by the Over-Seas Club to counteract the evil Americanization of the motion picture business. In trying to form a British-Canadian Film Company, a very provocative advertisement appeared in the *Times:*

Films of Canadian Life and History

An Eager and Profitable Market in the Picture Theatres of the World now Awaits the Production of Films to Take the Place of the American Desperado, Cowboy, and Civil War Films, of which audiences have grown Tired.

The full story of American movies in Great Britain must, however, be left for a later volume.[13] American producers leased or purchased cinema houses which sometimes used our methods and managers. New schemes of film renting were devised. In 1911 we shipped to the United Kingdom instruments and apparatus (including cinematograph films) to the value of £648,767; in 1912, £1,498,367. In 1915 the value of films alone was £47,486; this increased to £880,240 in 1927, and dropped to £130,847 in 1932 because of new trade policies and duplications of negatives in England. In 1933, 330 of 476 important films shown in England, Scotland, and Wales were American. In 1931 the contents of such films were: drama, 110; melodrama, 78; western, 82; romance, 45; comedy-drama, 33; sex, 24.

As a factor in the American impact, it is difficult to make comparisons of the pre-1914 and contemporary cinema.[14] The American origin of films became more conspicuous, and the force of the Hollywood product more definite, when sound films became popular. The silent subtitles were crude—the talkies much worse and more potent so far as Britain was concerned. Scores of commercial observers in England insisted that quite innocently the talkies, more than the silent films, stimulated the sale of American products. Journalists, if they admit their readers like America's sensationalism, are ready to attribute this to the cinema. The press coverage of Hollywood is comprehensive, and it has become a lodestar for the British traveler as significant as British sporting adventures in the bison days of the Golden West. The sale of our movie magazines fluctuates with the fortunes of the American film.

A large majority of influential Britons speak of movies as the principal Americanizing influence on the less educated masses. And these more sophisticated observers find it difficult to resist being completely taken in by the same medium. Almost unanimously, the British state that they are able to detect immediately whether a film is of American origin, and are conscious of national differences in outlook and treatment. Only 65 per cent thought they paid much attention to anything but the story. But it is easily seen that the language and opinions of the remaining 35 per cent were also affected. Only 30 per cent thought they were moved to purchase products used in these pictures. Taking various social groups together, seventeen years of age or more, about 60 per cent acquiesced in the domination of the industry by American producers; about 70 per cent concluded that American films were representative of American life. In Wales, Scotland, and Northern Ireland, less was said about the "Hollywood touch." The American "Colony" in England believed our prestige was lower because of the cinema.

The generalizations obtained from such a survey cannot be stated dogmatically. Because of the cinema, some knowledge existed where none existed before. The United States is viewed as a paradise of entertainment where a faster mode of life and a less rigid social code provide more sensations. Any country which is so entertaining and unregimented will in time attract attention that will carry beyond the mere sensational. This tendency is discernible among the younger people, who will, however, be subjected to stereotypes other than cowboys and Indians. The screen, especially of our prohibition era, left a haunting memory of a glorified American woman, sometimes much-divorced and intoxicated. The gangster film may arouse indignation at home—in England it often produces contempt. Although there is now closer Anglo-American coöperation in films, our cinema has kept British censors busy. But the fact remains that no foreign censors will cut anything that may slander American life. Films such as *The Life Machine, I am a Fugitive,* and *Scarface* are censored to preserve morality, not America's reputation; a film such as *The Informer* (129 deletions) is censored to sterilize an American viewpoint. Even though our work first persuaded British sceptics to consider seriously the teaching film, the Commission on Educational and Cultural Films explained: "The U.S.A., however unjustly, have suffered much in this country from the popular estimate of their worst films."

Were somebody to attempt a needed comparative anatomy of pleasure, Anglo-American relations would offer strange instruction. Especially in its international aspects, entertainment is a serious and important element for the study of social and cultural history. While sharing our joyous exuberance and taste, no doubt more noticeably in the era characterized by new, international, mass instruments for pleasure and information (the radio and motion pictures), American culture became an incalculable, intimate influence upon British life.

[1] See Escott, *National Links,* 185, 187; Clement Scott, *The Drama of Yesterday and To-Day* (London, 1899), II, 309–11, 317, 425; H. G. Hibbert, *Fifty Years of a Londoner's Life* (London, 1916), 113, 116; Stead, *Americanization of the World,* 119–20. Also Hibbert's *A Playgoer's Memories* (London, 1920), chap. xvi.

[2] Lee, *Times,* Mar. 24, 1902; I. F. Marcosson and Daniel Frohman, *Charles Frohman: Manager and Man* (London, 1912), 252, 230, 232–38, 247–52, 308–09 and App. B.

[3] *D. Mail,* Jan. 8, 1898; Cosmo Hamilton, *Unwritten History* (London, 1924), 84, 150, 151, 160, 176; Hamilton first visited in 1912, drawn by the good-natured curiosity of Am. audiences. *Academy,* Apr. 23, 1898; *P. Debs.,* 1900, 83:276–85.

[4] Daniel Frohman, *Memories of a Manager* (London, 1911), 172, 185, 187–88, 190, 194; cf. Richards, *John Bull,* 201, on Charles Coghlan in *The Colonel; Scotsman,* Apr. 29, 1907; Marcosson and Frohman, *op. cit.,* 300; *West. G.,* June 27, 1907; *M.A.P.,* Sept. 8, 1906, p. 297; *Times,* Jan. 29, 1914; *Manch. G.,* Mar. 23, 1911.

[5] Reported in *The Stage Year Book, 1913* (London), 245ff., 290ff. This annual is valuable for other years.

[6] *West. G.,* Apr. 13, 1898; *Globe,* Apr. 13, 1898; Edna May was the Salvation Army girl in the play; Hibbert, *Playgoer's Memories,* p. 73; *West. G.,* Apr. 24, 1901.

[7] James Huneker, *Dramatic Opinions and Essays with an Apology by Bernard Shaw* (London, 1907), II, 332ff., 437, 443; *Academy,* Apr. 16, 1898, p. 428.

[8] D. A. Jones, *The Life and Letters of Henry Arthur Jones* (London, 1930), 235; Henry Arthur Jones, *The Foundations of a National Drama* (London, 1913), 41, 63, 65, 67, 121, 124; Hicks, *op. cit.,* 210; *Seymour Hicks: Twenty-Four Years of an*

Actor's Life (Lond. 1910), 180, 184, 190, 192, 258; Mrs. Clement Scott, *Old Days in Bohemian London* (London, 1919), 208.

[9] *World Almanac, 1934*, p. 800; *P.P.*, Copyright Committee 1910, XXI: 23, 64, 104, 105; *Punch*, Apr. 9, 1913, p. 275; Peggy Webling's "An American Toe Dancer, a story," *Pall Mall M.*, 16:419; *Bispham* v. *Bispham et al.* reported in *Times*, June 18, 1903. Tunes may become Anglicized; "Stars and Stripes Forever" was the first tune heard at the beginning of the Coronation procession, May 1937.

[10] The B.B.C. has a representative in this country. The talks given by the Am. R. G. Swing penetrated remarkably into the mind of the British radio audience. In the development of the international radio union, Am. influence has been noteworthy, clashing at times in pre-War years with G.B.; the U.S. supported unrestricted interchange of communications between all stations and obligatory ship-to-ship exchange. See Keith Clarke, *International Communications: The American Attitude* (New York, 1931), chap. iv.

[11] It was not until the author analyzed British comments on the "good" picture "Mr. Deeds Goes to Town" that he realized the final court scene left very bizarre impressions of disrespect for law. See also, D. W. Churchill, "Hollywood's Censor Is All the World," *N.Y. Times Mag. Sect.*, March 29, 1936. *P. Debs.*, 1901, 98:1306ff.

[12] The Council was later known as the National Council for Race Renewal. Its report is *The Cinema: its present Position and Future Possibilities* (London, 1917), pp. xxxi, xxxii, xxxviii, lxi, lxxxii, 15, 26, 46, 51, 54, 55, 60, 63, 106, 110–13, 119. An investigation of 4,000 boys and girls in Worcester City, 1917, showed that cowboys and Indians, and then, comics, ranked in popularity, *ibid.*, 143–44. Note the use of Am. females in early *Photo-Bits, New Photo Fun, Snap-Shots*, etc. *Times*, May 7, 1914, p. 20.

[13] *Annual Statement of Trade of the U.K.*; "The Motion Picture Industry in the U.K. in 1931," *Trade Information Bulletin*, No. 801 (U.S. Bureau of For. & Dom. Commerce, Washington, 1933), 8; *Kinematograph*, Jan. 6, 1910, 465. G. B. Shaw, *The Political Madhouse in America and Nearer Home* (London, 1933), 10, hopeful of Am. saving the world's soul; also mentions the Mormons. Charles Merz, *Harper's*, Jan. 1926, 160–63. Per cent of Am. films to total in U.K., 95 in 1925, 72 in 1931; see H. T. Lewis, *The Motion Picture Industry* (1933), 397, 425.

[14] Observations made during August 1936–July 1937. See also *The Film in National Life* (London, 1932), 11, 46, 61. Wanger, "120,000 American Ambassadors," *Foreign Affairs*, Oct. 1939, 45–60. Currently, about 600 pictures (or 120,000 prints) are abroad.

XIV

THE AMERICAN IMPACT IN BRITISH
SOCIAL AND CULTURAL HISTORY: I

OUR shortcomings no doubt decreased our influence abroad, and created a state of mind which disposed the British to resist America's impact. Had the United States covered less territory and fewer extremes, it might have been easier, in everything from machinery to social evolution, to adduce American experience. The British, perhaps not unlike ourselves, did not master American analogies, and were easily led astray by incidentals. Just as New York often threw visitors into a feverish coma, so America hypnotized many Britons. England fully recognized our optimism and brag, but she also derived some courage from our development of vigorous and extended organizations to carry out ideas; one might cite the Sunday schools, the Student Volunteer Movement, the Y.M.C.A.'s. Some optimism must have been infectious because at least one-half of the British comments predicted that the crudities of our civilization would disappear. Probably a much larger proportion still regarded us as hypersensitive. Our chase after excitement and novelties appeared even more definite. The British realized, perhaps imperfectly, that it was important for world progress to know America's contribution to the philosophy and outlook of this modern epoch.[1] Even though sociology first gained an established position here, our social history was not drawn upon in the fullest way either for illustration or theory.

Benjamin Kidd (1858-1916), who had been inspired by us to extol the "white man's burden," made little use of our story, except for trusts and collective organization, in his sociological writings. Yet he recorded a typical, almost poetical, impression:

When we stand in the midst of the rushing tide of the life of New York or Chicago, and catch sight of the actual relationship between the

341

deep-seated, inherent antinomies of the English-speaking world . . .
and the fierce stress and freedom of American life, industry, and progress
at the present day;—an overwhelming sense of the character of the
future takes possession of the mind.

There were a few, such as Sir Robert Giffen, who analyzed our
population statistics to discover a new, growing force in international affairs. America helped to make J. A. Hobson an "economic heretic"; his vivid experiences here gave him a clearer understanding of the defects of political democracy divorced from
economic equality. "Repeated visits to America during the past half-
century," Hobson declared, "have perhaps taught me more of the
ethics and politics of the economic system in its modern capitalistic
shape and development than any experience available in England. . . ."

Frederic Harrison, a jurist, historian, and leader of the English
Positivist Committee, after a visit of seventy days, became conscious
of a new world if not a new race. In spite of all the vulgarities and
quacks we exported, he believed that Americans had more real interest in Comte, that since the Civil War we had given more new
impulse to Europe's social life than it had given to us. Americans
lacked, however, according to H. G. Wells (who here did not diverge far from Bryce), a real, sustaining conception of a collective
interest embodied in the State. Individualism was burning itself
away—the residual was excitement; the fetish of freedom was de-
stroying freedom. One suspects that nothing up to 1914 so inspired in Wells the need for synthetic knowledge and effort as his
experiences in America. Wells, it may be added, acknowledged
exposé volumes so prevalent in 1906 as well as our advances in
sociology, social psychology, and pedagogics. C. R. Enoch, who
cited the importance of America's evolution, concluded in 1910:
"The Americans are on the full tide of their material prosperity,
such as precedes a more humane civilization."

America deeply inspired Ebenezer Howard, the famous town-
planner, who came over at the age of nineteen. "My stay in Chicago," he wrote, "had great influence on my life—giving me a fuller
and wider outlook on religious and social questions than I should
have gained in England." He came under the religious spell of
the Christian Humanism of Emerson, Lincoln, Lowell, and Whit-

tier; he returned to England in 1879 where he was incited to
practical social reform by reading Edward Bellamy in 1898. Letch-
worth and Garden City were the results. His English biographer
discovered "typical" Americanism in his make-up—the ability to
get the ideal first which made him an inspirational rather than an
authoritative leader. George Jacob Holyoake (1817–1896), secu-
larist, late in life "attained that comfortable assurance of success in
English public life, a triumphant tour through the United States."
He frowned upon our tariff protection, political system, giantism,
and impetuosity; besides trying to devise a handy American guide-
book to facilitate emigration, he started correspondence with American organizations, and brought our social lessons to British workers in the coöperative movement.

The British Institute of Social Service, organized in 1904 as a
clearing house for social workers, drew inspiration and guidance
from our organizations. Dr. Josiah Strong of the American Institute
came over to help; Bryce told the Institute that he knew no country
to which England could better go for instruction in working out
social problems. But such a problem as America's public relief was
viewed as too chaotic for the Royal Commission on Poor Law and
Relief of Distress (1906) to use to advantage. Contrariwise, the
Standard, which approved the investigation of our treatment of
imbecility, declared, "America has always shown enterprise in its
methods of grappling with social problems. . . ."

One of the socio-cultural problems which teased Britain was the
American woman who became a significant factor in our prestige
abroad.[2] Imagination conjured up a sunny, carefree land inhabited
by desirable women who could capture the attention of a relaxed
moment. There has seldom been any agreement between the real
woman and opinions about her; indeed, one may insult the other.
Partly because of language they affected England first and most
strongly. Many observers have been surprised by the exaggerated
interest in American women who apparently fascinated Britons
more than Continental males who were sufficiently captivated by
their own or aboriginal women. In the late nineteenth century she
was a social phenomenon about which even the most cautious Britons would generalize. She emerged in British pages as a "type" before the American male ever achieved his identity.

Evidently the American woman was different, yet not too exotic. While not accepting the *fin de siècle* type overdrawn by French writers, Englishmen were surprised at her capacity for pleasure. Was it the Puritan merging into determined gaiety, carefreeness, "nasal" forthrightness, into a sterility prompted by decisive sophistication? She apparently possessed a delicate pallor, graceful features, and vitality which approached nervousness. She was anarchical, exhilarating, and capable of primitive hoydenishness which disturbed boredom. The American girls in England may not have represented the arrogant beauty, self-absorption, self-satisfaction, and over-cultivation of the types in British or American fiction, but she might hunt without neglecting the boudoir. Oscar Wilde thought our females dainty, without Goddess of Liberty proportions. In the pages of *Punch* it was always the "Fair" American— sentimental, overwrought, aggressive, and originator of crack-pot fads such as training courses for wives, professional bridesmaids, and leagues to enforce politeness. Emil Reich concluded that Englishmen labored under an odd conception of American womanhood, especially since he found it deficient in true femininity. One might suggest that Britons actually overemphasized the sex consciousness of the American woman.

Foreign novelists, according to Andrew Macphail, attributed their heroine's caprices to her American origin; "It is luxurious idleness alone which appeals to the 'American Woman' of foreign fiction"—a type, it may be added, which existed before Columbus. Shaw wrote in a preface of 1905:

I did not understand the British peerage, just as I did not understand that glorious and beautiful phenomenon, the "heartless" rich American woman, who so thoroughly and admirably understands that conscience is a luxury, and should be indulged in only when the vital needs of life have been abundantly satisfied. The instinct which has led the British peerage to fortify itself by American alliances is healthy and well inspired.

Because, thanks to such alliances, a few people could still maintain the tradition of a proud, free, costly life. Created by one who disliked Anglo-American marriages and heiress hunters, the Gibson Girl became the rage in England when her popularity was already waning at home. Perhaps it was only natural that Ford Madox

Ford in *An English Girl* (1907) should use a well-bred English girl as a vehicle for describing New York's blatant and vulgar standards.

Upper class, which did most of the traveling, saw upper class. By 1870 our sisters began to take themselves, with papa's millions, to England. Even before that, a prominent English diplomat feared the Americanization of the international diplomatic corps. By the eighties American women appeared in British memoirs and candid recollections; myth-building and fictionalizing began. It was not until post-War days that England saw the poorer, but attractive, American.

At delightful intervals Anglo-American marriages have caused sensations.[3] The social historian is tempted *a priori* to assume the important cultural significance of hyphenated marriages. There are conditions which obviously affect such marriages. It may be assumed that the parties involved have a denationalized outlook or an international contact. The American woman, whose position was usually considered enviable, may have entered into such marriage with a very definite urge to identify herself completely with another's national outlook and customs. Very probably, the masses based their opinions upon Americans not married to Englishmen. But it is by this time clear that many of those quoted in this volume had American wives. The possibility of influence might be conditioned by the success of such marriages, yet success often depended upon the abnegation of American ways. T. P. O'Connor, who ultimately separated from his American wife, wrote:

> On the whole an American woman is unwise to marry outside her own country. It's the only country in the world which gives to woman her proper place—or at least something approaching it.

His wife, Mrs. Elizabeth Howard, wrote, "The American man expects to make his wife happy—the Englishman expects his wife to make him happy." The other view, which was more true of post-War marriages contracted on a broader basis, held the adjustment easily made.

Lady Randolph Churchill (who became Mrs. G. Cornwallis-West in 1900) recorded that if an American conducted herself properly she was complimented: "I should never have thought *you* were an American." Later, G. W. Smalley noted that British mothers (with daughters) disliked the invasion; further, "The English girl has been encouraged to copy her American cousin . . . and it is the faults, not the merits, that are copied." According to Smalley, however, animation and a sense of equality gained her a foothold in English society. One of the first modern enterprises for the British peerage in the field of commerce was the discovery of New York as a matrimonial market. Although money was not always a factor—nor were "old American families" necessary—American women and money were inextricably connected. It was said:

> Had the heir to the throne [later Edward VII] been more insular in his views, marriage with an American heiress would not have become a recognized method of reviving the family fortunes of impoverished patricians.

No doubt American women did gain a social position which was easily exaggerated for our benefit. An exposure which perturbed even Queen Victoria was based upon the newspaper work of the American Elizabeth Banks, who was known as an exponent of the "newer and American journalism." She received most impressive and influential replies to an "ad" in the *Morning Post* in the early nineties—"Young American Lady of *Means* wishes to meet with a chaperon of highest social position who will introduce her into the best society. Liberal terms. Address, 'Heiress.'" Thus, for £2,000 to £4,000 for one season in society, Americans could be helped up the social ladder, sometimes to marriage, a business which *Punch* commented on in 1905:

> Envy of our unrivalled race
> May prompt the alien's vulgar sneer:—
> "It is her fortune, not her face,
> That captivates the British peer. . . ."

American women helped to break down insularity. Nor did Edward VII ever say about our women what he said about American men whom he didn't like—"They are not adaptable, that's the r-r-reason!" The King once observed that American women were hard on each other, a minor fact which helped to spread gossip. However, this woman was more than a passing fad, like Buffalo

Bill. By 1903 more than seventy Americans had married British peers or titled men; by 1914, at least 130.[4] The Roxburghe-Goelet marriage caused so much American boasting that the sober *Scotsman* became sarcastic. Escott described a garden party at Windsor, June 1907, and

. . . the American heiresses whose acceptance of British coronets had infused wealth, smartness, sometimes art and wit into the peerage of their adopted country.

"The House of Lords," remarked the *Times*, "is getting a good many American mothers." When Locker-Lampson sought to introduce a bill on May 19, 1914, to prohibit traffic in titles, an opponent pointed out that there was no tariff on the importation of our heiresses who brought foreign capital. Sensational American careers did not prevent Mrs. Victoria Claflin Woodhull and her sister, Tennessee Claflin, from being accepted in English circles as Mrs. Martin and Lady Cook. The former, whose marriage into a banking family took place in 1883 after some years of delay, founded the magazine *Humanitarian* (1896), and later curbed her radicalism.

In spite of dollars, Marie Corelli credited the American with enough brains to evaluate men and win popularity in English society.[5] But the "American Bounder" was very obnoxious. Bret Harte wrote, August 15, 1898:

There is no flunky anywhere so atrociously servile and mean as the average American who haunts London society. And I am sorry to say that the American woman is even worse than the American man.

A theme of such international, cultural significance loosed a flood (especially between 1898 and 1907) of British and American novels and plays which has not yet been exhausted. This literature did not do justice to the theme, especially when treating marriages. In bulk, British comments reflected some apprehension at this social invasion. For dramatic purposes, writers sharpened the contrasts between the Old and the New World. By 1910 the American woman had lost some literary value because the superficial life marked out for her—in contrast to the prosaic activity of the neglected American male—led to dramatic poverty.

Perhaps the earliest recorder of the growth of American smartness in England was the cranky Laurence Oliphant (1829–1888). (Lord Houghton declared in 1875 that the eccentricities of Oliphant and Whistler prepared England to look for American freakishness.) Oliphant fell under the influence of Thomas Lake Harris, an American spiritualistic prophet, and came to the Brotherhood of New Life at Brocton on Lake Erie, a clear illustration of the gravitating pull of queer America upon the unstable fringes of British society. In *Piccadilly* (1870), Oliphant portrayed a mercenary aristocrat who introduced moneyed nobodies to fashionable circles, a common pattern of cultural contact. In *Masollam* and *Altiora Peto* (1883), he described unconventional girls and deplored our financial wizards who put a sanctimonious covering on their operations.

"It is almost impossible," said Gertrude Atherton, "for an American woman ever quite to understand Englishmen, and this adds to their fascination." She questioned hyphenated marriages, claiming "no woman with individuality can get along with an Englishman," and described one of her characters as "curiously like an Englishwoman's affectation of American animation." She satirized the marrying peer in *His Fortunate Grace* (1897), and wrote one of the better novels on this subject, *American Wives and English Husbands* (1898). While supposedly dealing with an American wife who schemed to captivate her husband's wealthy friends, Lady Sykes in *Algernon Casterton* (1903) proved that English society was being corrupted by these women and German financiers. The adaptability of our girls, whether heiresses or not, was preached by the C. N. Williamsons in two popular novels: *Lady Betty Across the Water* (3d ed., 1906) and *Lord Loveland Discovers America* (1907). Israel Zangwill in *The Grey Whig* (1903) married American love to English ambition; Mrs. Burton Harrison's *Transplanted Daughters* (1909) contrasted stereotypes—the American millionaire against the effete British aristocrat. "Americans were odd, anyway," said H. G. Rhodes in *The Lady and the Ladder* (1905), "but they certainly helped to pass the time, so people felt."

For personal reasons Frances Hodgson Burnett, author of *Little Lord Fauntleroy*, delayed the publication of *The Shuttle* until

1907.[6] Slowly and unwittingly bonds had been built up, she argued, upon a money basis; she wrote to R. W. Gilder, December 4, 1900:

It is not in the least anti-international. . . . (We are merging you know, and it's an absorbingly interesting thing to look on, and give thought to.) It is only anti—a certain order of particularly gross, bad bargain.

Mrs. Everard Cotes wrote *Those Delightful Americans* (1902) and *Cousin Cinderella* (1908); the latter paid tribute to imperial preference by allowing a Canadian to win the English lad in competition with an American heiress. A genial portrait of an adaptable New England girl was painted by Mrs. Humphry Ward in *Eleanor* (1900) where Lucy, the American, interloped in a love affair with remarkable restraint and elusiveness which suggested anemic femininity. In H. G. Wells's *The Soul of a Bishop* (1917) the bishop lets himself become a prophet through Lady Sunderland, a wealthy American widow; rich and beautiful ones crossed the paths of the heroes in *The Sea-Lady* and *Secret Places of the Heart*. Oddly enough, the hero of *The New Machiavelli* (1911) came to America to avoid a mistress. To show that the theme had not been exhausted, Anne Douglas Sedgwick wrote *Adrienne Toner* (1921) which was analyzed by E. A. Baker as a serious study of a typical American girl—soulful, self-assured, and ignorant; in her relations with an English family she exhibited the virtues and defects of the type—superficial efficiency and instability because of lack of tradition. Little wonder that W. L. George with his press advice to the lovelorn, and the custom of "Saying it with Flowers" also crossed the Atlantic! Or that a Bostonian went to London in 1901 to organize a branch of the "Amulet League of Love" to preach the gospel of love and romantic marriage!

The marriages helped to persuade English aristocrats that our democracy was conservative and stable, and convinced the masses that we were becoming plutocratic. Greater friendliness in Britain's upper classes was inspired by dollars which appealed to personal and family self-interest, and merged politics into a social background. The severe training of our debutante broke down the preconception of rawness and extravagant get-up; business and advertising soon stepped in to stress the American's charm and physical consciousness. Mrs. John Lane (an American married to an

English publisher) declared: "In no way has the American invasion proved more triumphant than in the subtle change it is producing in the new generation of English girls," that is, a new charm and vivacity. The American, accustomed to an environment of publicity, thrived better in London and smart society than in the provinces, but many important words besides "swank" were adopted. It was said these women destroyed the backbone of the aristocrats by "choosing" them, injected free and easy ways into society, and promoted a lenient view on divorce, unpunctuality, midnight hansom rides, and hotel and apartment life. "Sorry" replaced "I beg your pardon." Summer hotels were projected on models of those near New York City. Americans popularized the "rest cure" (but Britain never appreciated our improvements in the wares and organization of the funeral business).

"Rita" (Mrs. Desmond Humphreys), the prolific romantic novelist, added other details in 1904:

What of the "Smart" women from Transatlantic shores, who have brought their slangs . . . their vulgar modes of eating and drinking and speaking, into halls made sacred by a long race of noble ancestors? Most of the loss of dignity and delicacy . . . may be traced to the influence of the "Smart" American woman.

They had introduced "notions" (which once meant mechanical gadgets, then social antics, and now "Beauty aids"). They brought "hen" luncheons, surprise parties, appendicitis dinners, bathing-dress picnics, floral teas, "color" suppers, and novelties in cotillion figures. Said "Rita":

To Fancy Dress a Charity, to flaunt a Bazaar, to self-advertise a Hospital, these are the things we have learnt from our Transatlantic neighbours.

The cake-walk prompted her to say, "The nigger has indeed cast off his yoke; he has set the fashion to modern London." Americans pushed casino and poker, helped to introduce bridge into London about 1894, and popularized auction bridge. An American firm of roller-skate makers, first arranging for a rink in Liverpool, popularized the pastime throughout the country in 1908. Girls' teas became acclimatized by 1898. American dishes became popular: terrapin and canvas-back ducks, grapefruit, apple and celery salads, small turtles with Indian corn as dressing, fruit to begin the meal, iced dishes, and special *plats* from New York. But apparently few Americans made much impression upon British domestics. When L. H. Armstrong brought out *Etiquette up to Date* (1908), she included many American party delights which had or might become popular—"favours," progressive dinner parties, jig-saw puzzles, silver and golden cake, sherry ice, decorations of smilax, "all the lively dances," the barn-dance and cake-walk parties; "American sweetmeats," she added, "are already so well known I need not dilate upon them further." Iced champagne was a gift to London, like the American bartenders. Women who drank brandy and soda, declared Mrs. Lynn Linton, had learned from Americans!

Many concluded that we surpassed England in applied and domestic arts. Our household novelties began to supersede heavier utensils. Following American fancies and tourists, "Anglo-American" laundries helped to eliminate the British washerwoman. After fifteen years of struggle to inculcate the soda-fountain habit, a company got under way in the hot summer of 1899; the ice habit also grew. (The recent extension of the "milk bar" amounts to almost a craze, in spite of the fact that it takes several generations to produce skilful "soda-jerkers.") The *Daily Mail* in 1901 deplored the Automatic Restaurant; an American Quick Lunch Restaurant ran afoul of the R.S.P.C.A. by advertising "broiled live lobsters." Capitalizing upon the deference paid to American methods in 1901, the Postum Cereal Company tried to make England like "Grape-Nuts" by boldly declaring: "American Brains—Brain Workers require special food." American "nature cures," health fads, and diet rules (such as a no-breakfast plan) spread through the country.

American-made ladies' shirtwaists, which were feebly introduced in the summer of 1898, combined neatness, low price, and novel designs; by 1899 they completely dominated the market. Captivating, straight-front, three-laced corsets also entered the London market in 1900. Mrs. A. M. Palmer campaigned in 1902 to popularize short skirts; she commented ruefully, "They admire our short skirt, and will eventually adopt it, but they don't like to take suggestions from American women." The pointed-toe shoe, for indoors and walking, and designed to give an impression of extreme slenderness, caught on in 1905. By 1906 Americans, in league with Parisians, frowned upon *frou-frou* in walking gowns, and pushed tailor-made coat-and-skirt costumes. To capture migratory trade, tailors in the Strand and Regent Street displayed Americanisms, "Fall Goods Now Ready," in addition to the "distinct advantages of American-made shirts" for men.

Lady Randolph Churchill praised her compatriots for improving English decoration, house furnishing, and dress. But Moreton Frewen's observation was much more important:

> All this humour and cheerfulness must enter into one's happiness and play a part for him who marries amongst them. My composite American, do I then respect him? Not exactly. Do I admire him? Yes! inordinately. . . . My mood when I think American is laughter, and that mood will last my time.

This is as socially significant as his lessons in piquet and poker under American tutelage. Judging from more recent evidence, British women admit that the American woman is a "very finely polished instrument for social success." Others see the lower classes imitating our working girls' absorbing interest in personal appearance. But partly because of the movies, the real American woman (whatever she is) has been almost lost in a haze of simplified conceptions held by British males. She has become unduly associated with entertainment, captivating play, even looseness. Indeed, the reformers of the English divorce laws have had to combat throughout modern history the real or alleged playful, capricious, sex-conscious American female. The author would not deprive England of this mental outlet and luxurious dream.

Britain has had a morbid interest in our marriage legislation and high divorce rate.[7] This aspect of our social life, which elicited strong opinions, pushed forward the reformers of the stricter marriage and divorce code, but probably has been more of a stumbling block to liberalized legislation. American divorce laws or decrees were frequently before English courts. The most dramatic case was that of Earl Russell who was prosecuted for bigamy by the House of Lords, 1901, which established the principle that an American divorce would not be recognized where a divorce had been refused in England. The president of the English divorce court, Sir Gorell Barnes, who sent his son to an American law school, reluctantly recognized the validity of a divorce decree granted by a Circuit Court in South Dakota (1906).

In 1901 Parliament again discussed the Marriage with Deceased Wife's Sister Bill; Sir Henry Fowler cited, along with Australian opinion, Justice Story, who had no complaint against such marriages. But our appalling divorce rate was brought forward by the opposition who thought one look at America would raise the question: "Dare we tamper with our marriage laws?" Discussion, with American references, continued in 1902. The Vanderbilt wedding in London, 1902, set Father Black and High Anglicans on the war path against remarriage. Again, in 1903, marriage legislation prompted Sir Gilbert Parker, who had married an American heiress, to recall that many Britons contended we had less respect for the bond of matrimony:

He had heard remarks made on this subject in this House regarding the United States which were extremely offensive to all people who understood what domestic life in the United States was . . . and it was in order to prejudice opinion in this country that it was said that because divorce was so easy there, the United States was extremely lax in its views of the marriage ceremony. That was not so.

In 1907 Earl Nelson and the Marquess of Salisbury agreed with the Archbishop of Canterbury, who quoted Gladstone's solemn warning: "We are not to make the United States our model." The United States and the Colonies drew a distinction between consanguinity and affinity. In spite of many warnings, the bill for the Deceased Wife's Sister passed.

Mrs. Humphry Ward castigated our marriage and divorce, and New York's smart society, in *Daphne or Marriage à la Mode* (1909), written after a lecture tour to get money for London playgrounds. Lord Rosebery, however, told the Society of Comparative Legislation about Michigan, which prohibited the marriage of epileptics and feeble-minded persons, and Wisconsin, which prohibited the marriage of first cousins. Smiles would disappear, he added, if this legislation worthy of Plato's republic should succeed; the *Times* disagreed because our tradition and constitutional checks did not apply to England. When it was proposed in 1909 to extend divorce jurisdiction to the County Courts, the Archbishop of Canterbury and Viscount Halifax painted our evils; Lord Gorrell withdrew his resolution. On the second reading of the Matrimonial Causes Bill in 1914, our social conditions were again criticized. Bryce reported a counter-movement against the divorce evil which he attributed to administration rather than to the law itself.

Between 1909 and 1912 a Royal Commission on divorce and matrimonial causes secured a broad analysis of the situation. For the Minority's report, the United States was the best foreign case, even though the Colonies and European countries had similar causes for divorce. Written by the Archbishop of York, Sir W. R. Anson, and others, the report stated (correctly):

In the United States of America the excessive percentage of divorce is notorious, but the actual facts are not perhaps so well known in England as they ought to be.

The Minority continued by drawing a similarity between our system and that desired by the Majority:

After making all allowances for differences of national temperament, climate, and circumstances between England and the United States we are bound to recognise that the two countries have too much in common to make it probable that if we in England adopt what are substantially the American grounds for divorce, we shall escape the grave disasters which have admittedly followed their adoption in the United States. . . . We cannot but be profoundly influenced by the example of America. . . .

The Minority cited a feeble American organization to prove the need of saving our decaying home life.

The Majority's report, which counseled further facilities for divorce, gave close attention to America; but they preferred not to argue by analogy. Several American witnesses felt compelled to remark that our morality was as good as England's. England had the impression that many states allowed divorce for incompatibility of temper. Harsh rumors grew in the pulpit, platform, and press; the number of decrees said to have been granted mounted higher day by day. The Minority even believed that conjugal fidelity was best in South Carolina (which abolished divorce in 1878). The

Times printed the Minority report *in toto,* but gave a mere summary of the Majority's. In 1912 the Secretary of the English Church Union in his annual letter to members predicted correctly:

English people are not prepared to see a condition of things such as that which exists in the United States . . . reproduced here to please a few theoretical lawyers and social faddists.

The Bostonian Dr. Charles Knowlton's *Fruits of Philosophy,* first introduced and circulated quietly in 1833 with a chapter on birth control, when reprinted by Charles Bradlaugh and Annie Besant in 1876 brought on legal proceedings which made the reprinters famous and sold over two hundred thousand copies in a week. Knowlton affected England's birth rate by promoting voluntary parenthood. Mrs. Woodhull's London lecture in 1877 on stirpiculture (eugenics) aroused considerable attention. The practice of sterilization in this country had been submitted as evidence to the Royal Commission on Divorce. The president of the Eugenics Education Society, it was suggested, had facts but no proposals; he replied, "I point to the legislation of the United States which is not only practicable but practised." The *Lancet* in 1911 commended the work done by the Eugenics Record Office. An American report in 1912 which favored sterilization did not help the eugenics movement abroad. England had also heard much about "free love" and the "affinity" between sexes in America. The National Vigilance Association, interested in suppressing the white slave traffic, reported in 1911 that the most remarkable accession of strength to the English cause was the "sudden awakening of a more determined attitude" in the States; "in reality, this is a symptom of a great rise in the moral feeling . . . in public matters."

Few doubted that the American man did not know how to live; he lacked passion, adaptability, and, as the *Times* put it, appeared too busy to regard opinions about himself. Even the *Daily Mail,* which had extolled the merits of "hustling," began to doubt the true economy of our speed. Perhaps Americans helped to drive the beard from England and, according to *Hearth and Home,* taught all classes to expectorate in carriages. Some, like Northcliffe, thought the spread-eagle American was passing away. Our children did not enjoy a good name abroad; the *Scotsman* once said, "The fewer monstrosities like the American Child the better." Others were dumfounded by child labor in America as described by Wells. But as a social reformer and editor of the *Sunday Magazine* from 1874 to 1896, Benjamin Waugh had watched New York, and he called a meeting in 1884 which developed into the London Society for the Prevention of Cruelty to Children. Very few details concerning our home life penetrated British opinion, but it was generally agreed that the home gained in comfort but lacked privacy.

Americans have constantly complained of the European attitude which makes us the leading golden-calf worshippers.[8] The Dickensian tendency to portray us as kindly barbarians enjoying only a materialistic culture still spiced literature. To Sir Walter Raleigh, writer and Oxford professor, Americans were "incredible"; "their culture would choke you. But their dollars are a bit all right." Hopeful as he was, Sir William Mather regretted that in character, virtue, and refinement we had not kept pace with skill and energy. While reviewing Roosevelt's message to Congress in 1902, the *Spectator* was impressed by "the space which the accumulation of wealth occupies in American thought." Sumptuous weddings and bizarre parties gave the popular imagination something to conjure with. *Punch* commented:

> Your arts are new to our benighted shores,
> Yet now and then we read a Yankee rumour
> Of some portentous meal like this of yours
> And say, "We hoped they had a sense of humour!"

England was convinced of our drift toward plutocracy. The *Spectator*, November 2, 1907, feared plutocracy "may win the day, and if it does, the hopes of mankind, which have been so greatly raised by the success of American institutions, will once more be overthrown." G. Lowes Dickinson's gentleman hoped,

> The Plutocracy of the West may yet be transformed into an Aristocracy; and Europe re-discover from America the secret of its past greatness.

But the American world of O. Henry, lamented W. S. Blunt, author and poet, a world with virtues as ugly as its vices and only an upper class of wealth, would engulf England; "people of the usual Yankee type, well-meaning but altogether wearisome," Blunt added in 1916, would bring manners and money into Europe under the label of democracy, an evil perhaps worse than the aristocratic Hun.

Recklessness was another trait which impressed the British. Hardly a collision or disaster was overlooked; our carelessness made this country the home of horrors. The sinking of the *General Slocum* could mean nothing but complete disregard for life. Some disasters, such as a theatre fire in Chicago, made Britons examine their own safety measures. Both disasters and crime made America an escape from boredom. America was viewed as a criminals' refuge. Our underworld had to be sensational; we seemed to so regard it, and the British eagerly agreed. A few Americans swindled, robbed banks, and counterfeited in England: Dan Noble, Charles Lister, George Engels, Neill Cream, and others.

Mrs. Maybrick, who married a Liverpool cotton merchant in 1881, was accused of disposing of her husband; transatlantic efforts were made to secure her release. The "gold-brick swindles" were hailed by British police as a "triumph of American ingenuity." A clever witness and a beautiful female adventuress like Miss Wilberforce could be plausible only by claiming an American origin; Lord Russell of Killowen broke down her story by what he considered his best piece of cross-examination. A clever use of the "millionaire" fixation led in 1902 to the Humbert-Crawford case in France, which excited England; like the defrauded French, Englishmen must have considered a Yankee a man of boundless wealth and *capable de tout*.

So widespread was the morbid interest in the Harry Thaw trial that the Theatres and Music-halls Committee of the London County Council took steps to restrict the presentation of a music-hall sketch, "The Unwritten Law," based upon it. Thaw entered Madame Tussaud's, a mark of British fame. The trial was hailed as a "burlesque"; the *Saturday Review* was comparatively mild:

America is millionaire-ridden, that is one of the morals of the Thaw case, but it is also lawyer-ridden as is no other country in the world, and this is another moral of the Thaw case.

Even a magazine like *Hospital* was interested: "The moral issues involved in this case have a very serious bearing upon the government of all civilized countries." The trial aroused opposition against a Court of Criminal Appeal and other needed changes in the English criminal system. Curiously enough, W. M. Chase felt that English sympathy favored Thaw not White, and he visited London to rehabilitate the dead architect's reputation. No graft or crime was missed, but it is necessary to add only the *Glasgow Herald's* comment in 1912 on the Becker-Rosenthal case:

A country which has made a worship of the Money Power to the neglect of social or moral ideals, needs more than a political revolution to develop a soul.

The Dean of Canterbury affirmed the value of denominational instruction by reminding his listeners that in a comparable period of time America's homicides exceeded England's losses in the Boer War. These episodes must not be isolated from a social context because they mar a nation's eloquence.

The meat-packing scandals were additional evidence that we were careless in vital matters, and in view of England's excited criticisms it was impossible to put the moral stigma merely on the trusts and not on the American people.[9] "It is impossible to understand," commented the *Manchester Guardian*, "this complete absence or breakdown of inspection and regulation in a civilized country." The *Scotsman* concluded, "The whole scandal raises in acute form the problem which awaits solution as between modern industrialism and modern capitalism." England wanted criminal prosecutions. All of Liverpool believed the meat scandals; cheaper restaurants in Soho had to close; in mining districts cheese temporarily replaced tinned meat. As Sinclair once complained, his *Jungle*, designed for the public heart, hit instead its stomach; but many British papers did not overlook the evil working conditions. The scandals bolstered British inspection. The shadows grew deeper in debates on the Army Estimates, and the government, in order not to add to lurid press stories, hesitated to publish its experts' reports. *Punch* parodied the poet Coleridge:

In Chicago did Kubla can
A Mastodon from dim B.C.

And called it beef, the wily man!
And sent it in a baggage van
For England's heavy tea.

The Franco-American Company and Armour combated the rumors by advertisements; the former declared, "What distinction does the foreigner . . . make between the packer in Chicago or in New York?" Geography might not be clear, but England could not escape America. The *Jungle* gave America's refrigerated beef export trade to the United Kingdom a severe blow, just as the Argentine supply began to expand.

Racial assimilation and the American Negro were also problems which England did not underestimate.[10] Opinion about our ability to assimilate the hordes of Europe was evenly divided. The English were impressed by the nationalizing process carried on in the schools. Sir William Butler, a soldier who knew our frontier, noted a developing uniformity of type; so did the *Spectator*, "Ian Maclaren," and Charles Whibley. Bryce did not fear immigration, but by 1900 English opinion, mindful of Charles Henry Pearson's prophecy, began to feel that immigration must stop if America was to remain as she was. Wells also doubted the process of assimilation. In a shrewd article, A. E. Zimmern concluded that America was not a nation but a state of mind, unable to assimilate, or to nurture the soul.

Not one lynching was missed by the British press, and throughout these years one would have concluded that hatred was growing between Negroes and Whites. This treatment of the Negro foreboded ill for America's tropical expansion. Nor could a nation that professed to be civilized permit lynching, which weakened America's protests against Jewish pogroms. William Tallock, at one time secretary of the Howard Association, advocated a "State Board of Charities and Corrections" for the Southern states to alleviate peonage. Viscount Morley, just after being immersed in the difficulties of Indian reform, viewed the American Negro as a harder problem than India. The writings of W. Laird Clowes and Pearson had attracted much British attention in the nineties. William Archer wrote a book on the Negro in the South for imperial guidance; his purpose "was heightened, moreover, by the feeling that a great deal of what passes in England as advanced thought on the subject of race-relations is very superficial and remote from the realities of the case." Wells could see no reason for the Southern frame of mind; Archer could, but curiously advocated a Negro state. Sir Sydney Olivier, a colonial official in Jamaica, told the Church Congress in 1913 that America's difficulty could be solved only by resolutely disclaiming the color line. Sir Harry Johnston's articles on the Negro first appeared in the *Times* in 1909; his *Negro in the New World* was unpopular in England and almost tabooed in the States. Col. H. B. Jeffreys, like Sir Harry, professed to see some danger in Africa from the importation of American Negroes to Liberia and the theory of equality. But a Prime Minister acknowledged Booker T. Washington's aims as useful for the Empire's problems.

At the risk of underestimating the social and cultural effects of American gifts to Great Britain, charity may be discussed here as a factor in the formation of attitudes.[11] The planetary consciousness of our philanthropists has embraced the wealthy British Isles in a way that is remarkable, and the flow of gifts has been extremely one-sided. This is partly explained by admiration for the value of a mother country, as witnessed by the Edward Stephen Harkness gift to the Pilgrim Trust in 1930. There have been few complaints that our charity would Americanize the islands or pauperize the generosity of the British, partly because nowhere have American gifts been so denationalized in application and less talked about. Therefore it is not surprising that only a select few have been influenced in their views about the United States by any American munificence, and outside of that group the donations merely served to build up pictures of our excessive wealth.

American money brought scholars to the United States and American books to England; but the improvement of contacts, so far as British knowledge about America is involved, has not yet been remarkable. Probably no American gift to England has meant as much to the national sentiment of the donor or the recipient as the mutual gain to France and the United States by the gift of the Statue of Liberty. It is extremely doubtful whether the Scottish Trust, quietly or not, brings the English-speaking peoples together as Mr. Carnegie's biographer suggests. But in another sense, the things done with American money may affect profoundly British life. As G. M. Trevelyan said in 1933, prompted by gifts for preserving the pristine charm of Cambridge,

The amount of good that is daily being done in this island by American trusts of this motive and character—Carnegie, Rockefeller, and now the Pilgrim Trust—is a thing that Englishmen should never in these days be tempted to forget.

In their management the foundations have followed closely British feeling, methods, and desires, perhaps more closely now than in pre-War days. Yet the possibility of receiving American donations unnerves Britain; it is as unbalancing as the vision of a triumphant American lecture tour; it gives opinions, especially among academics, a touch of unreality.

Andrew Carnegie personified one form of the American impact.[12] In the eighties he thought that he might give his money to republicanize Great Britain; he joined with Samuel Storey to form a chain of popular newspapers in industrial regions. The syndicate controlled eighteen papers in two years (including Passmore Edwards' London *Echo*). Carnegie (who wanted to extend the vote to agricultural laborers), Thomas Graham, and the *Midland Echo* coöperated in the "Black Country." The *St. James's Gazette* denounced him and declared,

. . . the present agitation originated in America, and is an attempt to infuse republican sentiments into English politics. The movement, with all its paraphernalia of banners, processions, monster meetings and other factious machinery, which American politicians know so well how to handle, is entirely foreign to English sentiment, and is the result of American influence and paid for by American dollars.

Mr. Hendricks claimed that Carnegie's various *Echoes* helped to create the background for Gladstonian reforms—universal franchise, payment of M.P.'s, restrictions on the House of Lords, and Home Rule. Under the challenging title *Triumphant Democracy*, Carnegie gave Britain in 1886 a glorification of republicanism and a forecast of his preaching at the turn of the century. In spite of the contempt of Marston, his English publisher, sixty thousand copies were circulated in Great Britain. As propaganda, Carnegie quoted Salisbury's praise of the Senate's strength and efficiency and the Supreme Court's stabilizing influence; he preached the conservative character of our democracy, and identified the American as a "true Briton." Carnegie also thought:

The influence of America and of American ideas upon England is seen in various ways. We meet frequently one who has visited the Republic, whose advanced ideas, in consequence of the knowledge derived from actual contact with American affairs, are very decidedly proclaimed.

His donations to libraries and education gave rise to mixed feelings. According to Rosebery and John Morley, the gifts to Scotland had improved education and awakened Britain to the need of more physical equipment and greater funds. Nor did Morley share the widespread fear that the payment of fees would demoralize students and encourage "bad debts." The *Spectator*, which would have praised Carnegie if he had given some money to Oxford and Cambridge, did not look upon the £2,000,000 as an unmixed blessing; the *Manchester Guardian* feared such funds might distort teaching. There was not much doubt what J. A. Hobson had in mind when he argued that *nouveaux riches* funds in universities encouraged wasteful intellectual competition. In 1911 Haldane supported the Trust's efforts to establish postgraduate scholarships, a feature which had lagged in Britain. The success of the Hero Fund in North America prompted Carnegie to extend it to Great Britain in 1908, with some opposition on the charge of professionalizing the heroic spirit. Nor were the grants of free libraries always welcomed, partly because it was felt that they were unnecessary and a vulgar display of money power.[13] Opposition arose, as in Manchester, frequently from laborers and their press because the money was "tainted." But Carnegie gave tremendous encouragement to the public library movement; from 1900 to 1910 about 163 local bodies gained by this stimulus and the extension of public lectures under library auspices. These gifts directed attention to the scientific tone of American librarianship, coöperative cataloging, bibliographical aids, and reading rooms for the blind. Between 1882 and 1910, 120 libraries adopted the Dewey decimal system of classification. The Bristol Public Library bought American apparatus; Manchester investigated our libraries before erecting its own. The American Library Association had also assisted the organization of a similar British body in 1877.

Carnegie preached and denounced from many platforms on subjects ranging from American rivalry to peace, and there is no doubt that his idealism and ideas, backed up by money, were viewed as more than half American. He probably received more press space than any other American during the pre-War years. His generosity acted as a challenge to Britons' purses, and our patrons were held up as examples in pleading many causes.

Charges of political or social bias were easily brought against Joseph Fels's donations.[14] In 1901 Fels came to England with Walter Coates as a co-worker. George Lansbury, who had met him in 1903, recalled:

I had heard very little of him, and confess I was somewhat prejudiced against him because he was a rich American.

Fels, who applied American advertising to political propaganda in England, won over Walter Long, G. Balfour, and Colonel Lockwood at the Local Government Board Offices, and set plans for rural repopulation. In 1903 he began advocating small holdings and farms. He bought one hundred acres at Laindon for the first farm colony for the unemployed; later he took over estates at Hollesley Bay and Mayland. He used his American experience in working with the London Vacant Land Cultivation Society, which was similar to the parent organization in Philadelphia. He wanted every British voter to get a bundle of Single Tax literature; he joined a non-party organization formed in London, March 23, 1907, the United Committee for the Taxation of Land Values. In 1911 Fels, accused of undue interference in the General Election, denied that he had any interest in maintaining free trade. He aided the cause of woman suffrage and established health centers in London, school clinics, and the first open-air nursery.

Between 1913 and 1936 the Rockefeller Foundation donated over $19,500,000 to the United Kingdom in the medical, natural, and social sciences and the humanities, about 70 per cent being devoted to medical sciences.[15] Over three hundred British scholars have enjoyed Foundation fellowships. This is just one of the gestures which have been added to the picture as drawn for the pre-1914 years.

How did America add to the religious heritage?[16] Anglo-

American ecclesiastical contacts, according to British churchmen, were perhaps stronger before 1914 than at present. Greater appreciation rose for our mission work in all parts of the world. Although England suspected that American theology might suffer without wealthy benefices, high salaries attracted eminent British divines to our shores, and yet our religious history was not so well known as one might expect. The "hustling" messages of our evangelists stirred the British masses; their deeper spiritual tones touched responsive chords as though America, as in business, was rousing new enthusiasm and appeals to primordial instincts. But Britain, in spite of its stability, or because of it, became a happy hunting ground for religious freak-fashionists or quacks.

Emerson's teachings carried over to the new century. W. T. Stead, who was influenced by Lowell, has said:

To those who have been brought up in the sectarian seclusion of the Anglican cult, it is difficult to realize the extent to which American books, American preachers, American hymnody, mould the lives of the Free Churchmen of this country.

The formation of an American Committee for revision of the Bible, part of a movement begun in the seventies by the Church of England, was an early step in scholarly coöperation which indicated our progress in biblical scholarship and the desirability of keeping us in touch with any changes in English usage. Partly through the efforts of W. Evans Darby of London, the Anglo-American churches had consulted each other in the cause of arbitration; the atmosphere of Chicago in 1893 inspired the Peace Congress to ask churches to rally to this cause.

Many of our ministers, especially from the Eastern seaboard, encouraged liberalizing moves in England, but this channel often became ineffective because our styles of eloquent pulpit oratory diverged from English taste. An audience in the last decades of the century had been prepared for Rev. T. De Witt Talmage, a Presbyterian, by his best-seller sermons; his manager wrote: "It seemed incredible that there could be such a craze over a minister, and yet that it caused no comment whatever in the daily newspaper . . . in any way." The secular nature of Talmage's sermons soon caused a revulsion. Rev. C. M. Sheldon, author of *In His Steps* (1896), was hailed in 1900 by the *Daily Mail* as the American best known to England's poor. One of his compatriots known in Established circles was H. B. Whipple (1822–1901), Bishop of Minnesota, who gained an English hearing through his work among the Indians; he was offered the bishopric of the Sandwich Islands. Dr. J. H. Jowett helped to draw together the Congregational pulpits. Dr. Charles Albert Berry (1852–1899), who declined an invitation to succeed Henry Ward Beecher in 1887, succeeded in interpreting America to England's evangelical churches; his American "call" quadrupled his salary at home. After hearing Dr. Lyman Abbott about 1890, Dr. John Clifford concluded: "Christianity in America is advancing and coming into line with the best element of English theology." Contacts which were not all ineffective or for ulterior motives had been established by Beecher, Brooks, Bishop Gore, George Dawson, Charles Kingsley, Deans Farrar, Hole, Stanley, and Stubbs, and the Bishop of Ripon.

What offended Hugh Price Hughes (1847–1902), particularly after a five weeks' visit as a delegate to the Methodist Œcumenical Conference in 1890, was America's ideal of shallow, personal piety; this did not prevent him from conceiving of an imperial Anglo-Saxon Federation in which Methodism would have a leading rôle. Principal James Denney, who preached here in 1894 and 1905, noted the absence of a healthful connection between churches and public life but imbibed courage from our "hope" even if it were "without measure." Likewise Dean Hole, who also suggested that Oxford should imitate courses in sacred harmonies for preachers; but Sir Robert Perks decided that our churches were too much like music halls. The Bishop of London contrasted America's quiet (*sic*) toleration with England's sect battles. The *Glasgow Herald* in 1909 hoped that American Protestants' coöperation would be taken to heart by Scottish Presbyterianism. As we have shown, it was to the advantage of those favoring any change in Britain's Church Establishment to paint a rosy picture of our religious life. Nowhere was religious knowledge more general or religion more genuine and earnest, according to John Morley, who was pleased by our secular education and church structure. Asquith, during a debate on the Welsh Establishment in 1914, declared that here

. . . the religious life of the community was as strong and vital as it could possibly be under the aegis of an Established Church, and with at least as large and liberal an atmosphere of thought and an infinitely greater power of elasticity.

Definitely considered then and now an American importation, Christian Science was greeted as a product of a commercial society and first struck roots among the upper classes.[17] Ties were maintained with British members, and no doubt American viewpoints reached groups which hitherto had been left untouched. The spread of this faith was made more difficult because England regarded us as the home of medical quacks; Mary Baker Eddy, who toyed with the Anglo-Israel racial theory, had been over-certain that she could introduce it more readily than in America. Among the earliest pioneers was Miss Dodge, who came from New York in 1889 at a time when only a few copies of Eddy's *Science and Health with Key to the Scriptures* (1875) were in the entire country. Huxley had placed a copy in the British Museum, Arthur Stanley had presented one to the library of Westminster Abbey. The first members in the British Isles were probably Mr. Graves Colles and Mrs. Marjorie Colles (often called the first "teacher") who lived near Dublin; among the pioneers were others who lived in Ireland. Mrs. Julia Field King, who later disagreed with Mrs. Eddy, possibly over genealogies, went to London in 1896 and secured Lord and Lady Dunmore, Sir Douglas Galton, Sir William Marriott, and Colonel Hamilton. Regular services began in Hammersmith by 1894; on November 7, 1897, in Bryanston Street, the first church in the Old World opened its doors.

The *Times* (May 26, 1885) first referred to mental healing in Boston as "entertaining"; the *Westminster Gazette* in 1898 called it "The Latest West End Religion," and stressed the ignorance of Mrs. Eddy. The *St. James's Gazette* also spoke of the "prominence now given to the methods of enterprising American ladies who are making a fat living out of the weak-minded. . . ." By 1901 the *Times* reported fifty "practitioners" in London. Dr. Stephen Paget condemned the movement before the Church Congress in Swansea. The Society of Emmanuel, which originated in America and borrowed some hints on mental therapy from the Christian Scientists, was received more kindly by leaders of the Church of England.

In June 1937 there were about 290 churches and numerous reading rooms in the British Isles, and some 1,055 registered practitioners; 242 lectures were given by members of the Mother Church.

By their glowing accounts of Utah, the Mormons, since the time of their onslaught upon Liverpool in 1837, had brought the color of a romantic frontier to British life. The mother of Brigham Henry Roberts (1857–1933) left England and a husband to bring her children to Utah; between 1886 and 1888 Roberts returned to the British Mission, where he edited the *Millennial Star*. Plural marriage had injured the Church, and many Britons transferred to the Reorganized Church of Jesus Christ of Latter-Day Saints. The Mormons and Utah drew large numbers of over-excited tourists; they received ample publicity, and Britain's curiosity is still greater than that of non-Mormon Americans. In 1910 the Mormons distributed about six million tracts and 117,000 pamphlets, and got five hundred persons, mostly women, to go to Utah. In 1911 there was a brief Mormon "scare." They were asked to quit Birkenhead; a public manifesto in Maidstone, signed by the mayor and others, warned parents; the vicar of Little Hornsea cried, "Beware of Mormons." The *Daily Mail*, after ten bishops had favored drastic action, wanted the Aliens Bill to include Mormons. A crowded meeting in the Birmingham Town Hall, April 10, condemned their campaigns as subversive to young womanhood. A Home Office inquiry discovered 323 elders (there had been two hundred teaching in 1901) and eighty thousand members whose activities centered in northern industrial centers. There were rumors that the anti-Mormon campaign was managed by American money and the sensational press. Two slightly uncomplimentary plays, *The Girl from Utah* and Edwin George's *At the Mercy of the Mormons*, capitalized upon Britain's curiosity in 1913.

Anglicans cannot now remember any contributions which came from us, and any liberalizing tendency has been in appeal rather than theology.[18] Bishop Hopkins of Vermont suggested periodical assemblies of bishops in 1851. One can find a few more references to America in the Lambeth Conference of 1908 as compared with those of 1867, 1878, 1888, and 1897. English clergymen, with English orders and letters from their bishops, were numerous in American churches; but there had been little reciprocity. American bishops first appeared on the platform of the Church Congress at Wolverhampton in 1868. Among the few Anglicans interested in our religious life was the liberal dean A. P. Stanley (1815–1881) whose tour in 1878 refreshed his last years; he once said, "I have often felt that I could never quite understand Europe till I had seen America." J. P. Morgan told the Archbishop of Canterbury, Randall Davidson, that nothing would help Anglo-American friendship or the Church more than an American tour. The Primate went in 1904, inquiring into immigration, divorce, education, and the licensing systems, "with their possible bearing on the contemporary controversies in England."

At the fourth Lambeth Conference, 1897, the proposal for a "tribunal of reference" was withdrawn partly because American bishops preferred a "consultative body"; Davidson, then Bishop of Winchester, said, "I did not realize that it was wholly unpopular even in the United States. . . ." The Pan-Anglican Congress and the Lambeth Conference of 1908 enabled Anglo-American co-religionists to get together. The Report of the Committee on Supply and Training of Clergy drew attention to the canon of the Episcopal Church which allowed ordinations to the diaconate at the age of twenty-one. The Committee on Religious Education also reported:

The preparation of a teacher for religious instruction is a far more serious matter today than it was when most of the existing schemes of Bible instruction were prepared. This fact is far better understood in the United States than in England, and there is much to be learned from the Bible Schools which are being established there.

At the Congress, the Bishop of Auckland, supported by others, attributed most of our evils to secular education. In a curious letter in 1912 to bishops and laity, the Archbishop of Canterbury asked their services for a World Conference on Truth and Order since its American origin and probable meeting place would facilitate matters in England. Mandell Creighton, conscious of national differences in religious outlook, spoke of visiting American bishops as "good fellows, full of fun, and with a breezy way of looking at the world which was useful to contemplate."

The *Freeman*, a Baptist organ envious of America's church expansion and the success of the Baptist Tract and Book Society, used such examples to prod British Baptists.[19] The Baptist World Alliance formed in 1905 at the first Baptist World Congress, London, which received its impetus from an American, found the "American host naturally jubilant" and the British awakened by a large delegation. Dr. John Clifford explained that America also wanted to show that it supported the Britons who were fighting priestism. No doubt we encouraged Dr. Clifford's "passive resistance" to the Education Act of 1902 which provided denominational religious teaching. America could not be ignored at the Methodist conference at London in 1881, at Washington in 1891, or again at London in 1901. At the latter, we brought the "race question" immediately to British attention; a large public meeting discussed "The Moral Unity of the English-speaking Peoples." Bishop Matthew Simpson of the American Methodist Episcopal Church received a window in 1902 at Wesley's Chapel, City-road, London.

"Americanism" came upon the Catholic faith at home and abroad, stimulated by Father Hecker, the New York founder of the Paulists, who aimed at Christian perfection consistent with national characteristics, an adaptation of Catholic discipline to our institutions, in reality a form of Anglo-Saxon religious imperialism. The outcry against this doctrine broke out in France because contemporary problems there inspired the clergy to study Catholicism in a democracy; but despite the alleged appeal to Anglo-Saxon temperament, the controversy aroused little interest among English Catholics. Leo XIII condemned this doctrine in 1899. It did not escape Lecky that "The future of America and democratic Catholicism is a very interesting question."

Mr. and Mrs. Robert Pearsall Smith, the parents of Logan Pearsall Smith, went to England in 1872 to triumph in evangelical circles and embellish the work of Moody and Sankey.[20] Smith, an exponent of the "Higher Life" movement, preached a type of perfectionism and sanctification by faith alone. Two notable meetings were held, at Oxford, August 1874, and, after an excursion to Germany where he fostered the *Heiligungsbewegung*, at Brighton, June 1875. His English career closed abruptly, partly because of lapses into heresy and unpleasant gossip. His rush to secure full salvation reminded Britons of our "Get rich quick!" spirit where

"Jesus saves me *now*." But out of their work grew the Keswick Movement. Rev. W. E. Boardman, also a Perfectionist, remained in England and later became a faith healer. Many of our enthusiasms had extravagant elements, as shown by the Welsh revival in 1905 and the Pentecost Movement ("Los Angeles Revival").

Dwight L. Moody and I. D. Sankey enjoyed remarkable gospel campaigns in Britain, 1873–75, 1881–84, and 1891–92, popularizing at the same time their *Gospel Hymns* and Moody's colloquial sermons. Much opposition came from their embodiment of America's muscular Christianity. Moody's translation of the Bible into American vernacular shocked and stimulated; he organized daily noon prayer-meetings. The great mission of 1875 might have been thought sensational by Queen Victoria, but its influence spread to all classes. Disraeli, when opposing reforms on behalf of British seamen, called Plimsoll a "Moody and Sankey in politics." Yet *Vanity Fair* concluded that Moody had "every cause to be satisfied with the amenability of the English to American methods." Their work helped to draw together British and American students; Moody inspired George Adam Smith and Henry Drummond, and got Glasgow to overhaul herself. Australian emissaries, who failed to locate in England the religious men they needed, invited R. A. Torrey and C. M. Alexander; news of their revivals reached the Convention at Keswick with the suggestion of forming prayer circles. The London Evangelical Council welcomed them to Great Britain in Exeter Hall, January 9, 1903. Torrey's anecdotes, very much like frontier "tall stories," jarred English audiences; their songs were translated into Welsh. Their mission spoke with great self-possession in harsh American accents.

Because of its organization the Salvation Army never lost touch with its American branches. Ballington Booth resigned from the American body on March 9, 1896, explaining that Anglo-American tension over Venezuela might harm their work. The Ballington Booths later said of "General" William Booth:

We loved and understood this country. He exhibited prejudice and misconception of it and its people. He said that the time had arrived to cease carrying the Stars and Stripes at the head of our parades. He objected to the use of the eagle upon our crests and insignias, and constantly spoke depreciatingly of the country, its people and its institutions.

"Americanism" in the evangelical ranks! They wanted less control from London and objected to the "General's" plan for merging some of the states with the Canadian organization. Ervine, William Booth's biographer, denied this accusation, claiming that the "General" foresaw a great future here and merely wanted to preserve unity. A demonstration held in London, July 1904, tried to show by the remarkable dimensions of the American work that a shrewd people had endorsed the Army. Yet "Commander" Railton became rather impatient with American customs where women came very much to the front.

England also observed our foreign mission expansion.[21] Lord Cromer referred to a mission in these terms:

It is conducted on those sound, practical, common sense principles which are, indeed, thoroughly characteristic of American mission work in Egypt.

Robert College in Constantinople and American missions in Asia Minor were almost viewed as imperialistic inroads. In April 1909 the Archbishop of Canterbury told the S.P.G. that Americans were doing more than his countrymen to evangelize India. Lord William Cecil preferred our mission's educational work in the East. Members of the Laymen's Missionary Movement journeyed to England in the spring of 1907 to describe America's growing interest in foreign missions; the British and Foreign Bible Society in June 1907 seemed willing to have Britain and Ireland join this movement. Many at the World Missionary Conference of 1910 felt that European missionary societies had much to learn from our methods of forwarding native industry and education.

Six years after its American origin in 1886, England prepared to foster the Student Volunteer Missionary movement. Henry Drummond, J. E. K. Studd, and others brought back information about this and the Y.M.C.A.'s student departments. "The British students," said Tatlow, "were impressed by the skill with which the Americans were organizing, and were anxious to secure a visit from [Robert P.] Wilder to help them organize a movement." Wilder came to London, July 1891, and described the work to the Keswick Convention. English leaders kept in contact with the American program and spoke of the Northfield Student Conferences as "a wonderful inspiration and means of opening the eyes of the delegates to the possibilities of organized Christian work in the colleges." A summer conference for students was imitated in 1893, also specially prepared textbooks and group leader guides. By invitation John Mott went over to help perfect the organization and program of what came to be the British College Christian Union. The go-getting American watchword was adopted in 1896—"The Evangelization of the World in this Generation."

The suggestion for the World's First Sunday-School Convention was made at Chautauqua, New York, in 1886.[22] The convention took place at London in 1889 with many overseas delegates. At the third convention, London, 1898, Britons advised copying our "Home Department," Sunday school literature, and house-to-house visitation. The President discussed teacher-training:

Our friends in America are more successful than we are in England. The title "Normal Graduate" frightens us English teachers somewhat. But how much more satisfaction . . . if the teachers would take the trouble to go through the courses adopted by our American friends.

Our increasing attendance jogged Britons.

"So far," said the *Western Mail* in 1902, "the American system has revolutionized our schools"; it also referred to the Cardiff and District Sunday schools which now had rolls of honor, gold badges for regular attendance, and shields for the best classes. By 1908 British leaders agreed with the American committee on the International Sunday School Lessons. The World's Sunday School Convention at Washington, 1910, gave great impetus to the work in England. American leaders also conducted "inspirational tours" in the British Isles.

A young English emigrant mechanic who met Francis E. Clark, founder of the Christian Endeavor Societies, informed his former pastor, Rev. M. Potts of Crewe, who started the first society in England about 1885. In 1888 Clark told the Sunday School Union in England how Christian Endeavor might stop the leak between the Sunday School and the Church, but the idea did not at once commend itself. From a weak beginning, however, a large number of societies developed. The Christian Endeavor convention of 1900 at London heard many speeches which extolled the unity of Anglo-

American youth. A few months later, after a gospel tour, the president told the British Christian Endeavour Society that sensationalism was giving way to religion in American pulpits. The National Home Reading Union was modeled on the lines of the Chautauqua Literary and Scientific Circle; the name had also become known through the series "Chautauqua Girls."

As Percival Chubb has said, "If England drew upon America for new ethical inspiration, America has drawn liberally upon England for its exponents." The English Ethical Society was formed in the eighties in an atmosphere of ideas which emanated from America; Felix Adler's *Creed and Deed* (1877) had circulated with some effect. But despite American recruits, such as Stanton Coit at the South Place Ethical Society, the English hesitated to institutionalize the movement along American plans. Coit, in England since 1888 and founder of the Moral Education League, had hoped to reproduce in England's societies a fierce passion for conversion.

Spiritualism, table-turning, rapping, etc., had invaded Europe in mid-century in the person of D. D. Home, a Scot by origin, who received greater attention from British big-wigs than more substantial Americans.[23] Another spiritualistic prophet, Thomas Lake Harris (removed from England at the age of five), came to Britain from time to time after 1859, and secured some converts by appeals not entirely free from eroticism. Through the efforts of the Theosophical Society (founded 1875) and especially Colonel H. S. Olcutt, England received stimulus from America as well as India. William James's *Varieties of Religious Experience,* which was fairly well received, surprised Britons by treating seriously such persons as Madam Blavatsky and Mrs. Besant. Conan Doyle, whose first production, *A Study in Scarlet* (1887), was inspired by Utah and two brutal Mormons, throughout his life received sustenance, as did A. R. Wallace, from American spiritualism. "The Californian Psychic," Florence Montagu, attracted attention by her Sunday meetings at London in 1901; she formed the London Psychic Society. Despite his Scottish and Australian antecedents, John Alexander Dowie, founder of Zionism, and his wife and son were viewed as American freaks and were mobbed in London in 1903 and 1904. The American founders of "Theocratic Unity," Theodora and Laura Horas, found themselves in London courts,

October 1901. An Irish-American hailing from Detroit established himself near Chatham in 1905 as "Prince Michael" of the "New Eve" or "House" or "Body of Israel."

The difference between American and British free-thought history, according to J. M. Robertson, was to be attributed to our unleisured population, which had little time for disinterested thinking.[24] J. T. Merz, in his *History of European Thought* (1904), noted that our "steady growth and peculiar civilization" increased the task of the intellectual historian, but he could say nothing about the tendencies of this new culture which were to him "vague and enigmatical." The Scottish philosopher and educator Thomas Davidson (1840–1900), who taught under W. T. Harris at St. Louis and associated with the Concord school of philosophy, tried to lay a religious basis for democracy. Post-graduate work at Harvard in 1886 and C. E. Norton and William James were mentally liberating for L. P. Jacks, who helped to bring American thought to Britain. The Gifford Lectures at Edinburgh (1899–1901) and the Hibbert Lectures at Oxford (1908) brought William James's philosophy to the fore. Pragmatism, received as a typical American product, was first put into print in 1898. In England it was taken up by W. Caldwell and F. C. S. Schiller in 1900 and 1902. It was sometimes described "as a transatlantic importation of the debasing slang of the Wild West . . . as an outbreak of the sordid commercializing of the Anglo-Saxon mind." Bertrand Russell declared, "The influence of democracy in promoting pragmatism is visible in almost every page of James's writings."

Thus, in many different ways, the United States was adding to Britain's social and cultural history. The complicated pattern will be examined further in the concluding chapter.

---

[1] H. G. Wells, *An Englishman looks at the World* (London, 1914), 250–328, and *Future in America* (1906); Frederic Harrison, *Autobiographic Memoirs* (London, 1911), II, 188–90, 206; Harrison had great enthusiasm for Roosevelt; see also his *George Washington* (1901). J. A. Hobson and M. Ginsberg, *L. T. Hobhouse: His Life and Work* (London, 1931), 59; C. R. Enoch, *Farthest West*, viii. Joseph McCabe, *Life and Letters of G. J. Holyoake* (London, 1908), 109–13, 124, 131–32; his volume of impressions, *Among the Americans*, was not successful; see also Holyoake's *Bygones Worth Remembering* (1905). *Report of Royal Commission on Poor Laws, etc.*, P.P., 1910 (Cd. 5441) in LV, Pt. 1, 4–45, 185–211, 417–66,

Dugald Macfayden, *Sir Ebenezer Howard and the Town Planning Movement* (Manchester, 1933), 10, 11, 20; Kidd, *Principles of West. Civ.*, 339–40, 404–73; J. A. Hobson, *Confessions of an Economic Heretic* (London, 1938), 68, 27, 48, 57, 64, 67.

[2] Bernard Shaw, *Prefaces* (London, 1934), 654; preface to *The Irrational Knot* whose hero is an Irish-American electrical engineer. Emil Reich, *Imperialism* (London, 1905), 34, 55ff., 121; Andrew Macphail, *Essays in Fallacy* (London, 1910), 4–5; Fairfax Downey, *Portrait of an Era, as drawn by C. D. Gibson* (New York, 1936), 86, 106, 176, 192, 295; Coleridge, *Lord Coleridge* (II, 344–45) found Am. women pretty and graceful in mind and body. H. B. Marriott-Watson, "Deleterious Effect of Americanisation upon Woman," *19th Cent.*, Nov. 1903, 782–92; Kipling, *American Notes* (Boston, 1899), 37ff.; Shaw, *Cosmopolitan*, Sept. 1907, 561; *ibid.*, Feb. 1905, 38:371–82. Note the sentimental comedy by J. K. and W. I. Paulding, *Bucktails; or, Americans in England* (Philadelphia, 1847)—an original idea: an Am. girl living in England marries a visiting American! F. E. Greville, *Life's Ebb and Flow* (London, 1929), 123, 211; Bancroft's *Directory, 1903* and *An.-Am. Year-Book, 1916* for list of hyphenated marriages. *Lippincott*, Jan. 1903, 71:68–77; M. V. Ponsonby, *Preposterous Yankee* (London, 1903), chap. xiv; E. A. Baker and J. Parkman, *A Guide to the Best Fiction* (London, 1932).

[3] H. Fyfe, *T. P. O'Connor*, 119ff., 200; Mrs. T. P. O'Connor, *I Myself* (London, 1910), 150, 151, 159; Mrs. G. Cornwallis-West, *Reminiscences of Lady Randolph Churchill* (London, 1908), 4, 47, 48, 209, 308ff.; G. W. Smalley, *London Letters and Some Others* (London, 1890), II, 120, 122, 126–27, 131, 137; see also J. A. Hobson, *Modern Outlook*, 171, 179. See "The 'Almighty Dollar' in London Society" in Elizabeth Banks, *Campaigns of Curiosity: Journalistic Adventures of an American Girl in London* (London, 1894), 99–113; Banks, *The Re-making of an American* (London, 1928), 38ff., 47, 56, 287, and *Autobiography of a 'Newspaper Girl'* (London, 1902). Ralph Nevill, *The World of Fashion: 1837–1922* (London, 1923), 273; F. T. Martin, *Things I Remember* (London, 1913), 126. Sir Sidney Lee, *King Edward VII, A Biography* (London, 1925–27), II, chap. xviii; see also *Fifty Years of London Society, 1870–1920* (London, 1920). R. Nevill and C. E. Jerningham, *Piccadilly to Pall Mall* (London, 1908), 25. Stead, *Americanization*, 124. One writer in 1906 estimated that since 1870, 500 Am. girls married titled foreigners with dowries amounting to $208,000,000; *M.A.P.*, Sept. 29, 1906. The marriages of Misses Vanderbilt and Shouts prompted a long-smouldering proposal to tax dowry and settlement; Foreign Marriages Bill in the N.Y. Assembly, reported in *Times*, Feb. 3, 1908, p. 5.

[4] The author has not forgotten Englishwomen married to Americans, but this aspect is not so important. *P. Debs.*, 1914, 62:1796; Escott, *Natl. Links*, 34, 225; Emanie Sachs, "*The Terrible Siren*," *Victoria Woodhull (1838–1927)* (New York, 1928).

[5] G. B. Harte, *Letters of Bret Harte* (New York, 1926), 331; see also Pt. iv, 281ff. Marie Corelli, *Free Opinions Freely Expressed on Certain Phases of Modern Social Life and Conduct* (London, 1905), 117, 120, 121; also Corelli *et al.*, *Modern Marriage Market: a discussion* (London, 1898); Atherton, *Adventures of a Novelist*, 298; Escott, *Natl. Links*, 214, 222; Margaret Oliphant, *Memoir of the Life of Laurence Oliphant, and of Alice Oliphant, His Wife* (Edin. and London, 1891), II, 154; *Piccadilly* was publ. in *Blackwood's* in 1865. See also Mrs. Everard Cotes,

An American Girl in London (London, 1891), and the traveling Senator in *A Voyage of Consolation* (London, 1898). Cleeve, *Anglo-Americans*, 289, 290, 299; Rhodes, *Lady and the Ladder*, 143. Ruth and Helen Hoffman, *We Married an Englishman* (New York, 1938), more about Iraq than marriage. At least twenty Englishmen married to moderately poor Am. told the author their friends won't believe they didn't marry "money."

⁶ Vivian Burnett, *The Romantick Lady: Frances Hodgson Burnett* (London, 1927), 299, 295, 29ff., 170; Frewen, *Melton Mowbray*, 196; Mrs. John Lane, *The Champagne Standard* (London, 1906), *passim.* Churchill, repr. in *Bancroft's Directory, 1903; Rita, *The Sin and Scandal of the 'Smart' Set* (London, 1904, repr. from "The Gentlewoman"), 63ff.; D. G. Phillips, *Reign of Gilt* (London, 1905), 130; Lady Dorothy Nevill, *My Own Times* (London, 1912), 153; Ralph Nevill, *Fashions, Fads, and Fancies* (London, 1913), 4–7, and *World of Fashion*, 272–74; L. H. Armstrong, *Etiquette* (London, 1908), chaps. vi, xv; Lady Jeune St. Helier, *Memories of Fifty Years* (London, 1909). Walter Besant tried to popularize Am. women's clubs which he thought helped to clarify social problems; some clubs served as models.

For fiction see also: S. Tytler, *American Cousins* (1897); B. M. Croker, *Infatuation* (1899); W. E. Norris, *Flower of the Flock* (1900); Mrs. Burton Harrison, *The Anglo-Maniacs*; Mrs. Urban Hawkeswood, *American Countess* (1900); Elliott Preston, *An American Venus: Emotional Romance* (1900); A. S. Swan, *An American Woman* (1900); Stuart, *Son of Gad* (1902); Arabella Kennedy, *American Duchess* (1906); Mrs. Henry de la Pasture, *The Man from America* (1905); G. H. Jessop, *His American Wife* (1913); Cosmo Hamilton, *Indiscretions* (1910), *Princess of New York* (1911), *Undelivered Letters* (1925); Lucas Cleeve (Mrs. Adelina Kingscote), *Anglo-Americans* (1903), *Dollar City* (1907).

⁷ Rosebery, *Times,* July 1, 2, 1908; *P. Debs.*, 92: 1200, 1209, 1214, 1238; 1902, 102: 439; 1903, 121: 1078–79, 1104; 1907, 169: 1183, 1200; 181: 405, 407; Lords, 1909, 2: 493, 496–97; in 1914 Viscount Halifax also cited Edith Wharton's *Custom of the Country*, Lords, 17: 217–22. Prof. J. D. Lawson demonstrated that Am. opinion opposed insanity as grounds for divorce; particular attention paid to National Congress on Uniform Divorce Laws (1906). See *Report, etc.*, P.P. 1912–13 (Cd. 6478–82), vols. 18–20. J. Arthur Barratt, "The English Divorce Reports from an American Standpoint," *Am. Law Review*, 48: 514–29. Norman E. Himes, "Charles Knowlton's Revolutionary Influence on the English Birth Rate," *N. Eng. Journ. of Medicine*, cxcix (1928), 461–65. *National Vigilance Association, Annual Report, 1911* (London), 8.

⁸ Gustavus Myers wrote *America Strikes Back* (New York, 1935) to attack this charge of materialism; note that Myers described Am. graft in Eng. magazines and had to go to London to find a publisher for his *History of Tammany Hall* (1901). Mather, *Mather*, 193–94; Tweedie, *America . . .* , 201, 275; G. L. Dickinson, *Appearances*, 207, 217; Edith Finch, *Wilfred Scawen Blunt, 1840–1922* (London, 1938), 172, 351; Lady Raleigh, ed., *Letters of Sir Walter Raleigh*, I, 254, 257–58; II, 335, 350, 370, 414. The author has not seen Rudolf Gauger's *Amerikaner Gestalten in der englischen Literatur der Gegenwart* (Dissertation, Tübingen, 1933). The *Spec.* believed Am. divided life into water-tight compartments; Shaw, J. A. Hobson, and W. W. Massingham thought us intellectually "intolerant."

Dickinson, *A Modern Symposium* (New York, 1927, written in 1905), 143; see also Gertrude Atherton's *The Aristocrats* (1901) which caused a sensation in England. Cf. William Watson's poem, "To the Invincible Republic." Sir Robert Anderson, *The Lighter Side of my Official Life* (London, 1910), 254; Dean of Canterbury, *Times*, Jan. 31, 1908.

[9] Adulterated lard annoyed England between 1880 and 1890. Inspection for tuberculosis in pigs did not come up to standard recommended by Royal Commission of 1898. *P. Debs.*, 1906, 158: 544–45, 618, 705–06, 949–50, 1354–57; 159:631, 651, 767–68, 1634; 163:1102, 1311; 1907, 170:471; 1910, 19: 2111ff.; 1914, 63:964–65.

[10] Sir William Butler, *An Autobiography* (London, 1911), 89, 95; he won a literary reputation by his *Great Lone Land: a narrative of travel and adventure in the North-West of America* (London, 1872); see also his *Light of the West* (Dublin, 1909). A. E. Zimmern, "Seven Months in America," *Sociological Review*, July 1912, 202, 205ff.; W. L. Clowes, *Black America* (1891); B. Kidd, *Social Evolution* (London, 1920), 50–51; C. H. Pearson visited U.S. in 1868 to gather material for *National Life and Character* (1893); W. Archer, *Through Afro-America: an English Reading of the Race Problem* (London, 1910), x, 199, 200, 237ff.; Sir Sydney Olivier, *White Capital and Coloured Labour* (1907); Sir Charles Lucas, *Partition and Colonization of Africa* (London, 1922), 57; Sir Harry Johnston (who had been impressed by Martin Chuzzlewit), *My Life*, 429, and *Liberia*, I, 348, 354, 370. Morley, *Recollections*, II, 336–37. The American play *Strongheart* (Am. Indian marries white girl) created controversy in London in 1907.

[11] Beginning in 1862, George Peabody gave £500,000 to improve living conditions of the London poor. The author could not find any tenants in the Peabody Buildings who thought of their Am. origin; nor does the Fund's literature mention it. See also Winkler, *J. P. Morgan*, 56. *Punch*, May 10, 1899, 219, suggested England's poor seemed too happy to attract attention of Am. millionaires. Dean Fry collected £32,000 on three Am. visits to aid restoration of Lincoln Cathedral. For details, see pamphlets and annual reports of the Pilgrim Trust, the various Carnegie Trusts in the U.K., Rockefeller Foundation, etc.

[12] Hendricks, *Carnegie*, II, 218–19, 224–25, 260–69; *Andrew Carnegie, The Trusts and Their Work* (Edinburgh, 1935); Carnegie, *An American Four-in-Hand* (Garden City, N.Y., 1933), published in 1883, 228, 167–68, 230. James Howard Bridge, *Millionaires and Grub Street: Comrades and Contacts* (New York, 1931), 37–38, 42–46; aided in writing *Triumphant Democracy*. Carnegie's *Triumphant Democracy or Fifty Years' March of the Republic* (New York, 1886), 45, 356, 369, 471, 486, and the cover! J. A. Hobson, *Crisis of Liberalism: New Issues of Democracy* (London, 1909), chap. iv.

[13] Marie Corelli, *Free Opinions*, 107; Manchester City Council meeting, *Manch. G.*, Sept. 7, 1911.

[14] Mary Fels, *Joseph Fels, his life work* (London, 1920), *passim*, a volume that reads like Harold Laski's. George Lansbury, *Looking Backward and Forward* (London, 1935), 223–26. Percy Alden, Patrick Geddes, Lansbury, and Zangwill were responsive to some of Fels's proposals. Miss Rye, a pioneer in Eng. movement for emigrating poor children to the Colonies, had been inspired in 1868 by the plan of the Am. philanthropist Van Meter for transporting New York street arabs to the Far West. Rider Haggard's visit to Am. as Commissioner for the British Govt. brought a favorable report on the free land settlements of the Salvation Army in Calif., Col., and Ohio.

[15] Other bodies supported by Rockefeller have also made sizable contributions,

e. g., $3,500,000 in 1928 for the University Library at Cambridge. Eastman's dental dispensary was perhaps a natural gift for an Am.; C. W. Ackerman, *Eastman*, 467–80. Pierpont Morgan's numerous gifts (wiring St. Paul's Cathedral, etc.) produced fewer outcries and publicity.

[16] Escott, *Natl. Links*, 206; George W. E. Russell, *One Look Back* (London, 1912), 351; L. P. Jacks, *My American Friends* (London, 1933), 12, 18, 25, 57; James Moffatt, ed., *Letters of Principal James Denney to his family and friends* (London, n.d.), 56; Stead, *Americanization*, 102; on Talmage, see Pond, *Eccentricities of Genius*, 91, 96ff.; D. P. Hughes, *Life of Hugh Price Hughes* (4th ed., London, 1905), 325–27, 556–57; Marchant, *Clifford*, 84; Hole, *Little Tour*, 145, 162; *P. Debs.*, 1914, Commons, 61:814, 806; Balfour also pointed out that when the Supreme Court disestablished the Church in Virginia it did not disendow it.

[17] C. P. Smith, *Historical and Biographical Papers* (Boston, 1936), Second series, chap. xi; Fred Dixon in *The World To-day*, Feb. 1908; E. S. Bates and J. V. Dittemore, *Mary Baker Eddy* (New York, 1932), 345–49; Viscount Elibank became a member through Lady Astor. Stephen Paget, *The Faith and Works of Christian Science* (1909), is a detailed criticism.

[18] G. K. A. Bell, *Randall Davidson, Archbishop of Canterbury* (London, 1935), I, 301, 443; G. M. Royce, *The Note Book of an American Parson in England* (New York, 1918), chaps. xxi, xxiv; R. E. Prothero, *Life and Letters of Dean Stanley* (London, 1909), 526, 530–31, 543; the cautious Bishop of Truro, C. W. Stubbs, *In a Minster Garden* (London, 1901), chap. viii, and sermons in *Pro Patria* (London, 1900). H. R. Haweis, delegate to the Chicago Parliament of Religions, 1893, wrote *Travel and Talk* (1896). Mrs. Creighton, *Mandell Creighton*, II, 240, 393; Creighton thought our writers "thin," substituting "gush for real perception." *The First Six Lambeth Conferences, 1867–1920* (London, 1929), 352, 371, 418. The diocese of Honolulu, formerly under the jurisdiction of the Archbishop of Canterbury, was transferred in 1900 to the Episcopal Church which organization also holds missionary jurisdiction over North Tokyo, Kyoto, Shanghai, and Cape Palmas.

[19] Rev. A. C. Dixon, Am., became pastor of Spurgeon's Metropolitan Tabernacle, London, 1911, and president of the London Baptist Association and the London Christian Endeavour Federation. *Record of Proceedings, Baptist Congress, London, 1905*, pp. v, vi, 1. Lecky, *Lecky*, 223; F. J. Kinsman, *Americanism and Catholicism* (1925). Archbishop Ireland (an Am.) wrote a letter in 1900 to the Duke of Norfolk on the advantages of union between English-speaking Catholics; this was denounced by the Jesuits, and Ireland reassured the Vatican.

[20] L. P. Smith, *Unforgotten Years* (Boston, 1939), 41ff.; Warfield, *Perfectionism* (New York, 1931), I, chaps. 6, 7; II, 471, 508. Mrs. Greene, a cartoonist-preacher, worked on England in 1901. W. R. Moody, *D. L. Moody* (New York, 1930), 107, 210ff., 218, 229, 345, 358; in 1881–82, Moody inspired the Inter-Collegiate Christian Union at Cambridge; Henry Drummond, *Dwight L. Moody: Impressions and Facts* (New York, 1900). W. T. Stead, *The Torrey-Alexander Mission, the Story of the Men and their Methods* (London, 1905), 68, 70, 76ff.; H. J. Jennings, *Chestnuts and Small Beer* (London, 1920), 141, 162; St. John Ervine, *God's Soldier: General William Booth* (London, 1934), I, 501; II, 761, 763, 770.

[21] Cromer quoted in Hall, *Empire to Commonwealth*, 383; L. J. Gordon, *American Relations with Turkey, 1830–1930; An Economic Interpretation* (Philadelphia, 1932), 225–27; Cecil, *Times*, Jan. 7, 1909; *World Missionary Conference* (9 vols., Edin., 1910); Basil Matthews, *John R. Mott, World Citizen* (London,

1934), 112; Tissington Tatlow, *The Story of the Christian Movement of Great Britain and Ireland* (London, 1933), *passim*.

[22] See *Proceedings* of 1898 World Convention, 242; F. E. Clark, *Memories of Many Men in Many Lands, An Autobiography* (Boston, 1922), 100–01. Percival Chubb, *On the Religious Frontier* (New York, 1931), p. vii and "Background: Anglo-American." The Am. author, Moncure Daniel Conway (1832–1907) was minister at South Place Chapel (London) from 1863 to 1884; see Conway's *Autobiography* (London, 1904). Lord Snell claims Conway did more for Anglo-American friendship than anyone else. Snell, *Men, Movements, and Myself* (London, 1936), 45, 58, 159–60, 202, 225, 228. McCarthy, *Reminiscences*, II, 61ff.

[23] On Home, see Robert Browning's "Sludge the Medium" (1864); Sir William Crookes believed in his pretensions. *Hibbert Journal*, 1902, I, 187; Jacks in *Cont. R.*, 1911, 99: 32. Alfred Austin in his *Poetry of the Period* (1870) devoted a chapter to Harris. Note Doyle's *Our American Adventure* (London, 1923) and *Our Second American Adventure* (London, 1924); in the latter he describes the Abrams system of medicine based on etheric vibrations and the work of Dr. and Mrs. Wickland and Dr. Littlefield. Doyle's "Adventure of the Five Orange Pips" is based on the K.K.K. Wallace, *My Life*, II, 123, 277, 337ff.

[24] J. M. Robertson, *History of Freethought in the Nineteenth Century* (London, 1929), II, 448, 480. T. B. Muller, *Die Kennisleer van het Anglo-Amerikaansch Pragmatisme* (Hague, 1913); Schiller, later teaching in the U.S., dedicated his *Formal Logic* to James—"the last great Liberator of the Human Spirit." D. L. Murray, *Pragmatism* (London, 1912), 1–4; H. V. Knox, *Philosophy of William James* (London, 1914). Dewey and the "Chicago School" were not overlooked in logic and philosophy. Thomas Davidson, "American Democracy as a Religion," *Int. Journ. of Ethics*, x (1899–1900), 21–41.

XV

THE AMERICAN IMPACT IN BRITISH
SOCIAL AND CULTURAL HISTORY: II

DURING the discussions of education and industry the American Government and people were credited with a great interest in science, perhaps surpassing England's. But *Punch* shrewdly summed up popular opinion of a sort which would affect the recognition of our achievements:

> We know that our kin
>   Work wonders not small;
> A yarn they can spin
>   Out of nothing at all,
> And on the most slender foundations
>   Build stories amazingly tall.

We may sketch the nature and importance of individual or organized Anglo-American professional contacts. Attention to another country may be aroused by professional interests which, although often narrow and technical, contain a modicum of definiteness which is helpful in international understanding. The volume of professional traffic varied eastward and westward year by year, and in different specialties. The American civil engineers met their brethren at London in 1900, the mechanical engineers at Birmingham in 1910. One may conclude that these efforts at contacts have not been well-coördinated or persistent; that they have not been so numerous as a common language would suggest; that they were not very effective before the last decade of the nineteenth century; and possibly, that they have increased only slightly since the World War.

One way of tracing the acknowledgment or use of our endeavors is to study the foreign learned societies which have honored American workers by memberships or medals. These recognitions infer that in one way or another a contact has been established. Honors may not always carry the same weight because learned societies suffer vicissitudes of fortune, and the recognition or non-recognition may run counter to the critical opinion of one or both countries.

The Royal Society, London, deserves first attention.[1] James Bowdoin in 1788 became the first "foreign" American member. The long period of neglect lay between the years 1818 and 1852, between Nathaniel Bowditch's and Benjamin Peirce's elections. Louis Agassiz, elected in 1838, could scarcely have drawn attention to America until some years after his emigration to that country in 1845. And by chance Audubon, the ornithologist, was elected as a "home" member in 1830, although it was largely because of his work in the States. American membership increased progressively in the nineties and again immediately after the World War. Between 1889 and 1914, the following Americans were elected as Foreign Fellows (a group limited to fifty: Henry A. Rowland, Alexander Agassiz, B. A. Gould, H. A. Newton, Samuel P. Langley, J. Willard Gibbs, G. W. Hill, A. A. Michelson, E. C. Pickering, S. Weir Mitchell, and George Ellery Hale. Between 1886 and 1914, eight Americans received medals from the Royal Society: S. P. Langley (Rumford Medal, 1886); J. Willard Gibbs, G. W. Hill, and A. A. Michelson (Copley Medal, 1901, 1909, 1907); T. W. Richards and E. W. Morley (Davy Medal, 1907, 1910); W. C. Gorgas (Buchanan Medal, 1912); and Alexander Graham Bell (Hughes Medal, 1913).

If we turn back a few years we see that the first award since we had become a nation went to a famous immigrant! In announcing the award of the Copley Medal to Louis Agassiz, Sir B. C, Brodie said in his presidential address, November 30, 1861:

> The results of these inquiries, and those of his fellow-labourers, Clark and Weinland, are embodied in the magnificently illustrated monograph entitled "Contributions to the Natural History of the United States," works which do equal credit to the naturalists who planned them, and to the State and people whose intelligent munificence renders their publication possible.

When awarding the Copley Medal to our first indigenous product, James Dwight Dana, mineralogist and geologist, Sir Joseph Hooker, November 30, 1877, described his recent American visit.

He detailed the work being done at the Harvard College Observatory, the survey conducted by Dr. Hayden, and his own interest in American flora;

> I must not end without expressing my admiration of the spirit and the manner in which the Government and people have coöperated in making known the physical and biological features of their country, and my conviction that the results they have given to the world are, whether for magnitude or importance, greater of their kind than have been accomplished within the same time by any people or government in the older continent.

Simon Newcomb was proposed for the same award for his investigation of the moon's secular acceleration, solar parallax, and the determination of the velocity of light. In 1884 two Americans were considered for the Rumford Medal, S. P. Langley and Henry Rowland; Langley for his studies in solar physics, and Rowland for his spectroscopic study of radiant heat and light, and as a founder of the *American Journal of Mathematics*. Willard Gibbs was before the Society for his work in chemistry and the "Phase Rule." William Huggins proposed A. A. Michelson again in 1907 in these terms: "Michelson's genius has opened up new ground in experimental optics." S. P. Thompson wrote of Elihu Thomson, 1907: "He has been conspicuous in maintaining a high scientific level in his work as an electrical engineer." G. W. Hill was proposed for the Copley Medal in 1907 for his work in the determination of perpetual orbits and their stability, and it was suggested that he laid the point of departure for Poincaré, Sir G. Darwin, E. W. Brown, and others. Herbert B. Baker, who supported T. W. Richards for the Davy Medal in 1910, wrote:

> It is probably no exaggeration to say that he has done more to raise the standard of accuracy in physico-chemical work than any other living chemist.

And Ronald Ross's nomination of William Crawford Gorgas in 1912 for the Buchanan Medal paid tribute to his knowledge of sanitary organization in the tropics:

> Colonel Gorgas has been called to lead the way for the first time in the prevention of a new class of diseases, namely, those carried by insects. His first work in this direction in 1901 coincides with my first recom-

mendations on the subject, but was, I believe, largely independent of them.

These few selected tributes illustrate an increasing appreciation of American science.

Such events as the meeting of the British Association in Canada in 1884 had brought the British into personal touch with activities below the border; likewise, visits of men like Sir Joseph Hooker and Huxley. Lord Kelvin (1824–1907) also told his British colleagues of America's progress; he even hoped the two countries might be under one flag and government. The third Baron Rayleigh, who had met Simon Newcomb, A. A. Michelson, Pickering, and Trowbridge, wrote October 18, 1884:

> [Henry A.] Rowland of the Baltimore University is about the first physicist in America, and happens to have worked at much the same things as myself so that we appreciate one another! and had good talks.

Members of the Empire, especially Canadians, frequently acted as interpreters. In addition, part of America's penetration depended upon the interchange of her scientific literature; the Royal Society claimed that it had done everything to promote such exchange. With democratic zeal the Smithsonian Institution had begun to send literature to organizations ranging from lunatic asylums to Lloyd's. By 1912 the Carnegie Institution at Washington also made an impression; Sir Robert Ball, Lowndean Professor of Astronomy at Cambridge, declared: "In the history of the world there has never before been so efficient a force for the advancement of knowledge."

The Royal Society of Edinburgh has had twenty-six Americans as Honorary Foreign Fellows since 1895.[2] Almost without exception those Americans who achieved membership in the two Royal Societies were elected first by the Royal Society, London. On the Royal Astronomical Society's list of Associates (an honor given to foreign scholars), Nathaniel Bowditch (1829) was the first American.[3] By 1847 the Council reported that we no longer neglected astronomy; American observatories soon came definitely into the Society's field of view. W. C. Bond became an Associate in 1849, and many of his compatriots soon joined him. In 1858, seven of the fifty-two Associates were American; in 1901, fourteen of forty-three; in 1934, twenty in a list of forty-five. One can count fifty-nine American Associates since the origin of the Society in 1820, but the interchange of ideas might also be forwarded by Americans who were ordinary Fellows. In 1865 G. P. Bond was the first American to receive the Society's Gold Medal; between 1865 and 1906, ten received the Medal; between 1917 and 1936, seven. G. B. Airy, the Astronomer Royal, stated December 14, 1849:

> The Americans . . . although late in the field of astronomical enterprise, have now taken up that science with their characteristic energy, and have already shown their ability to instruct their former masters.

The Astronomer Royal in 1903, while praising comprehensive advances, attributed some of the success to the coöperation between astronomers and engineers.

The Geological Society of London (1807, incorporated 1825) gave medals to ten Americans between 1858 and 1918, only one since then.[4] There have been thirty-seven on the Foreign Member lists; in 1828, three in a group of fifty foreigners; in 1862, five; in 1932, ten; paleontologists predominated. The Royal Institute of British Architects has given its greatest honor, the Royal Gold Medal, to three Americans: Richard Maurice Hunt, 1893; Charles F. McKim, 1903; and Thomas Hastings, 1922.[5] Americans were first added to the list of the British Academy (1902) in 1907, at which time Lord Reay wanted a similar Academy here "because the co-operation with such a body would ensure excellent work on both sides of the Atlantic." Between 1864 and 1913, the Royal Society of Arts conferred its Albert Medal upon Eads (1884), Edison (1892), and Bell (1902).

Since Honorary Fellowships were established in 1900 by the Royal College of Surgeons, thirteen Americans have been elected.[6] In 1899 Frederic S. Dennis was elected to the Fellowship of the College, an "unprecedented honor" according to the *Lancet*. There have also been some American members of the Royal Society of Medicine. But there never has been medical reciprocity between the two countries. Part II of the Medical Act (1886) which governs the General Medical Council's recognition of medical qualifications granted abroad has never been applied to the United States. But as a footnote one may cite the American degrees registerable (if obtained prior to June 25, 1886) *as additional titles:*

University of Pennsylvania   — Medicine, Surgery, Obstetrics
Jefferson Medical College, Phila.   — Medicine and Surgery
Miami Medical College, Cincinnati   —   "   "
University of Buffalo   —   "
Harvard University   —   "
University of New York   —   "
University of City of New York   —   "
University of Vermont   —   "
Bellevue Medical College, New York —   "

American medical students had also centered at Edinburgh. The career of Elizabeth Blackwell, who emigrated to America and entered medicine after attending school at Geneva, New York, was closely watched in England. She settled in England in 1868 where she drew upon her experience to sow the seeds of women's medical education and to help in the founding of New Hospital.[7] While traveling here to learn about female education, the feminist Sophia Jex-Blake (1840–1912) met Dr. L. Sewall of Boston who demonstrated to her the need for women doctors; she returned to England where she aided in starting the London School of Medicine for Women (1874). Dr. Francis J. Campbell (1832–1914), an American knighted in 1909, was largely instrumental in establishing in 1872 the Royal Normal College and Academy of Music for the Blind at Upper Norwood. From 1858 to 1869 Campbell had been associated with the Perkins Institution, Boston.[8] After a visit in 1899 Mr. Thomas Burns wanted the Royal Blind Asylum modernized by adding a gymnasium. With the Prince of Wales in 1860 came Sir H. W. Acland (1815–1900) who returned laden with reports on American medicine; on later visits he was impressed by the possibilities of the Johns Hopkins University.

According to Sir D'Arcy Power, from 1885 onward medical congresses, mostly in Europe, brought English and Americans together.[9] John Ashurst (1839–1900) and Samuel D. Gross (1805–1884) had an English following in the latter part of the nineteenth century. Sir Arbuthnot Lane, Will Mac Cormac and G. H. Makins came here frequently as medical ambassadors; eastward went the Mayos, W. W. Keen, William Welch, William Osler, Harvey Cushing, and others. Members of the American Society of Clinical Surgery visited England in 1910.[10] The Clinical Congress of Surgeons of North America also met in London; the *Lancet* remarked that the idea was ours and that the practical nature of the successful clinical meetings pleased Americans. Sir Squire Sprigg visited in 1893 and submitted articles to the influential *Lancet* which led to an invitation to join the staff as assistant editor; he became sole editor in 1908, and the journal increased somewhat its American reporting. But earlier, in 1905, the *Lancet* sent a special sanitary commissioner to report on conditions. The Corporation of Liverpool benefited by sending a representative to the 15th International Congress of Hygiene and Demography, Washington, 1912. Contacts in homeopathy have been persistent. The International Homeopathic Congress in 1896 apparently derived encouragement from the work being done here. Britons praised the coöperation of the American secretaries and our model schemes at the English-speaking Congress on Infant Mortality held in London, 1913.

American dentistry, with trumpets blaring, invaded the Old World. The American Dental Society of Europe (established about 1873) tried to maintain legitimate contacts and prestige. According to the *Medical Register* of 1903, twenty-four were practising in the United Kingdom, but those who claimed "American" training, which usually meant success and skill, were numbered by scores. In a comparative discussion carried to extremes, the *Dentist* observed:

We think every English dentist or medical man who has had experience with American patients will tell you that they are rather difficult patients to handle. They know almost too much; or, at least, they think they do.

If the general level of our dentistry was higher, argued British professionals, it was because the public had been made mouth-conscious. The *British Journal of Dental Science* in 1905, goaded into action by the American Mrs. John Lane, admitted that organized teaching of dentists originated here; but times had changed:

When the American invasion of Europe began, from a dental standpoint, digital skill and knowledge of the operative treatment of diseases of the teeth was not so widespread in Europe as it is now. . . .

The phenomenal reputation gained by a few men descended upon a host of others.

Superlatives in advertisements and pernicious circulars convinced the *Dentist* it would be desirable to abolish two-thirds of our dental colleges; an American dentist wrote in 1902 to the *Lancet:*

"American Dentistry" seems to have a great fascination, and though it is obvious that it possesses no claims to superiority over dentistry as practised over here, yet even medical men who ought to know better are lured by the magic expression "American." We Americans practising in this country look on the term "American dentistry," "Teeth on the American system," and such like expressions as advertising dodges. How long will this be allowed?

Attacks on British dentistry irritated Mr. Charles Fox who reaffirmed the view that our colleges granted diplomas after a few months; he asserted that textbooks, machinery, tools, and methods were international; "To claim credit for crown and bridge work and even gold stoppings as an American prerogative is absurd." (From the Old World came the first strong protests against the exposure of gold in American mouths.) However, W. Booth Pearsall, who was hostile before his visit, discussed "Technical Training in American Dental Schools" before a general meeting of the British Dental Association; he concluded that dental technics as organized here were superior and should be imitated. An American Association of Painless Dentistry offered practical dentistry courses in 1903 at London. The British Dental Association successfully prosecuted unregistered practitioners who used titles which implied "special qualifications," such as "D.D.S., U.S.A." Americans practising in England (and in India) should have used "Mr." Said the *Lancet*, July 22, 1906:

A large amount of the ill-feeling that exists towards American graduates in this country would cease if they could conform to the etiquette of the profession here.

The General Medical Council fought the American Dental Institute Ltd. which had been incorporated under the Companies Act for the purpose *inter alia* of "promoting the adoption of advanced American and other scientific methods of dental surgery" in London, Manchester, and Liverpool; the Council disliked unlicensed assistants, misleading advertising, and derogatory remarks about English dentistry. Under our influence, house-to-house canvassing and advertising increased. "Hygienic Institutes," which flourished everywhere between 1905 and 1912, pretended to our inspiration and methods. The *Report of Committee on the Extent and Gravity of the Evils of Dental Practice*, published in 1919, was due in part to "American" dentists' activity since 1900.[11]

The discovery of a new continent gave meaning to the phrase— "We repair our bodies by the drugs from America." As we grew into a nation the phrase became even more significant.[12] Some extended space must be given to patent medicines and the like because their penetration into Britain produced many ideas about America, to say nothing about the curative powers which worked wonders upon the health of the British Isles! Since some quacks were involved, it accounted for much of the suspicion that we were "over-enterprising," even crooked. In 1932, about $30,000,000 of American money was invested in some thirty-two companies manufacturing medicines in the British Isles. The years 1900 to 1903 marked a period of growth in these enterprises which flooded Britain with clever advertising and a tremendous mail-order business. In 1911, fifteen million packages of proprietary remedies had come from the States. Prominent in the pre-1914 American colony was J. Morgan Richards, who altered British advertising in order to push remedies; he testified to the medical profession's approval of our better drug preparation for accurate dispensing. He was the first to get support for our digestive ferments based on pepsin and pancreatin.

The *Lancet*, November 22, 1902, commented at length:

Recent years have added a new danger to life for the denizens of these islands—viz., the American quack. American progress . . . is much adduced nowadays . . . but when examination is made of any concrete example . . . it is not unusual to find that the benefit to be derived . . . is obtained by the sacrifice of something the retention of which many of us might value more than the new thing. . . . We owe to American pharmacy many very convenient therapeutic preparations and much ingenious application of laboratory knowledge, but it would seem as if we are bound to have hand in hand . . . the malignant American quack. . . . To the American quack all other quacks must give place.

Appeals sent out by firms showed that they expected to benefit by the contemporary interest in our prosperity and expansion; for example, the J. L. Pulvermacher Institute in London claimed that England must imitate America, which used more curative electricity. An American in Newcastle-on-Tyne was publishing in 1905 *The American X Ray Messenger*. The *Lancet* cudgeled the "Dr. McLaughlin Company" and the "Electric Vigour" treatment whose advertisements and letters had spread everywhere. It even criticized a Chicago medical equipment house for sending letters to England which began "My dear Doctor." In 1905 it wanted to follow the rules made by the American Medical Association to regulate proprietary remedies. It also saw the need for modifying the British Pharmacopeia, especially in Canada, since "the influence of American practice on medical work there is sufficient to warrant the inclusion of several new drugs and preparations in an addendum of Imperial scope."

The evidence taken in 1912 and the report of the Select Committee on Patent Medicines were an exciting summary of one heroic phase of our impact. Imports had increased because of restrictive legislation here; Professor Cushny declared, "We are getting a lot of quack remedies which were formerly confined to the United States." Throughout, the Committee gave attention to our legislation for such things as misbranding. The Report referred to the Irish-American Macaura, who was said to have gained $300,000 by a strenuous British campaign with a vibratory cure for many ailments; for the same activity, he received a jail sentence in France. Two of the most familiar remedies were "Mother Siegel's Syrup," which received much attention as being typical, and "Mrs. Johnson's American Soothing Syrup." A versatile Pennsylvanian, Mr. Harry Sweet, brought over "a whole variety of Yankee notions . . . which have been advertised enormously"—fat-producing concoctions and beauty parlor cures for baldness. One of the first fat-curers to arrive in England was a Dr. Turner, who achieved world-wide fame. A chameleon-like New York company offered an increase in stature; as "Harriet Meta" it posed as a wrinkle eradicator, as "Kathryn B. Firmin" it removed superfluous hair, and as "Everett Wood" it grew hair on bald heads. Another American doctor was selling an "Oxygenator" (gas-pipe therapy) as a cure-all. Most of the eye treatments were coming from us, such as the instrument called the "Ideal Sight Restorer," a gymnasium for the eye. Yankee deafness quacks were also numerous. Failing to find gold in the Klondike, a Mr. Pointing, declared the associate editor of *Truth*, picked up his store of quackery from American newspapers and died a rich man with a cure for drunkenness.

There was some evidence that British physicians still prescribed nostrums which could not be advertised in reputable American journals. Relying upon its American experience, Dr. Chase's Chemical Company decided that English clergymen were favorable agents for introducing remedies. Mr. Paternoster objected to the method of the Viavi Company (in England since 1902) which held public meetings supervised by women called "health lecturers." Flamboyant circulars sent out in 1911 described the enormous profits to be made by selling highly polished American chocolate drops. Americans who invaded England brought enough funds to start a campaign; in three months they expected to get back all their money and much more. From liquor cures to a specific called "Tuberculozyne," we had entered Britain's daily life.

The great diversity in medical legislation, sanitation, education, and progress in the various states made British generalizations very cautious, and attention seemed especially confined to regions east of the Mississippi River.[13] During the Spanish-American War, a medical journal was not above reporting that "the Anglo-American race is one," and naturally the medical experience gained in that conflict was noted by British medical officers. When Professor Jacobi described the growth of our medical profession and education before the Thirteenth International Congress of Medicine, Paris, 1900, the Lancet observed: "This was all quite new to the greater part of the audience." In a speech entitled "A Century of Medicine in America," Dr. J. C. Wilson commended the work of J. K. Mitchell on infective diseases, Brand on the treatment of enteric fever, and S. W. Mitchell on neurasthenia; American surgery, and Johns Hopkins. The *Lancet* did not accuse him of exaggeration, and praised many American textbooks, the Index Catalogue of the Surgeon-General's Office, and Wilson's suggestion for a Minister of Public Health. While looking enviously at our libraries and laboratories, British opinion did not extend its full praise to America's medical journals, education, or backward legislation.

By 1903 the *Lancet* did not appreciate all the boasting before the

American Medical Association, except for the discovery of the anaesthetic properties of ether. However, the surgeon Samuel D. Gross had received honorary degrees from Cambridge, Oxford, and Edinburgh. A review in 1898 of the *Treatise on Surgery by American Authors* spoke of the "high level of theory and practice which surgery has attained." In his *Glimpses of American Surgery in 1906*, C. Hamilton Whiteford, with the *Lancet* in agreement, declared that with the exception of the treatment of the vermiform appendix our surgery was of the highest merit. Interest was also aroused in brain surgery as developed by Harvey Cushing and in gynecology. A Texan's paper on pellagra before the Medical Congress of 1913 started a scare in England and Scotland.

American medical education was insufficient and impractical, according to predominant opinion.[14] Fake degrees did much to harm the professional interchange. Among the British visitors to Sir William Osler in 1884 were Dr. Struthers of Aberdeen and Dr. Cunningham of Dublin; Struthers was impressed by sad deficiencies. In 1889 Osler himself declared the American "system" was a byword among nations; but in the nineties he was able to report constructive work, particularly at Johns Hopkins. In July 1905 he presided at the luncheon of the Continental Anglo-American Society organized to foster international amities. Osler began his Oxford period in 1905, but his enthusiasm was not so effective in England as in America. He helped to organize the Association of Physicians of Great Britain and Ireland, 1907, a replica of the Association of American Physicians. The Association of Provincial Surgeons, started in 1914, rather followed the example of our interurban clinical societies. H. A. L. Fisher said of Osler:

> His remarkable evidence given before the Royal Commission on London University was especially important as helping a professional opinion in favour of the clinical unit system of teaching which he had himself perfected at Johns Hopkins, and is sufficient to give him an enduring importance in the history of English medical teaching.

By 1898 some who felt that London's post-graduate students could not obtain enough at home broached a scheme for a Medical Graduates' College and Hospital on American lines, that is, an institution where only qualified men were taught. The *Lancet* thought there was much to recommend it, but another Johns Hopkins would have to arise.

The Mosely Education Commission (1903) also looked into medical education. Dr. J. Rose Bradford lamented the lack of the clerk and dresser system and clinical facilities comparable to London's; but he was favorably impressed by the systematization of instruction, the close inter-relationship between the clinical laboratory and clinical medicine in out-patient and in-patient practice, clinical records, well-equipped laboratories, and methods of teaching in such subjects as pathology. Dr. W. H. Gaskell would have imitated the Harvard method of concentrating upon two subjects at a time, and the extension of classes in experimental psychology. Although we had achieved excellent results in the education of the deaf, such schools as Gallaudet College (Washington) had been ignored. However, not only did Henry Rayner (1841–1926), a future editor of the *Journal of Mental Science* and pathologist, become a Protectionist after his visit, but his conversation with Mr. Gallaudet opened to him new fields of thought on the problems of individuality and environment. Others urged an institution like Gallaudet's for England. At the request of the Royal College of Physicians and Surgeons, Mr. Frederic G. Hallett went to obtain information relating to the standards of general education and the range of curriculum required for various University degrees recognized by the English examining board. By 1910 some Britons were beginning to sense that we had too many medical men. A Carnegie Report inspired the *Scotsman* to say, November 12, 1910, "Medical education in the United States has long been connected in the public mind with bogus universities and quack doctors."

The *Lancet* did not want a new profession of optometry; others disliked the increasing specialization, e. g., the American Proctological Society. Others cited the American Roentgen Ray Society, which had received much help from medical colleagues and had gained an edge on x-ray work and apparatus. An experimental boarding school with a regulated diet of adulterated foods was greeted with a mixture of laughter and enthusiasm. What we really needed, it was asserted, was a national registration of the causes of death as accurate as Europe's. The increase of accident litigation indicated demoralization. The laws of professional secrecy in medicine were

held to be misconceived. The expert medical evidence for the Harry
Thaw trial prompted the *Lancet* to say:

Recent legal procedure in America, in relation as much to medical
evidence as to any other subject, may not be expected to furnish this country with any valuable examples to copy.

However, in 1908 the same journal thought English courts might
well look to our medical laws and decisions where English law was
silent.

Improvements in hospital construction in such cities as Boston,
New York, and Baltimore were carefully followed. However, Sir
Isambard Owen told the Medical Society in 1904 that we "regarded
buildings and sites of more importance than men," and he hoped
the University of London would not follow the example. But an
object lesson was the intelligent link between home and hospital
carried on through the social work of the Massachusetts General
Hospital which enlisted the sympathy of a large body of voluntary
female workers. The honorary president of the International Council of Nurses, Mrs. Fenwick, made a partly successful plea in 1901
for a scheme of organization based on a graduate nurses' system
which had proved eminently successful in America. Although district nursing originated in Britain, opinions were now expressed
which showed that lessons might be learned from its very complete
organization here. Others would have imitated a school of pre-
ventive medicine for social workers. London in 1899 was also urged
to copy the ambulance service of leading American cities.

Sir John Hibbert, after comparing the treatment of the feeble-
minded in both countries in 1898, found no reason for discourage-
ment in England.[15] But the United States was the only country
to which a special report was devoted by the Royal Commission on
the Care and Control of the Feeble-minded, 1904. A committee
composed of W. P. Byrne, W. H. Dickinson, and others was amazed
by the variety of legislation; but many progressive and successful
details were closely followed, especially for facilitating education,
in the final report of the Commission. Lunatic asylums were better
designed, more cheaply built, and more successfully managed than
the majority in England. We avoided the word "asylum" and used
a higher proportion of medical men on the staffs. Many American

osteopaths and chiropractors stimulated their British colleagues. One is reminded of Mark Twain, who said in 1900: "Presently the Osteopath will come over here from America and will soon make himself a power that must be recognized and reckoned with." Among those who carried abroad the principles of Andrew Taylor Still, picturesque founder of osteopathy, may be mentioned Wilfred A. Streeter who went to Glasgow in 1907; he founded the Osteopathic Defence League (London) in 1929. The major expansion occurred after the World War.

A few comments may be made on sanitation and public health.[16] Our methods of controlling milk supply were frequently brought up as examples, especially by those who considered the Model Milk Clauses of 1899 antiquated. Generally health authorities viewed our peaks of success as higher than England's, while traders objected to such paternalism. The Local Government Board sent Dr. A. Eastwood, who reported New York's system with recommendations for the control of tuberculosis in cows and a sanitary milk supply. Dr. F. M. Sandwith in 1907 spoke highly of the control of the sale of milk; in 1913 the Congress on Infant Mortality made much use, pro and con, of our experience with pasteurization and certification. In 1914 in the Commons, Mr. Astor and others who wanted milk classification advised legislation like New York's; but such suggestions were not then considered practicable, even though Astor said the best milk in New York contained only ten thousand bacteria per cubic centimeter while that served in the House of Commons contained seventy-two million bacteria!

The *Lancet* also wanted medical inspectors who were specially detailed for the inspection of phthisis, and Dr. J. T. Neon urged compulsory notification before the Royal Institute of Public Health in 1902. Others carefully noted our farm colonies for patients with arrested tuberculosis; Arthur Newsholme and J. P. MacDougall's report on the Tuberculosis International Congress of 1908 contained impressive accounts of the successful coördination of private and public agencies for the prevention of tuberculosis. By 1907, via Ireland, the educational value of itinerant tuberculosis "exhibitions" had became known. Statistics from the Chicago Health Department on the treatment of diphtheria by antitoxin were considered remarkable proof of success. Those urging regular medical inspection (also feeding) of school children gained some guidance from us. Journals also advocated similar facilities for washing and dressing in factories, and ventilation. The *Lancet's* special sanitary commissioner did not convince its readers that our law or administration was to be copied; but a few details, such as Boston's municipal bacteriological laboratory, might be imitated. The commissioner criticized the water supply of many American cities. In discussing the purification of sewage, Percy F. Frankland recorded British progress, "although we are deeply indebted to America for the extraordinary diligence with which some of its men of science have conducted a truly monumental series of experiments, demonstrating the great possibilities of intermittent filtration." Only feebly could England believe that our public health had been placed under the effective protection of competent authorities.

The *Standard* felt that a Senate bill in 1897 for more stringent quarantine against yellow fever would dislocate trade; "It is singular to find any civilized country contemplating so retrograde a step at the present day." In 1900 the *Lancet* added:

The methods adopted for dealing with plague-infected vessels would be regarded in this country as altogether impracticable, but it has, of course, to be remembered that the internal sanitary machinery of America is behind that of this country.

The Liverpool School of Tropical Medicine organized a commission in 1900 to study yellow fever here and in Brazil; by April 12, 1902, the *Lancet* hesitatingly praised our work on yellow fever.

But America's sanitary progress was used to attack unsatisfactory conditions in England. Said the *Times*, November 21, 1905:

When we look at the sanitary problems with which we are confronted, both in civil life and in military administration, it is difficult not to envy our American cousins the possession of President Roosevelt and Governor Magoon.

At the London School of Tropical Medicine, Sir P. Manson referred to our generosity which supported medical research in the Philippines; he wished the British Government realized as thoroughly that prosperity depended upon health. Compared with the failure of the West Indies to get money for anti-malarial measures, Viscount Elibank was impressed by the sums given Gorgas. Lord Kitchener drew unfavorable comparisons between our success at Panama and the British in India. But when controversy was laid aside, it was realized that we gave new hope for the white man's future in the tropics. Gorgas had a great ovation on his visit to England. When the Rand mine owners were worried by a plague of pneumonia which was killing off the Negroes, they turned to Gorgas because Samuel Evans of the Transvaal Chamber of Mines happened to read a reference to him by Sir William Osler. Sir Arthur Slaggett, Surgeon General of the British Army, related in 1914:

> After we have accomplished so much in preventive and tropical medicine, we cannot but feel disappointed that the mine owners have gone outside of our service and even out of the Empire for a consultant. Yet we feel, too, that they are right. On those subjects which he will study there, General Gorgas is the greatest authority in the world.

Thus, at least in one way, our imperialism worked to advantage.

What learned societies and professional contacts are for the few, sporting events are for the masses.[17] Contacts gained momentum in the nineties, and by 1900 England became conscious of a formidable rival whose sporting victories were expanding into traditional strongholds. There were many undercurrents of suspicion and revulsion concerning the alleged professionalism of American sports and training which led to the impression that we were more absorbed than England in athletics. These contests often inspired discussions of national characteristics. Some events turned sour, for example, the Palma Trophy meet when Americans did not use regulation rifles. Our victory in 1909 startled England's polo players from complacent stagnation; the *Times* declared, "For the fact that England did not win, the national characteristics are perhaps partly to blame." It was extreme energy which warped football. Our enthusiasm and tempo might even extend further; *Punch* observed, October 1, 1902:

> In cricket, just as in Combines,
> *Fas est ab hostibus doceri,*
> And played on Transatlantic lines
> The game no longer need be dreary.

America's Olympic victories, especially in 1908 and 1912, often suggested possible imitation. Startled by our supremacy in field events in 1908, England was reminded once again of the complicated system of inter-school competition. The *Saturday Review* thought England would be beaten so long as she did not make pleasure a business, and it criticized the Duke of Westminster, Lord Roberts, and others for trying to industrialize Britain's sports. When Americans began to criticize themselves, the *Manchester Guardian*, February 25, 1914, rejoiced:

This American discussion should certainly make us thankful that the recent appeal for the formalizing and perfecting of our athletes on the American model fell on deaf ears in England.

The tour of the Pilgrims in 1905 hardly spread Association football in American colleges; nor did the London visit of the Chicago White Sox and the New York Giants promote baseball in England. But an exhibition of baseball before the King in 1914 made the *Spectator* observe that

. . . in various games and athletics America's workmanlike methods and capacity for getting to the heart of the game, and consequently of playing it without pause or dead-points, have impressed our players at home.

Anglo-American collegiate matches boomed in England after 1894, drawing attention primarily to two eastern schools, Harvard and Yale. In 1899 and 1904, at Queen's Club, London, the combined American teams beat Cambridge and Oxford. Some explanations had to be made when American Rhodes scholars won all the firsts in 1913 at the Oxford Freshmen's sports. Yachting races and Sir Thomas Lipton's career were usually hailed as productive of good understanding. Yachting was invigorated by Lipton's challenge in 1899, and the publicity was almost American. Those who did not wish to internationalize the Henley regatta in 1901 argued that American crews were trained under conditions which were virtually professional. A. A. Zimmerman's English tour in 1893 stimulated cycling. Jay Gould's English victories at "court tennis" appeared remarkable to the *Manchester Guardian* in 1906. Francis Ouimet's golf triumph in 1914 was not regarded as a national calamity. Tod Sloane, the hard-riding spearhead of American jockeys in

England, became for a short time in 1899 a dazzling figure with myth-making qualities; his great victories while riding short stirrups, the saddle shifted forward on to the animal's withers ("the American seat") convinced English sportsmen. Although Lord Durham denounced American jockeys and methods before the Jockey Club, Newmarket in 1901 was a blaze of triumph for America. "Doping" was added to England's vocabulary about the same time.

The impact of American prize-fighting was more significant.[18] Britons eagerly followed the career of Jack Johnson, who was often denounced as a "menace to the ring." His fight with Jeffries at Reno made the *Times* wonder whether England might have the same racial hostility. Elaborate arrangements had been made to hear the results of the match in England, including special telephones in principal clubs and announcements in provincial theatres. Two Negro performers leaving a London music hall were assaulted by rowdies trying to vindicate Aryan superiority. The *Daily Express* commented, "Of course, America has gone mad over the business. . . ." How could a nation which idealized women, added the *Standard*, possibly allow women to grace the ringside? The *Saturday Review* observed, "There has been no equivalent to the Reno prize-fight since the Gladiatorial shows of the Roman Empire in its decay," and expressed a common fear that the movies and any subsequent English bouts by Johnson might stir up the Empire's color problem. American mass methods were being used to exploit the proposed fight between Johnson and Bombardier Wells; the opposition to the fight, undertaken in part by Rev. F. B. Meyer, indirectly raised the whole question of ring ethics. Boxing was to be brought out of the privacy of the National Sporting Club. Although the panic was full of humbug and sentimentalism, there was great relief when the fight was postponed. R. H. Gretton concluded:

The interest of the whole incident is that the real inhibition of the fight lay in public opinion still capable of revulsion from American exploitation of "bruising."

We may now turn to American artists who scattered to Old World studios without entirely losing their nationality, but without

creating an impression that there was any art movement worth observing here.[19] In subject matter, technique, or outlook, it is conceivable that they may have conveyed some idea of American life;
by migrating, their personal influence may have spread, but it was
uncommon to speak of American art. Almost to this day, such art
is an unknown quantity and quality among British artists or the
public. This, in spite of the careers of West, Copley, and Stuart,
and the later achievements of Whistler, Sargent, and others. Paris
Americans, London Americans, American Americans confused the
British who said what they pleased about one or the other. One
senses a prejudice among artists as deep as that in any other class
of society. Public speeches denied that we ever had an artistic history. American artists were gathering together world traditions,
but this was not considered important in international culture. Even
those whose work and influence were important in England, such
as Sargent and Whistler, were British for the mass of people and
were not identified with American culture. Hung with the "British
Schools" or in "British Rooms," they were appropriated—by logic
which would also put Holbein and Van Dyck with the British—like
Copley, Stuart, and West. This practice irritated Pennell who said,
"They even went so far as to say there is no American School—as
if ignorance could go so far." Since 1783, ten Americans have been
members of the Royal Academy.

By eccentricity in dress and poise, his biting humor and "a sort
of transatlantic impudence," Whistler helped to prepare British
opinion to expect almost anything from an American. In 1886 he
became president of the Royal Society of British Artists; he helped
the foundation of the International Society of Sculptors, Painters
and Gravers at London, 1898, and was its first president. G. H.
Boughton, who always called himself an American, became an R.A.
in 1896. Francis Davis Millet (1846–1912), who exhibited at the
Royal Academy in 1878, formed a colony at Broadway, England,
in 1884 along with Alfred Parsons, Abbey, and Sargent; he also
served as *Times* correspondent in Manila, was a member of the
Institute of Painters in Oil Colours, and was represented in English collections. Edwin Austin Abbey, who was sent to England in
1878 by *Harper's* to gather material for illustrations, was elected
to the Royal Institute of Painters in Water-Colours in 1883, and

became a full R.A. in 1898; he painted the Coronation of Edward VII. J. S. Sargent, whose influence in portrait painting was admitted, became an R.A. in 1897, and declined a knighthood in 1907. Americans were represented in the New English Art Club in 1885. Charles Dana Gibson exerted an important influence on English line illustration. The award of a gold medal to John Gardner Lowes (1835–1907) in 1880 for his tiles in competition with old English potters created a sensation in the Five Towns. London knew practically nothing about American sculpture until Hiram Power (1805–73) sent his work to London; not much more filtered in although we taunted England for the poverty of its sculpture.

Americans were discriminated against, Joseph Pennell concluded, in the Painters' and Etchers' Annual Exhibition, 1885, and some resigned, having lost confidence in the management because "British members feared their influence and competition." Pennell described a lecture by W. J. Linton (1812–1897), an ardent republican who went to America in 1867 to improve his finances, in which Linton abused our wood engraving; "They had," Pennell continued, "no use for American wood engravers who believed their business was to interpret." Pennell, it should be noted, also felt that the "Englishman's attitude to the American was one of tolerance and he was pained if the American failed to be grateful." Overwhelmed by our "over-hopefulness and getting-on-ness," John Ruskin (1819–1900) never found time for his "most earnest inquiry into the condition of [American] art." He only said that our deficiency in landscape painting was deep rooted—"the want of historical associations"; he attacked the worship of William Merritt Chase, president of the Society of American Artists; and as an old man, he hoped piously for a national school of American art. He never appreciated our landscape, neither the Mississippi, nor New Hampshire, whose abbreviation "N.H." meant "New Hell."

Contacts with America did not mean much to the work of British artists, but we may note that Herkomer, who planned to lecture and paint here, wrote to his uncle, July 22, 1881:

The American race is one with a great future to it, and I might stimulate the growing art feeling and fan the spark into a flame. I have a longing to get to the hearts of the Americans. I know much about them and feel I shall like them.

Another artist, Sir Philip Burne-Jones, came because he was bored, and he observed, not American art, but the land of El Dorado, speed, and smart-looking women. Sir Alfred East, R.A., who made frequent visits, said in 1909:

Of American illustrations we know a little, but of the work of American painters, strong and virile as much of it is, England is without knowledge.

This suggests that Charles Dana Gibson was one of the few artists known in England as an American.

Reporting on the Philadelphia Exposition in 1876, Charles West Cope became puzzled by our great diversity of aim and treatment in plastic and graphic art. Despite the Paris Exhibition in 1900, our art still remained unrecognized in England, but there was a dawning consciousness (already expressed by Cope) that landscapes by Americans who remained at home warranted appreciation, not as mere catalogues of exotic items but as expressing a distinctive nationality. Pennell believed that unless American men and dollars managed exhibitions, our art would not take the place it deserved. Arthur B. Davies, Abbott Thayer, and De Forest Brush were seen in London in the first decade of the new century, and Augustus Saint-Gaudens had his first comprehensive showing. There was also an exhibition of American water-colors in 1905. While urging Harrison S. Morris to make a good showing at Venice, Pennell wrote on January 17, 1909,

The reception that has been accorded to Saint-Gaudens and other Americans who are showing in the International this year proves incontestably what I have preached to you. . . Saint-Gaudens' work has been universally damned, and why, because they don't understand it—because they hate it and all Americans and have taken advantage of every fault in detail—and magnified it a million times. . . . Davies has been mentioned but once in the *Athenaeum*, and then only to be dismissed as the best thing shown—in three or four words.

The four hundred American canvases at the Anglo-American exposition, 1914, were grouped significantly according to the foreign or American residence of the artists. Necessary exhibitions were held at Paris and London in 1938, and generally reinforced the conviction that there was little American art with a native outlook.

What strength we lacked in art was manifested in art-collecting.[20] Our yearning for artistic masterpieces led to the formation of the National Art-Collections Fund in 1903, stimulated British interest in its own treasures, and dramatically personified America's dollar and unholy greed, apparently without ever building up a reputation abroad for true cultural aspirations. Bishop Lloyd's Palace in 1899 had to be protected from American hands. At the eleventh hour in 1909, Holbein's "Duchess of Milan" was saved for the National Gallery from rapacious collectors by a national exercise in donating £72,000 and a campaign filled with discourteous language which did not idealize us. The American bogey is still a good weapon for the Fund. The *Saturday Review* sneered at a lavish book called *Elizabethan Interiors;* "In pictures such as these the American millionaires can gloat over their English plunder." Pierpont Morgan's library might indicate good taste and a civilizing influence, but the westward migration of excellent collections of Shakespeare, Caxton, and the like was alarming. *Punch* suggested a course of training for the unfeeling millionaire. While justifying his request for power to act quickly to preserve ancient buildings and monuments, the First Commissioner of Works in 1913 referred to our behavior. Visiting here in 1912, William Rothenstein expressed a typical response: "I admired the museums; but I wondered whether the acquisitive passion was not detrimental to the rise of a vigorous school of American art."

Sir Aston Webb, when presenting the Royal Gold Medal of the Royal Institute of British Architects to Charles F. McKim, explained that it was in appreciation "not only of what Americans are doing, but also of what we expect them to do untrammeled by traditions, full of youth, energy, imagination and initiative, and supported by almost boundless resources." [21] Sir Banister Fletcher in his *History of Architecture* viewed America as handing on "the torch of freedom." Manning Robertson declared in 1925:

Although there is an active exchange of ideas between us and America, there exists there no particular school of thought from which we are borrowing, but we are still learning a great deal from their development of high buildings where the vertical line is always predominant.

An Anglo-American syndicate which included Earl Grey and F. B. Elser of New York projected an American office building for the north side of the Strand as part of the invasion of 1901. Buildings such as Bush House, which was of pioneer service to London, the new Devonshire House, and others stand as examples of American designing. English designers, according to some authorities, admired in American architecture the ability to grasp opportunities, to make use of mechanical resources, and to "ride the whirlwind." According to H. H. Statham, the first symptom of original spirit in American architecture was a desire to escape conventions, especially in country-house architecture, by returning to mere building with rock-faced masonry, chimneys which were plain shafts of masonry, and woodwork "simply hewn and squared," a development which affected English architects. One can fancy some evidence of our influence in flatter relief, lighter moldings, less projection, and smaller cornices, which give a hard plainness. But John Lane concluded in 1905 that England was still ignorant of the originality and dignity of our architecture.

Charles Godfrey Leland (1824–1903) in his *Minor Arts* (1880) aimed to bring art and beauty to the daily life of workers; this movement to widen the range of home work was taken up by Mrs. Jebb for the Cottage Arts Society, and by Sir Walter Besant and Lord Brownlow. But more important was the indirect influence of America's architectural schools. With analyses of various American institutions before the Royal Institute, Mr. Arthur Cates discussed the Annual Report in 1899:

> The time would come if they continued sluggish and dullards as they were now, when their young men would go to America to learn that architecture which they ought to be able to acquire at home.

And the next year Mr. Cates again warned that we were outstripping England in training architects, and the president of the Architectural Association, W. Howard Seth-Smith, urged his organization to start a systematic and thorough course as offered by American universities. The successful American School at Rome also suggested a similar British School. Under American pressure there seemed to be an extension of technical training before entering offices. Courses at

Liverpool were designed on American lines, partly under the influence of Professor C. H. Reilly, who had a high opinion of the training of our architects. S. D. Adshead praised the eminence of our architecture to the Leeds and Yorkshire Agricultural Society in 1909, attributing progress to well-directed, scholarly study.

The glass-and-girder, or factory style, spread into England, e. g., Sir John Burnet's Kodak building in Kingsway.[22] Upper stories were stepped back. Iron and steel construction was closely but slowly followed. Legislation relating to steel construction, particularly from the Building Act Amendment of 1909 onward, borrowed from New York's building experience. Stereotyped building laws prevented the full use of our reinforced concrete construction. Regulations for fire escapes, fire precautions, fire-resisting material, and fireproof construction were observed and frequently copied. Along with other technical information, Sir William Mather brought back automatic fire-sprinkler protection from Frederick Grinnell of Providence. American improvements in the brick-making industry—in firing-plant, machinery, organization, and standardization—were used. Some concluded that our domestic architecture excelled in comfort and convenience, including plumbing. At the Congress of the Royal Institute of Public Health, 1900, the British were urged to imitate small apartment dwellers who used all rooms as day-rooms, and Fletcher hoped to use roof spaces as in Chicago. Occasionally Britons were impressed by the aggressiveness of our town planning. Young Prince Edward told Queen Victoria that London might take some hints from the Government buildings at Washington. Efforts to establish official boards of experts to pass upon building designs were stimulated by us. J. M. Brydon and F. J. Burgoyne urged architects to study public buildings in America, especially libraries, landscaping, and general construction. The rebuilding of the Quadrant in Regent Street, London, followed designs carried out in our cities. One may possibly conclude that builders and architects were susceptible to America's progress. The position of American architecture has become stronger in Britain since 1914. From straw and bricks and stone we may turn to Mother Earth.

The great interest of the eighties in America's agricultural evolution, and its repercussions in Britain, had died down.[23] Echoes of popular ditties lingered faintly in farmers' ears:

To the West, to the West, to the land of the free,
Where the mighty Missouri rolls down to the sea.

But that land of opportunity now appeared less satisfactory for the Briton. As a class, rural Britons know little about us, and have little reason to discuss American agriculture which is so different. (To a great extent farmers also miss the constant stimulus of the movies.) Nor does one sense that the majority of Britons ever think of us as an agricultural country despite our historic significance as a source of food supply. Many times since 1877 more than half their wheat came from the States. The importance of the fluctuations in the American supply of wheat or beef can hardly be exaggerated. Sir William Crookes included a pessimistic note in his presidential address to the British Association in 1899:

It is almost certain that within a generation the ever-increasing population of the United States will consume all the wheat grown within its borders, and will be driven to import like ourselves.

Leiter's ambition to corner markets sent up the stock-in-trade arguments of those desiring national granaries. Whenever America showed signs of buying meat in world markets, as was apparent in 1913, such organizations as the Home Produce Association urged British farmers to attempt greater production. We also had a real grip upon agricultural machinery which was attractive because of low prices and varied uses, although Britons usually preferred machinery of heavier appearance. Such machinery had been hailed at the World's Fair in London, 1851, as opening a new era in agriculture. Nor should readers forget the refreshing story of America as a hunting gound for Old World naturalists, and the variety of American plant life which aided English garden art of the eighteenth century.

Interest in our agricultural training has been persistent. The *Scotsman* commented in 1908 on the Agricultural Education Committee: "This experience of America is regarded by Lord Reay's committee of great importance." T. H. Middleton, one-time professor of agriculture at Cambridge, testified that our agriculture had improved since 1889 partly because of experimental stations. Those who visited the United States or Canada could not doubt that Great Britain had been remiss in expenditures on agricultural science. England copied an association of agriculture teachers; farmers' institutes seemed to interest the Committee. Others were convinced that we had shown that specialization was necessary in agricultural instruction.

Members of Parliament urged upon the Government the benefits of the Bureau of Chemistry to American agriculturists, and the desirability of following the example of our Bureau of Agriculture, which disseminated information more rapidly and issued daily weather forecasts at public cost.[24] The President of the Board of Agriculture admitted that he was impressed by Roosevelt's message in 1901 on the prosperity of the American farmer; he added that it might be because our Government did more for the farmer. He also advised more governmental assistance, as in Germany and the States, to develop evaporating processes for fruits and vegetables. From 1890 to 1900 our canning and evaporating processes had been used profitably in the East Midlands. The value of experimental fruit farms was often cited.

American homestead policies and exemptions were copied in the colonies and, to an extent, in Europe; in England, the Social Democratic Federation used American examples to revive agitation. Sir Horace Plunkett's ten years in Montana (1879–89) brought him wealth and experience for the Old World. While illustrating urban dependence on rural prosperity to the Midland Farmers' Association, he quoted Roosevelt's insistence upon the productivity of natural resources as a measure of national efficiency; policies which were maturing in America led him to write *The Rural Life Problem of the United States* (1910). The Colonial Office, which had a scheme in mind for South Africa, sent H. Rider Haggard, the novelist, to inspect the farm colonies established by the Salvation Army at Fort Romie (California) and Fort Amity (Colorado). Haggard was on the whole satisfied with the settlements, and his report in enlarged form, *The Poor and the Land* (1905), advocated a scheme of national land settlement for Great Britain. Mrs. Victoria Martin, a reformer with American antecedents, founded the Agricultural Society at Bredon's Norton.

The American limpet, not a pest in American waters, harmed oyster beds and worried the Kent and Sussex Sea Fisheries Commission. American products, it was claimed, brought in the Colorado beetle, the codling moth, the American river weed, and the American gooseberry mildew. Our products often furnished other forms of excitement. One of the tariff reform proposals in 1907 was designed to protect the hop growers who, by fair means or foul, were being injured by excessive imports; at Canterbury embattled farmers aroused by Americans cried, "Chuck 'em out!"

Many Britons kept a close watch on America's cotton, which partly accounted for the feeling of intimacy with the South. The songs of unemployed Lancashire operatives had resounded throughout the kingdom in 1863:

> We can't get no cotton from old Kentucky Shore,
> Oh, hard times come again no more.

The Civil War had brought about great speculative transactions and extended the system of "grading"; trans-oceanic telegraphy upset for some years the organization of the Manchester cotton market. The Amalgamated Association of Operative Cotton Spinners in 1903 believed that New York's cotton speculation was managed by a "gang of gamblers." An American speculator, J. A. Patten, caused a riot at the Manchester Exchange, March 1910. The exorbitant demands of American planters, poor crops, or cotton "rings" drove England to seek new cotton-growing regions; in turn a good American crop hindered the British Cotton-Growing Association, which was formed June 12, 1902, as a result of our gambling in cotton. Mr. C. W. Macara, chairman of the International Federation in the Cotton Industry, was largely responsible for the interest taken in American cotton and cotton manufacturing; Sir Daniel Morris, Imperial Director of Agriculture for the West Indies, went to the United States to study methods of growing and marketing cotton. The Lancashire Private Cotton Investigation Commission, which visited in 1906, was probably more concerned about reforming us than in gathering information for its own use. Those who wanted more governmental support for tropical agriculture pointed to the aid given American cotton by our federal Department of Agriculture. "King Cotton" could at times have dramatic significance.

These two chapters, integrated at best on the principle of diversity, round out the many repercussions of our civilization—and temper the Epilogue.

¹ For details of proposals, bibliography, etc., see author's article, "Americans and the Royal Society, 1783–1937," *Science*, March 25, 1938, 267–72. S. P. Thompson, *The Life of William Thompson, Baron Kelvin of Largs* (London, 1910); R. J. Strutt, *John William Strutt, Third Baron Rayleigh* (London, 1924), 146, 41, 145–47; *Proceedings*, vol. xi, 461–62. Hendricks, *Carnegie*, II, 214. Author's articles, on Peter Stephen DuPonceau, *Penna. Hist.*, July 1936; on mss. in Acad. of Natural Sciences, Philadelphia, *ibid.*, Jan. 1938; on O. W. Gibbs, *Science*, Sept. 16, 1936; on James Jackson, *Journ. of A.M.A.*, Oct. 16, 1937. Note premature and unsuccessful journal, *English and American Opinion on Science* (London, Feb. 13, 1873).

² Details in the Society's *Transactions* (1783–) and *Proceedings* (1832–); communication from Mr. G. A. Stewart, Edinburgh. Henry Fairfield Osborn was elected at Edinburgh in 1908, at London, in 1926.

³ For details see author's article, "Americans and the Royal Astronomical Society, London," *Science*, June 24, 1938, p. 575. Electrical apparatus for recording occultations of the stars as used at the Harvard Observatory was known in Europe as the "American method." See *Monthly Notices*, Mar. 11, 1859, 192; Airy, *ibid.*, 1849, vol. 10, p. 26; misfortunes of Schumacher, ed. of *Astronomische Nachrichten*, prompted some observations on Am. to be found in the R. Sheepshanks Mss. at the Society. Up to 1856, an Am. astronomer with an "official" position was preferred to facilitate coöperation with the Society. Contacts outside the organization, for example, the correspondence of Sir David Gill and Simon Newcomb, are just as important. George Forbes, *David Gill, Man and Astronomer* (London, 1916); also R. A. Sampson, *History of the Royal Astronomical Society 1820–1920* (London, 1923).

⁴ See author's article, "Americans and the Geological Society, London," *Pan-American Geologist*, Nov. 1937. The first Am. member was probably Professor Parker Cleveland (1818), and the first medalist, James Hall (1858). Fellows of all groups, resident in the States: 22 in 1874; 36 in 1884; 40 in 1890; 42 in 1900; and 22 in 1936.

⁵ There were in 1937 eleven Honorary Corresponding Members from the U.S. Its library contains many Am. books and publications.

⁶ Philip Franklin, and one or two others, were the only Am. Fellows of the R.C.S. before the War. Honorary Fellows are: W. S. Halstead (1900), W. W. Keen (1900), J. C. Warren (1900), R. F. Weir (1900), J. B. Murphy (1913), G. W. Crile (1913), H. Cushing (1913), W. J. Mayo (1913), J. M. T. Finney (1920), C. H. Mayo (1920), R. Matas (1927), E. L. Keyes (1933), W. B. Coley (1935). Cushing received the Lister Medal in 1930; George W. Corner delivered one of the Thomas Vicary Lectures. Communication from Registrar, G.M.C., June 9, 1937. *Medical Register, 1937*, Table H, p. xcix.

In a very sketchy list, the *An.-Am. Year Book, 1914* noted in London: 8 Am. doctors, 17 mining engineers, 17 authors, 26 dentists, 20 osteopathic doctors, 13 artists, 6 lawyers, and 3 clerics. Honorary Fellows of the Medical Society of London were J. S. Billings (1881), J. M. Costa (1881), T. A. Emmet (1881), S. Weir Mitchell (1878). Billings and Mitchell were the only Am. on the honorary lists in 1898 of the Clinical Society of London and the Royal Medical and Chirurgical Society. See *The Citadel*, a film based on A. J. Cronin's novel.

⁷ Elizabeth Blackwell, *Pioneer Work for Women* (London, 1914 ed.); M. Todd, *The Life of Sophia Jex-Blake* (London, 1918).

[8] See *Dict. Am. Biog.* In 1868 Dr. Armitage founded the British and Foreign Blind Association. J. B. Atlay, *Sir H. W. Acland* (London, 1903), 297, 408, 410, 486.

[9] Interviews. John Weir went to Chicago in 1908 for post-graduate work in homeopathy; one of Sir Arbuthnot Lane's visits was in 1913. G. H. Nuttall, Director of the Molteno Institute at Cambridge, was one of Welch's students.

[10] *English-speaking Congress on Infant Mortality* (London, 1913), 6, 95; *International Homeopathic Congress, 1896,* 9, 16, 31. *The Dentist,* Apr. 20, 1899, 267; *Brit. Jour. of Dental Sc.,* Apr. 15, 1901, 349–50.

[11] Committee on Dental Practice, Rt. Hon. F. D. Acland, chairman; see *P.P.,* 1919 (Cmd. 33), XIII, 8. Am. dental books circulated widely. C. R. Coffin, Baltimore, was probably the pioneer (c. 1854) Am. dentist in England.

[12] Prof. A. R. Cushny (1866–1926) returned to England from Ann Arbor in 1905 to become the first occupant of the chair of pharmacology at University College, London. *Lancet, passim; Report from the Select Committee on Patent Medicines, etc., P.P.,* 1914, IX, pp. viii, x, xv, 17, 31, 138, 312ff., 345.

[13] *Lancet,* Apr. 23, Aug. 13, Nov. 12, 1898; June 24, 1899; Aug. 11, 1900; July 26, Sept. 27, 1902; May 16, 1903; R. H. Nesbitt, "Operative Surgery in America," *19th Cent.,* 1901, 50:598.

[14] Cf. A. Flexner, *Medical Education* (New York, 1925), who says (p. 50) that in 1915, independent of Am. movement, the General Medical Council established a full time teacher in the Univ. of London. Mosely, *Report,* 64–78, 147–61; cf. *Lancet's* series on post-graduate work abroad, Nov. 28, 1903. Harvey Cushing, *Life of Sir William Osler* (Oxford, 1925), I, 226, 255–56, 307, 400, 402; II, 184, 296, 388, 402, 420, 427, 600; the Duke of Cambridge in 1901 said to Osler, "Oh, you Americans are so joky. I do like you."

Henry Rayner, *Intimate Recollections, 1842–1926* (n.p., 1929), 40–41; Am. educ. of the deaf was carefully explained in the 11th ed. of the *Ency. Brit.* by A. H. Payne of the Oxford Diocesan Mission to the Deaf and Dumb, a former fellow at the National Deaf Mute College, Washington; Alex. Morgan, *Education and Social Progress* (London, 1916), 213. Joseph Chamberlain had visited the school at Washington in 1888; satisfied with the "sign" system, he so testified three months later to a Royal Commission.

[15] Hibbert, *Manch. G.,* June 22, 1898; *Report, etc., P.P.,* 1908, XXXIX (vols. 7 and 8 of the Commission are relevant); see esp. 132ff., and chap. xli of the Final Report (vol. 8). Twain, *Letters* (1912), II, 690.

[16] Sir H. D. Rolleston, *The Rt. Hon. Sir Thomas Clifford Allbutt* (London, 1929), 167, 221, 234–35; Dr. A. Eastwood, *Report on American Methods for the Control and Improvement of the Milk-Supply* (Local Govt. Board Health Reports, New Series, No. 1, London, 1909); *Congress on Infant Mortality* (London, 1913), 161, 209, 213, 217, 230; *P. Debs.,* Commons, 1914, 61:1027–40, 1044, 1067; 63:245, 250; 65:1284, 1292, 1295; 1899, 74:741. *Lancet,* Feb. 4, Apr. 15, 1899; June 1, 1901. Newsholme and MacDougall report in *P.P.,* 1909 (Cd. 4508), LXXI; Neon, *Times,* Aug. 26, 1902. John Beard, *Scots.,* Jan. 21, 1905. Factory Report in *P.P.* (cd. 223), 1900, XL, 292. *Stand.,* Jan. 13, 1898; *Lancet,* Mar. 3, 1900; Elibank, *Man's Life,* 177; Manson, *Times,* Oct. 22, 1907; M. C. D. Gorgas and B. J. Hendricks, *William Crawford Gorgas* (London, 1924), chap. ix.

[17] Chesterton said, "The American is a bad sportsman because he is a good Jingo"; *Pub. Opinion,* Sept. 18, 1908. It was noted in 1906 that Cambridge rowed a "scull-

ing style" more like that of Am. crews. H. J. Whigham, "American Sport from an English Point of View," *Outlook*, 1909, 93: 738–44. Invasion of English turf began with Richard Ten Broeck in 1856; not until M. H. Sanford went over in 1875 were Am. horses raced again in England. Lord Durham, *Manch. G.*, Oct. 18, 25, 1900. Horace G. Hutchinson, discussing a projected country club, declared, "The American analogy really misleads almost as much as it guides and inspires."

[18] R. H. Gretton, *Modern History of the English People: 1880–1922* (London, 1930), 825; *Times*, July 7, 1910; Sept. 29, 1911; Aug. 26, 1913; Jan. 21, 1914; *Daily Express*, July 4, 6, 1910; *Sat. Rev.*, July 9, 1910; Sept. 23, 1911.

[19] E. W. Hudson, "Notes on American Sculpture, chiefly in relation to Gothic Work," *Jour. RIBA*, Sept. 26, 1908, 605–16; also *Punch*, July 3, 1901, p. 16. E. T. Cook and A. Wedderburn, *Ruskin* (39 vols., 1903–12); most of Ruskin's Am. observations are in footnotes; see esp. 36: 194–95, 37: 563. Linton wrote *History of Wood-Engraving in America* (1882), returned to England in 1890. Note also English career of Mark Fisher and J. J. Shannon. E. R. and J. Pennell, *Life of James McNeill Whistler* (London, 1908), *passim*; Frank Harris, *Contemporary Portraits* (London, 1915), 63; F. Whyte, *Heinemann*, chap. 10; E. V. Lucas, *Abbey* (London, 1921). East, *Times*, Tariff Supp., July 20, 1909. J. Saxon Mills, *Life of Sir Hubert von Herkomer* (London, 1923), 122; cf. Maxwell Armfield, *An Artist in America* (London, 1925). D. C. Thomson, "The Art Movement in the U.S. and Canada," *Art Journal*, London, 1898. *Edin. R.*, July 1900, 192: 183; E. R. Pennell, *Life and Letters of Joseph Pennell* (Boston, 1929), I, 138, 309, 317, 318; II, 22, 29, 30, 61.

[20] Henry James, *The Outcry* (1911). *P. Debs.*, 1913, *Lords*, 13: 298; W. Roberts, *Natl. R.*, 1912/13, 60: 98. *Punch*, Jan. 6 to 27, 1904. *Men and Memories: Recollections of William Rothenstein, 1872–1922* (New York, 1932–35), II, 257, 37, 87–88, 172, 258; I, 78, 81.

[21] During the last few years, Messrs. A. D. Miller, J. Russell Pope, Thomas Hastings, and Harvey W. Corbett have made important contributions to London architecture. Manning Robertson, *Laymen and the New Architecture* (London, 1925), 103; Fletcher, *Hist. of Architecture* (9th ed., London, 1931), 886; Webb, *Jour. RIBA*, June 27, 1903, 441; see also Wm. Emerson, *ibid.*, 1901/02, 12. John Lane, *Sir Caspar Purdon-Clarke* (London, 1905), 10; H. H. Statham in 11th ed. *Ency. Brit.*, "Modern Architecture"; C. and A. Williams-Ellis, *The Pleasures of Architecture* (London, 1924), 57; R. Langton Cole in *Arch. Assoc. Notes*, May 1898, 57; A. W. Cleaver, "An American Hospital: Its Heating and Ventilation," *ibid.*, Feb. 1898, 24; *Jour. RIBA*, 1899, 6: 65. E. R. Pennell, *Charles Godfrey Leland, a Biography* (Boston, 1906), II, 253, 255–56. Since 1925, ten Commonwealth Fellows came here to study architecture. Robert Atkinson, *Report on the Education of the Architect in the U.S.A.* (London, 1922), studied in Am. and active in Arch. Assoc. School of Architecture.

[22] Lee, *King Edward*, I, 99; Lord Windsor, *Times*, Nov. 3, 1903; "American Architecture: with especial reference to work at Washington," *Jour. RIBA*, 1909, 325, 355; "American Methods of Erecting Buildings," *Jour. RIBA*, 1905, 13: 44; *ibid.*, 1912, 19: 331–39. *Transactions, Congress of Public Health* (Aberdeen, 1901), 427, 433, 444; Mather, *Mather*, 17; Paterson, "Study of Domestic Architecture in Eastern States of U.S. in 1896," *Jour. RIBA*, 1898, 309–30; Webb, *Times*, Jan. 10, 1907. R. A. Cram read a paper before the RIBA on university arch. in U.S., May 20, 1912. C. A. Daubney, *Jour. RIBA*, Dec. 6, 1902, 70; *P. Debs.*, 1899, 69: 136.

[23] F. W. Grey, *Seeking Fortune in America* (London, 1912), not enthusiastic. When councillor at the British Embassy, Esme Howard wrote a *Report on Agricultural Educ. in the U.S.* (London, 1908), supplement to *Jour. of Board of Agriculture*, Jan. 1908, vol. xiv. *Agricultural Educ. in England and Wales; Reports, etc.*, *P.P.*, 1908 (Cd. 4207), XXI, Pt. ii, 185, 225ff., 474, 558, 562ff.; and Mr. T. W. Cowan. *P. Debs.*, 1906, 165: 1464–65; *Mosely Report*, 7–25; *Education*, Jan. 7, 1910. Cf. J. B. Botsford, *English Society in the Eighteenth Century, as influenced from oversea* (New York, 1924), and essay by E. D. Merrill, "Plants and Civilization" in *Independence, Convergence, and Borrowing in Institutions, Thought, and Art* (Cambridge, Mass., 1937). June Rainsford, before Philadelphia meeting of the Bibliographical Society of America, 1937, "America a Hunting Ground for 18th Century Naturalists."

[24] Raymond P. Stearns, "Agricultural Adaptation in England, 1875–1900," reprint from *Agricultural History*, VI, Nos. 2 and 3, 1932, 139. Palmer, *P. Debs.*, 1905, 144:46; 146:51. Hanbury, *Times*, Dec. 11, 1901 and *P. Debs.*, 1901, 97:690; Milward (using pamphlet prepared by Professor Shaw who was sent to investigate U.S. by the Royal Agricultural Society), *P. Debs.*, 1901, 90:751. British horticulturists objected to some of Luther Burbank's novelties. Wallace, *Times*, Oct. 21, 1907. C. S. Read and Albert Pell traveled 9,000 miles in U.S. in 1879 on behalf of the Royal Commission on Agriculture. Implements extensively used here might come late to England, e. g., the disc harrow which arrived about 1900. U.S. owed much to Sir Horace Plunkett for such things as the Country Life Commission; the Horace Plunkett Foundation of London is considered by the American Institute of Coöperation as correspondent for British and Colonial information. Haggard's report also published as a command paper, Cd. 2562; Sir H. Rider Haggard, *The Days of My Life* (London, 1926), II, 173, 177–78, 193–94. Note also, on rice, *Ac. & P.*, 1905 (Cd. 2237–6), LXXXVI; on beet sugar, *Ac. & P.*, 1901, LXXX, Mis. Ser. No. 548.

P. Debs., 1908, 190:410; 1909, 10:966; 1911, 23:322, 323; 26:1581; 1913, 52:2006. S. J. Chapman, *The Lancashire Cotton Industry* (Manchester, 1904), 121, 125; *Memorandum on Government Action in encouragement of Cotton-Growing in Crown Colonies*, *P.P.*, 1910 (Cd. 5215), LXVI. On Californian David Lubin's activity in England, see A. Hobson, *The International Institute of Agriculture* (Berkeley, Calif., 1931), 21, 29, 49, 56, 57.

EPILOGUE

FOR good or evil, the American impact increased from 1898 onward. Our civilization was coming to mean more to the British
Isles. Commercial fanaticism—akin to a wave of religious fanaticism
—stirred England in the first years of the twentieth century and
elicited a new interest in us which in turn encouraged a growing
spirit of commercialism in British life. The interplay of the Atlantic
nations was difficult to escape. The differences in these two countries,
no doubt trivial if compared with occidental and oriental variations,
were comprehended by Englishmen later than by Americans. A
prophet would be needed to say whether these differences would
grow more marked with each generation. The world may be inter-
dependent, but international contacts and channels of information
have not kept pace with deceiving technical improvements. In the
spread of culture, as in the pacific treatment of international affairs,
this deficiency or abnormality of information affects the progress of
the world.

*

Two contradictory aspects of this Anglo-American history must
have constantly impressed the reader—a marked neglect of American civilization and very ineffective channels which cut down the
possibilities of our influence and, on the other hand, what many may
view as unexpected and unhoped-for interest in American activity.
This apparent contradiction may be quite normal as between any
two nations. And yet, underlying the first is an immobility in British
mentality—a lack of sympathy and certainty concerning America
and Americans. But it would be foolhardy to judge, as some have
tried to do, Britain's total intelligence or insularity as manifested
by its response to America. Nevertheless, more from our pressure
and evolution than from any British influence upon us, the years between 1898 and 1914 mark an important convergence of the two
nations.

*

There are great difficulties and dangers in making full use of channels of information. It would seem that deficiencies can be improved only by sincere, mutual efforts. Just as Britain did not seem to extract the greatest amount of value from America's experience, neither did we, in spite of our great itch to know foreign opinion, extract the full measure of corrective help from her judgments on us. There are signs that many gaps in the channels are being repaired, although much really depends upon the increasing worth of American culture. While dramatic events and political fortunes may help to exploit channels as they exist, it is well to remember what Professor Pollard said in 1925: "Even the conclusive demonstration of the power and wealth of the United States in the Great War has failed to carry conviction in the educational importance of its history very far." But in spite of all such handicaps, America has been an important laboratory for experience and thought.

*

No doubt those who have pet hobbies to ride when attempting to modify the course of Anglo-American relations have found herein some cues which await their further exploitation. But far more important, such riders of hobbies—and, we may add, grinders of axes —should be somewhat sobered. One nation does not enrich or benefit another by catch phrases. And it is not obvious that many of the accepted methods of facilitating international understanding or the spread of national achievements have the power or the good results commonly attributed to them. This book may be useful for those who are thinking of applying American experience in proposals for a durable peace.

*

Obviously, parallelism in the two countries may be due to the same causes acting in both countries rather than to any direct influence of America upon Britain. Though it may be too early to isolate our "influence," certainly America has altered British history in no small way, and much more than Britons at first glance are likely to realize.

*

When citing American experience England was unable to satisfy itself that there was "such a parity" of conditions as to justify the use of that experience; although this was frequently a polemical dodge, the attitude was basically sound. But impacts and cultural diffusion are not always logical. However, these pages should have made "American Contributions to Civilization" or "The United States as a Factor in World History" more concrete, even if sometimes more trivial. They may suggest sanity and realism to those who are interested in our foreign prestige.

*

Whether its reaction to America has been as intelligent as that evoked by any foreign nation, Great Britain should decide for itself. If the response has not been sound—and such a case could easily be made from parts of this book—it is Britain's loss as much as ours. For whether the response is correct or not, America's influence may increase, with changing results, in everything from politics to spirit.

*

It is only this complex interweaving of the elements of civilization, and the conditioning of one nation by others, which constitute meaningful international history. Studies in diplomatic relations or analyses of international organizations are really only convenient subdivisions of international history, not its totality. So long as "nationalism" has any force, a nation's foreign repercussions may be legitimately studied. Yet in spite of a vigorous era of nationalism, this has not been done to any great extent for several reasons. Diplomacy seems to absorb so much of the external history of a nation as to leave little else. Further, cultural historians cling praiseworthily to an unbounded world of thought in which such studies as the present one are at best mere pettifoggery. Then too it is much more convincing for a patriotic historian to write about his nation's contributions if he does not try to track abroad what might prove to be really insignificant so far as all the nations in this civilization are concerned. Nevertheless, this suggested type of international history would add immeasurably to the total picture of man's world.

*

Without elevating British judgment to heights of unnecessary prestige, the preceding pages should challenge those Americans who are vitally aware that much of the future of history depends upon our own work and thought. A cautious person would have to admit that our influence, whether mighty or not, has not always been beneficent. Faulty channels of information cannot always be blamed for this. There are inadequacies in our civilization which we can ponder without foreign encouragment; but if our horizons be extended, these deficiencies are revealed in a harsh light, and at the same time the challenge of removing them becomes more significant for our own position in world history. While one need not accept Seeley's thesis that "the whole future of the planet depends upon the mutual influence of the branches of the English race"—indeed, that would be unduly restricting the American imagination, and harmful to the accumulated variety of our heritage—this book should convince the most sceptical that we have an external history which is a vital part of international history. In the migration of national experience, so many things other than the usefulness or value of the ideas or methods govern interest and reception that foreign opinion frequently has to be discounted in estimating the real meaning of our experience. Competition thickens the smoke screens laid down by selfish national pressure groups, and bounding American prosperity or commercial failure may warp foreign judgment. Experience conflicts with prejudice. But we are not likely to understand or recognize our own nationalism until we estimate its force upon other nations. The term "American" gains new meaning when we look abroad.

*

One might speculate endlessly and idly whether the impact as discussed here was more important for Great Britain or America. I would suggest that America is coming to occupy a most effective strategic position for altering the course of British history, that our influence may be greater than any future British influence upon this country. The World War, which temporarily increased our power, demonstrated this; our financial and armed participation did much to save the Allies, to upset the balance of power in Europe, and enable the victors to impose rather than negotiate a peace. Nor did that war seem to disturb or distort our development as much as that of Britain and other European nations. In later decades, the dawn of the twentieth century is likely to be taken as the birth years of this alteration in position. "When America has been bright Britain has seldom remained thoroughly gloomy." Is it not conceivable that one may extend Professor Clapham's observation to fields other than economics?

*

The institutions and customs of British life were not easily affected by outside influences, but America, almost as much as any other force, acted as a solvent. The vastness of the United States made it very difficult for any good practice or reform to be developed uniformly throughout the nation; this spottiness enabled foreign commentators who wished to combat allusions to America to paint very dark pictures. But we flatter ourselves if we think that during these years conservative Britons distrusted us merely because we were too progressive, too democratic, and too socially minded. Indeed, time may prove America to be the most conservative force in the twentieth century. Had America been able to convey the impression that it was not superficial, corrupt, or lawless, a poet would be needed to sing the song of a much greater and more noble influence. Should we not pause to reflect that our democracy may have lost some of its world-wide inspirational value? That progress is not inevitable? That our world influence for good does not inevitably increase like a rolling snowball?

INDEX